THE CZECH AND SLOVAK REPUBLICS:
TWENTY YEARS OF INDEPENDENCE, 1993–2013

THE CZECH AND SLOVAK REPUBLICS

*Twenty Years of Independence,
1993–2013*

Edited by

M. MARK STOLARIK

Central European University Press
Budapest–New York

Copyright © by M. Mark Stolarik, 2016
Published in 2016 by

Central European University Press

An imprint of the
Central European University Limited Liability Company
Nádor utca 11, H-1051 Budapest, Hungary
Tel: +36-1-327-3138 or 327-3000
Fax: +36-1-327-3183
E-mail: ceupress@press.ceu.edu
Website: www.ceupress.com

224 West 57th Street, New York NY 10019, USA
Tel: +1-732-763-8816
E-mail: meszarosa@press.ceu.edu

All rights reserved. No part of this publication may be reproduced,
stored in a retrieval system, or transmitted,
in any form or by any means, without the permission
of the Publisher.

ISBN 978-963-386-153-0 Cloth

Library of Congress Cataloging-in-Publication Data

Names: Stolarik, M. Mark, 1943-
Title: The Czech and Slovak republics : twenty years of independence, 1993-2013 / edited by M. Mark Stolarik.
Description: Budapest ; New York : Central European University Press, 2016. | Includes bibliographical references and index.
Identifiers: LCCN 2016008449 (print) | LCCN 2016010948 (ebook) | ISBN 9789633861530 (hardbound : alkaline paper) | ISBN 9789633861547 (pdf)
Subjects: LCSH: Czech Republic—Politics and government—1993- | Slovakia—Politics and government—1993- | Czech Republic—Economic conditions—1993- | Slovakia—Economic conditions—1993- | Social change—Czech Republic—History. | Social change—Slovakia—History. | Czech Republic—Social conditions—1993- | Slovakia—Social conditions—1993- | Post-communism—Czech Republic—History. | Post-communism—Slovakia—History.
Classification: LCC DB2243 .C98 2016 (print) | LCC DB2243 (ebook) | DDC 943.705—dc23
LC record available at http://lccn.loc.gov/2016008449

Printed in Hungary by
Prime Rate Kft., Budapest

Table of Contents

Acknowledgments ix

Abbreviations xi

Introduction
M. Mark Stolarik 1

Part I:
THE DISSOLUTION OF CZECHOSLOVAKIA

CHAPTER 1:
The "Velvet Split" of Czechoslovakia (1989–1992)
Jan Rychlík 23

CHAPTER 2:
Czechoslovakia's Dissolution Twenty Years After
Michael Kraus 47

CHAPTER 3:
The Dissolution of Czechoslovakia. The Slovak Perspective
Jozef Žatkuliak and Adam Hudek 55

CHAPTER 4:
The Dissolution of Czechoslovakia: The Slovak Perspective
Stanislav J. Kirschbaum 79

CHAPTER 5:
The Slovak Republic After Twenty Years
Jozef Moravčík 85

CHAPTER 6:
The Czech Republic After Twenty Years: Gains and Losses
Petr Pithart 95

Part II:
POLITICAL DEVELOPMENTS AFTER 1993

CHAPTER 7:
Of People, Mice and Gorillas: Slovak Politics Twenty Years After
Juraj Hocman 105

CHAPTER 8:
Thinking Big About a Small Country: On Juraj Hocman's
"Of People, Mice and Gorillas"
Kevin Deegan-Krause 129

CHAPTER 9:
Letting Czechoslovakia Go: Czech Political Developments
Since 1993
Adéla Gjuričová 143

CHAPTER 10:
Czech Political Developments Since 1993: Some Comments
Carol Skalnik Leff 155

Part III:
ECONOMIC DEVELOPMENTS AFTER 1993

CHAPTER 11:
Economic Developments in Slovakia Since 1993
Ľudovít Hallon, Miroslav Londák, and Adam Hudek 177

CHAPTER 12:
To Neoliberalism and Back? Twenty Years of Economic Policy in Slovakia
John A. Gould 197

CHAPTER 13:
Economic Developments in the Czech Republic, 1993–2013
Martin Pospíšil 211

CHAPTER 14:
The Czech Economic Transition: From Leader to Laggard
Sharon Fisher 237

Part IV:
SOCIAL DEVELOPMENTS AFTER 1993

CHAPTER 15:
Reflections on Social Developments in Slovakia, 1993–2013
Martin Bútora and Zora Bútorová 247

CHAPTER 16:
Social Developments in Slovakia after Twenty Years: The Impact of Politics
Sharon L. Wolchik 281

CHAPTER 17:
Social Developments in the Czech Republic Since 1993
Oldřich Tůma 289

CHAPTER 18:
Some Comments on "Social Developments in the Czech Republic"
James W. Peterson 311

Contributors 321

Bibliography 325

Index 347

Acknowledgments

The editor is grateful to many individuals who helped him to compile this volume, a comparative treatment that had not appeared in either of the newborn republics since the breakup of Czechoslovakia in 1993. Thanks are due to the University of Ottawa for hosting an international scholarly conference in 2013, on the twentieth anniversary of the historic event, and to the outstanding mix of scholars who participated in it. The editor is particularly grateful to Professor Jan Rychlík of Charles University in Prague, Professor James Ramon Felak of the University of Washington in Seattle, and Dr. Slavomír Michálek of the Historical Institute of the Slovak Academy of Sciences in Bratislava who helped him in identifying and recruiting the participants in the conference. The editor is also grateful for the assistance of Dr. Milan Kollár, former Ambassador of the Slovak Republic in Canada, and to Dr. Karel Žebrakovský, former Ambassador of the Czech Republic in Canada, for helping to find and persuade Dr. Jozef Moravčík and Dr. Peter Pithart, former prime ministers of Slovakia and the Czech Republic, who were eyewitnesses to the breakup of Czechoslovakia, to present co-plenary addresses based on their recollections and experiences.

The editor is also indebted to the following individuals and organizations who contributed financially to the success of the conference and to the publication of this informative and insightful book. Patrons ($5,000+): A Friend, and the Slovak Community Circle of Oshawa; Benefactors ($2,500–$4,999): Anne Stolarik, the University of Ottawa Faculty of Arts, La Maison Slovaque, Inc., Philip A. Taylor, and Sean

Adams; Supporters ($1,000–$2,499): Dušan Miklas, the First Catholic Slovak Union, Global Atomic Fuels Corporation, Jaroslav Slaba, Margaret Ridzon, National Slovak Society, Pauline Ridzon, Slovak Catholic Sokol, and US Steel Canada; Honorable Mention ($100–$500): First Catholic Slovak Ladies Association, and Sonja Bata.

Abbreviations

ANO	Akce nespokojených občanů [Action of Dissatisfied Citizens] [Czech Republic]
ANO	Aliancia nového občana [Alliance of the New Citizen] [Slovak Republic]
ANO 2011	[YES 2011] [Czech Republic]
CEFTA:	Central European Free Trade Agreement
CEFTA 5:	Central European Free Trade Agreement
CERGE-EI:	Center for Economic Research and Graduate Education, Charles University, and the Economics Institute of the Academy of Sciences of the Czech Republic
COMECON:	Council for Mutual Economic Assistance
ČSFR:	Česká a slovenská federatívna republika [Czech and Slovak Federative Republic]
CSK:	Česká koruna (Czech Crown [currency])
ČSL:	Československá lidová strana [Czechoslovak People's Party]
ČR:	Česká republika [Czech Republic]
ČSR:	Česká socialistická republika [Czech Socialist Republic]
ČSSD:	Československá sociální demokracie [Czechoslovak Social Democratic Party]
ČSSR:	Československá socialistická republika [Czechoslovak Socialist Republic]
ČTK:	Česká tisková kancelář [Czech News Agency]

CVVM:	Centrum pro výzkum veřejného mínění [Center for Public Opinion Polling]
D-92	Demokraté 92 [Democrats 1992]
DS:	Demokratická strana [Democratic Party]
EBRD:	European Bank for Reconstruction and Development
EU:	European Union
FDI:	Foreign Direct Investment
GDP:	Gross Domestic Product
HSD-SMS:	Hnutí za samosprávnou demokracii—Společnost pre Moravu a Slezsko [Movement for Self-Governing Democracy—The Society for Moravia and Silesia]
HZDS:	Hnutie za demokratické Slovensko [Movement for a Democratic Slovakia]
IMF:	International Monetary Fund
IPB:	Investiční a poštovní banka [Investment and Postal Bank]
IRB:	Investičná a rozvojová banka [Investment and Development Bank]
IVO:	Inštitút pre verejné otázky [Institute for Public Affairs]
Kčs:	Koruna Československá [Czechoslovak crown]
KDH:	Kresťanskodemokratické hnutie [Christian Democratic Movement]
KDS:	Kresťansko-demokratická strana [Christian Democratic Party]
KDU-ČSL:	Křestanská a demokratické unie—Československá strana lidová [Christian and Democratic Union—Czechoslovak People's Party]
KOZ:	Konfederácia odborových zväzov [Confederation of Labor Unions]
KSČ:	Komunistická strana Československa [Communist Party of Czechoslovakia]
KSČM:	Komunistická strana Čech a Moravy [Communist Party of Bohemia and Moravia]
KSS:	Komunistická strana Slovenska [Slovak Communist Party]

ĽSNS:	Ľudová strana Naše Slovensko [The People's Party Our Slovakia]
LSU:	Liberálně-sociální unie [Liberal-Social Union]
MOS:	Maďárská občianska strana [Hungarian Civic Party]
NATO:	North Atlantic Treaty Organization
NBS:	Národná banka Slovenska [National Bank of Slovakia]
ODA:	Občanská demokratická aliance [Civic Democratic Alliance]
ODS:	Občanská demokratická strana [Civic Democratic Party]
ODÚ:	Občianska demokratická únia [Civic Democratic Union]
OECD:	Organization for Economic Cooperation and Development
OF:	Občanské forum [Civic Forum]
OH:	Občanské hnutí [Civic Movement]
OK'98:	Slovak Citizens Campaign, 1998
Oľ aNO-NOVA:	Obyčajní ľudia a nezávislé osobnosti – Nová väčšina [Ordinary People and Independent Personalities – New Majority]
RFE/RL:	Radio Free Europe/Radio Liberty
SaS:	Sloboda a solidarita [Freedom and Solidarity]
SDKÚ:	Slovenská demokratická kresťanská únia [Slovak Christian and Democratic Union]
SDĽ:	Strana demokratickej ľavice [Party of the Democratic Left]
SKDH:	Slovenské kresťanskodemokratické hnutie [Slovak Christian Democratic Movement]
Smer:	Direction
SKK:	Slovenská koruna [Slovak crown [currency])
SMK:	Slovenská maďarská koalícia [Party of the Magyar Coalition]
SNS:	Slovenská národná strana [Slovak National Party]
SOP:	Strana občianského porozumenia [Party of Civic Understanding]

SPR-RSČ:	Sdružení pro republiku—Republikánská strana Československa [Association for the Republic—Republican Party of Czechoslovakia]
SR:	Slovenská republika [Slovak Republic]
SSR:	Slovenská socialistická republika [Slovak Socialist Republic]
SZ:	Strana zelených [Green Party]
TOP 09:	Tradice, Odpovednost, Prosperita 2009 [Tradition, Responsibility, Prosperity, 2009]
Úsvit:	Dawn of Direct Democracy
US-DEU:	Unie svobody—Demokratická unie [The Freedom Union—Democratic Union]
V4:	The Visegrád Four
VV:	Věci veřejné [Public Affairs Party]
VAT:	Value Added Tax
VPN:	Verejnosť proti násiliu [Public Against Violence]
VSŽ:	Východoslovenské železiarne [Eastern Slovak Steel Works]

Introduction[1]

M. Mark Stolarik

In 2013, the Czech and Slovak Republics celebrated twenty years of independence. Not all citizens welcomed the split. Furthermore, the new countries' subsequent trajectories, which were sometimes painful and controversial, have received little comparative scholarly attention within the two republics. For observers on the outside, however, the new states have provided a rare opportunity to study political and social change in two closely related countries, an experiment of significant importance. Without emotional and political restraints, Western scholars quickly seized upon the causes of the split and the subsequent paths taken by the two new independent republics.

One of the first works to appear was by Carol Skalnik Leff, an American political scientist. She briefly described the history of Czechoslovakia from 1918 through 1989 and its 1993 breakup. Her main focus, however, was on the period from 1989 to 1996 in the two republics with respect to the evolution of political parties, the economic challenges, and the desire to join the European Union (EU). While recognizing the difficulties both countries faced, she remained cautiously optimistic about their future.[2]

While Leff presented the first attempt at a broad comparative analysis of the new states, other Western scholars dug deeper into

---

[1] I would like to thank Kevin Deegan-Krause for having critiqued and strengthened this introduction.
[2] Carol Skalnik Leff, *The Czech and Slovak Republics: Nation Versus State* (Boulder, CO: Westview Press, 1997).

issues of national identity, political parties, local communities, and European integration. The British literary historian, Robert B. Pynsent, led the way by looking at the issue of national identity, and he found the Czechs exhibited an individualistic, non-national outlook while the Slovaks were community-oriented.[3] The American historian, Hugh Agnew, followed up with his survey of Czech historical thinking, which centered on the history of the Kingdom of Bohemia, while the Slovaks emphasized "natural rights," based on their language and culture.[4] Nadja Nedelsky, meanwhile, found that, starting in the late nineteenth century, Czechs increasingly adopted a civic identity, whereas the Slovaks continued to focus on their ethnic identity. That is why, she concluded, the Czech Republic stresses citizenship, while the Slovak Republic views nationality as important.[5]

Politics in the Czech and Slovak Republics also interested Western scholars. Thus, Petr Kopecky, a Czech political scientist at the University of Leiden in the Netherlands, carefully described the creation and democratic functioning of political parties in the Czech and Slovak Republics.[6] Meanwhile, Kevin Deegan-Krause, in the United States, showed the differential impact of issue dimensions—primarily economics in the Czech Republic and nationalism in Slovakia—on the success of early democratization efforts in the two countries.[7] The American political scientist, James W. Peterson, compared and contrasted the foreign policy of the Czech Republic with that of Slovakia and found that, in the initial years of their independent existence, the Czechs looked westward, while the Slovaks turned their attention east-

---

[3] Robert P. Pynsent, *Questions of Identity: Czech and Slovak Ideas on Nationality and Personality* (Budapest – New York: Central European University Press, 1994).

[4] Hugh Le Caine Agnew, "New States, Old Identities? The Czech Republic, Slovakia and Historical Understandings of Statehood," *Nationalities Papers* 28, no. 4 (December 2000): 619–50.

[5] Nadja Nedelsky, *Defining the Sovereign Community: The Czech and Slovak Republics* (Philadelphia: University of Pennsylvania Press, 2009).

[6] Petr Kopecky, *Parliaments in the Czech and Slovak Republics: Party Competition and Parliamentary Institutionalization* (Burlington, VT: Ashgate, 2001).

[7] Kevin Deegan-Krause, *Elected Affinities: Democracy and Party Competition in Slovakia and the Czech Republic* (Stanford: Stanford University Press, 2006).

ward. However, after the defeat of the Vladimír Mečiar government in 1998, Slovak governments switched to cooperating with the West.[8] The American political scientist, John A. Scherpereel, meanwhile, asked why the Czech and Slovak Republics did not decentralize into regions in the 1990s or create an independent civil service and why they identified the EU as the driving force for regionalization and civil service reforms in the 2000s.[9] The American sociologist, Simon Smith, edited a book of readings that compared the environmental movement, civil society, community life, and group strategies in the Czech and Slovak Republics.[10] The British political scientist, Kieran Williams, teamed up with American Dennis Deletant to compare the newly established security services in the two republics and found mismanagement and incompetency within the Czech Secret Service, while its Slovak counterpart, under the Mečiar regime, evolved into a political police linked to organized crime.[11] The American defense analyst, Jeffrey Simon, showed how *both* the Czech and Slovak Republics had to change their military policies and strategies when they were admitted into NATO at the turn of the millennium.[12] Finally, in the field of political economy, John Gould, an American, delved into the flaws of the initially well-received Czech privatization plan, which he compared with the deliberate politicization of the privatization process in Slovakia.[13]

While Western scholars compared various aspects of the two independent republics after 1993, Czech and Slovak scholars, working in their home countries, opted to focus on other questions. As Jan Rychlík

---

[8] James W. Peterson, "Separate Paths: Czech and Slovak Foreign Policies since 1993," *Slovakia* 38, Nos. 70–71 (2005): 121–45.
[9] John A. Scherpereel, *Governing the Czech Republic and Slovakia: Between State Socialism and the European Union* (Boulder: CO: First Forum Press, 2009).
[10] Simon Smith, ed. *Local Communities and Post-Communist Transformation: Czechoslovakia, the Czech Republic and Slovakia* (London: Routledge, 2003).
[11] Kieran Williams and Dennis Deletant, *Security Intelligence Services in New Democracies: The Czech Republic, Slovakia and Romania* (New York: Palgrave, 2001).
[12] Jeffrey Simon, *NATO and the Czech and Slovak Republics: A Comparative Study in Civil-Military Relations* (Lanham, MD: Rowman & Littlefield, 2004).
[13] John Gould, *The Politics of Privatization: Wealth and Power in Postcommunist Europe* (Boulder: Lynne Rienner, 2011).

pointed out, even though certain Czech scholars still are interested in Slovak history, they focus only on the nineteenth and twentieth centuries, especially on the history of Czechoslovakia. Since Slovakia is no longer a part of their former common state, they do not compare and contrast their experiences since 1993.[14] Similarly, scholars in Slovakia, while they have produced comparative works and analyses of Slovakia's development since 1993, often do not compare and contrast what happened in the Slovak Republic versus the Czech Republic since separation.[15] Time, however, has produced a new generation of scholars, who came of age after the split and the independence of the two countries, and time has given the more senior generation the ability to reflect on the intertwined stories of the Slovak and Czech republics.

This volume emerges from the valuable insights of some of the best and brightest Slovak and Czech scholars, who came together with the explicit goal of comparing Czech and Slovak achievements and failures in the twenty years since independence. With support from the University of Ottawa and the Czech and Slovak communities in Canada, the editor put into motion, in 2011, an effort to promote discussion among Czech, Slovak, and Western scholars that resulted in an international scholarly conference entitled "The Czech and Slovak Republics: Twenty Years of Independence, 1993–2013" at the University of Ottawa on October 3–4, 2013. This volume presents the papers and responses from that conference, all of which the authors extensively revised and reworked to take into account the conference discussions, external reviews, and subsequent events. The chapters are clustered in thematic sections, each containing papers by leading Slovak and Czech

---

[14] Jan Rychlík, "České, slovenské, československé dejiny—vztahy a souvislosti," [Czech, Slovak, Czechoslovak history: relations and continuities] in *Československo 1918–1938. Osudy demokracie ve Střední Evropě I* [Czechoslovakia 1918–1938. The fate of democracy in Central Europe], ed. Jaroslav Valenta (Historický ústav ČAV, 1999), 163–9; and Jan Rychlík, "Výskum slovenských dějin v České republice," [The study of Slovak history in the Czech Republic], *Historický časopis* 52, no. 2 (2004): 363–74. Rychlík confirmed this observation to the editor in an e-mail sent on September 12, 2015.

[15] Adam Hudek confirmed the opinion of the editor via e-mail on September 14, 2015. He edited *Overcoming the Old Borders: Beyond the Paradigm of Slovak National History* (Bratislava: Historický ústav SAV, 2013), which is the latest and most comprehensive historiography of the Slovak Republic.

scholars along with the responses of North American experts. They cover the causes of the breakup of Czechoslovakia and the political, social, and economic developments over the subsequent twenty years.

Although the chapters deal with a wide range of topics and vary significantly in their methods and the type of evidence they present, they share quite a few common theoretical perspectives and recurring themes. The most striking of these is the implicit (and sometimes explicit) debate over issues of individual agency and deeper political structures that, in this volume, take shape around questions about the inevitability of the split and the subsequent trajectories of the two countries. In this sense, many of the chapters represent thoughts about broader questions of political change and stability. On a slightly smaller scale, the chapters address the relative impact of cultural variables against economic ones and some discussion about the specific leadership styles that may (or may not) have made a difference in the split and subsequent events. Finally, the chapters address the underlying issues of national identity: what it might mean to be a Czech as opposed to a Slovak and why that might matter.

Jozef Moravčík's and Petr Pithart's plenary addresses could not have been more different. While both had initially opposed the breakup of Czechoslovakia, Moravčík, the interim prime minister of the Slovak Republic in 1994, recognized that, by 1992, the two sides continued "to face a permanent political crisis"; therefore, the best solution was to "divide the state." After retracing historical developments, especially over the past twenty years, Moravčík concluded that the division made sense and that "my conscience is clear." Pithart, the prime minister of the Czech Republic in 1990–1992, by contrast, lamented that, "for the first time in our more than one-thousand year history, we Czechs are living in our 'state-house' alone." He blamed Czech intellectuals and politicians for having failed to recognize the legitimate demands of the Slovaks for home rule, for having been unwilling to compromise, and for carrying most of the blame for the breakup. He bitterly concluded that the breakup was legal but was "without any legitimacy." While neither former politician is typical of the populations they led, their comments subtly reflect on the relative trajectories of the two countries: Slovakia avoided the worst-case scenarios that seemed likely during the government of Vladimír Mečiar in the 1990s and, for most citizens of Slovakia, the split has proved the source of relatively few regrets.

Czechs, too, have regretted little, but they are also unlikely to see the split as "freeing" them from the burden of Slovakia. Pithart focused on the role of human agency. He saw the split not as a structural inevitability but as the result of the personal failure among his colleagues to see a bigger picture and keep the two peoples together. Czechoslovakia, he suggested, probably should have—and could have—been saved.

In the section on the breakup of Czechoslovakia, Jan Rychlík's chapter presents a comprehensive set of underlying factors that led to the breakup of the country. Rychlík, who had served as one of Petr Pithart's advisors during the latter's premiership of the Czech Republic, points out that the basic reason why Czechoslovakia split was that there was no strong "Czechoslovak" identity, in spite of the efforts of Tomáš G. Masaryk (1850–1937), his colleagues, and their successors to promote it. In 1968, the republic federalized, and the Slovaks acquired veto powers in the House of Nations, where their representatives enjoyed parity with the Czechs. Consequently, if the Communist Party ever lost control over Czechoslovakia, which happened in 1989, the Slovaks could paralyze federal legislation. Furthermore, no Czechoslovak political parties arose after 1989 because the Slovak Public Against Violence (VPN) movement forbade them in Slovakia. The first inkling that all was not well in relations between Czechs and Slovaks arose in the winter and spring of 1990, when president Václav Havel (1936–2011) proposed that Czechoslovakia drop the word "socialist" from its official name (it became known as the Czechoslovak Socialist Republic in 1960).[16] The Slovaks agreed but wanted to reintroduce the hyphen into the name so that it would be spelled as Czecho-Slovakia, as it had between 1918 and 1920 and again between 1938 and 1939. The Czechs refused because the hyphen reminded them of the ill-fated post-Munich Second Republic (1938–1939).[17] On April 20, 1990, the

---

[16] See the *Ústava Československé socialistické republiky* [Constitution of the Czechoslovak Socialist Republic] in the S*bírka zákonů Československé socialistické republiky,* částka 40, vydána dne 11. července 1960 [Compendium of documents of the Czechoslovak Socialist Republic, Part 40, published on June 11, 1960].

[17] Stolarik explained the "hyphen war" of 1990 to American readers in "For Slovaks, a Hyphen Means Recognition," on the editorial page of the *New York Times,* April 22, 1990.

two sides finally compromised on the "Czech and Slovak Federative Republic," which appeared on official stationery and on embassy buildings, but the Czechs continued to spell the country Czechoslovakia, while the Slovaks preferred Czecho-Slovakia. This so-called "hyphen war" reflected the two different interpretations of what Czechoslovakia meant to the Czechs and Slovaks. To the Czechs, it meant a strong "functioning federation"; whereas to the Slovaks, it meant two sovereign republics in a loose federation. In the June 1992 elections, Václav Klaus's Civic Democratic Party (ODS) won the largest number of seats in the Czech Republic, while Vladimír Mečiar's Movement for a Democratic Slovakia (HZDS) gained the largest number in Slovakia. These parties and their leaders reflected the two different conceptions of what Czechoslovakia should be, and since they could not come to an agreement, they decided to dissolve the state. Finally, Rychlík reminds us that "states come and go, and no state on earth is eternal" and that "all multinational states are unstable," and offers the examples of the Ottoman Empire, Austria-Hungary, the Soviet Union, and Yugoslavia as multinational states that failed. He also points to the United Kingdom, Belgium, and Spain as states that continue to experience disunity.[18] He concludes that the breakup of Czechoslovakia was not necessarily a bad thing because today "Czech-Slovak relations are excellent. Nobody could want more."

Michael Kraus's commentary largely agrees with Rychlík's analysis. Kraus, too, summarizes the scholarship related to the breakup of Czechoslovakia and concludes that the field still lacks consensus. He gives former president Havel credit for helping to keep the negotiations on the breakup "civilized." He also agrees with Rychlík that "the Czechs and Slovaks today get along better than at any point in the seventy-four-year history of their common statehood."

With their Slovak perspective on the breakup of Czechoslovakia, Adam Hudek and Jozef Žatkuliak offer a comprehensive historiographical discussion of the problem that rejects the interpretation of some

---

[18] On September 18, 2014, Scotland held a referendum on separating from the United Kingdom, which failed to pass by a vote of 55% against and 45% in favor. See "A Kingdom Still United," *The Globe and Mail* (Toronto), September 20, 2014, A9, and "Three Cheers for Pluralism Over Separatism," *The New York Times*, September 21, 2014, SR1.

scholars that an underlying conflict between Slovak *ethnic* nationalism and Czech *civic* nationalism caused the split.[19] The authors agree with Abby Innes that, on both sides, post-communist elites, who retained a pre-1989 mindset to the effect that politicians can do anything without the approval of the people, facilitated the split.[20] Having surveyed events between 1989 and 1992, Hudek and Žatkuliak find a critical juncture in the decision of the dissident Civic Forum, in the Czech Republic, and Public Against Violence, in the Slovak Republic, both of which negotiated the transfer of power from the collapsing Communist Party of Czechoslovakia in November of 1989, to call for early elections in 1992. The authors suggest that the decision did not leave enough time for Czech and Slovak politicians to come to a mutually acceptable agreement on the future form of their state. Ultimately, Czech politicians following Klaus, favored the breakup of Czechoslovakia over the confederal model that Mečiar and his associates proposed. Interestingly enough, the authors conclude that the breakup of Czechoslovakia into two independent states bodes ill for the future of the EU, which attempts to promote more, rather than less, unity in Europe.

Stanislav J. Kirschbaum's commentary on the Hudek-Žatkuliak chapter takes the authors to task for what he argued was their incomplete historiographical discussion and inadequate historical background. Kirschbaum asserts that a discussion of independence should reach back to the period of the first Slovak Republic (1939–1945) to show that the Slovaks were capable of running their own affairs and that "independence was the only solution."

Juraj Hocman's chapter begins the section on politics since 1993, and his detailed, step-by-step analysis of Slovak politics since independence traces, in great detail, the rule of the autocratic Mečiar between 1992 and 1998. Hocman sees it as part of a wider process by which Slovak politicians have evolved into "an autonomous political class which opened itself to the public only in times of elections." He argues that, initially, the members of this political class shaped economic developments

---

[19] Nedelsky, in *Defining the Sovereign Community*, was among those who presented this interpretation.
[20] Abby Innes, *Czechoslovakia: The Short Goodbye* (New Haven: Yale University Press, 2001).

because they allowed their friends to gain control over state assets during the privatizations of the 1990s. Within a decade, however, the tables were turned, and the winners in the privatization process began to dominate the politicians. As a result, ordinary Slovaks became disillusioned with politics and opted for the left-of-center populist, Robert Fico, and anyone else who sought to stop the oligarchs. Hocman concludes that the Slovak political system still showed signs of political immaturity, that Slovak citizens still had to learn how to become good patriots, and that Slovak politicians needed to start behaving in the public interest.

In his commentary on Juraj Hocman's chapter, Kevin Deegan-Krause argues that, in a sense, "Slovakia is everywhere" since Slovak politics are typical in East-Central Europe. Deegan-Krause supplements Hocman's analysis with attention to other issues. Among these is the relatively successful accommodation between the ethnic Slovak and ethnic Hungarian populations and the far-from-resolved situation of 400,000 Roma citizens in Slovakia, whose poverty and exclusion from mainstream society has posed challenges for every Slovak government since independence.[21] Deegan-Krause also focuses on the role of political institutions and the "authority issue," noting that Mečiar tried to undermine the democratic system in Slovakia but ultimately failed to do so, unlike in Belarus and Russia, and that Prime Minister Fico's loss in the presidential elections of 2014 reflect the continued unwillingness of the Slovak electorate to put all power into the hands of one party, unlike in neighboring Hungary, where Fidesz was simultaneously consolidating its rule. The rise and fall of new political parties in Slovakia is a cause of concern to Deegan-Krause, but it is not unique to Slovakia and is a worldwide phenomenon. In spite of these open questions, Deegan-Krause concludes, independent Slovakia has become "ordinary" in East-Central Europe and is, therefore, a success.

---

[21] According to the 2000 census, 520,528 Magyars and 89,920 Roma lived in Slovakia. The number of Roma is too low since many of them self-identify as Magyars, Slovaks, or others. For more on minorities in Slovakia, see Pál Csáky, "Human Rights and Inter-Group Relations in Slovakia," in *The Slovak Republic: A Decade of Independence (1993–2002)*, ed. by M. Mark Stolarik (Waucondia, IL: Bolchazi-Carducci, 2002), 95–104.

In her succinct chapter on Czech politics since independence, Adéla Gjuričová focuses on the main trends. She agrees with Jan Rychlík that the Czechs always regarded Czechoslovakia as "their" state and look upon the Czech Republic as a direct (if somewhat truncated) continuation of that state. She then asserts that, in the two decades after independence, individual agents, particularly Havel, Klaus, and Miloš Zeman, dominated Czech politics. While Havel was a bohemian, in the literary sense of the word, and anti-political, Klaus and Zeman were pragmatic economists from different sides of the political spectrum, Klaus being a right-wing "neoliberal" and Zeman a Social Democrat. In spite of their ideological differences, both Klaus and Zeman rejected Havel's humanism and managed to isolate him and other political parties so that, for the next two decades, Czech governments were under the leadership of either Klaus's Civic Democratic Party (ODS) or Zeman's Social Democrats (ČSSD). Indeed, in spite of their ideological differences, Klaus and Zeman often supported each other's legislative policies, even as they criticized each other. In addition, Klaus was a eurosceptic who, in spite of having supported the inclusion of the Czech Republic into the EU and NATO, heavily criticized the EU and rejected adopting the euro as the Czech currency. The other main anomaly in Czech politics, Gjuričová continues, was the enduring popularity (15 percent support) of the old Communist Party (now called the Communist Party of Bohemia and Moravia or KSČM), although none of the other major parties were willing to accept it into a coalition. By the time of the 2013 elections, Czech voters had grown so disillusioned with the "old" parties that 18.6 percent of them voted for a brand new pro-business party under the leadership of the expatriate Slovak billionaire, Andrej Babiš, who became a deputy prime minister in the new coalition government under the Social Democrats. It remains to be seen if the ODS, which received only 7.7 percent of the vote, or the Social Democrats, who fell to 20 percent, will be able to maintain their support at these lower levels.

In her commentary on Gjuričová's chapter, Carol Skalnik Leff focuses on the paradox of the Czech Communist Party and the continuities and discontinuities among other parties. To the question as to why the Czech Communist Party survived with strong electoral support in the new Czech Republic, in contrast to the failings of such parties in other East-Central European states, she answers that it had stronger historical roots than elsewhere, and was thoroughly purged of reformers in 1969–

1970, so that only the more "rigid" and "ossified" members remained. Since the Social Democrats refused to form coalitions with the Czech Communists, the SDs have found it very difficult to form coalitions, and this has led to unstable governments (twelve of them) between 1996 and 2014. Political parties, by contrast, were quite stable in the Czech Republic until 2010. After that, newcomer protest parties gained a solid foothold against the establishment. Among them were two pro-business, populist parties under the leadership of Babiš and the Czech-Japanese Tomio Okamura. Interestingly enough, even though 70 percent of Czechs were either atheists or non-religious, a viable Christian Democratic Party has endured, largely based in Moravia. It attracts voters who prefer traditional Christian values, whether or not they are atheists.[22] Finally, even though only 40 percent of Czechs expressed pride in their nation, Klaus and Zeman both raised the specter of Czech nationalism, when, in the 2013 presidential elections, they questioned the Czech identity of Zeman's opponent, former foreign minister Karel von Schwarzenberg![23]

The section on economic development begins with a chapter on Slovakia by Ľudovít Hallon, Miroslav Londák, and Adam Hudek. In a survey of Slovakia's place in Czechoslovakia's economy since 1918, they show the process by which the Slovak economy, which started out much weaker than the Czech economy, climbed to within 13 percent of Czech per capita GDP by 1989. In the section on development after 1993, the authors argue that, unlike the economists at the Czech

---

[22] For Czech attitudes towards organized religion, see Paul Froese, "Secular Czechs and Devout Slovaks: Explaining Religious Differences," *Review of Religious Research* 46, no. 3 (March, 2005): 269–83. Karel D. Bicha dealt with Czech hostility towards the Roman Catholic Church in "Settling Accounts with an Old Adversary: The Decatholicization of Czech Immigrants in America," *Histoire sociale—Social History* 8 (November, 1971): 45–60.

[23] Klaus and Zeman's alliance against the "suspect" Czech Schwarzenberg refutes the claim of the former communist historian, Jiří Kořalka, who, in a very flawed historiographical article, wrote that Czech nationalism is "unthinkable." See his "Czechoslovakia," *American Historical Review* 97 (October, 1992): 1026–40. For critiques of this article, see "Communications" by M. Mark Stolarik and Milan Hauner, (*American Historical Review* 98 (April, 1993): 650–1). For a general discussion of Czech nationalism, see Ladislav Holy, *The Little Czech and the Great Czech Nation: National Identity in the Post-Communist Social Transformation* (New York: Cambridge University Press, 1996).

Academy of Science, some Slovak economists rejected the principles of a "standard economy" and preferred one based on "national sentiments." Therefore, they disagreed with the "voucher privatization" of the federal minister of finance, Klaus, in favor of direct sales to the managers of various large industries in Slovakia, a position that supported the desire of Prime Minister Mečiar to create "a strong group of Slovak businessmen," who would support his policies. The same approaches, however, led to tunneling of large Slovak enterprises, such as the Eastern Slovak Steel Works in Košice, and the creation of instant billionaires, such as Alexander Rezeš. Only the National Bank of Slovakia, they conclude, managed to remain independent of Mečiar's influence, and its continued independence prevented more damage to the Slovak economy. By 1998, the Slovak public had tired of Mečiar's authoritarianism and voted in a right-wing electoral coalition under Mikuláš Dzurinda, who reversed Mečiar's policies. During its two terms in office, Dzurinda's governments opened up Slovakia to foreign investment, floated the currency, and replaced existing taxes with a 19 percent flat tax, which attracted many new foreign investors. While the rest of Europe approved the political transformation and admitted Slovakia into both the EU and NATO, the policies had less positive impact on Slovak citizens, who suffered from high unemployment and relatively low wages. The left-wing populist Fico replaced Dzurinda in 2006 and has remained in office since then, except for the brief interregnum of Iveta Radičová's pro-market government between mid-2010 and early 2012. Fico proceeded to dismantle many of Dzurinda's reforms, even making some modifications to the flat tax.

According to the authors, the true impact of these policy shifts remains to be seen. They note that Slovakia's economy did not collapse after independence, as many western observers had predicted,[24] and

---

[24] For misgivings about Slovakia's future, see Stephen Engleberg, "Czechoslovakia Breaks in Two, To Wide Regret," *The New York Times*, January 1, 1993; and Paul Koring "Breakup of a Nation, a Split Decision," *The Globe and Mail* (Toronto), December 31, 1992. The Canadian political scientist, Robert Young, even used the breakup of Czechoslovakia and the supposed dark future of independent Slovakia as a warning to French separatists wanting to proclaim the independence of Quebec from the rest of Canada. See his *The Breakup of Czechoslovakia* (Kingston: Institute for Intergovernmental Relations, 1994).

the Slovak GDP increased from 57 percent of the EU average, in 1993, to 75 percent, in 2013. However, Slovak unemployment remained at 14 percent, 160,000 Slovaks were working in Western Europe, and the significant disparity between western Slovakia and the rest of the country continued.

John A. Gould's commentary generally supports the Hallon-Londák-Hudek analysis and underlines the mistaken belief of many economists and political leaders in East-Central Europe, the Balkans, and Eastern Europe that the privatization of industry in the former Soviet Bloc countries would lead to political reform and democratization. Instead, Gould argues, it frequently led to "a short-term, high-stakes battle for the wealth and power of the country." Slovakia's example is notable. Mečiar cancelled voucher privatization in Slovakia in 1994, largely because he wanted the managers of the large firms to become his allies and supporters. Gould credits the Dzurinda governments with reversing Mečiar's policies and notes that, despite the problem of unemployment, Slovakia performed very well economically, until the worldwide recession hit in 2008–2009. Gould argues that, in the process, "Slovakia has now fully hitched its wagon to the global economy," and how well it will do in the future depends heavily upon the performance of the world economy, as well as on the policies of Fico's Social Democratic government.

Martin Pospíšil, in his chapter on economic developments in the Czech Republic since 1993, covers three periods: the initial transformation (1991–1997); crisis and convergence (1997–2007); and the global crisis (2008–2014). In the first part, he focuses on the transition from communism to capitalism under the leadership of economists from the Prognostic Institute of the Czech Academy of Science. He points out that there was no game plan for this transition, so Czech economists, under Klaus, adopted neoclassical economics, based upon the "Washington consensus," which stressed privatization, liberalization, and stabilization.[25] Unfortunately, this "Washington consensus" ignored his-

---

[25] In spite of the Cold War between the Soviet Union and the West from 1947 to 1989, and American hostility to communism, the American government never developed an economic game plan for Eastern Europe should communism collapse. Jean Kirkpatrick, the American ambassador to the United Nations in the early 1980s, best summarized the American attitude in one

toric and institutional differences among countries. Thus, the Czech Republic, using Klaus's voucher system, privatized 75 percent of all businesses. However, Czech law enforcement, corporate governance, and business ethics were unprepared for the rapid changes, and the privatization led to the tunneling of businesses and much corruption. In addition, Klaus did not shut down inefficient enterprises for fear of rising unemployment. So low productivity continued, and income stagnated below 1989 levels until 2001. In the second part of his essay, Pospíšil pointed out that state-owned banks were under the control of privatization funds until 1997, and they made tunneling possible by lending money to companies under their control. This led to a banking scandal in 1997, the defeat of Klaus's right-wing government, and its replacement by Zeman's Social Democrats. Ironically, it was the Social Democrats who privatized Czech banks and stopped tunneling, and this led to the 1998–2007 economic recovery. The fickle Czech electorate returned Klaus's party to power between 2006 and 2013, and the new prime minister, Mirek Topolánek (Klaus had become President), asked Czechs to tighten their belts when the world recession hit in 2008. He also moved the Czech economy closer to that of Germany, and this helped Czechs weather the storm. Thus, Pospíšil concludes, "despite mistakes made, Czech economic development over the last decades has been a success."

Sharon Fisher, in her commentary on Pospíšil's chapter, sharply disagrees with his assessment of success. She points out that Czech per capita GDP, as compared to that of the EU improved only from 77 percent in 1995 to 80 percent in 2013. Slovakia's GDP, by comparison, shot up from 48 percent to 76 percent. In fact, Fisher argues, "Slovakia experienced one of the fastest convergence rates of all new member states [of the EU]." According to Fisher, Pospíšil did not explain this huge difference. Indeed, she continues, there was very little economic

---

of her speeches, when she tried to justify American support for right-wing regimes in Latin America and hostility towards communism. She declared that she had seen many instances of right-wing governments eventually becoming democratic, but she never had heard of a communist regime reverting to democracy. She based her speech on an article that she had published as "Dictatorship and Double Standards," *Commentary Magazine* 68 (November, 1979): 34–45.

reform in the Czech Republic after 1993, and the coupon privatization failed to create an adequate legal and institutional framework. The Czech "economic miracle" that Klaus bragged about in the early 1990s had disintegrated by 1997, and Social Democratic governments were left to clean up the mess, while Klaus played the nationalist card and became a eurosceptic. As a result, Fisher concludes, the Czechs now "appear to be happy with neither EU membership nor the Czech-Slovak split."

In the final section on societal changes, Martin and Zora Bútora use empirical data and many public opinion surveys to offer a comprehensive overview of developments in Slovakia between 1993 and 2013. They present seven snapshots of Slovak society, over the last twenty years, which depict a country that "has muddled through," succeeding in some ways and lagging in others. Slovakia, they argue, has joined the club of the most successful countries in the world; but it scores high in corruption, with an inefficient bureaucracy and a corrupt judiciary. Slovakia's citizens are deeply concerned with unemployment and "civic helplessness," but 64 percent of Slovaks take pride in their country, and ethnic pluralism has become the norm, in spite of the nagging difficulties related to integrating the Roma into Slovak society. Civil society survives, even though most Slovak governments do not like NGOs and often set up roadblocks in their way. Although the Bútoras worry that Slovakia still needs a clear vision for the future,[26] they nevertheless echo the message "Don't be afraid!" that the late Pope John Paul II delivered to Slovakia, and they finish with the cautiously optimistic conclusion that, no matter what the difficulty, Slovak society has always been able to "stand up after falling down."

In her commentary on the Bútoras' chapter, Sharon Wolchik raises four follow-up questions: Why, if Slovakia ranked so high on the corruption index, did its citizens not perceive the problems with the judiciary? How, in light of the 2012 Gorilla scandal, which pointed to the major financial institutions' widespread illegal financing of parties, can Slovakia deal with the inability (or unwillingness) of political parties

---

[26] They may have taken the need for a vision for the future from Tom Nicholson's chapter, "Je čas dať tomuto štátu zmysel" [It's time to give this state some meaning], in *Odkiaľ a kam?* ed. Bútora et al., 281–91. A revised and expanded version of this article appeared as "Corruption in Slovakia: Time to Reclaim the State," in *Slovakia* 42, nos. 78–79 (2015): 112–25.

and their leaders to act in the public interest?[27] How should Slovakia deal with those who are economically disadvantaged, especially women, the poor, and young people who are leaving for work elsewhere? And finally, what kind of "new narrative" would serve to achieve these various goals? Wolchik suggests that observers still need to understand Slovakia as a post-communist society, whose leaders have yet to overcome communist ways of thinking and doing, and that Slovakia's citizens need to broaden their definition of democracy from simply free and fair elections to include the rule of law, a well-cultivated civil society, and democratic political values. Thus, Wolchik concludes, "Slovakia still has a way to go."

In his chapter on social developments in the Czech Republic since 1993, Oldřich Tůma claims that outsiders could perceive this story as "boring," and that Czech society, over time, had fallen into "a bad mood." He blamed this situation on post-communist society, which saw the Czech Republic turn from a fairly egalitarian society to a stratified one, with former communist functionaries, members of State Security, and black marketers gaining a jump on others in social mobility. His statistical analysis finds that the share of Czechs defining themselves as "middle class" dropped from 61 percent in 1991 to only 37 percent in 2007, and that the Czech Republic's unusually low unemployment rates of only 4 percent, in the 1990s, reached higher levels, between 6–9 percent, depending upon the region. Nevertheless, while only 10 percent of young people studied at university in the 1980s, 50 percent did so in 2013. He argues that, even as the Czech Republic came closer to Western Europe in economic terms, it continues to suffer from political division, constant squabbling, and prevailing feelings of frustration, failure, and skepticism. He finds it to be "spiritually stagnant."

In his commentary on Tůma's chapter, James W. Peterson called for more research on the relationship between public opinion and the actions of politicians that might yield insights into the disconnect between political activity and the general public's reaction of feelings of "frustration." Peterson also asked whether there was a relationship between political behavior and economic conditions, particularly with

---

[27] For an exposé on the Gorilla scandal, see Tom Nicholson, *Gorila* (Bratislava: Dixit, 2012).

regard to the continuing strength of the Communist Party in the Czech Republic and specific examples of the communist legacy.

A number of conclusions can be drawn from the first two decades of Czech and Slovak independence. The new findings range from the immediate and factual to deeper insights into the methods by which we compare large-scale social transformations. The evidence suggests a strong similarity of outcomes, despite potentially large initial differences in leadership and institutional paths between the two republics. While the Czechs privatized their state-owned industries, largely with the voucher system, and the Slovaks did so through crony sales (as Petr Pithart put it, the Slovaks stole openly while the Czechs stole discreetly), both ended up with thoroughly tunneled industries and rampant corruption that no one seems capable of eliminating. While the Czech party system experienced twenty years of continuity in players and alliances and Slovakia's system changed seemingly with each election, both ended up with a political class that demonstrated contempt for the electorate, ushered in widespread dissatisfaction, and engendered a rapid influx of new outsider-led parties. The similarity of these outcomes at the macrolevel suggests the need for a serious reconsideration of the underlying factors that produced the result. If Czech and Slovak cultures are truly different, as some Slovaks and Czechs would suggest, then the similarities suggest the existence of powerful homogenizing influences, old ones, such as the legacy of communism and persistent aspects of political culture, or perhaps new ones, such as economic globalization and the spread of new political technologies.[28] Another possibility may be that, despite the appearance of fundamental differences in culture between Slovaks and Czechs, their underlying similarities in certain areas, such as in tolerance of corruption, orientation toward the market, xenophobia, and national pride, may be greater than many care to acknowledge.

The difficulty in finding answers to such questions reflects the deeper challenges of scholarly research in the social sciences. The complexity of societal change means that even the most experienced scholars are unable to agree about the interpretation of data. Where

---

[28] See Steve Forbes, "Investor's Paradise," *Forbes*, August 11, 2003; Matthew Reynolds, "Once a Backwater, Slovakia Surges," *The New York Times*, December 28, 2004, and "Slovakia: Unleashing the Tatra Tiger," Special Advertising Feature, *Business Week*, August 7, 2006.

the questions are so fundamentally difficult, circumstances stand in the way of efforts to find answers. The baseline of expectations plays a big role in how scholars judge outcomes. This leads to relatively more sanguine views of progress for Slovakia, which seemed in greater danger than the Czech Republic in 1993, even though both have arrived at much the same destination. Perspective also matters: one's national origin—whether Czech or Slovak or outsider—shapes what one expects to see. It is for this reason that this project's goal of creating a focused dialogue directly between Slovaks and Czechs has been so important. Putting these accounts side by side and then provoking a direct dialogue was essential for the participants in the conference to filter out what was superficial from what was essential. Whether the split of Czechoslovakia was inevitable or preventable, whether the (re)convergence of the two countries' paths is ingrained or merely superficial are questions that have too many variables for crafting easy answers. Nevertheless, academic projects, like the chapters in this book, help guide researchers and rule out glib answers about "those Czechs" and "those Slovaks" that are more easily repeated than researched.

Any increase in understanding should lead to an improvement in action. The chapters in this book lead the reader to a few immediate conclusions about what might have been done and what could be done better. Tunneling and corruption arose because there was no game plan for converting a communist economy and society to capitalism and democracy. This was a major failing of the West, which railed against communism for forty-five years but made no plans about converting the so-called captive nations into democratic and capitalist states should Soviet rule and its Marxist-Leninist ideology disintegrate. At the same time, the relative success of the separation of Czechoslovakia into the Czech and Slovak Republics does not bode well for the EU, which is struggling to promote deeper integration among its member states.[29] The Czech-Slovak split may even contribute, in a

---

[29] At the time of this writing (September 2015), the European Union was deeply divided over whether or not to accept hundreds of thousands of Middle Eastern, African, and Afghan refugees. Generally speaking, the wealthier western and northern European countries were willing to accept them; the poorer eastern European countries were not. See "Hungary Shuts its Border to Refugees," *The Globe and Mail*, September 16, 2015, A3.

small way, to movements that aim to break up the United Kingdom, Belgium, and Spain. That may not be a bad thing because, as Rychlík pointed out, "states come and go, and no state on earth is eternal." Finally, all the scholars who contributed to this book agreed that, ever since the split, relations between the Czechs and Slovaks have never been better. Thus, the breakup of Czechoslovakia in 1993, like Norway's secession from Sweden in 1905, may be a good model for other nations who live in a common state but wish to go it alone.[30] After all, there were only fifty independent political states on the face of the earth in 1914.[31] Today there are 193.[32] Most of them became independent through armed struggle. The Slovak and Czech model can provide, for many states facing dissolution, a reasonable alternative.

---

[30] For this story see Stuart Burch, "Norway and 1905," *History Today* 55, no. 6 (2005): 2–3.
[31] *The Statesman's Year-Book: Statistical and Historical Annual of the States of the World for the Year 1914* (London: Macmillan, 1914).
[32] See the official website of the *United Nations*: www.un.org.

Part I

THE DISSOLUTION OF CZECHOSLOVAKIA

CHAPTER 1

The "Velvet Split" of Czechoslovakia (1989–1992)

Jan Rychlík

The main reason Czechoslovakia disintegrated in 1992 can be explained quite simply: there was no strong Czechoslovak identity. Starting with its creation in 1918, the Czechs identified with Czechoslovakia as their nation-state, but they considered it in fact as their Czech nation-state. The Slovaks never saw Czechoslovakia this way, but rather as a loose union of two nation-states. Language similarity between Czech and Slovak was not enough to span two fully conscious nations with different histories. By 1992, the Czechs and Slovaks did not need each other any more.[1] However, the split took place in a concrete political situation and in the specific constitutional system of Czechoslovakia, which did not offer many alternatives.

---

[1] For the main literature about the split of Czechoslovakia in English see Michael Kraus and Allison Stanger, eds., *Irreconcilable Differences? Explaining Czechoslovakia's Dissolution* (Lanham: Rowman and Littlefield, 2000); Jiří Musil et al., *The End of Czechoslovakia* (Budapest: Central European University Press, 1995); Eric Stein, *Czecho/Slovakia: Ethnic Conflict, Constitutional Fissure, Negotiated Breakup* (Ann Arbor: University of Michigan Press, 1997). For literature in other languages (mainly Czech and Slovak) see Jan Rychlík, *Rozdělení Československa 1989–1992* [The dissolution of Czechoslovakia, 1989–1992] (Prague: Vyšehrad, 2013), 402–8.

Constitutional Law number 143/1968 of 27 October 1968[2] established two new states on the territory of the former unitary Czechoslovak Socialist Republic (ČSSR): the Czech Socialist Republic (ČSR) and the Slovak Socialist Republic (SSR), each with its own parliament (the Czech and the Slovak National Councils) and its own government, effective January 1, 1969. According to the preamble of the constitution, the ČSR and the SSR were, in theory, two completely sovereign states, which voluntarily delegated part of their sovereignty to federal organs, the Federal Assembly, and the federal government in the new Czechoslovak Socialist Republic. The federal government could make decisions only in a narrowly delimited realm.

To properly understand the background of the split of Czechoslovakia, it is necessary to understand first the mechanism of the Czecho-Slovak federation. The Czecho-Slovak federation was based on the principle of consensus between the representatives of the Czech Republic and the representatives of the Slovak Republic. The Federal Assembly had two chambers, the Chamber of the People (in Czech: *Sněmovna lidu*/ in Slovak: *Snemovňa ľudu*) and the Chamber of the Nations (*Sněmovna národů*/ *Snemovňa národov*). The Chamber of the People had 200 deputies (from 1990 on, only 150 deputies) elected on the basis of proportional representation throughout the country. Because there were ten million Czechs and five million Slovaks in Czechoslovakia, the number of Czech deputies elected to the Chamber of the People was about twice as many as those elected in Slovakia. The Chamber of the Nations had equal representation; each republic had seventy-five deputies. There were two types of laws: simple laws (*obyčejné/obyčajné zákony*) were adopted if they were approved in both houses by a majority of deputies in attendance. The House of the People could act, if more than half of all deputies were present, while the House of the Nations could act, if more than half of the deputies elected in the Czech Republic and half of the deputies elected in the Slovak Republic were present. The peculiarity of the constitutional system was the so-called minority veto *(zákaz majorizace/zákaz majorizácie)*, which made it impossible for the (Czech) majority to override the votes of their Slovak counter-

---

[2] *Sbírka zákonů Československé socialistické republiky* (Sb.) 1968, č. 143/1968 Sb. Explanatory note: *Sbírka zákonů/Zbierka zákonov*—Collection of Laws) was printed simultaneously in Czech and Slovak versions; both versions have the same legal validity. The laws are available on the Internet at http://aplikace.mvcr.cz/sbirka-zakonu/.

parts: legislation concerning issues of economic significance required the votes of a majority of the deputies in the Chamber of the People and a majority of deputies elected (not just present) to the Chamber of Nations in the Czech Republic and deputies elected to the Chamber of Nations elected in the Slovak Republic (voting separately). Further, constitutional amendments and the election of the president required a three-fifths majority of deputies in the Chamber of the People and a tree-fifths majority of both Czech and Slovak deputies (again voting separately) in the Chamber of the Nations. This consensus principle in fact embodied a strong confederative element and signaled the potential for a constitutional crisis. If a consensus was not reached between Czech and Slovak representatives, the state was paralyzed. The constitution did not offer any solution for a political deadlock.

For the majority of Slovaks, the establishment of the federation in 1968 seemed to be a sufficient guarantee for their further national development. Most Slovaks truly believed that the federation would make possible both Slovak statehood and a common Czech-Slovak state. Therefore, the Slovaks did not raise the question of an independent Slovak state in 1968. The Czechs would have preferred the unitary Czechoslovak state as it was established in 1918; however, being aware that such a solution was unacceptable to the Slovaks, they accepted the federation and regarded it as a necessary concession, hoping that it would secure long-term, if not permanent, stability for Czechoslovakia.[3]

In fact, the 1969–1989 federal constitution and its "minority veto" had a minimal effect because real political power was vested in the Presidium of the Central Committee of the Communist Party of Czechoslovakia (KSČ). The parliaments—federal, Czech, and Slovak—had no significance. Nor did the elections in which voters were always presented with only a single list of candidates chosen and approved by the leadership of the Communist Party. Subsequently, the deputies voted according to the directives of the government, which were in fact the directives of the KSČ. The possibility of a deadlock due to different votes by Czech and Slovak deputies was unthinkable. Just like the parliaments, the governments—federal and republican—were mere transmission belts for the Communist Party of Czechoslovakia.

---

[3] See Jan Rychlík, *Češi a Slováci ve 20. století. Spolupráce a konflikty* [Czechs and Slovaks in the 20th century: cooperation and conflicts] (Prague: Vyšehrad, 2012), 533–64.

For all these reasons, the federation had, in its own way, a strange impact on Czech-Slovak relations. The Czechs saw the federation only as an endless increase of Slovak officials in the federal ministries and as a transfer of resources from the federal budget to Slovakia. From 1969 to 1987, the First Secretary of the Communist Party of Czechoslovakia was a Slovak, Gustáv Husák (1913–1991), who was also president of the republic from 1975 to 1989. The *éminence grise* of the communist leadership was another Slovak—Vasil Biľak (a Slovakized Rusyn). Consequently, a widespread feeling arose in the Czech Lands that the state was run by Slovak communist "normalizers,"[4] who were shifting resources from the federal budget to benefit Slovakia. In effect, they believed that the Czech Lands were subsidizing Slovakia.

The Slovaks, no less than the Czechs, were also dissatisfied with the federation, because it did not fulfill their expectations. The Slovaks wanted local matters to be decided in Bratislava and not in Prague. They also expected that the federation would give Slovakia increased visibility on the world stage. Neither of these aims was realized. The outside world continued to view Czechoslovakia as a Czech state, so that the adjectives Czechoslovak and Czech were frequently interchangeable in foreign languages. Husák and Biľak were just as unpopular in Slovakia as they were in the Czech lands. In general, Slovaks regarded the federal ministers, deputies, and bureaucrats in Prague as turncoats and traitors who did not defend Slovak interests. A significant segment of the Slovak population continued to feel that they lived in Czech bondage and that Slovakia was being economically exploited by Czechs.

Arguably for Slovakia, the normalized federation had some positive effects. A strong Slovak managerial class arose from a previously small one. The federation meant the creation of a Slovak government and Slovak ministries in Bratislava, which, though for the time being functioning only as branches of Prague federal offices, could begin to work quite independently at any time.

The fall of the communist regime in November of 1989 reopened the question of Czech-Slovak relations, a problem with which Czechoslovakia had wrestled since its very inception in 1918. In November

---

[4] The period after the Soviet occupation (August 21, 1968) is called the "period of normalization." The communist politicians of that period are called "normalizers."

1989, two different organizations were founded: Public Against Violence (*Verejnosť proti násiliu*—VPN) in Slovakia and the Civic Forum (*Občanské forum*—OF) in the Czech lands. Attempts to create branches of the Civic Forum in Slovakia where the citizenry traditionally felt strongly pro-Czechoslovak (especially in Eastern Slovakia) were quickly blocked by Public Against Violence. The Civic Forum, bowing to the will of Public Against Violence, abolished those chapters of the Civic Forum in Slovakia that had already formed. At the outset of 1990, it became evident that no political force in Slovakia could ignore the question of Czech-Slovak relations. Czech political parties, especially those that had been active before the communist takeover in 1948, attempted to make inroads in Slovakia, but they encountered a total lack of voter interest because they were unable to offer any new ideas on Czech-Slovak relations. Conversely, the Slovak Democratic Party (*Demokratická strana*—DS), the largest anti-communist Slovak political party during 1945–1948, could not gain any influence in the Czech Lands, since its emphasis on Slovak issues did not interest Czech voters.

After November of 1989, Slovakia's status within Czechoslovakia was a plank in the platform of every political party in Slovakia; the differences among them turned only on the degree of Slovak autonomy they required. In this regard, Public Against Violence and the Democratic Party were moderate parties, which supported the modification of the existing Czechoslovak Federation, while the Christian Democratic Movement (*Kresťanskodemokratické hnutie*—KDH) was more radical. At the extreme end, the Slovak National Party (*Slovenská národná strana*—SNS) of Víťazoslav Moric and Jozef Prokeš demanded only a very loose Czech-Slovak Union. In both the KDH and SNS, there were many proponents of an independent Slovak Republic, but in the first half of 1990, even the SNS had not yet formally introduced this demand. While Czech and Slovak communists gradually parted ways, and an independent Slovak Communist Party was born (KSS, later the Party of the Democratic Left, *Strana demokratickej ľavice*—SDĽ), the latter's embrace of the Slovak national program positioned the Slovak communists nicely into the new political scene.

The first open Czech-Slovak conflict took place in connection with the Federal Assembly's deliberations on the country's new name. Given the political and socioeconomic changes that had occurred since November 1989, in early 1990, President Václav Havel proposed that the officially used title—the Czechoslovak Socialist Republic—be amended to the Czechoslovak Republic, which had been in use before 1960. A similar proposal had been made at the end of December 1989. It had been rejected because the communists still held a majority in the Federal Assembly and in both national parliaments at the time. Constitutional law 14/1990, passed on January 23, 1990, however, removed this obstacle. All the legislative assemblies underwent reconstruction: a portion of the deputies lost their mandates and were replaced by new representatives, mostly from the ranks of the Civic Forum and Public Against Violence. That is why Havel assumed that his proposal would be accepted without any problems. That was not the case.

The Slovak National Council fundamentally opposed the proposed name change (to the Czechoslovak Republic), demanding instead that the new state be called the Federation of Czecho-Slovakia. In this fashion, the world would be put on notice that Czechoslovakia was not simply a Czech state, as was seen from abroad, but instead consisted of two nation-states—the Czech and the Slovak ones.[5] This proposal was supported by a clear majority of the Slovak people, but rejected in the Czech Lands. For the Czechs, the name Czecho-Slovakia evoked bitter memories of the post-Munich (or the Second) Republic, when it was officially used until March 15, 1939, when the rest of the Czech Lands were occupied and incorporated into Nazi Germany. On March 29, 1990, after long discussions,[6] the Federal Assembly approved Constitutional Law 81/1990, which established the official name as the Czechoslovak Federal Republic. Demonstrations against the new name immediately erupted in Slovakia, and for the first time, slogans demanding an independent Slovakia appeared. The VPN had accepted the new name during deliberations of the Federal Assembly, so Slovak critics now charged that party with betraying Slovak national interests. Czech deputies in the Federal Assembly backed

---

[5] In this aspect it should be noted that the demand for more "visibility" from abroad was understandable. However, the world community always thinks in the category "one nation=one state." Czechoslovakia, even written with a hyphen, would be still seen from abroad as a Czech state, as was the case after its new name, the Czech and Slovak Federative Republic, came into being.

[6] The shorthand reports of all lawmaking bodies on the territory of the former Czechoslovakia (including the former Federal Assembly, the Czech National Council and the Slovak National Council) are available on www.psp.cz/eknih/index.cz. We do not refer to this source again in the text.

down and on April 20, 1990, another Constitutional Law (101/1990) proclaimed the official name to be the Czech and Slovak Federative Republic (ČSFR). The unofficial name, Czechoslovakia, and the adjective, Czechoslovak, could thereafter be written in Czech as one word but in Slovak with a hyphen (e. g., Czecho-Slovakia).[7]

The so-called hyphen war indicated that subsequent discussions were not going to be easy and that the Slovak side would propose a maximum loosening of the federation. While the VPN participated in the negotiations that produced the interim federal government (December 1989–June 1990) and the first federal prime minister, Marián Čalfa was a Slovak, Slovaks did not trust the federal organs of government. Even the pro-Czechoslovak VPN insisted that the issues concerning the new framework for Czech-Slovak relations were beyond the purview of the federal government and that they should be negotiated on a bilateral, republic-level basis. The first such unofficial talks took place on April 11, 1990 between Czech Premier Petr Pithart and Slovak Premier Milan Čič. The Slovak premier outlined for Pithart the principles of a future Czech-Slovak relationship. These, in turn, were based on key principles that had been developed by the VPN. The program was also based on the principles of 1968, anticipating two essentially independent republics, which would delegate some of their competencies to common federal organs. Formal negotiations were to begin after the June 1990 elections.

The Czechoslovak Federative Republic's first free elections took place on June 8 and 9, 1990. The elections were based on the principle of proportional representation, but parties that did not receive at least 5 percent of the vote, and in the elections to the Slovak parliament, 3 percent, won no seats. In Slovakia, the VPN received the largest percentage of the votes, 29.3 percent, followed by the KDH's 19.2 percent, the SNS's 13.9 percent, the KSS–SDUs 13.3 percent, and the Hungarian coalition (Coexistence and the Hungarian Christian Democratic Movement) with 8.7 percent. The Democratic Party and the Green Party also made it in into the Slovak National Council. In the Czech Republic, the Civic Forum came first, followed by the Czechoslovak People's Party (ČSL), the Communist Party, and the Movement for Self-Governing Democracy—the Society for Moravia and Silesia

---

[7] For the "hyphen war" see Milan Šútovec, *Semióza jako politikum alebo "pomlčková vojna"* [Semiotics as politics or "the hyphen war"] (Bratislava: Kalligram, 1999).

(HSD–SMS), which proposed a three-way federation of Bohemia, Moravia, and Slovakia, also won seats in the parliament.[8] The new federal government consisted of a coalition between the VPN and the Civic Forum, with the support of the Czech and Slovak center-right parties (the coalition of ČSL–KDS, that is, the Christian Democratic Party and KDH), and it was headed again by Marián Čalfa. The Czech government was again led by Petr Pithart, but the leadership of the Slovak government changed: Milan Čič was replaced by former Slovak Minister of the Interior Vladimír Mečiar. Negotiations between the Czech and Slovak governments continued. In addition, there were also negotiations between Chairman (Speaker) of the Slovak National Council František Mikloško (VPN) and his counterpart in the Czech Lands, Dagmar Burešová (OF), and their colleagues.

Official negotiations between the Czech and Slovak governments took place on August 8 and 9, 1990 in Trenčianské Teplice. They continued on September 10–11 in Piešťany, on September 27 in Kroměříž, and on October 28 in Slavkov, where President Václav Havel also participated. On November 5, 1990, the Czech-Slovak relationship was the subject of negotiations between the Prime Ministers of all three governments. Four days later, in Luhačovice, Premiers Pithart and Mečiar met again.

The negotiations showed that an agreement was impossible, because both sides approached them from very different points of view. The Czechs wanted to preserve Czechoslovakia, and took its continued existence for granted. They understood the federation as a shift in competencies. Their criterion for any shift was the functionality of the federal state. This meant that certain prerogatives—foreign policy, army, finances—had to be retained by the federation without interference from the republics.

By contrast, the Slovak side's approach assumed the existence of two republics, which then were to delegate powers to common organs in a federal state. The question of functionality was secondary and subordinated to the principle that Czech and Slovak governing elites had the prerogative either to maintain the state or to divide it. Because a fundamental agreement proved impossible, representatives from the governing parties, along with President Havel and representatives of all three governments, issued

---

[8] The results differed slightly in the Chamber of the People, the Chamber of the Nations, and both National Councils. For the results see Rychlík, *Rozdělení Československa*, 149. See also *Wikipedia*, http://cs.wikipedia.org/wiki/Volby_1990.

a declaration on October 28, 1990, which emphasized their will to maintain the ČSFR. The Czech and Slovak sides also agreed that the division of powers would be rearranged and a definitive solution would subsequently be arrived at. The final shaping of the division of powers took place in the presence of President Havel and all three premiers in the Prague Castle on November 12, 1990. The proposal was then evaluated by the National Councils and passed on to the Federal Assembly.

In the version of the power-sharing law presented to the Federal Assembly, the Czech National Council and the Czech government proposed several changes (to the November 12, 1990 proposal). In this context, an expanded Presidium of the Slovak government, headed by Mečiar, suddenly came to Prague on December 6, 1990. Mečiar presented Pithart with an ultimatum: if the power-sharing law was not adopted in its original form, that is, if the Czech National Council or the Federal Assembly amended the draft version of the law, the Slovak National Council would declare the supremacy of Slovak laws over the laws of the federation. This would mean de facto paralysis and dissolution of the Czecho-Slovak federation. The Slovak side further emphasized that the Federal Assembly had no right to interfere in the Czech-Slovak negotiations. The Czech government and the Czech National Council acceded to his demands. The government parties, especially the Civic Forum, instructed their deputies to vote for their original version of the power-sharing law, which was adopted on December 12, 1990 as Constitutional Amendment 556/1990.[9]

The new power-sharing law significantly reduced the power of the central (federal) organs. In contrast to the 1968 constitutional amendment that created the federation, this law eliminated the exclusive prerogative of the federation in foreign policy and defense, which opened up the future possibility of separate international treaties and even the creation of republic–level armed forces. The power-sharing law, however, did not remove the crux of the problem and, therefore, represented only a temporary compromise. While the Czechs viewed the amendment as their maximum concession, for the Slovaks it was only the first step towards their final goal—the attainment of a loose Czech-Slovak Union (commonwealth), in which Slovakia could reap the benefits of its own statehood while retaining all the advantages of a common state.

---

[9] *Sbírka zákonů ČSFR*, ústavní zákon č. 556/1990 Sb.

In 1991, the changing political landscape in the Czech and Slovak Republics transformed the negotiating atmosphere. On February 24, 1991, the Civic Forum splintered into Václav Klaus's right-of-center Civic Democratic Party (*Občanská demokratická strana*—ODS) and Jiří Dienstbier's Center-Left Civic Movement (*Občanské hnutí*—OH). Immediately after the elections of June 1990, the Slovak National Party declared full Slovak independence as its ultimate goal. Simultaneously, several smaller parties and movements emerged, which openly evoked the traditions of the authoritarian Slovak State (1939–1945). On March 3, 1991, the conflict between Vladimír Mečiar and the VPN's leadership—above all with Fedor Gál, the representative of its liberal wing—caused an acute crisis within the VPN. Under the auspices of the VPN, Mečiar founded his own platform, For a Democratic Slovakia, and after some time, he separated completely from the VPN, creating the independent Movement for a Democratic Slovakia (*Hnutie za demokratické Slovensko*—HZDS).

On April 23, 1991, the Presidium of the Slovak National Council recalled Mečiar from his position as prime minister of the Slovak government, as well as all his supporters, who refused to respect the decisions of the VPN leadership. As a result, the government was reconstructed, with Ján Čarnogurský, chairman of KDH, becoming the new prime minister. Čarnogurský was a proponent of Slovak independence, but for the time being, he did not regard it as the republic's most pressing issue. In his view, Slovakia would become independent only after Czechoslovakia had joined the then European Community. In contrast to the representatives of the VPN, who preferred an enduring bond with the Czechs, Čarnogurský viewed Czechoslovakia as a temporary formation, and made no secret of it. When negotiating with Petr Pithart, a former fellow dissident, Čarnogurský demanded that the foundation of Czech and Slovak cohabitation should rest on a legally binding treaty between the two republics, whose acceptance should precede the adoption of any new constitution.

Czech-Slovak negotiations continued throughout 1991. At first, Dagmar Burešová, Speaker of the Czech National Council, rejected the Čarnogurský notion of a treaty between the two republics. Eventually, the Czech side accepted it. By contrast, the Slovak side demanded that the treaty should have a binding nature, which meant, in effect, that it should assume the form of an international treaty, creating an association of two states. Such a solution was unacceptable to the Czech side, because it presupposed the transitory nature of the Czecho-Slovak state or commonwealth. The Czech side rightly feared that Slovakia would take advantage of the existence of any common state so defined to fortify its own position and then declare its independence anyway. In May and June of 1991, negotiations continued in a series of meetings: on May 12, in Lány (Czech Republic), at the end of May in Budmerice (Slovakia), and on June 19 in Kroměříž (Czech Republic), all without results.

A turning point in the balance of political power came when Mečiar's HZDS adopted a confederation stance, that is, its support for Slovak sovereignty (*zvrchovanosť*).[10] The notion of Slovak sovereignty, propounded in the spring of 1991 by the Slovak National Party and other nationalists, demanded the immediate transfer of all competencies to Slovak organs, and only thereafter would an agreement with the Czech Republic be possible. Mečiar, who until then had been a federalist, engaged in demagoguery by announcing that *zvrchovanosť* meant neither state independence nor the destruction of Czechoslovakia. The HZDS explicitly demanded international recognition of Slovakia as a separate subject of international law, with full diplomatic representation, while claiming (and the Slovak public had largely come to believe this claim) that even this demand was compatible with the continued existence of a common state.

Another contributing factor to the changing balance of political power was the gradual fragmentation of the KDH. A nationalistically oriented KDH splinter group, headed by Ján Klepáč, demanded a confederation, even though the Czech side repeatedly declared that such a formation would be unacceptable. On November 4, 1991, the HZDS, SNS, and the Ján Klepáč nationalist faction submitted a proposal for the declaration of Slovak sovereignty to the Slovak National Council, which they had already made public on September 12, 1991. Slovak public support for this project was by no means clear. In reaction to the proposal for a sovereign Slovakia, another petition was immediately born: for a common state, which received roughly equal support. Such conflicting responses demonstrated the deep divisions that existed in Slovak society.[11]

---

[10] In Slovak (and also in Czech) two words are used: *zvrchovanosť* (in Czech: *svrchovanost*) and *suverenita* (also in Czech). These words are synonyms and both are equivalent to the English term sovereignty. Vladimír Mečiar claimed, however, that *zvrchovanosť* meant something different from *suverenita*.

[11] The text of the declaration "For a Sovereign Slovakia" was published in the periodical *Literárny týždenník* [Literary weekly] on March 1, 1991. The declaration "For the Common State" was first published in the rival weekly *Kultúrny život* [Cultural life] on September 23, 1991.

In this situation, Čarnogurský was forced to seek a compromise with the Czechs. In the fall of 1991, it seemed that a compromise between Pithart and Čarnogurský, that is, between the Civic Movement on the one hand, and the KDH and the VPN on the other, would be possible. The Pithart government was willing to accept a treaty between the Czech and Slovak Republics, even though the matter was complicated by the formal legal conflict (in reality, groundless) over whether the republics could even enter into such a treaty while the federation still existed. The treaty was supposed to precede the federal constitution, which would then be bound by it. In October 1991, the Pithart cabinet was willing to agree that the federal ministries would be reduced to a minimum number in the areas of foreign policy, defense, and finance (or a ministry with broader responsibilities for the economy). On November 3, 1991, the top representatives of all three governments and parliaments gathered informally at the private villa of President Václav Havel in Hrádeček near Trutnov in the Czech Republic. With the exception of the Deputy Chairman of the Czech National Council, Jan Kalvoda (*Občanská demokratická alliance*—Civic Democratic Alliance—ODA), an agreement was reached on a binding Czech-Slovak treaty. The treaty was to be ratified by the National Councils, as well as the Federal Assembly (the Federal Parliament). In the future, neither the treaty nor the federal constitution could be amended or changed without the consent of both National Councils. The treaty, the constitutions of both republics and the constitutions of the federation (or rather: union) were to be prepared and approved separately, but they were to become active simultaneously (e. g., from the same date).[12]

There was another problem: who would be the legal subjects of the Czech-Slovak treaty? The Slovak delegation insisted that the subjects would be the republics themselves, while the Czech delegation proposed as signatories both National Councils. In fact, the Slovak demand meant that the Czech-Slovak treaty would have the standard form of an international agreement between two states, which the Czech delegation did not wish to accept. A compromise, however, was eventually reached. On January 10, 1992, representatives of the Czech and Slovak National Councils agreed in Prague that the treaty would be signed by the Czech and

---

[12] The transcript of the negotiations at Hrádeček was published as "Poločas rozpadu" [Halftime of the split] as a supplement to *Slovenské listy* (Prague) 2, no. 2 (1994).

Slovak Republics, represented by their respective National Councils. On January 23, 1992, a commission representing both National Councils was created in Bratislava and charged with the responsibility of preparing the final text. During February 3–8, 1992, in Milovy near Žďár nad Sázavou in the Czech Republic, there was a final round of negotiations between expert commissions of the Czech and Slovak National Councils and the governments of both republics, as well as the federation. The result was a draft treaty between the Czech and Slovak political representatives. The agreement was to be ratified by both National Councils.[13]

On February 12, 1992, the Presidium of the Slovak National Council considered the draft. Ten members voted for the proposal, and ten voted against it. Therefore, the proposal was defeated and could not be submitted to the Slovak National Council as a whole. On March 5, 1992, the Presidium of the Czech National Council declared that further negotiation with the Slovak side would be pointless. Furthermore, on March 7, the draft treaty from Milovy caused the definitive fragmentation of the KDH. The Klepáč nationalistic wing of the KDH became independent and created the Slovak Christian Democratic Movement (*Slovenské kresťanskodemokratické hnutie*—SKDH). As a result, the government coalition, comprised of KDH–VPN–DS,[14] became a minority government. On March 11, the Chairmen of the Czech and Slovak National Councils, Dagmar Burešová and František Mikloško, agreed that further negotiations should be left to the winners in the next elections.

New elections to the Federal Assembly and both National Councils took place on June 5–6, 1992. In The Czech Republic, Václav Klaus's ODS (in coalition with the tiny Christian Democratic Party (*Kresťanskodemokratická strana*—KDS), won the largest number of seats. The ODS–KDS coalition had entered the election campaign with a program of completing the economic reforms and the transition to a democratic

---

[13] For the text of the Milovy Treaty, see *Národná obroda* (Bratislava), February 12, 1992, 7. The text is reproduced in Jan Rychlík, *Češi a Slováci ve 20. století. Česko-slovenské vztahy 1945–1992* [The Czechs and Slovaks in the twentieth century: Czech–Slovak relations, 1945–1992] (Bratislava: Academic Electronic Press, 1998) doc. 32, 505–13.

[14] Part of the coalition included the Hungarian Civic Party (in Hungarian: Magyar Polgári Párt, in Slovak: Maďarská občianska strana—MOS), which closely collaborated with the VPN.

and capitalist society. On the matter of a constitutional framework, it had adopted the slogan, "Either a functioning federation or the division of Czechoslovakia into two states," while clearly preferring the former to the latter. In Slovakia, Vladimír Mečiar's HZDS won the largest number of seats with a program of social compromises that endorsed various populist demands. As far as the constitutional framework was concerned, it was a vague platform, which combined (in reality) mutually exclusive demands for sovereignty, international recognition for Slovakia, and the maintenance of a common state with the Czechs. Mečiar succeeded in persuading a substantial portion of the Slovak public that the demand for international recognition was fully compatible with the continued existence of Czechoslovakia. At the same time, he claimed that he had five variants of constitutional arrangements (including confederation, which in reality is not a common state) for Czech-Slovak relations, whose ultimate fate was to be decided by a referendum. The HZDS leadership chose to ignore objections that any of these variants would require the agreement of the Czech side, which had made it clear that it would insist on dividing the state if Slovaks rejected the federation. In this fashion, the HZDS won a substantial number of votes from supporters of the common state, especially voters who were less educated. The supporters of an independent Slovakia largely voted for the Slovak National Party.

The results of the elections to the Federal Assembly were the key to the fate of Czechoslovakia. The Civic Movement, which had been the mainstay of Czech politics until then, was defeated in the elections, failing to win seats in either the Federal Assembly or the Czech National Council. The results in Slovakia were even more catastrophic for the pro-Czechoslovakia, right-of-center forces. The VPN, renamed the Civic Democratic Union (ODÚ), campaigned independently, while the Democratic Party (DS) joined Klaus's ODS in a campaign coalition. Other pro-Czechoslovak forces forged a last minute electoral group called Democrats 1992 (D-92), while the Hungarian Civic Party joined the opposition Hungarian parties to create an electoral bloc. In addition, the ODÚ and KDH, expecting an election victory, raised the threshold for entering the Slovak National Council from the existing 3 percent to 5 percent. The result was that neither the ODÚ nor DS–ODS and D–92 gained any seats in either the Federal Assembly or the Slovak National Council. The KDH, after the departure of the Klepáč wing (which also failed to make it into parliament), was weakened. The ODS–KDS in the Czech Republic obtained 33.9 percent of the vote and forty-eight seats in the Chamber of the People, and 33.4 percent and thirty-seven seats in the Chamber of the Nations. The required majority in the Chamber of the People was seventy-six deputies; in the Czech part of the Chamber of the Nations, thirty-eight deputies. This meant that ODS–KDS was just one vote short of a majority in the Czech part of the Chamber of the Nations.[15]

As a result, the ODS–KDS was forced to look for allies, not only on the Czech, but also on the Slovak political scene. Since another potential ally, the rightist Civic Democratic Alliance, had entered the Czech National Council, but not the Federal Assembly, only the centrist Catholic Christian Democratic Union–Czechoslovak People's Party (KDU–ČSL) on the Czech political scene was a candidate for this role. It won seven seats in the Chamber of the People and six in the Chamber of the Nations, and the ODS–KDS was preparing to create a coalition with it in the Czech government. In Slovakia, Čarnogurský's KDH was another potential ally, but it won only six seats in the Chamber of the People and eight seats in the Chamber of the Nations. Therefore, the ODS–KDS–KDU–ČSL–KDH combination could not garner a majority in the Chamber of the People.

The situation in the Chamber of the Nations was even more critical, because the ODS–KDS needed allies in the Slovak part of the chamber to pass any law where the minority veto applied, such as the government program, votes of confidence, and the election of the president. Apart from the HZDS, however, there were no parties on the Slovak side that could become effective legislative partners. A conglomeration of smaller Slovak parties, which had emerged in the Federal Assembly after the elections, could not be relied upon, for they spanned incompatible ideologies and could never have agreed on a common program.

As early as Sunday, June 7, 1992, President Václav Havel had asked Václav Klaus to begin negotiations to form a new federal government and designated him as the next federal prime minister. Even though Klaus represented the largest party in parliament, Havel's move was most unfortunate. It violated an unwritten tradition according to which, when the president of the country was a Czech, the federal prime minister had to be a Slovak. Yet even in the event that Vladimír Mečiar had become the new federal prime minister, the underlying political situation could not have been

---

[15] For the results, see Rychlík, *Rozdělení Československa*, 299. Also see *Wikipedia*, http://cs.wikipedia.org/wiki/Volby_1992.

altered. The minority veto meant that the HZDS could not have created a new cabinet without the support of the ODS–KDS. As it soon turned out, however, Mečiar had not even considered entering the federal cabinet and instead intended to become the premier of the Slovak Republic. In the Slovak National Council, the HZDS had a majority, and for the passage of constitutional amendments, it could rely on the support of the Slovak National Party and, if needed, the Party of the Democratic Left (SDĽ).

The first post-election negotiations between the ODS and the HZDS took place in Brno (Czech Republic) on June 8, 1992. Both parties assumed that these negotiations would be difficult but not impossible. The ODS presumed that Mečiar's absurd demand for Slovak international recognition, which was fundamentally incompatible with Czechoslovakia's continued existence (if only because Slovakia and Czechoslovakia could not simultaneously be subjects of international law), was only a campaign trick by the HZDS, seeking to win SNS voters. The ODS was willing to accept a substantial devolution of the federal government's powers, as long as it would not endanger economic reforms. The HZDS was to be offered several key ministries, but had to make some concessions. The latter included, for example, recycling the demand of the Klepáč wing that Slovak soldiers wear separate insignias on their uniforms, that they might serve in separate units, as well as the request that only the Slovak part of the national anthem be played in Slovakia.

Along parallel lines, the HZDS approached the negotiations convinced that the ODS' claim that the only alternative to federation was a complete division of the state was only a campaign slogan. The HZDS leadership believed that the ODS in the end would accept a union or a confederation. The Czech and Slovak Republic would then each be independent subjects of international law, each having its own representatives on international bodies. For the purposes of defense, coordination of foreign policy, and economic affairs, they would create joint organs with equal representation of both sides. Each republic would have its own treasury, but both states would share a common currency. The HZDS leadership was incapable of grasping that such an arrangement not only would be dysfunctional, but also that for the Czech side it would only create problems. For, where the weaker and smaller unit has the same powers as the stronger and larger unit, what is involved is not equality but rather a minority veto over the decisions of the majority.

According to the testimony of one of the meetings' participants, Miroslav Macek (Deputy Chairman of the ODS), the negotiations began with a private meeting between Klaus and Mečiar. According to Macek, Mečiar was attempting, as usual, to use vague formulations to blur the irreconcilable conflict over international recognition. While the Klaus-Mečiar conversations were taking place, Macek spoke with Michal Kováč (Deputy Chairman of the HZDS, and later the first president of Slovakia), who described a Slovak proposal for an economic and defense union, apparently without previous consultation with Mečiar.[16] Macek, who subsequently dubbed this proposal a "Slovak state with Czech insurance," immediately realized that this project could not and must not be accepted by the Czech side because it signified an evolutionary approach to Slovak statebuilding, funded by Czech taxpayers. That is why after Klaus and Mečiar had joined the larger meeting, Macek declared that the matter had become quite clear; the only solution according to him was the dissolution of Czechoslovakia. Macek's testimony is generally confirmed also by the testimony of Michal Kováč (HZDS).[17]

Even after the Brno talks, Klaus apparently had not given up all hope that Mečiar would back away from some of his demands and that the dissolution of the state could be averted. That is why that subject was on the agenda at subsequent meetings in Prague on June 11 and 17 in 1992. At these negotiations, the ODS put pressure on the HZDS to give a clear response: either a functioning federation or two separate states. After six hours of futile negotiations, during which the HZDS again blurred the distinction between the two alternatives, relying on such contradictory formulations as "a common state in the form of a confederation" or "defense and economic union," Klaus's patience ran out. He asked the HZDS leaders whether they wanted to build a Slovak state with Czech money, and whether or not the Slovaks were a proud nation. Mečiar replied that each republic would be responsible for its own finances. With this response, Mečiar sought to return to the question of confederation, but the Czech side interpreted his declaration as yet another step towards Slovak indepen-

---

[16] There were several versions of this project—see Rychlík, *Češi a Slováci ve 20. století*, doc. 31, 494–513. For the testimony of Michal Kováč, see *Československá historická ročenka 2003* (Brno), 101.

[17] For Macek's testimony, see Kraus & Stanger, *Irreconcilable Differences?*, 244–6, see also Michal Kováč, *Pamäti. Môj príbeh občana a prezidenta* [Memoirs: My role as a citizen and as president] (Dunajská Lužná: Milanium, 2010), 57–8.

dence. In the end, they agreed on the composition of a reduced federal cabinet, which, in addition to the prime minister, would have only ten ministers. Apart from the premiership, which went to the ODS, there would be equal representation in the cabinet for each party, but the HZDS demanded the Ministry of Foreign Affairs and the Ministry of Defense.

Václav Klaus apparently had changed his mind as early as June 17, 1992, but the ODS made its position clear only after the fourth round of negotiations with the HZDS, which took place in Bratislava on June 19, 1992. The negotiations lasted a full twelve hours and confirmed that the only thing on which the parties could agree was the division of the country. Following the negotiations, both parties issued a declaration, which stated in part, "The ODS does not regard a confederation, in which both republics are subjects of international law (which was the HZDS proposal) as a common state, but instead as a union of two separate states. Rather than confederation, the ODS prefers two completely independent states, that is, a constitutional dissolution of the federation."[18] On June 24, 1992, a new Slovak government, headed by Vladimír Mečiar, was formed. On July 2, Václav Havel appointed the last federal cabinet of Jan Stráský from the ODS. On the same day, a Czech government comprised of the coalition ODS–KDS–KDU–ČSL–ODA was formed under the leadership of Václav Klaus.

Both the Czech and the Slovak opposition protested the agreement to divide Czechoslovakia. The SDĽ rejected the notion of a confederation and instead proposed a "cooperating federation." The KDH regarded independence as premature. On the Czech side, the Social Democrats (*Československá sociální demokracie*—ČSSD), the HSD–SMS and Liberal-Social Union (*Liberálně-sociální unie*—LSU), the Czech Communists, and the extreme right Republicans (the Association for the Republic-Republican Party of Czechoslovakia, or *Sdružení pro republiku—Republikánská strana Československa*—SPR–RSČ) also opposed the agreement. The opposition demanded that the dissolution of the state be decided by referendum. The opposition parties met with the new chairman of the Federal Assembly, Michal Kováč (HZDS), and welcomed the notion of a Czecho-Slovak union. Jiří Horák, the chairman of ČSSD, created a special commission of experts, which was expected to develop this project, in agreement with the

---

[18] *Mladá fronta Dnes* (Prague), 22 June 1992. The document is also reproduced in Rychlík, *Rozdělení Československa*, 398.

other opposition parties and the HZDS. The proposal was inspired by the notion of dualism along the lines of the 1867 Austro-Hungarian Compromise. While the HZDS was sympathetic to this idea, not even the ČSSD was able to solve the problem of international recognition for Slovakia. Lawyers considered the possibility that Slovakia could eventually receive special representation in the United Nations, much like Belarus and Ukraine had in the former USSR. There was also talk of Slovakia creating its own representation abroad, short of full diplomatic status. But since the HZDS demanded full diplomatic representation, the commission resigned and the project died.

Both the opposition and the government repeatedly considered the question of a referendum. Surveys of public opinion showed that when asked, "Are you for a common state?" most voters in both the Czech and the Slovak Republics responded positively. To rule out erroneous conclusions stemming from conceptual confusion promoted by the HZDS, the opposition (ČSSD) maintained that the question should be worded to make it clear that in a common state, Slovakia would *not* have international recognition. But the problem of the referendum had several layers: even if it had affirmed popular support for the maintenance of the common state, the opposing political forces would have remained in power, making a compromise impossible. At the same time, surveys of voters' preferences indicated that new elections would not have brought about any change. Irrespective of the outcome of the referendum and thanks to a political system with a powerful minority veto, the stage was clearly set for government paralysis and the gradual dissolution of the state. *Legal* means could not overcome the *political* stalemate. Only the use of force could do so, that is, the dissolution of the parliaments and the establishment of a Prague-based military dictatorship. Such a move would have created precisely the situation that the Slovak nationalists needed to sustain their claim that Slovakia was ruled by the Czechs. No one on the Czech side, however, actually considered this option. From 1990 on, there was consensus among Czech elites that if Slovakia wished to become independent, no one was going to stand in its way.

With the end of Havel's presidential term and new presidential elections in the Federal Assembly, the unfolding dissolution became apparent. Havel's term ended on July 5, 1992. The HZDS not only refused to support the candidacy of Václav Havel for another term, but it also declined to propose its own candidate. Given the minority veto and without the votes of the HZDS and the SNS, Havel could not be reelected. Such an attempt failed on July 3, 1992. On July 17, 1992, the Slovak National Council, with the support of the HZDS, the SNS, and surprisingly, the SDL, passed a "Declaration of Slovak Sovereignty" (*zvrchovanost'*), which declared Slovakia to be the state of the Slovak people.[19] The declaration passed over the dissenting votes of the KDH and the Hungarian parties. On the same day, Václav Havel resigned; no new president was chosen for the remainder of Czechoslovakia's existence.

Following the promulgation of the Declaration of Sovereignty, and during negotiations in Bratislava on July 22–23, 1992, the HZDS attempted to stop the further disintegration of the state because it wanted to take advantage of the existing federation to prepare for an independent Slovakia. The Czech side, however, had lost interest in Slovakia. It was afraid that slowing the dissolution would only create economic chaos and financial losses, which the Czech taxpayers would have to bear. Therefore, the Czech side insisted on a speedy and complete division. Klaus presented Mečiar with a draft law on the end of the federation, which the Federal Assembly was to approve by September 20. The draft assumed four possibilities: (1) a declaration by the Federal Assembly, approved by a constitutional law; (2) the agreement of the National Councils; (3) a referendum; and (4) a unilateral departure from the federation by one of the republics. Instead of a union, Klaus proposed a series of bilateral agreements. The final agreement was reached in Brno on August 26, where a timetable was established, and the date was set for Czechoslovakia's expiration on December 31, 1992, the end of the budget year. On the same day, the dissolution of Czechoslovakia was officially announced. On September 1, 1992, the Slovak Republic adopted a new constitution, which had been conceived for an independent state. It did not reckon with the existence of Czechoslovakia, except that the validity of some articles was to come into effect on January 1, 1993.[20]

As it turned out, the division of Czechoslovakia was not an easy matter. On September 11, the opposition forced a special meeting of the Federal Assembly, which again demanded that a referendum be held. The federal government refused this demand, arguing that if the referendum were to endorse the continued maintenance of the common state—which surveys of public opinion indicated was virtually certain—it would be in no position to act on such a result, for the disintegration of the state had already

---

[19] *Sbírka zákonů ČSFR, ČR, SR*, částka 84/1992, 28. 8. 1992, 2394.
[20] *Sbírka zákonů ČSFR, ČR, SR*, Constitutional law 460/1992 Sb.

gone too far. On October 1, 1992, the Federal Assembly voted on the constitutional amendment concerning the end of the federation. The opposition defeated the proposal. Miloš Zeman, then deputy chair of the ČSSD, took advantage of the situation and proposed a constitutional commission that would be charged with the transformation of the federation into a Czecho-Slovak union. The proposal, which enjoyed the support of the opposition as well as many of the HZDS deputies, was actually approved. The ČSSD's proposal presupposed the existence of two states with common organs for foreign policy, defense, and finance. Decisions were to be made on the basis of parity, but the question of international recognition was left open.[21]

The vote in favor of such a commission was a great victory for the opposition and the HZDS. Nevertheless, the ODS had already decided to divide the state at any price, and if no other way was open, it would proceed without the help of the HZDS. The Czech governing coalition refused to send any representatives to the new commission. Instead, on October 6, 1992, the ODS and HZDS delegations met in Jihlava (Czech Republic). Klaus insisted that the HZDS must explicitly reject union and confederation and commit itself to the division of Czechoslovakia into fully independent states. In the end, Mečiar agreed. As a result, the union project was shelved.

The next stage of the Czecho-Slovak development took place under the banner of deconstruction. On November 13, 1992 a constitutional amendment divided federal real estate property in a ratio of 2:1.[22] A new law on the devolution of powers of October 8 transferred further competences from the federation to the republics. On November 18, 1992, the Federal Assembly met to vote on a new version of the constitutional amendment concerning the end of the federation. The various modes of how the federation might end were no longer at issue. The new amendment was merely a modification of the existing law on the federation, which simply added a paragraph stipulating that the federation would end on December 31, 1992.

---

[21] See the text in Viera Hlavová and Jozef Žakuliak, eds., *Novembrová revolúcia a česko-slovenský rozchod. Výber dokumentov a prejavov november 1989– december 1992* [The November revolution and the Czechoslovak dissolution. A Selection of documents and speeches, November 1989–December 1992] (Bratislava : Národné literárne centrum, 2002), doc. 66, 266–8. The text of Zeman's proposal was approved as the Resolution of Federal Assembly no 58/1992.

[22] *Sbírka zákonů ČSFR, ČR, SR,* Constitutional law 541/1992 Sb.

By the time the assembly voted on this law, Czechoslovakia had already been de facto partitioned. The law, however, was passed only in the Chamber of the People, and another vote had to be held a week later on November 25. By lobbying the opposition deputies, the government coalition in the end persuaded some right-wing Republicans and some Czech and Slovak Social Democrats and succeeded in obtaining the needed votes. By a narrow majority and only on the second attempt, the constitutional law ending the existence of Czechoslovakia was finally passed.[23] On December 31, 1992 the Czech and Slovak Federative Republic officially expired.

The question that now arises was whether the split was inevitable or whether a Czech-Slovak compromise was possible. First of all, it should be acknowledged that, in general terms, the end of one state and the birth of another state or states is something quite normal. States come and go and no state on earth is eternal. Secondly, all multinational states are unstable.[24] To keep a multinational state (and specially a democratic multinational state) together requires permanent negotiations between its constitutional parts and nationality problems in multinational states are never definitively solved. In Europe, all multinational states failed (Austria-Hungary, the Ottoman Empire, the Soviet Union, Yugoslavia) or face serious problems (Belgium, Spain, and even the United Kingdom). Czechoslovakia was hardly an exception.

However, let's return to the question whether a Czech-Slovak compromise was possible. As the foregoing narrative makes clear, until the June 1992 elections, such a compromise was possible, for the Slovak side had not placed the issue of full international recognition on the agenda. A compromise, however, would have required that the Czech side accept the Slovak demand for a treaty arrangement. The Czech side made a critical error in clinging excessively to legalistic formulas. In actuality, the issue as to whether republics could or could not enter into treaties was subsidiary. It was an academic discussion without any practical significance. Entering

---

[23] *Sbírka zákonů ČSFR, ČR, SR*, Constitutional law 542/1992 Sb.
[24] In Europe, Switzerland is sometimes given as an example of a successful solution. This is, however, a mistake. Switzerland is not a multinational state; it is a nation-state of the Swiss nation, because all citizens have a common Swiss identity, not separate German, Italian and French identities. The fact that they speak different languages is not crucial.

into agreements, inasmuch as they would have assisted in the creation of functioning common organs, could have preserved Czechoslovakia, at least for a time. After the 1992 elections, however, there was no possibility of maintaining the common state. In the new situation, a peaceful separation was the only solution.

We should also explain why the Czechs, who considered Czechoslovakia their nation-state and identified with it, gave up so easily. There were two reasons: Václav Klaus was not prepared and not willing to change his concept of economic transformation, which did not and could not take into consideration the specific situation in Slovakia. The Mečiar concept of confederation would leave central authorities in Prague without any power in economic matters. This meant that the economic transformation, according to Klaus's concept, would be impossible. Because it was impossible to have two different economic transformations within one single customs and fiscal territory, the only possible solution for Klaus was a total separation. The main reason the Czechs gave up on Czechoslovakia, however, was political, or rather geopolitical: in 1918, when Czechoslovakia came into being, the main problem for the Czechs was Germany and the large German minority in the Czech lands. The Czechs needed Slovakia in order for Czechoslovakia to be stronger *vis-à-vis* 3.2 million ethnic Germans in the country and the Czechs also needed Slovakia as a corridor to prevent German encirclement to the east—to Poland and Russia. We should keep in mind that in 1918 the Czech lands were really encircled because Upper and Lower Silesia belonged to Germany and the inhabitants of Austria considered themselves mostly to be Germans, not Austrians. After 1945, the situation changed: the German minority was expelled from Czechoslovakia, Silesia was given to Poland and the Austrians gradually obtained a new, separate Austrian identity, which was very weak before 1918 and during the interwar period. In addition, the Soviet occupation of 1968 showed that the enemy was neither in Berlin nor Bonn, but in Moscow. The Soviet Union, not Germany, was now the main problem. Subsequently, in 1992, the corridors to the East were not only unnecessary, but unwelcome. After the breakup of the Soviet Union at the end of 1991, the situation in the East was very uncertain and nobody knew what would happen. By contrast, close relations with a unified Germany could bring the Czech Republic sooner and faster into both NATO and the European Union. Thus, the Czechs lost interest in maintaining

Czechoslovakia. In Czech policy, Slovakia was now to play another role: the role of a buffer against the East.

We should add that Slovak geopolitical situation in 1992 did not differ substantially from that of 1918. The problem for the Slovaks and Slovakia was Hungary and the Hungarian minority. Unlike the Germans in Bohemia and Moravia, the Hungarians in Slovakia were not expelled after the Second World War. In 1992, Mečiar was uncertain about their intentions and also about the intentions of Hungary. That is one of the reasons why Mečiar did not want a total separation in 1992 but insisted on some sort of defense and economic union. But this was unacceptable for Václav Klaus, who did not wish to involve the Czech Republic in a possible future Slovak-Hungarian conflict.

The process of disintegration of multinational states in general and of Czechoslovakia in particular should not be seen as something negative *per se*. More important than maintaining existing states are the relations between the new successor states. Both the Czechs and the Slovak Republic are now allies in NATO and both are members of the European Union. Czech-Slovak relations are excellent. Nobody could want more.

CHAPTER 2

Czechoslovakia's Dissolution Twenty Years After

Michael Kraus

January 1, 2013 marked the twentieth anniversary of Czechoslovakia's end. To account for Czechoslovakia's dissolution, Jan Rychlík states his thesis at the very outset: the Czechs and the Slovaks went separate ways in 1993 primarily because no deep sense of Czechoslovak identity had emerged over the previous decades that would hold them together. In his view, the seventy-four years of common statehood—interrupted by WWII—did not forge common bonds strong enough to withstand the trials and tribulations of the post-communist transformation. And, as Rychlík rightly points out, throughout Czechoslovakia's history, a palpable difference existed between the Czechs and the Slovaks regarding the strength of their identification with their state. While the Czechs tended to regard Czechoslovakia as "their" nation-state, the Slovaks historically displayed a weaker sense of identification with Czechoslovakia, resented to various degrees Prague's "centralism," and, in 1968, sought greater autonomy from Prague and federalization. Rychlík rightly emphasizes the poisonous institutional legacy of the "normalized federation," the constitutional provisions of which paralyzed the search for a viable formula in the post-communist transition. Further, he points out that, owing to the end of the Cold War, the Czechs and the Slovaks no longer needed each other for security reasons, certainly not as much as in 1918 when they had established a common home. Rychlík concludes that the fate of Czechoslovakia was sealed in the outcome of the 1992 elections, which produced two incompatible political elites in the Czech lands and in Slovakia, and he sees "no possibility of maintaining the common state" after that.

To assess the extent to which Rychlík's propositions are shared by other scholars, let us take a brief journey into recent Western scholarship on the subject of Czechoslovakia's dissolution. We are especially interested in the extent to which their findings add additional weight to one of the foregoing explanations or lend credence to alternative perspectives.

In the early 1990s, three socialist federations—the Czechoslovak, Soviet and Yugoslav—experienced disintegration simultaneously. The initial wave of scholarship on the subject tended to emphasize the common aspects of their dissolution, such as a socialist (or communist) past, federal (or "pseudofederal") constitutional structures, ethnic minorities, the "stateness" problems, economic drivers of nationalism, or the role of political elites in mobilizing and manipulating "unresolved" national questions.

This emphasis also informed our strategy in the 1990s, when, with Allison K. Stanger as my principal co-investigator, we set out to examine the roots of the Czechoslovak divorce. To do so, we also enlisted other contributors (both American specialists and leading Czech and Slovak political actors in the 1989–1992 developments) in this collective endeavor to consider seven explanations for the collapse of the Czechoslovak Federation. We suggested that the latter might be seen as the product of (1) the legacies of the communist and pre-communist eras, (2) the rational or erratic actions of post-communist elites, (3) constitutional deadlock, (4) the absence of political parties, as well as other associations and groupings that unite people across ethnic lines, (5) malevolent mass media, (6) regional economic disparities, and (7) demonstration effects (international factors fostering separatism).[1] As is in the nature of collaborative projects (involving some twenty participants, including two former prime ministers), we did not reach a clear consensus on the key issues. Some of our contributors emphasized pre-communist historical continuities or communist institutional legacies; others saw the breakup in terms of a broken down transition to democracy; and still others depicted the developments in terms of a consociational or power-sharing system that failed. Sev-

---

[1] Michael Kraus and Allison Stanger, eds. and transl., *Irreconcilable Differences? Explaining Czechoslovakia's Dissolution* (Lanham, Maryland: Rowman & Littlefield, 2000), Foreword by Václav Havel.

eral contributors blamed either Slovak or Czech nationalism that was rooted in either socioeconomic factors or manipulative media. In the concluding chapter, we emphasized that the tranquil nature of divorce Czecho-Slovak style was due, above all, to three factors: the absence of past violent conflict between the two nations; the very low degree of ethnic territorial interpenetration (simply put, few Slovaks and even fewer Czechs lived outside their republics); and finally, the distinctive contribution of Václav Havel's leadership.

Though over the past fifteen years, the list of publications dealing with Czechoslovakia's dissolution has expanded considerably, the range of divergent perspectives has also widened. Several of the most compelling explanations illustrate the whole gamut of competing analytical frameworks we now possess. To begin with, a number of scholars have attempted—though without much success—to solve the paradox of how a democratic state could "have disintegrated even though a majority of its citizens favored its continuance."[2] The problem with this oft-repeated proposition—as Rychlík persuasively argues in his recent book—is that the same public opinion polls also showed that the Czechs and the Slovaks who wished to maintain Czechoslovakia had completely different understandings of what actually constituted a "common state," and a large majority of Slovak respondents defined a "common state" so loosely that, in effect, they had two separate states in mind.[3] Robert Young has characterized the Czecho-Slovak separation as the only case of a "peaceful secession" "in a modern, highly integrated, industrial economy, where there was also a full democracy."[4] Considering that Czech and Slovak public opinion endorsed neither Czech nor Slovak independence, some scholars have argued that Czechoslovakia's dissolution was neither democratic nor inevitable and

---

[2] Carol Skalnik Leff, *The Czech and Slovak Republics: Nation versus State* (Boulder: Westview Press, 1997), 128.

[3] See Rychlík's *Rozdělení Československa 1989–1992* [The dissolution of Czechoslovakia, 1989–1992] (Prague: Vyšehrad, 2012). His study is the best documented and definitive—at least until we get the full record of the Klaus-Mečiar 1992 negotiations—history of the dissolution of Czechoslovakia.

[4] Robert Young, *The Secession of Quebec and the Future of Canada* (Montreal: McGill-Queen's University Press, 1995): 145. Though Young's focus is on Quebec and Canada, he dedicates an entire chapter to "The Breakup of Czechoslovakia," 144–67.

that Czechoslovakia "might easily…[have] remained in one piece."[5] Norman Davies in his recent book, *Vanished Kingdoms*, classifies Czechoslovakia as the clearest example of state "liquidation," namely "when the leaders of the two parts of Czechoslovakia reached agreement on their Velvet Divorce by consent in 1993."[6]

Yet Davies also points out that the "trickiest question is to determine which liquidations are genuinely consensual and which are not." On this issue, social scientists disagree widely. Some, like leading Slovak sociologists Martin Bútora and Zora Bútorová, have argued that the establishment of independent Slovakia "was more an unintended outcome of post-communist panic and confusion exploited by ambitious politicians than the culmination of Slovak national emancipation."[7] Abby Innes takes this proposition even further to argue that the decision to divide the state "was taken not only against the known majority will," but also "against the first preferences of a majority of voters" who cast their votes for both Klaus's and Mečiar's party, respectively.[8]

While many scholars have argued that federalism can assist the management of ethnic conflicts, others have claimed it exacerbates them. Carol Leff's explanation for the disintegration of the three "Communist Federations" links their fate to the process of democratization to conclude that, in all three cases, state dissolution was a function of the changing "balance of power between center and republics." The loss of central control over the transition facilitated the republics' "final defection from the existing state."[9] Addressing the same puzzle, Valerie Bunce focuses her study on the dynamics of center-periphery relations in each of the three countries and finds a linkage between the regime and state collapse in two crucial factors: the institutional design

---

[5] Mary Heimann, *Czechoslovakia: The State that Failed* (New Haven: Yale University Press, 2009): 321.

[6] *Vanished Kingdoms: The Rise and Fall of States and Nations* (New York: Penguin Books, 2012): 736.

[7] Quoted in Kraus and Stanger, 303.

[8] Abby Innes, *Czechoslovakia: The Short Goodbye* (New Haven: Yale University Press, 2001), 301.

[9] Carol Skalnik Leff, "Democratization and Disintegration in Multinational States: The Breakup of the Communist Federations," *World Politics* 51, no. 2 (January 1999): 227.

of socialism and the rapid expansion of opportunities for domestic and international change for both political actors and publics. Socialist-era institutions, she argues, "subverted both the regime and the state." The interaction between these two factors explains "why, when and how, socialism, the bloc..." and the three federal states disintegrated.[10] Central institutions in both Czechoslovakia and Yugoslavia were weak. Their power had been decentralized, she argues, weaker and more decentralized in Yugoslavia.

Bunce also tackles the question why Czechoslovakia and the Soviet Union expired peacefully while Yugoslavia did not. Though they had much in common, three factors (all institutional and all of socialist-era vintage) explain the violent Yugoslav break up: the confederal (decentralized) nature of the balance of power, tilted toward the republics over the center; Serbian expansionism, and the politicized military.[11]

Andrew Janos, to cite another approach, rejects factors such as historical animosities and interethnic intolerance as explanations and argues instead that "discernible differences of interest" "underpinned, most fundamentally, by economic disparities" were the main drivers of the dissolutions of Czechoslovakia and Yugoslavia.[12] Nadya Nedelsky's argument runs directly counter to that of Janos. Her study contrasts the Czech "civic" and Slovak "ethnic" conceptions of nationhood and finds them resistant to change over the course of a century and a half. In her interpretation, the contrasting nature of norms that constitute Czech and Slovak understandings of nationhood reflected fundamental continuities of Czech and Slovak political culture during a variety of twentieth-century political regimes—in spite of substantial equalization between Czech and Slovak levels of socioeconomic development. Where Janos emphasizes the primacy of material interests as the key factors, Nedelsky finds "no evidence" for this perspective and endorses

---

[10] Valerie Bunce, *Subversive Institutions: The Design and the Destruction of Socialism and the State* (Cambridge: Cambridge University Press, 1999), 130.
[11] Ibid.; see also Valerie Bunce, "Peaceful versus Violent State Dismemberment: A Comparison of the Soviet Union, Yugoslavia, and Czechoslovakia," *Politics & Society*, 27, no. 2 (June, 1999), 217–37.
[12] Andrew C. Janos, *The Political Economy of Ethnic Conflict: The Dissolution of Czechoslovakia and Yugoslavia*, NCEEER, contract no. 810-18, November 7, 1997, quotes from the executive summary.

Rogers Brubaker's proposition that "The central question is not 'who *gets* what?' but rather 'who *is* what?'"[13] Her thesis challenges those analysts of the region who explain ethnic politics by post-communist factors, such as the role of opportunistic political elites.

Opportunistic political elites (a topic we also explored in our volume with Stanger), however, are central to the perspective put forward by Abby Innes who portrays the story of Czechoslovak dissolution as a travesty of the democratic process. Her anti-hero is Václav Klaus, the Czech prime minister, whom she sees as "a vanguardist of the market—a Lenin for the bourgeoisie." His "particular genius as a leader," she argues, "lay in making the Czech partition look like a Slovak secession." Innes concludes that this was "a crisis more of governance than of ethnicity," with issues of leadership, reform philosophy, and democratization on center stage, impacting "constantly and pivotally." With Klaus in the saddle, she argues, it hardly mattered who got elected in 1992 in Slovakia, since the split was just about inevitable.[14] Yet in direct contrast to Innes, no less an authority than Václav Havel, in his 2006 memoir (critical of Klaus in many respects, including this one), suggests that with Vladimír Mečiar's 1992 election victory in Slovakia, "the fate of the federation was sealed. Though Mečiar never said that he wanted an independent Slovakia, he did everything for the federation to split."[15] Innes seems unaware that inside his own party, Klaus was in 1992 regarded as a "hardline federalist" whose willingness to accept a formula for "a dysfunctional federation" was feared by many.[16]

As Kevin Deegan-Krause notes, the shared history of the Czechs and Slovaks and the history of shared political institutions makes for

---

[13] Nadya Nedelsky, *Defining the Sovereign Community: The Czech and Slovak Republics* (Philadelphia: University of Pennsylvania Press, 2009). She quotes Brubaker on pp. 276–7.

[14] Ibid., 74–5, 209, 216.

[15] Václav Havel, *Prosím stručně: rozhovor s Karlem Hvížď'alou, poznámky, dokumenty* [Please be brief: Interviews with Karel Hvížď'al, notes and documentation], (Prague: Gallery, 2006), 95.

[16] Karol Wolf, *Podruhé a naposled aneb Mírové dělení Československa* [Secondly and finally or the peaceful dissolution of Czechoslovakia] (Prague: G plus G, 1998), 67; Miroslav Macek, "Fragments from the Dividing of Czechoslovakia," in Kraus and Stanger, 246.

a hospitable "natural experiment"[17] for testing hypotheses regarding post-communist developments. What the foregoing (of necessity) brief overview demonstrates, however, is that we have a surplus of competing explanations and still no scholarly consensus on some of the key questions concerning Czechoslovakia's dissolution. To be sure, this is to some extent due to the wide spectrum of interdisciplinary interest and to the different approaches to the subject matter, ranging from studies focusing on historical and ethnonational and identity issues to those privileging the analysis of political institutions or democratization. Yet the multiple, and often completely contradictory, explanations for Czechoslovakia's demise also testify to the field of opportunity that the research puzzle still offers some twenty years later.

A relative rarity for a state to disappear from the map without violence, Czechoslovakia's Velvet Divorce today serves as an attractive model for those who believe the costs of state dissolution—whether in Belgium, Canada, Great Britain or Spain—can be minimized. Dubbing it "the best example in postwar Europe of a relatively smooth parting of the ways,"[18] some observers have also brought the Velvet Divorce into focus again to suggest ways in which the EU (or the eurozone) can extricate itself from Greece and its financial problems, Catalonia from Spain, or how the divorce Czecho-Slovak style might serve as a strategy for dismantling the EU altogether.[19] Indeed, the demise of "federalized totalitarianism"—to use Havel's apt expression—in Czechoslovakia offers a sharp contrast to the violent nature of the Yugoslav breakup. While in the latter case, the role of the Yugoslav army as an extension of Serbian national interest and the virulent form of Serbian and Croatian nationalism stand out,[20] the Czechs and the Slovaks had no history of violent conflict (a factor that Bunce surprisingly ignores), nor did the

---

[17] Kevin Deegan-Krause, *Elected Affinities: Democracy and Party Competition in Slovakia and the Czech Republic* (Stanford: Stanford University Press, 2006), 2.

[18] Kate Connolly, "Is There a Lesson for Catalonia in the Czechoslovakian 'Velvet Divorce'?" *The Guardian*, November 19, 2012.

[19] For a sampling, see *Wikipedia*, http://en.wikipedia.org/wiki/Vlaams_Belang; Mary Dejevsky, "Breaking up Should Not Be So Hard to Do," *The Independent*, December 23, 2011; Oliver Kamm, "Euro Exit: How it Should be Done," *The Times*, January 30, 2012.

[20] See Bunce, "Peaceful versus Violent State Dismemberment."

emerging successor states contain any sizeable minorities of Czechs and Slovaks within them.

As we pointed out in *Irreconcilable Differences*, what also stands out is the critical role that political elites play in the process of the dissolution.[21] While for Slobodan Milošević and Franjo Tuđman the end justified the means, the moral force of Havel's leadership and the unsparing effort he expended over the course of 1990–1992 to explore every possible constitutional solution to the Czech-Slovak deadlock had won him credit in both lands. Small wonder that in December 2011, upon Havel's passing, the Slovak, much like the Czech, government marked the occasion by declaring a day of national mourning. Current opinion polls show that, two decades after the dissolution, most Slovaks have a positive view of Havel, while they give the once-lionized Mečiar, the reluctant founder of Slovakia's independence, only 16 percent approval.[22] They also show that, since 1993, when barely more than a third of Czechs and Slovaks embraced it, the support for dissolution has grown somewhat in both successor states. In November 2012, two thirds of Slovaks surveyed approved it, while only 46 percent of Czechs did. Yet about 70 percent of Czech and Slovak respondents continue to believe that dividing the country without a referendum was wrong.[23]

Rychlík concludes his excellent contribution by noting that the Czechs and the Slovaks today are close allies in the EU and NATO and "their relations are excellent." Indeed, owing to their historical and cultural ties, the proximity of their languages, their shared fate in Central Europe, and the relatively acrimony-free parting, the Czechs and the Slovaks today get along better than at any point in the seventy-four-year history of their common statehood.

---

[21] See Kraus and Stanger, "Lessons from the Breakup of Czechoslovakia," in Kraus and Stanger, ibid., 299–306.
[22] Martin Simecka, "After the Velvet Divorce," *Salon: Central European Forum*, 4/2/2012, http://salon.eu.sk/en/7482/english-after-the-velvet-divorce/.
[23] For the survey results, see *Centrum pro výzkum veřejného mínění*, http://cvvm.soc.cas.cz/politicke-ostatni/rozdeleni-ceskoslovenska-20-let-od-vzniku-samostatne-cr-a-sr.

CHAPTER 3

The Dissolution of Czechoslovakia: The Slovak Perspective[1]

Jozef Žatkuliak and Adam Hudek

In 1990, scholars and journalists abroad generally perceived post-communist Czechoslovakia as a country with a bright, democratic future. Only a few of them were aware of the existence and seriousness of the Czech-Slovak relationship and the significance this issue would have in the coming years.[2] The inability of political elites to solve this problem during the negotiations in the years 1990–1992 ultimately sealed the fate of the Czechoslovak Federation. However, only in the second half of 1992 did it became clear that there were no alternatives but the dissolution of the common state. For many observers the rapid breakup of the Czech and Slovak Federal Republic came unexpectedly. However, despite its surprising nature, the dissolution was more or less overshadowed by more dramatic events in other countries of the former Eastern Bloc. As Paal Sigurd Hilde wrote, "The break-up of the Czech and Slovak Federal Republic (ČSFR) took place in the shadow of the war in the former Yugoslavia and the crumbling of the

---

[1] This article is an outcome of VEGA Grant no. 2/0104/13, "Slovakia after 1968: From Normalisation to the Independent Slovak Republic and Democracy" and Slovak Research and Development Agency contract no. APVV-0628-11, "State Borders and Identities in Modern Slovak History in Central European Context."

[2] Juraj Hocman, *Slovakia from the Downfall of Communism, to its Accession into the European Union, 1989–2004. The Re-Emergence of Political Parties and Democratic Institutions* (Frankfurt am Main: Peter Lang, 2011), 83.

Soviet Empire."³ According to Hilde it was because of the smooth process of separation.

> With no shots fired and no lives lost, news from the ČSFR seldom reached front pages in Western Europe and North America. In the years following, too, with scores of academic and more popular books written about the break-up of Yugoslavia and the Soviet Union, the Czech-Slovak split has received comparatively little attention.⁴

In the 1990s, scholars and politicians alike mostly interpreted the Czechoslovak case according to examples taken from Balkan and Soviet cases. In the words of anthropologist Ladislav Holy, "The creation of independent Czech and Slovak states is generally seen as one particular instance of the general process of transformation which is taking place in the former socialist countries and in which the ideology of communism is replaced by that of nationalism."⁵

Considering the breakup of Czechoslovakia, two main questions emerged: was the Czech-Slovak split inevitable and who in the end was responsible for it? In the 1990s, a majority of commentators and scholars in Western Europe accepted a somewhat simplified explanation that the breakup of Czechoslovakia was caused by "traditional" Slovak separatism and anti-Czech attitudes.⁶ This assumption was based on the concept of the uneven "civilization" level of Czechs and Slovaks, resulting from different historical developments in the nineteenth century. Seldom taken into account were the discontent of a substantial part of the Slovak population with the centralist tendencies of the Czech elites, their lack of understanding of this Slovak discontent, and the existing desire of Slovaks for a democratic federation of two equal nations.

---

[3] Paal Sigurd Hilde, "Slovak Nationalism and the Breakup of Czechoslovakia," *Europe-Asia Studies* 51 (1999): 647.
[4] Ibid.
[5] Ladislav Holy, "Metaphors of the Natural and the Artificial in Czech Political Discourse," *Man* 29 (1994): 829.
[6] Ibid., 811.

The popular idea of "traditional Slovak separatism" was closely connected with a general belief on the part of Czech elites that Czech political discourse is based on the civic principle and nationalism plays only a marginal role in its development.[7] Western political scientists even defined two concepts of nationalism and argued that the Czech case represented the "Western, civic nationalism" which is different from the "dangerous" nationalism of the post-communist countries situated farther to the east.[8] The opinion of many Czech intellectuals was that "Czech patriotism" was rational, critical, and without fanaticism.[9] From this point of view, the dissolution of Czechoslovakia was understood as the result of a conflict between Czech rationality and Slovak emotionalism,[10] between "Western values" and "Eastern chaos." The subsequent contrast between political developments in the Czech and Slovak Republics in the second half of the 1990s only strengthened the stereotypical view of both nations.

In her book about the last years of Czechoslovakia, historian Abby Innes wrote, "[p]olicy-makers in the West viewed the separating Czechs and Slovaks as marching purposefully into two different worlds."[11] Many politicians and journalists were convinced that Czech liberal advocates of the free market prevented another nationalist conflict in Europe. This view was based on national stereotypes depicting the differences between "pro-Western Czech society" and the "nationalist and East-oriented Slovaks." In 1994, philosopher and former dissident Miroslav Kusý summarized the stereotypical statements in a Czech-Slovak comparison while emphasizing that, even if some of the assumptions could be correct, in general they were far too non-specific and superficial: [12]

1. The Slovaks are more nationalistic
2. Slovaks are separatists

---

[7] Stefan Auer, *Liberal Nationalism in Central Europe* (London: Routledge, 2004), 96.
[8] Ibid., 96.
[9] As an example S. Auer quotes Milan Kundera. See: Auer, *Liberal Nationalism*, 95.
[10] Holy, "Metaphors," 820.
[11] Abby Innes, *Czechoslovakia. The Short Goodbye* (New Haven, CT: Yale University Press, 2001), x.
[12] Miroslav Kusý, "Slovak Exceptionalism," in *The End of Czechoslovakia*, ed. Jiří Musil (Budapest: Central European University Press, 1995), 139–55.

3. Slovaks are more religious (Catholics)
4. Slovaks favor the political left

The concept of the "return of the history of ethnic conflicts" to the "frozen" communist societies became popular to explain the dissolution of the socialist federation. Political scientist Štefan Auer noted that even Slovak elites accepted the logic of historical determinism, whereby Slovak nationalism was interpreted as the inevitable result of the legacy of the past, characterized by collaboration with non-democratic ideologies—fascism and communism.[13] Auer himself rejected such arguments as absurd. However, many Slovak intellectuals saw the unresolved tension between the demands for national liberation and the advancement of personal liberties as the central force in Slovak political developments. According to political scientist Grigorij Mesežnikov, despite the fact that most leading Slovak politicians of the twentieth century interpreted the so-called "Slovak question" as a combination of historical, constitutional, social, and cultural issues, the ethnic-nationalist elements were usually in the foreground and this did not change, even after November 1989.[14] However, experts dealing with the Czech-Slovak split argued that the nationalism accompanying the breakup was more "phantom" than real. This means that while the decision-making Czech and Slovak political elites openly accused each other of nationalist tendencies, in fact they worked on achieving their own personal and political objectives. According to Sharon L. Wolchik:

> [T]he growing political importance of ethnicity that occurred after the ouster of the communist system in Czechoslovakia resulted in part from the ability of political leaders to channel the dissatisfaction and uncertainty that inevitably accompany large-scale economic and political changes into support for ethnic aims.[15]

---

[13] Auer, *Liberal Nationalism,* 134.
[14] Grigorij Mesežnikov and Olga Gyárfášová, *National Populism in Slovakia* (Bratislava: IVO, 2008), 8.
[15] Sharon L. Wolchik, "The Politics of Transition and the Break-Up of Czechoslovakia," in *The End of Czechoslovakia,* 240.

The phrase "national differences" only allowed for blaming economic problems on the "others" and the essential role in defining the "others" contained ethnicity. Such tactics had a long tradition in the case of Czechoslovakia—the best-known example is the never-ending discussion as to who benefited more from the federation. In fact, political elites very often exploited the national sentiments and their potential to mobilize the masses for their own political goals.

One of the main reasons for the breakup of Czechoslovakia was the difference between the main topics of discourse in Czech and Slovak society. The concepts of post-communist economic and constitutional developments were incompatible, and both sides believed that accepting the transition philosophy of their rivals would endanger their own future.[16] A comparison of statistical data regarding the economy and demographics shows that the history of Czechoslovakia was a process of gradual "equalization" of the social structure, the economy, the level of education and the living standards between the Czech and Slovak parts of the republic. Despite the gradual diminishing of these disparities, there were still distinctions between Slovakia and the Czech lands in 1989, mainly at the level of urbanization, as well as the ethnic and religious structure of the population.[17] According to anthropologist Juraj Buzalka, the changes in twentieth-century Slovakia did not last long enough for a complete cultural transformation, but long enough for structural changes.[18] This quick modernization resulted in a substantial gap between the economic and technical aspects of modernization, on the one hand, and cultural and social processes, on the other.[19] Demographic and social analyses in the early 1990s indicated that Slovak society remained more traditional than Czech society, with more stable behavioral patterns, stronger family relations, and greater isolation from external impulses. The Czech population was more receptive towards external (foreign) impulses,

---

[16] Jiří Musil, "Introduction," in *The End of Czechoslovakia*, 3.
[17] Milan Kučera and Zdeněk Pavlík, "Czech and Slovak Demography," in *The End of Czechoslovakia*, 36.
[18] Juraj Buzalka, *Slovenská ideológia a kríza* [Slovak ideology and crisis], (Bratislava: Kalligram, 2012), 67–8.
[19] Musil, "Czech and Slovak Society," 90.

responded faster and more rationally to them, and was more pragmatic and adaptable.[20]

We can say that growing structural homogeneity is not sufficient for permanent unity. According to Czech sociologist Jiří Musil, who utilized political scientist James McKay's theory of mobilization, the breakup would never have become a reality without a "system shock" in the form of the collapse of the communist regime. According to Musil, the fall of the communist dictatorship resulted in the establishment of a Slovak elite, which used the vision of an independent state as the means to mobilize the population.[21] As a result, Czechoslovakia fell apart despite the nonexistence of a mass separatist movement.[22] However, the profound differences between the Czech and Slovak sides regarding the future form of the federation effectively compensated for the absence of open separatism.

It is also true that the breakup was organized by politicians whose election program did not mention the dissolution of the federation. Abby Innes stated that, in the breakup process, the political elites (both Slovak and Czech) manifested a typical communist political culture, which survived 1989 without significant changes.[23] This political culture was based on the belief that elected politicians have the right to do whatever they want, shape the state according to their needs, and justify their actions with talk of "national interests." According to Innes, the dissolution of Czechoslovakia was a process "manufactured by a ruthlessly pragmatic Czech right, with the help of Slovak populists and opportunistic leaders."[24] In this context, political scientist Gil Eyal raised another crucial question, "Why and when were the political relations between Czechs and Slovaks shaped in the form of a bipolar elite constellation?"[25] The creation of such constellations was most visibly shaped by the unsuccessful discussions about the reconstruction of the Czechoslovak Federation. Finally, after the elections in 1992, we can

---

[20] Kučera and Pavlík, "Demography," 39.
[21] Musil, "Czech and Slovak Society," 91.
[22] Innes, *Czechoslovakia*, 73.
[23] Ibid., xii.
[24] Ibid., xi.
[25] Gil Eyal, *The Origins of Postcommunist Elites* (Minneapolis: University of Minnesota Press, 2003), xviii.

clearly identify two dominant, relatively homogenous groups of post-communist national elites with completely incompatible visions of the future, while the advocates of the federation were too weak and passive to reverse the course of events. Developments in the years 1990–1992, all the meetings, negotiations and declarations, prove that the formation of such a constellation began immediately after 1989.

From the second half of the 1980s, the Soviet style of communism exhausted its supplies and ended in an overall crisis. The influence of Moscow was weakening under the pressure of European integration and disarmament negotiations between the USSR and the USA. Slovak society of the 1980s became more socially, politically, culturally, and even psychologically differentiated, although the Slovak part of the socialist federation did not feel the social, economic and cultural stagnation as much as the Czech Lands did. In Slovakia, ideological and political persecution was less severe, and demographic and educational growth was more favorable.[26] However, dissatisfied citizens still formed various anti-establishment movements and groupings: the Christian and civil opposition, Chartists, Hungarians fighting for minority rights, ecologists, former reform communists of 1968, intellectuals or young reform communists. These groups published their own "samizdat" petitions and proclamations.

Alexander Dubček became a phenomenon of his own, even if he did not take part in any dissent activities (unlike many other former reform communists of 1968) and was not connected with any oppositional grouping. The former leader of the Czechoslovak Spring was more popular abroad and retained international appeal to the European left as a symbol of "socialism with a human face." In the second half of the 1980s, Dubček was interviewed by Hungarian television and the Italian leftist newspaper *L'Unità*, where he called for the rehabilitation of the Czechoslovak reform movement of the 1960s. On November 13, 1988, the University of Bologna awarded him an honorary doctorate in

---

[26] Maciej Koźmiński, "Skice k výkladu o hraniciach Európy a európskych hraniciach," [Attempts to explain European boundaries and the boundaries of Europe] in *Európska civilizácia: Eseje a prednášky* [European civilization: Essays and lectures], ed. Maciej Koźmiński (Bratislava: Kalligram, 2006), 231.

political science, praising his "struggle for democracy and the humanization of politics."[27]

At the end of 1988, even the communist MPs in the Slovak National Council (SNC) became discontented. They expressed disapproval with the process of the preparation of a new constitution for the federation. The proposed draft introduced centralizing tendencies with the argument that "it is necessary to strengthen the unified state politics of the federation on the whole territory of the Czechoslovak Socialist Republic." The reason for the protests was that the proposal failed to mention the national constitutions and national symbols of the two republics.[28]

In the years 1988 and 1989, a substantial gap grew between the official politics of the regime and the attitudes of the Czech and Slovak peoples. The March 1988 Candle Demonstration in Bratislava in support of freedom of religion constituted the most visible and open protest against the communist regime in Czechoslovakia since 1969. This growing discontent was mentioned in the samizdat publications *Palachiáda* and *Několit vět* [A few sentences] and demonstrated by the subsequent arrest of the so-called Bratislava Five (five representatives of the Movement for Civic Freedom) for their remembrance of the victims of the 1968 Warsaw Pact invasion. The last political trial (of the dissident Ján Čarnogurský) took place during the events of November 1989 (November 14–22, 1989) and was accompanied by mass protests.[29]

There is no doubt that November 17, 1989 was a significant milestone in the development of Slovak society and the Czechoslovak Fed-

---

[27] *Alexander Dubček: Od totality k demokracii: prejavy, články a rozhovory; výber 1963–1992* [From totalitarianism to democracy: A selection of speeches, articles and interviews, 1963–1992], eds. Jozef Žatkuliak and Ivan Laluha (Bratislava: Historický ústav SAV a Spoločnosť Alexandra Dubčeka vo vyd. Veda, 2002), 223–313.

[28] Jozef Žatkuliak, "Slovakia's Position within the Czecho-Slovak Federation, 1968–1970," in *Slovakia in History*, eds. Mikuláš Teich, Dušan Kováč, and Martin D. Brown (Cambridge, UK: Cambridge University Press, 2011), 315–29.

[29] Jozef Žatkuliak, "Sur la route des années 1988–1989 en Slovaquie," in *La Tchécoslovaquie sismographe de l'Europe au XXe siècle. Publié sous la direction d'Antoine Marés* (Paris: Institut d'études slaves, 2009), 258–63.

eration.[30] Thanks to their leading role in the termination of the communist regime, two new political movements arose in Czechoslovakia and attempted to introduce new, systematic democratic changes—the Civic Forum (Občianske fórum, OF) in the Czech Lands and Public Against Violence (Verejnosť proti násiliu, VPN) in Slovakia.[31] The VPN, together with the Coordinating Committee of Slovak Students, issued a manifesto on November 25 demanding full civil rights and freedoms, free elections and an "authentic" Czechoslovak Federation.

After the general strike on November 27, the communist leadership peacefully surrendered its role in leading the state. Gustáv Husák, the last communist president, resigned on December 10.[32] Despite strong support for Alexander Dubček, especially in Slovakia (the presidency of the Slovak National Council officially nominated him for the position of president), the VPN and the OF nominated the former dissident liberal Václav Havel as the next president. As a communist, Dubček supposedly could not become "a guarantor of the principles of the Velvet Revolution."[33] On December 28, an extremely disappointed Alexander Dubček became the Chairman (Speaker) of the Federal Assembly and, one day later, Václav Havel was elected (still by a communist majority in the Federal Parliament) president of Czechoslovakia. Both of them became leading figures in Czechoslovakia's democratic transition. However, they were significantly less successful in their efforts to influence the discussions regarding the future of the federation.

---

[30] Jozef Žatkuliak et al., *November '89: Medzník vo vývoji slovenskej spoločnosti a jeho medzinárodný kontext*. [November '89: A milestone in the development of Slovak society and its international context] (Bratislava: Historický ústav SAV in Prodama, 2009), 25–116.

[31] Jiří Suk, *Labyrintem revoluce: Aktéři, zápletky a křižovatky jedné politické krize* [Through the labyrinth of revolution: Actors, plots and intersections of one political crisis] (Prague: Prostor, 2003), 188–255; *Verejnosť proti násiliu 1989–1991: Svedectvá a dokumenty* [Public Against Violence 1989–1991: testimonies and documents] eds. Ingrid Antalová and Mária Mistríková (Bratislava: Nadácia Milana Šimečku, 1998).

[32] However, Marián Čalfa, a communist (until January 1990) became the federal prime minister, and the communist (until March 1990) Milan Čič became the new Slovak prime minister and another Communist Party member, Rudolf Schuster, led the Slovak National Council.

[33] Vladimír Ondruš, *Atentát na nežnú revolúciu* [Assassination of the Velvet Revolution] (Bratislava: Ikar, 2009), 43–57.

Constitutional developments in post-communist Czechoslovakia became one of the most important political topics, especially in Slovakia. The socialist federation, deformed by the centralizing laws of 1970 and the Communist Party's monopoly on power caused a serious problem in Czech-Slovak relations.[34] A majority of Slovak politicians called for a new constitutional law, which would provide the foundation for a new, democratic relationship between the two nations. Although November 1989 represented a discontinuity with the regime of the communist dictatorship, the democratic setting for Czech-Slovak relations should have been based on the Constitutional Law on the Czechoslovak Federation of October 1968.[35] The Preamble of the 1968 Constitution proclaimed the right of self-determination, even if it meant the dissolution of the state. The Czechoslovak Federation was characterized as a voluntary union, which was in accordance with the right of self-determination and national equality and in fact protected the national sovereignty of the Czechs and the Slovaks.[36] These declarations remained unchanged in the 1991 revision of the constitution. In theory, this could have been the basis for the dissolution of the federation. However, in reality it was not,

---

[34] *Realizácia a normalizačná revízia česko-slovenskej federácie (september 1968– december 1970)* [Realization and revision of the standards of the Czechoslovak Federation (September 1968–December 1970)] ed. Jozef Žatkuliak (Prague: ÚSD AV ČR, 2011), 253–68. About the social and economic disparities between the Czech Lands and Slovakia during the years 1948–1989 see Miroslav Londák, *Ekonomické reformy v Československu v 50. a 60. rokoch 20. storočia a slovenská ekonomika* [Economic reforms in Czechoslovakia in the 1950s and 1960s and the Slovak economy] (Bratislava: Historický ústav SAV, 2012), 24–5, 193–205, 474–515.

[35] Jozef Žatkuliak, ed., "Federalizácia československého štátu 1968–1970: Vznik česko-slovenskej federácie roku 1968" [Federalization of the Czechoslovak State, 1968–1970: Creation of the Czechoslovak Federation, 1968], in *Prameny k dějinám československé krize v letech 1967–1970, Díl 5/1 sv* [Sources for the history of the Czechoslovak crisis in the years 1967–1970, Part 5, Vol. 1], (Prague: ÚSD AV ČR; Brno: Doplněk, 1996), 346–75.

[36] See Constitutional Law 143/1968 regarding the Czechoslovak Federation, http://www.zakonypreludi.sk/zz/1968-143, and Constitutional Law 103/1991 regarding the Czechoslovak Federation, www.zbierka.sk/sk/predpisy/103-1991-zb.p-1017.pdf.

because, until 1992, the political elites spent their energy mostly on the preservation on the common state and the decision-making political forces of the post-1992 development did not really care about the formulations in the federal constitution. The development of the debates about the federation can be divided into four main stages, in which different views on Slovak, Czech and Czechoslovak statehood came into the foreground:

1. The formation of a democratic system and a return to the initial purpose of the federation (from November 1989 until the elections in 1990).

2. Quarrels about the division of competences between the federation and the two republics (until the end of 1990).

3. Negotiations from the beginning of 1991 until February of 1992, dealing with the contents of the federal constitution and the constitutions of the Czech and Slovak Republics.

4. Developments after the elections in 1992 and the dissolution of the federation.

The central discussion regarding the form of the new constitution was the "bottom up" versus the "top down" principle. The question was should a strong federation delegate some of its powers to the respective republics, or should strong republics delegate some of their powers to a weak federation? In general, the Slovak elite preferred the second model. Heated discussions about the name and the coat of arms of the Czechoslovak Federation were one of the symptoms of the growing divide between Slovak and Czech politicians. In January 1990, President Václav Havel suggested the removal of the word "socialist" from the official name of the country, renaming it simply the Czechoslovak Republic. However, many Slovak politicians rejected this name, which conjured up the "centralist past." According to them, the constitutional and national equality of the two federal republics should have been demonstrated by a new name for the common state—the "Federation of Czechia-Slovakia." The federal assembly rejected this proposal. The subsequent "hyphen war" demonstrated the serious problems of Czech-Slovak coexistence. The name of the federation became an important symbol, which could either accentuate the unitary character of the state or present it as a federation of two equal nations. Political discussions were accompanied by public nationalist outbursts strengthening anti-Czech and anti-Slovak resentments in both parts of the federation.[37]

During March and April 1990, both the Slovak and the Czech National Councils passed laws concerning the names of the federal republics (Czech and Slovak Republic, ČR and SR) and the new federal assembly agreed on the name of the whole federation (Czech and Slovak Federative Republic, ČSFR) as well as on the quartered coat of arms. At the first meeting of the new Slovak and Czech national governments (April 10–11, 1990), Prime Ministers Milan Čič (Slovak Republic) and Petr Pithart (Czech Republic) agreed on respecting the basic principles of Slovak and Czech national coexistence in the federation according to the Law on the Federation from 1968. Čič and Pithart issued a common statement that the former Czech-Slovak disagreements resulted from a "centralist, directive and bureaucratic system" and that future relations and federal competences would depend upon the free mandate of national legislative and executive bodies.[38]

Slovak politicians insisted upon considerably strengthening the competences of the national republics as the basis for the "stability of the Czech-Slovak Federation." According to these first Slovak drafts, the federal government should deal only with foreign policy, defense, the military, monetary policies, and federal legislation.[39] By this time, the different conceptions of federation among Czech and Slovak elites, and also concerning their national societies, had become clearly visible. Both sides declared that they wanted to maintain the federation (both sides were probably sincere in this), but their visions of the common state were radically different and ultimately incompatible. However, in 1990, discussions over these questions were postponed until after the first post-November elections.

---

[37] Paal Sigurd Hilde, "Nationalism in Post-Communist Slovakia and the Slovak Nationalist Diaspora (1989–1992)," (Ph.D. diss., Oxford University, 2003), 179–88, 206–13, 224–72.

[38] Jan Rychlík, *Rozdělení Česko-Slovenska 1989–1992* [The dissolution of Czecho-Slovakia, 1989–1992], (Prague: Vyšehrad, 2012), 141–2.

[39] Jozef Žatkuliak et al., *November 1989 a Slovensko: Chronológia a dokumenty (1985–1990)* [November 1989 and Slovakia: Chronology and documents (1985–1990)], (Bratislava: Nadácia Milana Šimečku—Historický ústav SAV, 1999), 526–34.

In the June 1990 elections in Slovakia, the VPN came in first, followed by the Christian Democratic Movement (Kresťansko-demokratické hnutie, KDH), the Slovak National Party, the Communists and the Hungarian Coalition.[40] The Czech OF and the Slovak VPN also dominated the federal parliament. The new prime minister of Slovakia, Vladimír Mečiar (VPN), declared that the future democratic development of Slovakia needed be based on a reevaluation of the mutual relations between the federation and its republics. For him, the fundamental bases for Czech-Slovak relations were "the primary rights of the republics, which delegate some of their powers to the federation, because it is favorable to their common development." According to Mečiar, the post-November legislative developments needed to be concluded by an agreement on three constitutions (two national and one federal). One of his main topics was also a change in the philosophy and practice of directing the Czechoslovak economy and the realization of economic reforms. Mečiar declared the principle of sovereignty of the national republics over their "national wealth" and the economy. However, this principle exceeded the definition of federalization and was much closer to a confederation model, which was unacceptable to the Czech side.[41]

This problem started a new round of negotiations between the Slovak, Czech and federal politicians. During a meeting in the spa town of Trenčianske Teplice on August 8–9, 1990, Mečiar denied that Slovakia wanted to return to the separatist and nationalist traditions of the wartime Slovak Republic (1939–1945). He opened the subject of rebuilding the Czech-Slovak Federation, including the redistribu-

---

[40] *Voľby do zákonodarných orgánov na území Slovenska 1920–2006* [Legislative elections in Slovakia from 1920 to 2006], eds. Vladimír Krivý and Milan Zemko (Bratislava: Štatistický úrad Slovenskej republiky vo vyd. Veda, 2008), 117–23.

[41] Czech Prime Minister Petr Pithart made this very clear during his speech to the Czech National Council on September 4, 1990, *Společná československá parlamentní digitální knihovna*, www.psp.cz, ČNR 1990–1992, stenoprotokoly, 4. schůze, 4. 9. 1990, část 1-3/26. On August 30, 1990, the CNC established a commission for the preparation of the Constitution of the Czech Republic (it was headed by Dagmar Burešová), www.psp.cz/eknih/1990cnr/predsedn/usneseni/ue072.htm.

tion of some federal competences between the two republics.[42] The Slovak view of the whole situation was manifested by the statement of František Mikloško, Chairman (Speaker) of the Slovak National Council, that the Czechs did not understand the Slovak demands, because "in the Czech case the notion of Czech statehood merges with Czechoslovak statehood."[43] However, according to Mikloško, this was a cardinal problem for Czech politicians, not for the Slovaks.

Vladimír Mečiar then started to prepare a so-called competency law, according to a November 6, 1990 proposal by the Slovak government. The proposed law dealt with the delimitation of the common competences of the federation and its republics. The SNC confirmed the draft of a competency law on November 20, 1990 and delivered it to the Federal Assembly. This proposal included the downloading of centralist economic policies to the national governments.

The Slovak side wanted to take control over the heavy machine and military industries in Slovakia, which were under the control of federal ministries and their budgets. In this sense, the draft involved the traditional demands of Slovak elites, which had been present in their political agendas since 1945. However, it was precisely this program which caused conflicts with the Czech side. In general, representatives of the Slovak government insisted on more competences for their national legislative and executive bodies, while their colleagues in the Czech and federal governments worked in favor of a strong federation.

The struggle over the competency law constituted one of the key conflicts over the functioning of the Czech-Slovak Federation during

---

[42] *Za naše Slovensko. Informácie z vlády Slovenskej republiky* [For our Slovakia. Information from the Slovak government], no. 13/90 (Bratislava: ÚV SR), 6; Slovenská národná rada. Stenografická správa o schôdzi Slovenskej národnej rady, 3. schôdza, 27. až 29. augusta 1990 (Bratislava: Kancelária SNR, 1990), 25. *Predsedníctvo SNR zriadilo 27. augusta spoločnú Komisiu SNR a vlády SR na prípravu Ústavy Slovenskej republiky v kompetencii prvého podpredsedu Ivana Čarnogurského*, www.nrsr.sk/dl/Browser/Document?documentId=1674.

[43] Slovenská národná rada. 6. schôdza, 1. októbra 1990. IV. volebné obdobie. Stenografická správa o schôdzi Slovenskej národnej rady (Bratislava: Kancelária SNR, 1990), 47 and 49f.

the years 1990–1992.⁴⁴ Its compromise version included the decentralization of competences from the federal to the national level, especially in the economy. However, the Czech side, represented by Dagmar Burešová, chair of the Czech National Council, refused six Slovak proposals giving more competences to the two republics. In response, on December 6, Slovak political bodies agreed to threaten declaring the superiority of Slovak laws over federal laws. The prime minister of the Czech Republic responded that, in such a situation, "there is nothing more to discuss."⁴⁵ The Czech and federal governments tried to discourage the Slovak side from some of their demands.⁴⁶ However, Chairman Mikloško of the Slovak National Council insisted on the original proposals. According to his records, Alexander Dubček declared during a meeting with Vladimír Mečiar and Ján Čarnogurský that he was still convinced that Slovakia should stay within the federation; however, if the Slovak demands were rejected, he was prepared to resign as chairman of the Federal Assembly.⁴⁷ This discussion occurred in December 1990 when the bipolar elite constellation was significantly weaker than in 1992 and compromise between the Slovak and Czech elites (or at least their majority) was theoretically still possible. However, no lasting agreement could be reached. In the next two years, relations between the Czechs and Slovaks worsened and in this sense it would be futile to expect that the politicians of 1992 could solve problems, which even their much less radical predecessors in 1990 could not.

---

[44] Eric Stein, *Česko-Slovensko: Konflikt—roztržka—rozpad* [Czecho/Slovakia: Ethnic conflict, constitutional fissure, negotiated breakup] (Prague: Academia, 2000), 65–77.

[45] Jan Rychlík, "Česko-slovenská jednání od roku 1990 do voleb 1992" [Czech-Slovak Negotiations from 1990 to the Elections of 1992], in *Česko-slovenská historická ročenka 2002* [Czecho-Slovak historical yearbook 2002] (Brno: Masarykova univerzita, 2002), 173; Společná česko-slovenská digitální parlamentní knihovna, ČNR 1990–1992, 10. schůze, 7. 12. 1990, část 1/1, www.psp.cz.

[46] E.g., the creation of national central banks other than the federal one, and the transfer of competences over railroads and customs administration from federal to national ministries. These were demands Slovaks already made in 1968.

[47] František Mikloško. *Čas stretnutí* [A time of meetings] (Bratislava: Kalligram, 1996), 19.

After a series of dramatic negotiations, the Federal Assembly approved a modified proposal of the Slovak National Council. However, unclear formulations about competences caused new disagreements between the Czech and Slovak representatives. In addition, a new highly divisive topic appeared—the so-called State Treaty. It was proposed by Ján Čarnogurský (leader of the Slovak Christian Democrats) in February 1991. He entered into negotiations between the Czech and Slovak governments with the draft of a state treaty between the Slovak Republic and the Czech Republic, implying that the federal constitution should be derived only from the constitutions of the two republics. In the preamble of Čarnogurský's draft, there was a statement about the right to national self-determination, even if it took the form of secession from the federation. The parties to such an agreement should have been the republics, represented by their National Councils as the supreme national governing bodies. As a result, the proposal was rejected by the federal government and the Czech National Council, with the argument that such a treaty between two sovereign republics would mean a confederation and not a federation.

However, even the proposal for a declaration of state sovereignty by the Slovak Republic, introduced by the Slovak government, described the SR as a sovereign state "based on the sanctioned right of self-determination of the Slovak nation and the sovereign right to decide its own destiny." The declaration emphasized that participation in the federation was a voluntary Slovak choice, and the SNC had the right to adopt a constitution of the Slovak Republic. In fact, this formulation was very similar to the preamble of the federal constitution. It was even less "radical" because explicit accentuation of the "right to secede from the federation" was not present in the declaration. The breakup of the VPN and the OF during the spring of 1991 also influenced constitutional negotiations. The growing heterogeneity of the Slovak and Czech political scene further complicated the entire process, and the first serious thoughts of a Czech-Slovak split began to appear. On May 22, 1991, the Czech National Council discussed a catastrophic scenario regarding the possible breakup of Czechoslovakia. Premier Petr Pithart stated that it was in reaction to Mečiar's politics.[48] At the same time, Mečiar's HZDS

---

[48] www.psp.cz/eknih/1990cnr/stenoprot/019schuz.htm.

denounced the activities of the Czech National Council as "a continuation of a policy reluctant to adopt a partnership with Slovakia."[49]

These separate lines of thought were strengthened by economic developments. A majority of Slovak political parties disagreed with the radical liberal economic transition enforced by federal Finance Minister Václav Klaus. His vision corresponded more closely to the situation in the stronger Czech economy and paid only limited consideration to growing Slovak economic problems. The June 1991 meeting in Moravian Kroměříž attended by representatives of the three parliaments, national governments, and political parties brought no new insights into the question as to how to realize a state treaty between the Czechs and Slovaks. The Slovaks preferred a contract between two sovereign republics. The Czechs proposed an agreement of the two National Councils, representing two federative republics. The representatives of the Slovak National Council interpreted the Kroměříž meeting as a gathering of the official representatives of the Slovak and Czech Republics, who would sign an agreement regarding the future constitutional structure of the Czech-Slovak Federation. It was also mentioned that the only legitimate method to decide the dissolution of Czechoslovakia was with a referendum.[50]

Opinion polls conducted in the Czech and Slovak Republics between 1990 and the following year showed a growing rift. According to opinion polls in October 1990, 47 percent of respondents in the Czech Republic and 53 percent in the Slovak Republic were in favor of an "authentic" federation; 6.7 and 9.7 percent, respectively, wanted a confederation, and 5.3 percent and 9.6 percent, respectively, were for dissolution. By October 1991, 38 percent of Czechs and 16 percent of Slovaks favored a unitary state; 31 percent and 34 percent, respectively, preferred a federation; 4 percent of Czechs and 25 percent of Slovaks wanted a confederation and 6 percent and 15 percent, respectively, pre-

---

[49] *Národná obroda*, February 25, 1991. The Slovak government discussed the possible economic consequences of the Czechoslovak dissolution in November 1991, www.nrsr.sk/dl/Browser/Dokument?documentId=4359.

[50] Hubert Maxa, *Alexander Dubček—člověk v politice (1990–1992)* [Alexander Dubcek—The man in politics (1990–1992)] (Bratislava, Brno: Kalligram—Doplněk, 1998), 139–44; Eric Stein, 97–102.

ferred two independent states.[51] It was clear that the majority of the population preferred the common state and secessionists were still in the minority. However, the strong support for a unitary state on the Czech side and growing sympathies for confederation in Slovakia suggested an increasing incompatibility regarding visions of the future state.

On September 6, 1991, the leaders of both National Councils agreed on a declaration to the effect that "the drafting of the new national constitutions will be based on the continuity of the ČSFR and in compliance with its constitutional principles." Although the materials of the CNC (An Agreement on the Principles of the Constitutional Alignment of the Common State), differed in some points from the Slovak version (A State Treaty between the ČR and the SR), both documents involved identical sections regarding the equality of the republics and their sovereignty, but also agreed on the sovereignty of the common state.[52]

The subsequent state treaty was meant to be a keystone for the federal constitution. According to these plans, the whole "drafting process" should have been finished by the end of 1991.[53] However, there was another problem; the various versions of the Slovak constitution already existed, while the Czech proposal still did not. This complicated the work on the federal constitution, which should have been drafted according to proposals submitted by both National Councils.

---

[51] Fedor Gál et al., *Aktuálne problémy Česko-Slovenska (Správa zo sociologického výskumu)* [Current problems of Czecho-Slovakia (sociological research report)] (Bratislava: Centrum pre výskum spoločenských problémov, November 1990), 12, 17–20, 38, 44–53, 81–93. Data from October 1991; Jozef Žatkuliak, "Transformácia česko-slovenského štátu na samostatné národné republiky," [The transformation of the Czecho-Slovak state into independent national republics] in *Národ a národnosti na Slovensku v transformujúcej sa spoločnosti—vzťahy a konflikty: Stav výskumu po roku 1989 a jeho perspektívy* [Nations and nationalities in the transforming Slovak society—relationships and conflicts: The state of research since 1989 and its prospects] ed. Štefan Šutaj, (Prešov: Univerzum, 2004), 26.

[52] Neither of the two documents included a sentence about the right to secession from the federation. See SNC 1990–1992, 9th term, Chairmanship, Parliamentary Press 2650, www.nrsr.sk/dl/Browser/Dokument?documentId=3820.

[53] Dubček, *Od totality k demokracii*, 427–34; Stein, *Česko-Slovensko*, 110–12, 310.

In December 1991, the SNC was dealing with proposals for a Slovak constitution. There were two primary alternatives:

1. The Constitution of the Slovak Republic would assume a common state, but would declare its own sovereignty and, therefore, demand a state treaty with the Czech Republic.

2. The Slovak Constitution would be based on the currently existing form of the Czecho-Slovak Federation, with the SR as its component.

Most Slovak politicians preferred the first variant. However, Prime Minister Ján Čarnogurský stated that the "form of the treaty and the procedure of its ratification is a permanent problem of Czech-Slovak negotiations." Čarnogurský then complained that "a substantial part of the Czech representation creates a false dilemma that either there will be an agreement on a relatively strong federation or we will split completely."[54] In January 1992, there was still no positive development leading to a compromise. However, the tensions between the National Councils quickly grew because the Czech representatives insisted on agreements between the National Councils while the Slovaks wanted a state treaty between the Slovak Republic and the Czech Republic.

Negotiations on February 3–8, 1992, attended by the leaders of the SNC and the CNC, a mixed commission, and representatives of the three governments (both national and federal), led to a new document. It was called A Proposed Agreement Regarding the Principles of the Constitutional Alignment of the Common State. However, this compromise did not define the republics as the contracting parties. The agreement was, therefore, not a state treaty because it did not specifically name the republics as the foundation for the existence of the federation, which was the Slovak side's central condition.[55] In addition, the proposal involved sections strengthening the competences of the federal political bodies.

---

[54] Hlavová and Žatkuliak, *Novembrová revolúcia*, 221–2.
[55] Stein, *Česko-Slovensko*, 128–40, 315–20; Vladimír Srb and Tomáš Veselý, *Rozdělení Československa: Nejvyšší představitelé HZDS a ODS v procese ČSFR: česko-slovenské spolunažívaní v rokoch 1989–1993* [The dissolution of Czechoslovakia: The leaders of the ODS and the HZDS in the process of the ČSFR: Czech-Slovak coexistence in the years 1989–1993] (Bratislava: Karpaty–Infopress, 2004), 43–8.

As a result, on February 12, the politically divided leadership of the Slovak National Council rejected the agreement by one vote. Although the Czech National Council ratified the document on March 11, both sides decided to suspend further negotiations until after the elections of June 1992. On April 1, 1992, the SNC postponed the negotiations with the CNC, as well as preparations for a new Slovak constitution. The Slovak National Council suggested that the future Slovak parliament should continue with preparations for a national constitution and also with negotiations about possible forms of coexistence in a common state with the Czechs.[56]

However, the failure to reach an agreement and to find a compromise between civic and national principles proved to be decisive for the fate of the federation. It was clear that the two-year electoral term was not long enough to achieve a compromise on the crucial documents, which would have enabled the proper functioning of the federation. These two years were not even enough to create a relatively stable plural political system. This situation had a negative effect on the quality of parliamentary democracy. The failures of the first post-November political elites opened the doors for more radical, technocratic and/or populist political movements, and the 1992 elections confirmed these trends.

In March 1992, Alexander Dubček expressed serious doubts about the future of the federation. According to him, "[t]he key to the solution is also in the hands of Czech political representatives; however on the outside it is presented as the problem of Slovak national bodies."[57] Another reason for the stalemate was the nonexistence of a "connecting" federal constitution accepted by both Czech and Slovak sides during the first two years after the fall of communism. In fact, the majority of Czech politicians were not concerned with this topic. They focused primarily on the economic and financial aspects of Czech-Slovak relations, as well as on economic reforms. In fact, one of the main objectives of the Czech rightist parties was to discard the federal Chamber of Nations (enshrined in the 1968 Constitution) in order to make federal legislation easier and faster.

---

[56] Hlavová and Žatkuliak, *Novembrová revolúcia*, 247–8.
[57] *Národná obroda*, March 13, 1992, 1–2.

The internal political situation in Czechoslovakia was developing contrary to the politics of integration in Europe. Czechoslovakia accepted Western liberal and democratic values, seemingly without any problems, and actively pursued integration into the European Union. This is one of the reasons why international observers regarded Czechoslovakia as a consolidated, relatively problem-free state. However, during the two years of its post-communist existence, the federation weakened significantly, and the definite solution to Czech-Slovak relations became more and more elusive, especially after the cancellation of mutual negotiations.

The election program of the Movement for a Democratic Slovakia (HZDS),[58] a party which won the largest number of seats in the 1992 elections, demanded a Czech-Slovak confederation, with both republics enjoying international subjectivity. It also called for a declaration of Slovak sovereignty, a new Slovak constitution and ratification of the state treaty with the Czech Republic. The HZDS was established by seceding from Public Against Violence in April 1991. It was formed by supporters of Vladimír Mečiar, Slovak prime minister from June 1990 until April 1991. Because of his arbitrary behavior and authoritarian tendencies, Mečiar came into conflict with the leadership of the VPN, which decided to depose him as prime minister. As a result, his supporters in the VPN established a new party under Mečiar's leadership. Because of his popularity, the HZDS overwhelmingly won the elections in June 1992 and Mečiar returned to the post of prime minister.

---

[58] For the preferences of Czech and Slovak political parties and the election results see: *Rozloučení s Československem: Příčiny a důsledky česko-slovenského rozchodu* [Farewell to Czechoslovakia: causes and consequences of the Czech-Slovak split], eds. Rüdeger Kipke and Karel Vodička (Prague: Český spisovatel, 1993), 87; Petr Fiala and Maxmilián Strmiska, "Systém politických stran v letech 1989–2004" [The system of political parties in the years 1989–2004], and Jozef Žatkuliak, "Politické strany a hnutia na Slovensku po novembri 1989 až do rozpadu česko-slovenského štátu 1992" [Political parties and movements in Slovakia after November 1989], in *Politické strany: Vývoj politických stran a hnutí v českých zemích a Československu 1861–2004 II. díl: Obdobi 1938–2004* [Political parties: the development of political parties and movements in the Czech lands and Czechoslovakia 1861–2004 II. Part: 1938–2004], eds. Jiří Malíř and Pavel Marek (Brno: Doplněk, 2005), 1366–67, 1405.

Vladimír Mečiar preferred a confederation as the most appropriate model, but was prepared also to negotiate a federation, a union, or even the establishment of two independent states.[59] The plan for a confederation was, in fact, an indirect call for independence, even if some members and sympathizers of the HZDS were probably not aware of it. It was clear that such demands were completely unacceptable, not only to most Czech political elites, but also to a majority of the Czech people.

The winner of the largest number of seats in the 1992 Czech elections was the Civic Democratic Party (Občanská demokratická strana, ODS), led by Václav Klaus. It was one of the successor parties of the Civic Forum, which ceased to exist in February 1991. ODS became a conservative party supporting economic liberalism. It preferred a strong federal government with broad and clearly defined competences. The ODS openly rejected any form of confederation.[60] In addition, the political program of the Czech government included the possibility of a Czech-Slovak dissolution, while the program of the Slovak government did not include such an alternative.[61]

When the election winners and their coalition partners secured control over the executive and legislative organs of the state, the bipolar elite construction, described by Gil Eyal, became a reality. However, representatives of both of the strongest parties had to continue the negotiations over the fate of the federation. Because of the radically different views of both main parties (and also their voters and sympathizers), the "twilight" of the federation occurred very quickly. During a meeting at the government-owned Hotel Bôrik in Bratislava, representatives from the ODS and the HZDS admitted critical differ-

---

[59] Jan Rychlík, *Rozpad Československa: Česko-slovenské vztahy 1989–1992* [The breakup of Czechoslovakia: Czech-Slovak relations, 1989–1992] (Bratislava: AEP, 2002), 274–5.

[60] Vladimír Leška, *Slovensko 1993–2004: Léta obav a nadějí* [Slovakia from 1993 to 2004: The years of fears and hopes] (Prague: Ústav mezinárodních vztahů, 2006), 12.

[61] Jan Rychlík, "Jednání ODS a HZDS o státoprávním uspořádání a rozdělení ČSFR v léte 1992" [Negotiations between the ODU and the HZDS regarding the constitutional arrangements and dissolution of Czechoslovakia in the summer 1992], in *Česko-slovenská historická ročenka 2003* (Brno: Masarykova univerzita, 2003), 63.

ences in their election programs and political agendas. The ODS once again declared that it would prefer the breakup of the federation over a confederation:

> The ODS considers a federation (with only one international legal entity) to be the only reasonable and functioning model for the present-day Czech and Slovak Federative Republic. The HZDS considers that it should have the form of a confederation with the international subjectivity of both republics. The ODS rejects a confederation with the international subjectivity of both republics for a common state, but desires a union of two independent states. Rather than a confederation, the ODS prefers two completely independent states, which means the constitutional dissolution of the present state. [62]

The main actors in these talks also took into consideration other disintegrating factors: different views on the necessity of a state treaty, as well as on the competences of the republics and the federation. In addition, Slovakia was much more affected by economic problems than the Czech lands, and the opinion that both republics required a different economic policy grew stronger. The decisions of the ODS and HZDS delegates in the Czech city of Jihlava (October 1992) definitely ended the existence of the Czech-Slovak Federation.

During these hasty political developments, the pragmatic decision to create two independent republics prevailed. Not passing a constitutional law regarding the procedures for the dissolution of the ČSFR efficiently eliminated any formal agreement between the SNC and CNC, as well as a referendum. The breakup was realized through the Constitutional Law Concerning the Dissolution of the Czech and Slovak Federative Republic (November 25, 1992) and twenty-eight intergovernmental agreements and treaties. The declarations of the National Councils confirmed the establishment of independent Slovak

---

[62] Jan Rychlík, *Češi a Slováci ve 20. století: Spolupráce a konflikty 1914–1992* [Czechs and Slovaks in the 20th century: cooperation and conflicts 1914–1992] (Prague: Ústav pro studium totalitních režimů v nakl. Vyšehrad, 2012), 606, 603–12. See also Srb and Veselý, *Rozdělení Československa*, 59–94.

and Czech Republics on January 1, 1993 as democratic states with full international legal entity.

In conclusion, we can quote the legal theorist Eric Stein that the construction of the socialist federation was not prepared for an option whereby the two republics followed radically different political programs.[63] Free elections brought with them nationalism as an important political agenda, and the socialist federation had no instruments to solve the problems of the post-communist transformation.[64] The fate of Czechoslovakia was determined by the fact that the central issues concerning Czech and Slovak societies were different, and thus political success demanded the accentuation of entirely different topics in the Czech Lands and in Slovakia.[65] According to this point of view, the breakup of Czechoslovakia was much more probable than its preservation. There are opinions that the dissolution was not a "historical inevitability" and there were alternatives which were not accepted. However, the further existence of the federation would have demanded very different elites on both sides and, in this sense, also voters with different preferences. In addition, as Jiří Musil pointed out, it is questionable if the breakup of multinational states is automatically a negative outcome. The supposed disadvantages of such an event can be balanced by greater political stability in the region. The peaceful breakup of the Czechoslovak Federation created two cooperating states without serious mutual conflicts, which made their admission into the EU significantly easier.[66]

---

[63] Stein, *Česko-Slovensko*, 230. English original: Eric Stein, *Czecho/Slovakia, Ethnic Conflict, Constitutional Fissure, Negotiated Breakup* (Ann Arbor: The University of Michigan Press, 1997).

[64] Carol Skalnik Leff, *The Czech and Slovak Republics. Nation Versus State* (Boulder, CO: Westview Press, 1997), 143.

[65] Václav Žák, "The Velvet Divorce—Institutional Foundations," in *The End of Czechoslovakia*, 266.

[66] Musil, "Czech and Slovak Society," 77.

CHAPTER 4

The Dissolution of Czechoslovakia: The Slovak Perspective

Stanislav J. Kirschbaum

Jozef Žatkuliak and Adam Hudek's presentation of the Slovak perspective on the dissolution of Czechoslovakia takes its cue from Western writings on the dissolution that focus on elites and process.[1] The approach of these two authors is best articulated by Abby Innes, whom they quote, that the dissolution was "manufactured by a ruthlessly pragmatic Czech right, with the help of Slovak populists and oppor-

---

[1] Some other titles to which they do not refer that have a similar approach are Jaroslav Krejčí, *Czechoslovakia at the Crossroads of European History* (London: Tauris, 1990); John O. Crane and Sylvia Crane, *Czechoslovakia: Anvil of the Cold War* (New York: Praeger, 1991); H. Gordon Skilling and Paul Wilson, eds., *Civic Freedom in Central Europe. Voices from Czechoslovakia* (New York: St. Martin's Press, 1991); Sharon L. Wolchik, *Czechoslovakia in Transition: Politics, Economics and Society* (London: Pinter Publishers, 1991); John F. N. Bradley, *Czechoslovakia's Velvet Revolution. A Political Analysis* (Boulder, CO: East European Monographs, 1992); Bernard Wheaton, *The Velvet Revolution: Czechoslovakia, 1988–1991* (Boulder: Westview Press, 1992); Shari J. Cohen, *Politics Without a Past. The Absence of History in Postcommunist Nationalism* (Durham and London: Duke University Press, 1999); Minton Goldman, *Slovakia since Independence: a Struggle for Democracy* (Westport, CT: Praeger, 1999); Michael Kraus and Allison Stanger, eds., *Irreconcilable Differences? Explaining Czechoslovakia's Dissolution* (Lanham, MD; Rowan & Littlefield, 2000); Robin H.E. Shepherd, *Czechoslovakia. The Velvet Revolution and Beyond* (London: Macmillan Press Ltd., 2000); Peter Toma and Dušan Kováč, *Slovakia. From Samo to Dzurinda* (Stanford: Hoover Institution Press, 2001); Karen Henderson, *Slovakia: The Escape from Invisibility* (London: Routledge, 2002); and Kevin Deegan-Krause in *Elected Affinities: Democracy and Party*

tunist leadership."² The greater part of their presentation focuses on the strategy and tactics of the Slovak side during the short period of negotiation that preceded it. They also offer some explanatory factors of a historical and social nature that underscore the political interests of the elite but they do not make an attempt to present them in a coherent and cohesive way that would actually enable one to define a Slovak perspective. The reason for this is found in their interpretation of historical developments and also in their explanation of elite behavior and outcome options.

The authors approach the question of Slovak historical development in a very narrow way. According to them, prior to the fall of communism, Slovakia had undergone some development, but had remained "more traditional, with more stable behavior patterns, a stronger orientation towards family relations and also … more isolated from external impulses;" nevertheless, they also acknowledge that it had been the part of the country where the only open opposition to the regime had manifested itself with the 1988 Candlelight Demonstration in Bratislava. They note that there exists a "Slovak question," "which is to be understood as a combination of historical, constitutional, social, and cultural issues" but that its "ethnic-nationalist elements" were usually in the foreground, that is to say articulating a nationalism, which Slovak elites saw as deterministic, and which, furthermore, was characterized by collaboration with non-democratic powers. The authors suggest, as a result, that Slovak politicians "simply exploited the national sentiments and their potential to mobilize the masses for their own political goals." They conclude, in fact, that "the nationalism accompanying the breakup was more 'phantom' than real."

Hence their focus on the elites and the goals that they were pursuing; they acknowledge that the main goal in Slovakia was the passing

---

Competition in Slovakia and the Czech Republic (Stanford: Stanford University Press, 2006). For an assessment of this literature, see Stanislav J. Kirschbaum, "Slovakia: Whose History, What History?" *Canadian Slavonic Papers/Revue canadienne des slavistes*, XLV (3–4), 2003: 459–467 and "Whither Slovak Historiography After 1993?" *Canadian Slavonic Papers/Revue canadienne des slavistes*, LIII (1), 2011: 45–63.

² Abby Innes, *Czechoslovakia. The Short Goodbye* (New Haven: Yale University Press, 2002), xi.

of a "proposed constitutional law which would provide the foundation for a new, democratic relationship between the two nations." In addition, they recognize that there was "discontent from a substantial portion of the Slovak population with the centralist tendencies of the Czech elites," and also that "constitutional developments in post-communist Czechoslovakia became one of the most important political topics, especially in Slovakia." The last two points are crucial, for they suggest that what was actually being discussed in Slovakia was its future and that, in theory, but also in fact, there was another option than to remain in Czecho-Slovakia, even in a reorganized form. What would explain choosing such a breakup option?

The socialist constitution of 1968, which defined the amendment process, and the very short period of two years in which the constitutional discussions took place, are the reasons, the authors write, why constitutional talks failed and dissolution turned out to be the only outcome. While there is truth to this assertion and another outcome might have been negotiated, if there had been more time, this does not tell us why Slovak politicians opted for an independence option that many actually feared was a dangerous leap in the dark. Must we conclude that they took such a decision simply because of the time factor, after they refused to submit Slovakia to centralist tendencies from Prague from which the Czech elite refused to part, and that no other forces played a role their decision? Was the dissolution ultimately really the result of political machinations, divorced from any further developments or perspectives other than the ambitions of the post-communist Slovak political elites involved in the process and able to manipulate public opinion? Such a perspective does not stand up to the light of the historical record, nor to any real understanding of Slovak history. The fall of communism did not present Slovakia with a *tabula rasa,* which is what the two authors seem to suggest.

Political elites, especially in a democratic system, usually deal directly with the realities they face, and only under extraordinary circumstances do they consider, perhaps even conceive, let alone put into effect, solutions for a future with a totally different outcome; yet some of their choices may result in just that. They make the decisions that appear to offer the best solution to the immediate issues with which they are dealing; from 1989 on, Slovakia faced a series of social, economic, and political challenges within Czecho-Slovakia that demanded solutions that were deemed acceptable not only to the elites, but, above all, to the population. The decisions Slovak politicians had to make were certainly against a backdrop of specific circumstances, but they were also part of an historical evolution that justified and defined them as a viable option. To acknowledge this enables one to explain the Slovak approach to the dissolution of Czecho-Slovakia and the choice of the independence option.

During this short period, there were two sets of intervening variables that had rendered independence feasible: First, there was the international environment. Independence was not being imposed as, in the view of many, it had been in 1939, nor was there any objection to it in either constitutional or international law. Particularly important is the fact there were no geopolitical imperatives at work that hindered it. If the Slovak elites who made the decision to opt for independence felt that it was the best option—as we know, constitutional solutions were the object of much discussion in Slovakia in 1990–1992—they did so because they knew that it not only was a possible option, but also a viable one. And it was viable also because of a second variable, namely the legacy of past struggles and decisions, which defined Slovakia's development over time. To fully understand the importance of these two variables, one has to take an historical perspective. To do so does not imply any sort of historical determinism.

There is no need to go too far back in the past; the history of Czecho-Slovakia will suffice. In 1918, the Slovak political elite knew that the only viable option for their nation, so as to protect it from further Magyarization and to ensure its development, was to leave Hungary and share a common state with the Czech nation; independence was simply not viable, however suitable it might have been as an application of the principle of self-determination that justified at that time the destruction of Austria-Hungary.[3] But their expectations, and indeed those of the population, that the Slovaks would enjoy an equal partnership were soon dashed, and, as a result, clouded the benefits that they were gaining from living in a common state. In consequence, within

---

[3] The independence option had been considered but was deemed inappropriate for a number of social, economic, and political reasons. See Stanislav J. Kirschbaum, "The Cleveland and Pittsburgh Documents," *Slovakia* 36, nos. 66–67 (1998): 81–97.

two decades, in 1939, under unexpected, exceptional, and dangerous external circumstances and pressures, their elites decided that it was best to secede and to run their own state, which they did successfully for six years. Then, in 1945, new elites, democratic and communist, in response to external circumstances, opted again for Czechoslovakia, expecting this time, as a result of the experience of 1939–1945, that they could alter the balance between the two nations that had defined the First Czechoslovak Republic with its ideology of Czechoslovakism; this happened only nominally. Another set of elites, not completely disconnected from the communist elites of 1945, succeeded in altering the balance in 1968 when they turned Czechoslovakia into a federation. A set of state institutions was created in Slovakia, which put an end, despite the monopoly of power and the centralism intrinsic to Communist Party politics, to the hitherto complete and obligatory reliance on institutions and decisions that emanated from Prague, and created an infrastructure in Slovakia that gave it a high degree of self-administration.

By 1989, Slovakia had once again acquired some considerable experience in self-administration from which the step to self-government was extremely small. But, if it was to be taken, it was also a gamble, given the regime change that was taking place. It depended on the extent to which Slovak society was ready and confident in its ability to take in hand its own future; it also depended on how the different Slovak political formations understood the extent of this development. There was division in Slovak political ranks and also among the public. At the same time, what became clear during the discussions that took place in 1990–1992, in the face of an inability to find an acceptable reorganization of the common state, is that remaining in a Czecho-Slovakia based on the centralizing Czech approach to the common state was an option that no longer had validity. The majority of Slovak citizens recognized this and public opinion polls backed this up. This is not to suggest that there was overt majority support for independence; indeed no major Slovak political formation articulated this option openly. Rather, what quickly became clear is that it was the default position. What many also understood was that this was an option that had an historical basis and justification along with the social, economic and political bases to make it viable. Past history, furthermore, suggested that it could work. The elections of 1992 gave democratic sanction to choose this option if no other solution were available; none was. In the end, not only was independence the only solution, but it was the only appropriate one for Slovakia. There is scholarship in the West[4] and in Slovakia[5] on such an approach to the dissolution of Czecho-Slovakia, but Jozef Žatkuliak and Adam Hudek chose to ignore it.

A Slovak perspective on the dissolution is one that focuses not only on the circumstances and the elites, but also on the historical process; to do so does not in any way diminish or deny the contribution of Czecho-Slovakia to the development of Slovakia and the Slovak nation. Rather, it helps to understand better the role of the parties and their leaders and the factors and conditions that made independence the option that was ultimately chosen and also how and why such an outcome occurred peacefully and democratically. No history of the dissolution of Czecho-Slovakia can be complete and fair unless it offers a Slovak perspective.

---

[4] See Stanislav J. Kirschbaum, *A History of Slovakia. The Struggle for Survival*, 2nd edition (New York: Palgrave Macmillan, 2005) and Stanislav J. Kirschbaum, *Historical Dictionary of Slovakia*, 3rd edition (Lanham, MD: Scarecrow Press, 2014).

[5] See Milan S. Ďurica, *Dejiny Slovenska a Slovákov v časovej následnosti faktov dvoch tisícročí*, 5th edition [A chronological history of Slovakia and the Slovaks over two millenia] (Bratislava: Lúč, 2013); Robert Letz, *Rozdelenie Česko-Slovenska v roku 1992* [The dissolution of Czecho-Slovakia in 1992] (Bratislava: Polygrafia SAV, 1997) and Robert Letz, *Slovenské dejiny* [Slovak history] (Bratislava: Literárne informačné centrum, 2008).

CHAPTER 5

The Slovak Republic After Twenty Years

Jozef Moravčík

Less than one year after the division of Czechoslovakia in 1993, a proposal to nominate Mr. Mečiar and Mr. Klaus for the Nobel Peace Prize was made by the leadership of a certain political party. Fortunately, the proposal remained in limbo.

It is a fact that the world greatly appreciated the peaceful division of Czechoslovakia, in the spirit of the Velvet Revolution. However, the very fact of the division was not so well appreciated. Generally speaking, the international community does not welcome the division of states, especially if such divisions could be seen as a precedent. Therefore, the question remains: can we defend what we have done? This question may seem irrelevant, as there is no tribunal before which we should stand. However, in this case, a tribunal is replaced by our consciences, with which we could be reconciled only after the consequences of this step had become clear.

The politicians who came to power in 1992 and had to make decisions, decided according to the best of their abilities and historical consciousness. The previous hundred years witnessed a century of intense ideological confrontation, of nationalism, of abandoning monarchical principles. Czechoslovakia was founded upon this tide. In 1918, Slovaks liberated themselves from under the weight of Hungarian assimilation in order to preserve their national identity. For this they have to be thankful for our first common republic with the Czechs.

At the same time, the idea upon which our common state was founded was markedly influenced by the pragmatism of our political leadership. This pragmatism drove the decision-making process. I refer to the concept of a homogenous "Czechoslovak" nation. However, when we take into consideration all the circumstances that had to be taken into account at the Paris Peace Conference after World War I, when the victorious Allies decided to recognize the new Republic of Czechoslovakia, we can only admire the abilities of our elite of that time. It is praiseworthy that they established themselves on the side of the victors. It would probably not have been possible without the concept of a single Czechoslovak nation.

It is paradoxical that the idea of the Czechoslovak nation helped the Slovak nation to stand firmly on its own two feet. It could then freely build its own schools and develop its own culture. Despite this, however, relations between Czechs and Slovaks were not ideal. Perhaps we lacked the same measure of pragmatism to strengthen the relations between our nations. Perhaps it was prevented by the problem of national minorities within Czechoslovakia. This was the other side of the coin for the countries of Central Europe, which had established their statehood upon a national base. Our first republic did not last long; just a bit over twenty years.

In the evaluation of our mutual relations it is necessary to skip over the period of the Second World War. Conditions in both the Czech Lands and in Slovakia were strongly deformed during this period and cannot be taken at face value.

The following period was constrained by Marxist ideology, paradoxically limiting even the development of this ideology. This period lasted two and half times longer than the first republic and no favorable conditions arose for the solution of the relations between Czechs and Slovaks. According to our communist rulers, such relations could be solved only on the basis of proletarian internationalism. However, in 1968, the principle of federalism entered into our historical consciousness and it was finally enacted into our constitution.

Nineteen eighty-nine witnessed a revolution in our country, wrapped in velvet garb, which demolished all existing ideas and concepts and, for a while, its participants had a feeling that they could change everything. This is probably the same in all revolutions. Did this revolutionary change justify the initiative towards the completion of the process of the establishment of our own national states, the completion of the principle of self-determination of nations? Ironically, it came at the end of a century which would witness a drive for the unification of

Europe, a period more marked by the process of linking states than by dividing them.

Here, we have to take into account that our historical consciousness was strongly influenced by past events in our region. I think that without these events it is not possible to properly assess our decisions at that time. The nations of Central Europe for a long time belonged to someone else—whether to the Ottoman Empire, the Austro-Hungarian Empire or the Russian Empire. After the demise of these empires, the region became fragmented. Therefore, it was easy, first for Germany and later for the Soviet Union, to fill that void. We, the nations of Central Europe, were not able to avoid being drawn into these struggles between superpowers. When the superpowers were defeated or retreated, Central Europe once again acquired the ability to solve its own problems. In the southern part of Central Europe, this solution led to war. Czechoslovakia, by contrast, chose a peaceful solution. This, in brief, was the historical consciousness that affected the winners of the 1992 elections in Slovakia. These coordinates marked the boundaries for their decision-making.

While history can provide a solid background, politicians, however, have to plan for the future. After 1989, our reintegration into Western values was, for a great majority of us, more or less a matter of course. But, how could we acquire these values again? The world we were rediscovering after fifty years of enforced isolation was quite different from the world we had left in 1939. Those who looked at Europe from behind the Iron Curtain admired, often uncritically, the vision of Europe, economically integrated, with a common currency, with the coordination of policies including foreign policy, drawn by the Maastricht Treaty. It then became necessary to solve the problem of national sovereignty, as well as of integration.

The question as to how Slovakia should enter Europe began to be tackled by Slovak politicians immediately after the revolution. One concept, represented by Ján Čarnogurský, was the entry of the common state, that is, Czechoslovakia into the European Union, providing that Slovakia and the Czech Lands would be independent members of the European Union—Slovakia into the EU with its own star. Ján Čarnogurský, then deputy prime minister of the federal government, relying on his good relations with the European People's Party, entrusted me, then dean of the Faculty of Law at Comenius University, with a mission to Brussels to discuss whether such a procedure would be feasible. The result of the consultation was an expert opinion, briefly summarized as follows: according to the rules, valid at the time, such a procedure would be very difficult, if not impossible. If, however, there was sufficient political will within the European Community, a way could be found. In diplomatic newspeak it meant that such an option was out of the question. This concept of a common entry into the EU with two stars had its origins in the possibility of a deterioration in Slovak-Hungarian relations, especially with regards to the Treaty of Trianon, the trauma of which among Hungarians could still be observed from time to time, even at present. In other words: a strong Czechoslovakia could better face Hungarian diplomatic pressure on Slovakia's southern border.

Ján Čarnogurský founded the Christian Democratic Movement in Slovakia. However, the decisive political force in 1990 was the VPN, Public Against Violence, a political movement founded in November of 1989 comprising a wide political spectrum from the left to the right—all those who were not yet politically clearly defined. Public Against Violence, however, could not long remain intact. Just like the Civic Forum in the Czech Lands, it eventually disintegrated. While in Bohemia the splitting up of the Civic Forum proceeded in a classical fashion, from conservative through liberal up to socialist-oriented parties, or their nuclei, in Slovakia the basic question in the splitting up of Public Against Violence Party was: are we for a federative or looser structure of Czechoslovakia? The wing represented by Vladimír Mečiar, opting for a looser union, prevailed. Fedor Gál, the advocate of a strong union of Czechs and Slovaks, was in the minority. The Movement for a Democratic Slovakia (HZDS), which broke off from the VPN, led by Vladimír Mečiar, won half the parliamentary seats in the 1992 elections. Fedor Gál, with his fraction, did not even get into parliament. That was a decisive moment regarding the future of a common state.

The development of political structures following November 1989 contributed in its way to the division of the state. No political party was established across the whole country. Political parties were founded on the basis of the individual Czech and Slovak Republics, which had existed on paper since 1969, but not on the whole state. The so-called "hyphen war" of April 1990 regarding the proper spelling of Czechoslovakia was just an episode; a hyphen between Czecho and Slovakia could not remove problematic issues between both nations.

The basic platform of the HZDS for the 1992 elections was to maintain the integration rate between the Czech and the Slovak Republics at the same level as stated in the Maastricht Treaty. This treaty took effect at the same time that Czechoslovakia was to split. It meant that the Czech and Slovak Republics would retain a common market with the free movement of people, commodities and capital as well, as a common currency. Moreover, the Slovak side proposed a common army and the coordination of other ministries, which would be on a republic level. That was the basis of the union, the voluntary association of two states.

The proposal of the union of the Czech and Slovak Republics was based on the prerequisite that Czechs and Slovaks would join the European Union, this being just a matter of time. Therefore, in our opinion, it would not be appropriate to lower the integration level under the level of integration of the EU member states

The preparation of the concept of the union of the Czech Lands and Slovakia in the form of legal documents was entrusted to Michal Kováč, Milan Kňažko, and myself. After the first consultations with the representatives of the winner of the Czech elections—the ODS (the Civic Democratic Party) led by Václav Klaus, it was evident that the ODS would not agree with our concept. Therefore, we did not continue further work on these legal documents.

Much later, when everything about the state's division had been decided, the idea of a union between Czechs and Slovaks met with a response on the Czech side. Miloš Zeman, the current Czech president, presented a proposal to form a Czecho-Slovak union in the Federal Assembly. The HZDS at first supported this proposal. However, due to an inner political crisis caused by this step, it had to change its standpoint.

During many negotiations before and after the elections of 1992, certain arguments were voiced that we had to take into consideration—that the Czech Republic was too poor to carry the burden of an economically weaker Slovakia by retaining a common currency. This reflected the Czech perception of Slovakia as an economic burden upon the more developed Czech Lands. At the same time, we (with a smile) rejected a suggestion by an ODS representative that the

Czech Lands would prepare some sort of Marshall Plan for Slovakia, which would raise it economically to a level close to that of the Czech Republic. The condition was that the HZDS would then agree to a strong federation.

These negotiations revealed a great degree of diversity of political opinion on the future of both states in the political representations of both republics, which had been elected by their citizens. Opinions presented regarding the form of a common state were so fundamentally different that it was not possible to find a compromise. The problem stood as follows: we stay in the common state and continue to face a permanent political crisis, or, we divide the state, concentrate upon building our own nation-states, finish building their political structure, based upon new values, and later we will meet in the European Union. Such questions could not be answered other than to agree upon the division of the common state. The only measure of integration the political representatives of both nations were able to agree upon, was a customs union.

Moreover, at that time concerns were voiced in Czech political circles regarding political development in Slovakia. Vladimír Mečiar's policies raised concerns that the Western world would have reservations, which could jeopardize the process of integration into the European Union. Unfortunately, it turned out that these concerns were justified. This was evident during my meetings with representatives of other European countries, as well as with American representatives.

To a certain extent, though not quite decisive, Slovak-Hungarian relations played a small role in the decision-making of the Czech representatives. They did not wish to be burdened with minorities issues. This can be demonstrated by an international issue, which, in a short six-month period of the federal government, was to be resolved—the problems were the one-sided damming of the Danube River on the border between Slovakia and Hungary and the building of a waterworks on the Danube, a dam with a hydroelectric power plant. The Czech part of the federal government supported the Hungarian government, which had requested halting the project, although the Slovaks went ahead with it, a procedure, which was justified as confirmed later by the International Court of Justice in The Hague. The Czech political representation was afraid that a diplomatic conflict with Hungary could jeopardize the ambitions of the Czech Republic to join the EU.

The division of Czechoslovakia in 1993 meant that the Czechs and Slovaks had to build borders between their two republics. When journalists asked me sometime before that whether there would once again be borders between our nations, I answered that if it happened, it would lead to my political defeat. Unfortunately, at the end of that year, when I was returning from Prague to Slovakia, I noticed intense preparations for building real borders. I was defeated. Fortunately, only for a short time.

The reconstituting of the federal government after the elections of 1992 on the basis of parity meant that the federation ceased to function, even though it still existed according to the constitution. For a short time, Czechoslovakia was practically a confederation. The last six months of 1992 were spent specifying conditions for the division of the state and concluding agreements necessary for introducing the customs union.

A very important task at that time was the need to convince the international community to accept the division of the state, as well as to secure a diplomatically recognized place for both republics in bilateral and multilateral relations. In this regard, an important role was played by President Václav Havel. Foreign representatives had considerable misgivings and concerns about the potential political destabilization of Central Europe. A more radical change came after the meeting of President Václav Havel with President George H.W. Bush at the Conference on Security and Cooperation in Europe in Helsinki in July 1992. The US president received the Czechoslovak president with manifestations of friendship and recognition. At this meeting, Václav Havel used his considerable authority, gained while visiting the USA in 1990, and stood up for accepting the division of the federation, in spite of the fact that he had never identified himself with the division and he did not fail to mention that. The press release by the American side recognized a peaceful division of Czechoslovakia as *de facto*. A change took place in the negotiations with representatives of other countries as well. A constructive approach dominated in those talks. In these negotiations, it was essential to secure an approach of equality towards both successor states by the international community, and this was successfully achieved. Absurd hints of blaming the division of the common state on one of the republics appeared here and there. However, not in the diplomatic environment. Such hints met with no response.

An equal approach by the international community towards the successor states, which had been secured without major difficulties, meant that both republics had the same starting point. Their fate was in their own hands. Shortly thereafter, however, the attitude of foreign countries, especially of our new allies, began to change to Slovakia's disadvantage. In subsequent years, Slovakia had to fight a difficult inner political struggle to gain the confidence of its allies.

Immediately following the official celebrations of the establishment of the independent Slovak Republic in 1993, I was asked by journalists whether I was looking forward to the new state; I had to answer: not yet. Part of Slovakia's political representation, which held leading positions in federal organs, the Prague Group, had analyzed the republic's possible development after independence. We came to the conclusion that Prime Minister Vladimír Mečiar did not guarantee the democratic development of Slovakia and could be a hindrance to Slovakia's integration efforts into the European Union. One important European diplomat told me that, in his opinion, the problem was not so much in the political decisions of the Slovak prime minister, as in his terrible rhetoric.

Regrettably, it was not possible to achieve a change either in Mečiar's rhetoric or in his policies. And my acquaintance stated that Mečiar's policies had begun to contain dangerous elements of totalitarianism. The first attempt at a change started to appear within the HZDS by the establishment of the Alternative of Political Realism within the party's framework. Its core comprised HZDS deputies who came to the same assessment regarding the person of the prime minister as the Prague Group had. Unfortunately, the Alternative of Political Realism did not gain support within the HZDS and its backers were expelled from the party. Consequently, this group initiated a no confidence motion in the prime minister in parliament. The motion carried in March 1994. The Mečiar government had to resign and early elections were called. The new government that was established for the six-month period until those elections, which I headed, won the support of the democratic world. It was based upon a wider range of all political groupings, including parties of the Hungarian minority. In the September elections, this grouping won a majority of the seats. However, because of the defection of a workers' faction belonging to our leftist ally, it was not able to form a government. The four years that followed demonstrated in full that our concerns about Vladimír Mečiar's policies had been justified.

The vote of no confidence in the government in 1994, however, was very important. It resulted in the creation of a pro-democracy opposition which returned to power in 1998. And when in 2002, I congratulated Mikuláš Dzurinda on forming his second government, I would have answered those journalists of 1993 as follows: "My conscience is clear."

CHAPTER 6

The Czech Republic after Twenty Years: Gains and Losses

Petr Pithart

Since January 1, 1993, for the first time in our more than one-thousand year history, we Czechs are living in our "state house," alone. This house has changed its name, size, form, ruling dynasties and presidents many times. But always here with us—Bohemians, Moravians, and Silesians—were other nations or national minorities: we were never alone. The transformation from a multinational state to a nation-state was significant: it changed our being, our way of life, but it happened and the inhabitants of the country were not asked to approve of it.

In Central Europe until 1938, Czechoslovakia, like Poland, had a high percentage of citizens who were not members of the theoretical nation-state. A few decades later we became the most homogenous of states; perhaps only some Icelanders are more homogenous. Non-members of the "nation-state" in 1938 formed 33 percent of the population, and even this was valid only because the nation-state consisted of both Czechs and Slovaks—a construct with which many disagreed. One marginal note: it is still an open question to what extent "Czechoslovakism" was a sincere attempt to establish a political nation of the Western European type, and to what extent it was only an expression of Czech paternalism toward Slovaks based on temporal need. It is also questionable whether anyone besides T. G. Masaryk took the idea of this political nation seriously.

Regardless, our state house was (even with the "Czechoslovaks") very mixed in the first years after the First World War. Our politicians wanted it that way and Edvard Beneš promised that we would become a "Central European Switzerland." By this promise (whether we wanted it or not) we accepted a very difficult task—to form in the mosaic of Central Europe a civic nation. The difficulty of this goal was appreciated and for some time even brought us some respect.

Democracy must face and solve difficult tasks; otherwise it degenerates. It should not give up on difficult problems by concentrating only on the easy ones. Our democracy tried to solve the difficult problems between 1918 and 1928, but then gradually gave up. At the end, it even abandoned such pro-Czechoslovak parties as the German Social Democrat, the Christian Democrats and the Confederation of Farmers—the courageous adherents of Masaryk's Republic, because they were Germans!

From the "state house" gradually disappeared first the Jews, then the Ruthenians, and finally the Germans. This happened in the tragic circumstances of the Second World War and the years that followed. But the Slovaks and Hungarians (of Slovakia), were "freed" from the union by the November 1989 politicians (or more precisely: the winners of the June 1992 elections) quite voluntarily. "At last we are alone"—this could be heard even from the famous Czech intellectuals like Ludvík Vaculík. They felt "relieved after that decision" because negotiations between the Czech and Slovak representatives lasted far too long and did not bring quick and definitive results. I personally was upset by their "relief."

Indeed, in 1992, the state was divided in half a year. Within six months, a state for which tens of thousands had fought and died on several fronts in both World Wars disappeared. Meanwhile, the Belgians, Canadians, and Spaniards, who for decades have faced the danger of separation, repeatedly tried to correct and reform their fragile states, attempting to make them stronger, because they obviously believe that it is worth it not to abandon the work of their forefathers. In the former Czechoslovakia, the initiative to divide the country was taken by the narrowest leadership of the two victorious political parties who, within a few weeks, decided that they would terminate the union in half a year.

Today, when one looks at the photos of these negotiations, one may ask: who are those young men (on the Czech side) and those old gentlemen (on the Slovak side) who are standing with stubborn faces around their leaders—Václav Klaus and Vladimír Mečiar? They have all gone. At the end, many of them were happy that they could quietly disappear. Their names are known today only to historians and to the people who remember this story with a quick ending, which still gives some of us nightmares.

Yes, the decision was taken within a few weeks, maybe even days. No political party (with the exception of the Slovak National Party) went into the elections with a program for the dissolution of the state. And it is known that electoral programs usually include everything that might eventually attract voters, even when it is evident that such a program cannot be fulfilled.

The 1992 elections were won by the Czech Civic Democratic Party (the ODS) and the Slovak Movement for a Democratic Slovakia (the HZDS). The Czech Václav Klaus ran as a candidate for the Federal Assembly. Vladimír Mečiar ran for the Slovak National Council. But Klaus soon rejected President Havel's appointment of him as federal prime minister. This was probably the first sign that things would develop differently than promised. It was a sign that the federal government would mean nothing, and that, later, it would probably not exist at all. The comments of the vice-chairman of the ODS, Miroslav Macek, a few days after the elections, showed that the negotiations about the dissolution would start a few days later. How was that possible?

At that time I was already out of active politics, because my party—the Civic Movement (OH)—did not pass the threshold into either the federal or the Czech Parliament. Throughout that extraordinary hot and dry summer, I watched the TV powerlessly, with the feeling that something wrong and inevitable was happening, and it was decided somewhere without any mandate. I never felt so miserable for such a long time as in the summer of 1992.

The Czech public was influenced mainly by the "phenomenon of Mečiar." Mečiar was really a difficult partner. He was extraordinarily emotional, but simultaneously had a strong will. With a light smile but with a deep, sonorous voice, he presented his demands in absolutely incoherent words and sentences. If he were to represent Slovakia forever, we really could not continue to live with the Slovaks in one state. He lied many times—and what was worse, he believed his own lies. If confronted with his own fabrications, he even cried—how could someone dare to accuse him of lying? His sincere belief that he was always right was the secret of his charisma, which attracted the minds and hearts of many Slovak women and men. Despite the fact that he was not a supporter of immediate independence, he served as proof to the Czech politicians that no alternative to independence was possible: Mečiar stubbornly insisted on maintaining the common state, but with a separate international legal subjectivity for Slovakia, two things which logically do not fit together. It was very easy to identify Slovakia just with him. "Don't you see, dear Czechs? It won't work. So let them go…" concluded the Czech politicians.

Everything moved quickly. The schools were on holidays and people were tired after the elections. When children went to school again in September, everything was already decided. But there was still the possibility of a referendum. On what else should citizens be consulted than on whether or not they want to live in one common state or in two separate states? Yes, to formulate the question would be difficult. It would also be difficult to decide what to do if the results were different in the Czech Republic and in Slovakia. The same question, formulated in public opinion polls, once positively and once negatively, brought answers which differed only by 16 percent. Certainly, everything like that meant problems. But should we only do easy things? Yes, with a referendum everything would be more complicated. But: why not? Because at that time it was already decided that all business ends at the end of the calendar year. The timetable for liquidation and division of federal authorities had been already been set up. Czech bank notes and coins were secretly and discretely ordered in Canada.

A referendum would definitely make things more complicated. If the results were as opinion polls showed (e.g. against the dissolution in both republics), all three governments would have to go. And before the new elections, the political parties would have time to openly explain to the voters what they planned to do with Czechoslovakia.

One and half million citizens signed a petition demanding a referendum (I can still see the bundles of petitions in the main hall of the Federal Assembly where they were delivered). The voice of the people was ignored. The referendum was rejected as a "complication." But democracy always means a complication: it complicates rule so that it is not easy. Democracy should not block the rule, but it should certainly complicate it. The argument then was that in Yugoslavia immediately after referendums people started to shoot at each other.

Political representatives light-heartedly rejected a referendum with demagogy, which can be described only as cynicism. It was acceptable to ignore the common people, who—according to the then political elites—do not understand anything. Confidence in democracy was seriously damaged at that time and it has not been fully restored to this day.

It was much easier to promise the newly elected Czech deputies of the Federal Assembly the seats in the not-yet established Senate. They were told not to worry about losing their mandates: if you vote for the dissolution of the state, you will automatically become senators (the deputies were to be "transformed," replacing one trough with another, as it was said in those days). That is why the "temporal Senate" was incorporated into the Czech Constitution. Despite morally problematic promises, a constitutional law on the dissolution of the Czecho-Slovak Federation was adopted on the twenty-fifth of November 1992 with only the slimmest majority. Yes, from a strictly legal point of view, it was legal.

I never claimed and do not claim that it was certainly possible to maintain Czechoslovakia. But I will always claim that very little was done to maintain it and what was done was done "pro forma." We were in a hurry. Klaus's ODS nominated the Czech Republic for a leadership role in Central Europe. We were expected to be the "Central European tigress" (as Minister of Economics Karel Dyba said). And we did not want the Slovaks to slow us down: Slovakia was described as a ball and chain on our leg, which we had to drag along. Where were we hurrying? To the European Union, naturally. We were expected to be there first and to connect with the European "money pipeline" (and to cut off the "money pipeline" to Slovakia). By the way, this awful word "money pipeline"—*penězovod*—was probably invented by the people from the Civic Democratic Alliance (ODA). It was awful: because once people at home start to talk about who is paying and who is subsidizing whom (the young family, the grandfather, the parents, the teenagers)— the family is finished. When such a word comes out of the mouth (that should have been washed out with soap), it is too late. But there was a dream about Czech exclusivity and all (pseudo)arguments were good, including demagogy.

I do not know if it was possible to maintain Czechoslovakia, but I know that we in fact never tried to implement the model "equal with equal." The model which was demanded by the Slovaks already existed in the first Czechoslovak Republic. Instead of that, the Czech side always implemented some sort of asymmetry. There was, for example, an illusion of a separate Slovak Communist Party, which should mask the fact that the real power was in Prague's Central Committee. Or the Slovak "Board of Commissioners" which was established in Slovakia after the war, with again an asymmetrical division of competences. This, in reality, did not mean "equal with equal." Even the last, federative form was rather problematic. In the fall of 1968, the federation was not formed by two legitimate political representations (let's forget for now the fact that without the approval of the Communist Party of Czechoslovakia, nothing could be changed). The country had just been occupied by the armed forces of the Warsaw Pact. The Czech National Council—the newly established Czech Parliament—was not elected by its citizens; it was handpicked by the Czech part of the National Assembly. And, after only two years, Party Boss Gustáv Husák took all the important competences from the two republics and back to Prague.

When, in the summer of 1990, we again started to negotiate the new division of competences, the Czechs got the feeling that the Slovaks wanted something more. The famous writer Ludvík Vaculík, in his essay "Our Slovak Question" (Naše slovenská otázka), probably was the first Czech to openly advocate the friendly divorce of the Czechs and the Slovaks. The Czech people did not understand that the Slovaks only wanted back what Husák had taken away at the beginning of the existence of the Czechoslovak Socialist Federation, in December of 1970.

During the spring of 1992 we were very close to the model "equal with equal": we negotiated the Czecho-Slovak state treaty, which would confirm the existence of a federation, this time represented and established by the democratically elected representations of both republics. But then came the elections of June 1992 and, with them, the opportunity for two leaders to strengthen their positions. That happened and the state was divided.

The situation in Slovakia with Mečiar as the leader was not easy. After January 1, 1993, a semi-authoritarian regime started to surface in Slovakia. Slovakia was no longer expected to join the EU and NATO. It started to be considered the "black hole of Europe." The prime ministers of both countries (Klaus and Mečiar) stopped visiting each other. Mečiar was threatening to shut down the oil pipeline from Russia; he allegedly organized the kidnapping of President Kováč's son, the murder of an investigative journalist, and the privatization of industry in favor of his friends, which was carried out openly, not secretly and discretely as in the Czech Republic. The cooperation of the Visegrád Group (e.g., the Czech Republic, Slovakia, Hungary and Poland) broke down.

In 1998, Mečiar expected to win the elections for a fourth time. He received the largest number of votes, but he did not gain enough seats to form a government. This can be described as a miracle. The Slovak right united; but mainly the Slovak people, the Slovak public, woke up. The civic nation was "resurrected." With the help of nongovernmental organizations (NGOs) from the democratic world, Slovak civic society activated itself, which, even today, deserves our admiration. Young people went from house to house; they visited every hut in every small village and explained to the people why should they vote. They did not tell which party the people should vote for; they just asked them to go to the polling stations (Mečiar counted on the passivity of most people who did not support him). The result was Mečiar's political defeat.

In 1998, the Slovaks lost their complex based on doubts that they could democratically rule their own state. In the past they had only one experience with their own state—the experience with a problematic independence during World War II, an experience which did not unite them but rather divided them, and even traumatized them.

What is the position of Slovakia towards the EU—and what is our stand today? Slovakia is not afraid of the EU, and admits that she needs her. Maybe even to look after her from time to time. And we the Czechs? We bought into the European Union subsidies—concretely twenty-four programs. There are so many because the politicians thought that, with so many, it would be impossible to control what the money would be used for. Fortunately, it was possible for the EU to control it.

We Czechs remained in our "state house" alone. Our state even lacks a generally accepted one-word name! (The Slovaks gave us such a word in their language, "Česko," but it does not work in English). We are tied to Czechoslovakia. Something like a *"reststaat"*—"rest state," as the Germans say. We remained here because we were not able to fulfill the goal which was given to us at the beginning—to live in tolerance with others. Our willingness and ability to negotiate and respect others is dying out. Only Romas and foreigners remain with us. It is significant that the Czech Republic very seldom grants asylum to refugees—we grant the smallest number of asylums in all of Europe.

We wish the Slovaks well in their independence and their state, despite our uncertainness about them in 1990–1992. And we congratulate the Slovaks because they did something for their civic character and democracy. They overcame their passivity and uncertainness. The man who led them so problematically to independence, and who started to establish an authoritarian regime in Slovakia, during the last elections was sent packing, along with his party (HZDS): the HZDS once had the support of 35 percent of the electorate; now it has a mere 0.93 percent. Nationalism in Slovakia is fading, while Slovak self-confidence is growing.

We in the Kingdom of Bohemia and the former Margraviate of Moravia did not use the division of Czechoslovakia to achieve anything positive. The question is whether we could even find anything positive, especially when we accept the fact that the dissolution was carried out legally, but without any legitimacy.

Part II

POLITICAL DEVELOPMENTS AFTER 1993

CHAPTER 7

Of People, Mice and Gorillas: Slovak Politics Twenty Years After

Juraj Hocman

When post-communist Czechoslovakia broke up, the public became perplexed. Few outside observers knew that there had been two nations in communist Czechoslovakia because its citizens had traditionally been referred to as Czechs. Nevertheless, with Yugoslavia torn apart by civil war at the time, the Velvet Divorce was easier to digest. In sharp contrast with the former, no war ruined the long-lasting and mostly friendly relationship between the Slovaks and the Czechs. Paradoxically, on January 1, 1993, the same date when Czechoslovakia ceased to exist, the Maastricht Treaty transformed a part of Western Europe from an economic community into an "ever closer (European) Union," which both Czechoslovakia's successor states desperately wished to join.

In 2012 and 2013, several conferences and seminars were held in the Slovak and Czech Republics with the aim of reflecting upon the common past and shedding new light on the dismemberment of the joint state.[1] They were accompanied by passionate public discussions, both formal and informal, on the gains and losses of the two "broth-

---

1 The most important was a conference hosted by the Slovak Academy of Sciences, "Konferencia 20 rokov Slovenskej republiky—jedinečnosť a diskontinuita historického vývoja" [Conference on 20 years of the independent Slovak Republic—the uniqueness and discontinuity of historical evolution], Bratislava, January 16–17, 2013. The papers from this conference, which were collected end edited by Miroslav Londák and Slavomír Michálek, were published under the title *20 rokov samostatnej Slovenskej republiky: Jedinečnosť a diskontinuita historického vývoja* [20 Years of the independent Slovak Republic: the uniqueness and discontinuity of historical evolution]

erly" nations. One thing soon became evident. Following the crippling consequences of the continuing economic crisis which started in 2008, and which has been considered by many the ultimate proof of the failure of the *laissez-faire* capitalist economic system in post-communist East-Central Europe, the traditional way of celebrating the Velvet Revolution by its flag-bearers as the beginning of democracy suddenly fell on deaf ears.[2] What's more, these reflections of past events made people in both countries weary of political sentiments. How come? Is it not true that a Czech or a Slovak can travel wherever he or she wants? Today, they can go to church without looking over their shoulders, fearing denunciation from their fellow citizens to the secret police and the Communist Party's ideological departments, with negative implications for their access to university education and advancement in professional careers. They also can buy a car of their choice instead of waiting for years for one to become available from a quota imposed by the state. So how did this gradual U-turn in the public mood happen? When looking for an answer, one may instinctively feel that statistics, plain facts, and formal logic alone are not enough to draw a picture of Slovak politics in the past two decades.

In the spring of 2012, the Gorilla Affair linked to corruption scandals among Slovak political and financial elites had already lost momentum.[3] Few expected a Czech version of the Gorilla syndrome to hit the domestic political scene. Within a couple of days, it struck and broke the neck of Petr Nečas's right-wing government. After a meeting held in mid-June 2013, a special unit of the Czech police raided the government's premises and arrested a couple of high-ranking executives, including the prime minister's aide and his intimate female companion Jana Nagyová, who served as the director of PM's office.[4] This

---

(Bratislava, VEDA, 2013). For details on the conference see http://www.sav.sk/index.php?doc=services-news&source_no=20&news_no=4823.

[2] Karol Moravčík, "Slovensko po roku 1989: Úpadok všetkých veľkých mýtov" [Slovakia after 1989: the fall of all great myths], *Britské listy* (www.blisty.cz), March 13, 2013.

[3] To be referred to on the following pages.

[4] "Nečas padl. Rezignuje z čela vlády i strany" [Nečas has fallen. Resigns as the head of the government and the party], *Parlamentní listy,* June 16, 2013, http://www.parlamentnilisty.cz/arena/monitor/Necas-padl-Rezignuje-z-cela-strany-i-vlady-275881.

led to Nečas's resignation on June 17. Robert Fico, his Slovak counterpart and the leader of the ruling left-wing party Smer—Social Democracy, brushed aside the police action, calling it "theatrical."[5] Once again, both countries switched roles.

Throughout the 1990s, the Slovaks had been solely held responsible for the breakup of their joint state with the Czechs.[6] In the following years, Slovakia not only proved that it could survive and exist as an independent state, but, by the 2000s, it had become the "Tatra Tiger" as a consequence of economic reforms introduced by the second Dzurinda government.[7] This new image of the country emerged shortly after American Secretary of State Madeleine Albright (herself of Czech extraction) had warned in 1998 that Slovakia might become a "black hole in the map of Europe."[8] This dramatic turnaround bears

---

[5] "Pre Fica bola česká razia teatrálna, podobné prípady boli vraj aj u nás" [To Fico the Czech police raid was theatrical: Similar cases happened here as well], *Sme*, June 16, 2013, http://www.sme.sk/c/6837955/pre-fica-bola-ceska-razia-teatralna-podobne-pripady-vraj-boli-aj-u-nas.html.

[6] The ouverture for such a perspective, which was instantly embraced by many Western journalists (see "For Eastern Europe Now, a New Disillusion," by Serge Schmemann The *New York Times*, November 9, 1990), was a famous essay written by Ludvík Vaculík "Naše slovenská otázka" [Our Slovak question] published on May 3, 1990 in *Lidové noviny*. As an addendum to Vaculík's essay appeared Irena Petřinová's "Plaidoyer za slovenskou samostatnost" [Plea for Slovak independence] in *Reportér* on May 19, 1990. For the interested public, not necessarily scholars, see the more recent Internet article "Rozdelení Československa" [Dismemberment of Czechoslovakia] published by an alternative source, *Zvedavec* [The enquirer], January 2, 2014, http://www.zvedavec.org/komentare/2014/01/5792-rozdeleni-ceskoslovenska.htm.

[7] "Once a Backwater, Slovakia Surges," by Matthew Reynolds, *The New York Times*, December 28, 2004. The article compares Slovakia with the Republic of Ireland, both of which progressed quickly from underdeveloped to fast-growing economies after having joined the EU.

[8] Albright told this to Slovak President Michal Kováč on his visit to Washington in 1998. See U.S. Department of State, http://www.state.gov./1997-2001NOPDFS/statements/1999/990122.html. See also "Slovakia's Election Another Direction," *The Economist*, May 20, 2010; Valerie Bunce and Sharon Wolchik, "Defining and Domesticating the Electoral Model: A Comparison of Slovakia and Serbia," in *Democracy and Authoritarianism in the Postcommunist World*, eds. Valerie Bunce, Michael McFaul, Kathryn Stoner-Weiss (Cambridge University Press, 2010), 134–154, 140.

some resemblance to the cinematic story of a tiny and plucky mouse called Stuart Little.[9] When Stuart's adoptive parents went to see a detective to find out what happened to the missing member of their family, he asked them politely, what kind of answer they expected from him. If they wanted to hear a good one, they should go home immediately because Stuart was already there. The second alternative, which seemed more plausible to the investigators, was that Stuart was kidnapped, tortured, and even killed. With Slovakia's evolution in the last two decades in mind, let us test the latter hypothesis.

From the beginning, Slovak politics has emanated from the masculine principle. This is, of course, not a Slovak specialty. What makes it specific within each particular context of modern Slovak history, apart from its most negative deviations, is the mixture of parochialism, conservatism, and the struggle for home rule and social justice.[10] It had all been about the leading political figures in Slovakia as a part of Austria-Hungary, the First Czechoslovak Republic, and communist Czechoslovakia. The Reverend Andrej Hlinka, the founder of the Slovak People's Party, Dr. Jozef Tiso, the president of wartime Slovakia, and Dr. Gustáv Husák, their ideological opponent and the successor of the two in one—all of them were men with undisputed authority, regardless of which side they stood on. Today it may seem a heresy, but Alexander Dubček, who gave a human face to the Czecho-Slovak Spring of 1968, and to an Eastern European variant of socialism translated as communism in the West, does not completely fit into this typological scheme. Speaking of political authority, not of popularity among the masses, Dubček, in a Machiavellian world of communist politics, seemed to have been a passive victim of circumstances rather than a lion tamer,

---

[9] *Stuart Little*, directed by Robert Minkoff, Columbia Pictures Corporation, 1999 (81–84 min.). Despite his limited physical abilities, Stuart was eventually able to overcome all difficulties and even to win the hearts of his opponents.

[10] See Elena Mannová, "Ideové smery, kultúrny a spoločenský život" [Major ideas, social and cultural life], in *Na začiatku storočia, 1901–1914* [At the beginning of the century, 1901–1914], eds. Milan Podrimavský and Dušan Kováč (Bratislava: Veda, 2004), 79–92. Dušan Kováč, "Nacionalizmus a politická kultúra v Rakúsko—Uhorsku v období dualizmu" [Nationalism and political culture in Austria-Hungary during the period of Dualism], *Historický časopis* 53, no.1 (2005): 45–56.

which was precisely what was needed during the turbulent 1960s.[11] Twenty years of normalization, which were personified by Gustáv Husák, the only Slovak president in communist Czechoslovakia, mostly produced sterile politicians, servile to their protectors in the Central Committee of the Soviet Communist Party.[12] The only ambition of Czech and Slovak Communists was to benefit from the advantages provided by the regime to its loyal followers and to survive in the petrified political environment which was dominated and controlled by one political party.

In the Czechoslovak variant of *perestroika* in the late 1980s, two Slovak politicians emerged as exceptions to the rule. The first was Marián Čalfa, a former communist who was to become the prime minister of Czechoslovakia during the country's transition to democracy before the first free elections in June 1990. The second was Rudolf Schuster, an ambitious communist politician, who was allowed by Public Against Violence (Verejnosť proti násiliu—VPN), the Slovak counterpart to the Czech Civic Forum (Občanské forum—OF), to serve as the interim Chairman (Speaker) of the Slovak National Council. After the elections in June 1990, Schuster was sent by the new federal Minister of Foreign Affairs Jiří Dienstbier, a former dissident and a

---

[11] A traditional 'humanistic' perspective on Dubček's personality and style of politics are reflected in his political autobiography, *Hope Dies Last* (New York: Kodansha International, 1993), translated by Jiri Hochman and edited by Paul De Angelis. More recently, a similar view on Dubček was presented by Slovak publicist Jozef Banáš in *Zastavte Dubčeka* [Dubček must be stopped!] (Bratislava: Ikarus, 2009). For opposite views on Dubček as an indecisive politician, see the well-known accounts by Pavel Tigrid, Zdeněk Mlynář and Petr Pithart.

[12] To this day, one of the best reflections of Husák's politics and his personality remains Vladimír V. Kusín's seminal book *From Dubček to Charter 77: A Study of Normalisation in Czechoslovakia, 1968–1978* (Edinburgh: Q Press Ltd., 1978). Numerous journal and newspaper articles have been written on Husák (they usually appear in January when Husák was born and in August, when both the anniversaries of the Slovak National Uprising of August of 1944 and the Warsaw Pact Invasion of Czechoslovakia of August 1968 are commemorated). The latest contribution on Husák is an extended scholarly monograph compiled by historians Slavomír Michálek and Miroslav Londák, *Gustáv Husák: Moc politiky—Politik moci* [Gustáv Husák: the power of politics – The politician of power] (Bratislava: Veda, 2013).

nominee of the Civic Forum, to Ottawa as Czechoslovakia's last ambassador to Canada.[13] After his return, he was elected mayor of Košice, the second largest Slovak city. Nobody expected Schuster, who, it was frequently insinuated, together with some other "new democrats" who had emerged in the early 1990s, from collaboration with the communist secret police, to jump from local to high Slovak politics in 1998 and to become the president of the country a year later. Before this could happen, the already independent Slovak Republic had to experience two Vladimír Mečiar governments with all their domestic and international repercussions.

When a hitherto obscure corporate lawyer began his meteoric political career on the pubescent Slovak political scene as Minister of the Interior in March 1990, it looked like a natural continuation of the country's masculine political tradition. Mečiar's robust dominance of Slovak politics expired four years later. Abandoned by his close collaborators and supporters, namely by Michal Kováč, the Slovak president at the time, Milan Kňažko, the former Minister of Foreign Affairs, and Peter Weiss, the leader of the Party of the Democratic Left that replaced the Slovak Communist Party, Mečiar was forced to resign a second time as PM following a tumultuous debate in the National Council on March 14th, 1994.[14] Having subsequently defeated the supporters and allies of the interim Jozef Moravčík government in the parliamentary elections in October 1994, Mečiar's Movement for a Democratic Slovakia (Hnutie za demokratické Slovensko—HZDS) triumphed and its leader became prime minister a third time. From the time of Mečiar's return to office, the feelings of betrayal, suspicion of others, and vindictiveness against opponents became his constant companions. Privatization, which was the primary reason for the division of the Slovak political elites, along with the personal animosities of political leaders, had a strong impact on Slovakia's path towards democracy

---

[13] See Rudolf Schuster's political autobiography *Ultimátum* (Košice: Press-Print, 1996).
[14] See "Stenografická správa o konaní 27. schôdze Národnej rady Slovenskej republiky konanej v dňoch 9.–25. marca 1994" [Stenographic report of the 27th plenary session of the National Council of the Slovak Republic held on March 9–25, 1994]. Digital Library of the National Council of the SR (www.nrsr.sk).

and its much desired membership in key international organizations. The period from November 1994 to October 1998, which became known as a Slovak variant of illiberal democracy called Mečiarism, resulted in an inconsistent and confrontational style of politics on the part of Slovakia's major representatives, inner political instability, and overall unpredictability of the regime in the eyes of external observers.[15]

In 1997, when the EU and NATO finally became fed up with the sharp contrast between the third Mečiar government's public statements and its deeds, Slovakia's fate in regards to its European and Euro-Atlantic integration was sealed. The political opposition in Slovakia, backed by democratic governments and, *sotto voce*, by the non-governmental sector, succeeded in making the 1998 parliamentary elections a tie. Unlike in the 1994 parliamentary elections, the Movement for a Democratic Slovakia lost 8 percent of its voters (35 percent in 1994) and could not find enough partners to form a new government, particularly because the Workers' Party of Slovakia, the former ally of the HZDS, did not gain enough votes to pass the 5 percent threshold. Although the Slovak National Party did receive 9.07 percent of the votes (5.4 percent in 1994),[16] HZDS was reluctant to form a coalition with nationalists who opposed the idea of Slovakia's integration with the EU and NATO. After a series of negotiations that lasted four weeks, Mikuláš Dzurinda, leader of the Slovak Christian and Democratic Coalition (renamed the Slovak Christian and Democratic Union or SDKÚ in the winter of 1999), formed his first coalition government. It consisted of five political parties—the SDKÚ, the SMK (Party of the Magyar Coalition), the KDH (Christian Democratic Movement), the SDĽ (Party of the Democratic Left) and the SOP (Party of Civic

---

[15] A plethora of scholarly accounts can be mentioned here, beginning with a typology of superficial democracies across the globe, including Mečiar's post-communist regime in Slovakia in "The Rise of Illiberal Democracy," by Fareed Zakaria, *Foreign Affairs*, No. 6 (1997): 22–43, continuing with Kieran Williams's *Slovakia after Communism and Mečiarism* (London: School of Slavonic and Eastern European Studies, 2000), to Tim Haughton's nuanced *Constraints and Opportunities of Leadership in Post-communist Europe* (Aldershot: Ashgate, 2005).

[16] Vladimír Krivý, "Election Results," in *Slovakia 1998–99: A Global Report on the State of Society* (Bratislava: IVO, 1999), 65. Rudolf Schuster, *Návrat do veľkej politiky* [Return to serious politics] (Košice: PressPrint, 1999), 139–40.

Understanding). Slovakia, which had begun its existence as an upstart in the early 1990s, emerged as a successful country under the following two Dzurinda governments.[17]

The results of the "success story" were both positive and negative. On the brighter side, Slovakia managed to catch up with the rest of the Visegrád Four (the other countries are Poland, the Czech Republic, and Hungary) by entering the OECD, NATO and the European Union between December 2000 and May 2004. On the darker side, the winners of the 1998 and 2002 parliamentary elections gradually lost support due to internal quarrels, as well as public scandals linked to party sectarianism, corruption, and nepotism.[18] They vehemently distanced themselves from the politics of Vladimír Mečiar and his appointee Ivan Lexa, the former head of Slovak Intelligence, who was linked to the scandalous kidnapping of Michal Kováč, Jr. (the former president's son) and the unsolved murder of Robert Remiáš (a key witness to the kidnapping) as the most visible symbols of Mečiarism. The appetite of the new rulers for political power in state institutions and economic influence in state-owned, as well as private enterprises based in Slovakia, did not lag behind that of their predecessors.[19] In fact, what had begun

---

[17] "Investors' Paradise," Steve Forbes, *Forbes*, August 11, 2003; "A European Powerhouse," Scott Steele, *Canadian Business*, September, 2004; "Slovensko je reformná jednotka" [Slovakia is a leading reformed country], Robert Grave, *Sme*, September 9, 2004.

[18] Peter Novotný, Daniel Forgács, Marián Velšic, "Non-Investors' Paradise," *Forbes*, August 11, 2003; "A European Powerhouse," Scott Steele, *Canadian Business*, September, 2004; "Slovensko je reformná jednotka." Peter Novotný, Daniel Forgács, Marián Velšic, "Governmental Organizations and the 2002 Elections," in *Slovak Elections 2002: Results, Implications, Context*, eds. Grigorij Mesežnikov et al. (Bratislava: IVO, 2003), 195–214. Oľga Gyárfášová, "Politické strany v spoločnosti: ich vnímanie a hlavné trendy volebného správania" [Political parties in society: Their perception and main trends in electoral behavior], in *Vláda strán na Slovensku: Skúsenosti a perspektívy* [The rule of political parties in Slovakia: experience and perspectives], eds. O. Gyárfášová and G. Mesežnikov (Bratislava: IVO, 2004), 113–26.

[19] See Erik Láštic, "Strany a štát na Slovensku: Osudová príťažlivosť?" [Political parties and the state in Slovakia: A fatal attraction?], in *Vláda strán na Slovensku*, 101–12. The author refers to the system of "patronage" (*patronát*), which allows the use of public resources for political purposes. Ibid., 108–10.

during the Mečiar era was more or less finished by the two Dzurinda governments. Before the state was to be kidnapped by political parties in the 2000s, it had been divided into their personal domains, regardless of the existing political alliances and personal animosities of their leaders.[20] Mikuláš Dzurinda's government lasted eight years, with the full support of Western democracies. The official approval of the Slovak government towards the NATO invasion of Iraq and the strengthening of close relations with the United States, which was regarded with suspicion by the leaders of the EU, materialized in February 2005, when the summit of George W. Bush and Vladimir Putin took place in Bratislava. It seemed that the Mečiar era was forgotten. This "success story," spread and echoed by the Western media, came to a halt in the summer of 2006, when the ruling coalition led by Dzurinda was soundly defeated by the leftist Robert Fico and his Smer (Direction) Party. Fico's ascension to power was initially interpreted by the right-wing parties and their supporters at home and sympathizers abroad as a return to the authoritarian style of politics, social demagoguery, and populism experienced during the third Mečiar government.[21] As the future was about to show, any comparison of Fico with Mečiar, insinuating their similarity, would be inaccurate and an oversimplification.

After negotiations with the representatives of the Christian Democratic Movement (KDH) and the Slovak Christian Democratic Union (SDKÚ) failed, the forty-two-year-old Fico formed his first government in July 2006. His coalition partners looked like ghosts from the past. They were Vladimír Mečiar and Ján Slota, leader of the Slovak National Party (SNS), who was known for his tendency to use offensive and derogatory language in communication with his opponents and the media. These two names were enough to alarm democratic politicians at home and abroad. However, following the constantly shrinking

---

[20] "Kusý: stále tu máme vládu strán" [Kusý: Political parties still rule over us], *Sme*, November 16, 2004.
[21] An unexpected comparison of the new Fico government with the third Mečiar government (1994–1998) was made by Monika Beňová, Deputy Chair and Party Deputy of Smer in the European Parliament. See "Fico začína s nepriateľom v zahraničí ako kedysi Mečiar" [Like Mečiar, Fico speaks about foreign enemies], www.hnonline.sk, July 10, 2006, http://hn.hnonline.sk/fico-zacina-s-nepriatelom-v-zahranici-ako-kedysi-meciar-200416.

number of votes cast for the HZDS (8.8 percent in 2006) in comparison with the previous elections in 1998 (27 percent) and 2002 (19.5 percent), Fico was firmly in control of the newly formed ruling coalition. This also happened because Slota and the SNS, which, after years of decline and an internal split, received an impressive share of the votes (11.7 percent).[22] Slota seemed to have been satisfied with Fico as the defender of Slovak national interests. Mečiar had more problems with accepting his position as a deposed king who was generously allowed to rule over his strictly limited domain by a new and younger contender.[23] The ambitious Fico, with his very good communication and organizational skills and fluent English, had abandoned the Party of the Democratic Left and its leading triumvirate: Peter Weiss, Milan Ftáčnik and Brigita Schmögnerová in the fall of 1999. This was in response to having allegedly been overlooked in the distribution of powers in the First Dzurinda government in November 1998.[24]

Despite promising election surveys before the 2002 parliamentary elections that had indicated 18.5 percent support for Smer among voters, Fico's first attempt to challenge the ruling coalition failed as his party received only 13.5 percent of the votes. This was probably because of his imprudent proposal to pass a law on the documentation of assets of the *nouveau riche*, which scared not only political leaders but also the public. Four years later, when Dzurinda and his peers may have thought that Mečiar and everything he had represented were already long gone, a new and widely popular leader arose on the Slovak political scene: Fico and his Smer, with 29.14 percent support, compared to 18.35 percent for the SDKÚ.[25]

Fico, who was seen by the supporters of the right-wing parties as a new, upgraded, version of Mečiar designed for the twenty-first cen-

---

[22] See the election results here: Statistics.sk, http://volby.statistics.sk/nrsr/nrsr2006/angl/obvod/results/tab3.jsp.htm.

[23] "Čarnogurský: Mečiar chcel radšej nás ako Fica so Slotom" [Čarnogurský: Mečiar preferred us over Fico and Slota], www.hnonline.sk, May 25, 2013.

[24] Grigorij Mesežnikov, "Vnútropolitický vývoj a systém politických strán na Slovensku" [Internal political developments and the system of political parties in Slovakia], in *Slovensko 2000: Súhrnná správa o stave spoločnosti* [Slovakia 2000: global report on the state of society], eds. M. Kollár a G. Mesežnikov (Bratislava: IVO, 2000), 17–124, 84.

[25] See http://portal.statistics.sk/showdoc.do?docid=4

tury, had to face the case of Hedviga Malinová, a young woman of Magyar descent from the Nitra Region. Malinová was allegedly beaten by Slovak extremists as a result of her ethnic origin while she was on her way to take an exam at a local university.[26] The news of this incident spread from the media to the Internet, stirring the rage of those who believed that Malinová had been beaten and those who claimed the case was fabricated to portray the new Slovak government in a nationalistic and chauvinistic way similar to that of Mečiar governments in the 1990s. To this day, the case has not been solved, as lawyers and medical experts on both sides claim that their versions of the story are true.

At the very beginning of his first government, Fico made clear that Slovak membership in the European Union was his government's first priority.[27] Despite his personal views with regards to the NATO invasion of Iraq, Fico kept Slovak soldiers in a country plagued by civil war and suicide attacks and later on sent Slovak troops to Afghanistan. Meanwhile, the European Commission investigated some of the public tenders held by the new government. The best known was the case of a billboard tender announced by the Ministry of Construction and Regional Development, which was under the control of the Slovak National Party. Fico insisted that the two ministers who held their offices consecutively resign due to the nontransparent procedures and favoritism, which were involved in the tender.[28] The SNS obeyed and

---

[26] For a concise summary of the case, see the article written on the first anniversary of the alleged attack "Chronológia prípadu údajného napadnutia Hedvigy Malinovej" [Chronology of the case of the alleged attack upon Hedviga Malinová], *Sme*, August 24, 2007. As of December 2013, Hedviga Malinová-Žáková was granted Hungarian citizenship and she left the country, thereby immediately losing her Slovak citizenship.

[27] See "Programové vyhlásenie vlády Slovenskej republiky, august 2006" [Program declaration of the government of the Slovak Republic, August 2006]. See the final part of the document "Zahraničná politika" [Foreign politics], 54–6, http://i.sme.sk/cdata/6/54/5475146/program_fico.pdf.

[28] For details see "Sumár najzaujímavejších aktuálnych informácií k tendru na Ministerstve výstavby s grafmi" [Summary of up-to-date information related to the (billboard) tender announced by the Ministry of Construction, including the graphs], *Monitoring fondov*, www.monitoringfondov.eu. See also the newspaper article "Prezident odvolal Štefanova, výstavbu povedie Mikolaj" [The president recalled Štefanov: The ministry will be led by Mikolaj], *Pravda*, March 11, 2010.

recalled both its nominees. Other tests of the inner compatibility with the European Union were the much-awaited accession of the country into the Schengen Area, which abolished visa requirements among its members and the acceptance of the common European currency—adopting the euro in 2007 was a breakthrough for the country's new political leadership.[29]

At first sight, this account of the first Fico Government's deeds may seem too rosy. Though Slovakia's place in the international community was not questioned, the exception was the still uneasy relationship with Hungary. This came to the fore with the visit of the Hungarian President László Sólyom to Komárno and his unsuccessful attempt to enter Slovak territory in August 2009, and with the adoption of a law that forbade dual citizenship to Slovak citizens.[30] This was how the first Fico government responded to a Hungarian law which gave ethnic Magyars living outside of Hungary the right to apply for Hungarian citizenship.

Meanwhile, the internal quarrels among political leaders, which have accompanied Slovak politics from the nineteenth century to the present, continued. To decipher this specific feature of Slovak politics, it is necessary to keep in mind that the majority of Slovak politicians started their careers between 1989 and 1990. They then evolved into an autonomous political class, which opened itself to the public only in times of elections. By the mid-2000s, the best-known individuals had been active in Slovak politics for a decade and a half; to the present

---

[29] "Belgický denník: Fico dostal Slovensko do Schengenu" [A Belgian daily: Fico managed to get Slovakia into Schengen], *Sme*, December 21, 2007. The original information appeared in *La Libre Belgique*, http://www.sme.sk/c/3647732/belgicky-dennik-fico-dostal-slovensko-do-schengenu.html.

[30] In October 2012, the European Court of Justice found the legal action taken against Slovakia baseless. See "Slovensko malo právo zastaviť maďarského prezidenta, rozhodol súd" [Slovakia had the right to block the Magyar president, court rules], http://www.ta3.com/clanok/1007763/slovensko-malo-pravo-zastavit-madarskeho-prezidenta-rozhodol-sud.html. "Robert Fico k avizovanému prijatiu zákona o občianstve Maďarskej republiky" [Robert Fico on the anticipated reception of the Law on State Citizenship in the Republic of Hungary]. See the website of the *Smer*, May 14, 2010, http://www.strana-smer.sk/1413/robert-fico-k-avizovanemu-prijatiu-zakona-o-dvojitom-obcianstve-madarskej-republiky.

day, their number of years in public service is even higher. The public became tired of many of them because they kept switching party allegiances for career purposes. Such politicians began resembling those against whom citizens of Czechoslovakia had fought in the late 1980s—the Communist Party apparatchiks.[31]

The political situation in Slovakia was further complicated by the global economic crisis that started in 2008. Real GDP growth fell from 10.6 percent in 2007 to 5.8 percent in 2008 and plummeted to −4.9 percent in 2009. The unemployment rate, which was kept under 10 percent in 2008, reached 14.4 percent in 2010; in some regions it rose to 20 percent.[32] The opposition political parties, led by the veteran politicians Mikuláš Dzurinda, Ivan Mikloš, Béla Bugár, chairman of the new Most—Híd (the Bridge) Party and Pavol Hrušovský, chairman of the Christian Democratic Movement, suddenly felt that the impact of the economic hardships stemming from the crisis allowed them to make use of the situation in Slovakia to challenge Fico and the left in the parliamentary elections of June 2010. The opposition's chances of defeating Fico had significantly increased by the emergence of a new political subject—the right-wing liberal Freedom and Solidarity Party (Sloboda a solidarita—SaS). Although Fico's Social Democrats won 34.8 percent of the votes,[33] they, like Mečiar and the HZDS in the parliamentary elections of 1998, could not find a partner to form a new government.

In the 2010 parliamentary elections, the masculine principle in Slovak high politics was briefly interrupted. The new prime minister, who was agreed upon by the leaders of the opposition political parties, became Iveta Radičová of the Slovak Christian Democratic Union. She had been a professor of sociology at Comenius Univer-

---

[31] "Šíri sa kontroverzné video výzvy k revolúcii: Politikov budeme súdiť ako najväčších zločincov" [Controversial video encourages people to revolt: Politicians will be tried as the worst criminals], www.topky.sk, October 15, 2013. The article had 1095 comments, http://www.topky.sk/cl/100535/1365136/Siri-sa-kontroverzne-VIDEO-vyzvy-k-revolucii---Politikov-budeme-sudit-ako-najvacsich-zlocincov-.
[32] Accessible at www.statistics.sk. The data were compiled according to relevant years.
[33] "Kompletné výsledky volieb: Parlamentné voľby 2010" [Complete election results: the 2010 parliamentary elections], *Sme*, June 14, 2010.

sity. In June 2009, Radičová ran for president of Slovakia but was defeated by Ivan Gašparovič, who was backed by Smer and nationally oriented voters in the second round of elections.[34] Her position as the PM was shaky, as she had to rely on the support of Mikuláš Dzurinda and his political twin Ivan Mikloš, who was the Minister of Finance and Dzurinda's deputy in the party. The Radičová government consisted of four political parties—the SDKÚ, the Most—Híd, the KDH and the already mentioned Freedom and Solidarity Party. The last was to become a maverick in the ruling coalition. At the beginning, it had played a role similar to Schuster's Party of Civic Understanding (SOP) in the 1998 elections and the Alliance of a New Citizen (Aliancia nového občana—ANO) in the parliamentary elections of 2002. Both of them had helped the opposition to gain enough votes to hold Mečiar at bay. The same scenario, this time to defeat Fico and Smer, was applied in 2010 when young and undecided voters, who felt close to the SaS slogans, cast 12.1 percent of their votes for it, thus making it the third strongest Slovak political subject after Smer and the SDKÚ (15.4 percent).[35] Since the SaS would play an important role in the period from July 2010 to October 2011, it deserves a closer look.

The leader of the SaS was Richard Sulík (born in 1968), a graduate of the University of Ludwig Maximilian in Munich, who became the new Chairman (Speaker) of the Slovak National Council. While Sulík himself was a proven economic expert and manager, he brought with him several *homines novi* who had a little or no political and administrative experience. The new Minister of Defense was Ľubomír Galko (1968) who had previously worked as a manager in a supermarket, and the Minister of the Economy was Juraj Miškov (born in 1973), the CEO of a mid-size trading company. The less their knowledge of political theory and diplomatic protocol, the more self-confi-

---

[34] "Kompletné výsledky II. kola prezidentských volieb" [Complete results of the 2nd round of the presidential elections], *Pravda*, April 3, 2009, http://spravy.pravda.sk/domace/clanok/161267-kompletne-vysledky-ii-kola-prezidentskych-volieb/.

[35] "Kompletné výsledky volieb: Parlamentné voľby 2010" [Complete election results: The 2010 parliamentary elections], *Sme*, June 14, 2010.

dent their approach to economic issues.[36] They challenged Fico's strict adherence to the fiscal policies of the EU. In terms of a generational change, Freedom and Solidarity truly represented a new generation of Slovak politicians. However, the party was in desperate need of more experienced middle-ranked cadres to tackle the demanding administrative and executive tasks. The party leadership, therefore, made an attempt to hire qualified people through public advertisements. Concerned with the weak economic situation in Slovakia, the party refused to share financial solidarity with the most endangered economies of the EU's southern wing, namely with Greece, Portugal, and Spain.[37] This critical approach to the EU, which would have been unthinkable six or seven years earlier, created problems and tensions within the Radičová government and raised the suspicions of Slovakia's partners in the EU. The European Commission became particularly concerned, after having listened to Sulík's derogatory statements regarding the economic policies of the EU in general and his remarks about the growing and ineffective bureaucracy of Brussels in particular.[38]

Under these circumstances, the ruling coalition led by Radičová, who was not even master in her own house (Mikuláš Dzurinda remained party chairman), could not survive. After sixteen months the coalition broke up over the issue of financial solidarity. After a vote of no-confidence in the National Council on October 11, 2011, Radičová resigned. She had previously made it clear that she would interpret the

---

[36] For Sulík's family background, his quite successful career as a financial advisor, and his political stances, see "Slovakia's Superman," *European Voice*, October 6, 2011, http://www.europeanvoice.com/article/imported/slovakia-s-superman/72212.aspx. An opposing picture of Sulík as an arrogant and inexperienced person was painted by Eva Zelenayová in "Falošný hráč" [The cheater], *Extra Plus,* September 2010.

[37] "Sulík: Slovensko nie je banka, aby si požičiavalo na Grécko" [Sulík: Slovakia is not a bank borrowing money to save Greece]. *Hospodárske noviny* online edition, April 26, 2010, http://finweb.hnonline.sk/spravy-zo-sveta-financii-126/sulik-slovensko-nie-je-banka-aby-si-poziciavalo-na-grecko-379925.

[38] On Richard Sulík as a politician see Stefan Auer's article, "Richard Sulík: A Provincial or a European Slovak Politician?" *Humanities Research XIX*, no.1 (2013): 81–100. The article indicates that it was Sulík's educational and cultural [German] background that made him a European rather than a provincial [Slovak] politician.

failure to support the Eurozone's bailout fund as a no-confidence vote. Sulík and the SaS were attacked by the right-wing Slovak press and media for destroying the government, who feared Fico's comeback.[39] Sulík argued that his party could not disappoint its voters and sympathizers who were skeptical about the EU's ability to solve the existing economic problems and, therefore, it acted principally and in accordance with its own political program.[40] In fact, the reason for the resignation of Radičová was twofold. It stemmed not only from her sense of responsibility with regard to keeping the coalition together, but also from her awkward position in her own party—the SDKÚ. In January 2011, when the PM insisted that one of the protégés of Minister of Finance Ivan Mikloš, who was the director of the regional tax office in Košice, resign because of his mismanagement of funds, Mikloš refused.[41] This was not the only time when her powers proved to be limited. Radičová remained the head of the government until March 2012 when the new parliamentary elections were held. Although she was still considered the only candidate who could defeat Fico in the presidential elections of 2014, Radičová repeatedly rejected this idea, nourished by the media and supporters of the Slovak Right. She has dedicated herself to her academic career in Slovakia and at St. Antony's College in Oxford.

Election surveys held before the 2012 parliamentary elections indicated that Fico and Smer were stronger than ever with 39.7 percent of public support.[42] The election results surpassed even the wildest expectations of the party and its leader. Having received 44.1 percent of the votes, Smer won eighty-three out of 150 seats in the National Council.

---

[39] "Radičová vyzýva Sulíka, aby odstúpil, ten na to nevidí dôvod" [Radičová urges Sulík to resign. He sees no reason to comply], *Sme*, October 11, 2011.

[40] In January 2014, Sulík anounced that he would run in the 2014 European Parliamentary elections. "Sulík, Nicholsonová a Oravec z SaS kandidujú do Európskeho parlamentu. Chcú získať viac ako jeden mandát" [Sulík, Nicholsonová and Oravec announced their candidacies for the European Parliament: They wish to win more than one seat], www.aktuality.sk, January 16, 2014.

[41] "Radičová alebo Mikloš?" [Radičová or Mikloš?] *Pravda*, April 19, 2011.

[42] According to the Focus Agency, http://udalosti.noviny.sk/volby-2012-preferencie/06-03-2012/predvolebn%C3%BD-prieskum-agentury-focus-februar-2012.html.

It did not have to seek an ally to form a government.[43] Some political commentators suggested that Smer might hesitate to create a one-party government and, given the grave economic situation in Slovakia, would prefer to share responsibility with another party.[44] Such comments seemed to have ignored two factors: 1) the intensity of personal animosities between the leaders of Smer and their counterparts from other parties, which can be traced back to the late 1990s, and 2) the determination of the Smer leadership to form a one-party government.

The second Fico government had to return to one of the most urgent cases in Slovak politics—that of who would become the new prosecutor general, an issue which had already arisen in 2010. The mandate of previous Prosecutor General Dobroslav Trnka, who was seen by the right-wing parties as sympathetic to Smer, had expired, and the office was vacant when the Radičová government was formed. The ruling coalition's candidate was Jozef Čentéš, an associate professor in the Faculty of Law at Comenius University. He was chosen as the candidate for the position of prosecutor general by the National Council in June 2011. However, President Gašparovič refused to approve Čentéš's election, claiming that he was a political nominee. The candidate appealed to the Constitutional Court. The president questioned the competence of the Constitutional Court, claiming that some of its members might be politically biased. Since the same objection had previously been raised by Čentéš, the Constitutional Court became paralyzed. In the end, President Gašparovič refused to appoint Čentéš on the basis that the candidate took an active part in "political games, publicly questioned the president's authority and became untrustworthy."[45] This situation, which centered around the control of the judiciary by political parties, became tragicomic. It served to dis-

---

[43] See Statistics.sk, http://app.statistics.sk/nrsr2012/sr/tab3.jsp?lang=sk (number of votes cast for political parties) and http://app.statistics.sk/nrsr2012/sr/tab4.jsp?lang=sk (number of seats in the national council).

[44] The origins of such speculation can be traced as far back as the fall of 2010. See "Politológ: Fico hľadá cestu späť do vlády" [Political scientist: Fico seeks to return to government], www.aktuality.sk, November 15, 2010.

[45] "Prezident SR Ivan Gašparovič nevymenuje Jozefa Čentéša za generálneho prokurátora" [President Ivan Gašparovič will not appoint Jozef Čentéš as Prosecutor General], Press communiqué, Office of the President of the Slovak Republic, January 2, 2013. Accessible at www.prezident.sk.

credit both political camps. The trust of ordinary citizens towards judicial institutions, which was already very low, decreased even more: 69 percent regarded their judicial institutions negatively in a survey held in April 2013.[46] In July, the National Council, completely dominated by Smer, elected Jaroslav Čižnár, a prosecutor and a recognized expert in the field, as the new prosecutor general, despite the objections raised by the opposition, which boycotted the vote.

In December 2011, a police file named "Gorilla" was leaked on the Internet. This document, the authenticity of which is still questioned, emerged as a result of a secret investigation by the Slovak Intelligence Agency of massive corruption among Slovak politicians during the Second Dzurinda government. The file insinuated an intimate (literally) relationship between politicians and financial figures in Slovakia.[47] Public disgust with the document and the practices described in it resulted in a series of protests in Bratislava and other Slovak cities. The public meetings, which started in January with 10,000 demonstrators on the streets of the Slovak capital alone, gradually decreased, and by March they were over. Reading the results of the 2012 parliamentary elections, it can be concluded that the Gorilla Affair was overwhelmingly associated with the Slovak Right, although Fico was also mentioned in the records as having had a meeting with a top representative of one of the two strongest Slovak financial groups in a conspiratorial apartment wire-tapped by the Slovak Intelligence Agency. To calm the public, old-new Minister of the Interior Robert Kaliňák and President of the Slovak Police Corps Tibor Gašpar from the second Fico government, created a team to investigate the case. As of today, the file contains over 60,000 pages and fifty persons have been investigated or called to testify. Canadian journalist Tom Nicholson, who has lived in Slovakia since the early 1990s, and knows the country's political ter-

---

[46] See "Záverečná správa z prieskumu verejnej mienky 'Postoje verejnosti k súdnictvu' pre Via Iuris, Apríl 2013" [Final report from the survey 'public opinion on justice,' for Via Iuris, April 2013: 4, http://www.viaiuris.sk/stranka_data/subory/postoje-verejnosti-k-sudnictvu.pdf. FOCUS Agency.

[47] For a complete document see "Slovenská Gorila: kompletní spis dokumentu" [Slovak Gorilla: complete list of documents], *Parlamentní listy*, January 9, 2012, http://www.parlamentnilisty.cz/zpravy/Slovenska-Gorila-kompletni-spis-dokumentu-221331.

rain very well, wrote a book with the same title, which by 2015 had sold 63,000 copies, an unprecedented number in a country as small as Slovakia. The financial group Penta secured a temporary court order to prevent the book being published.[48] The approach to this case from official quarters is lukewarm today and progress in the investigation is hidden from the eyes of the public. Questions raised by the media and concerned citizens regarding the current stage of investigation have received responses from state officials that use formulaic and evasive statements about the case's complexity.[49]

During the last two decades, politicians in post-communist Slovakia have become aware of the direct link between political and economic powers. Behind the broad shoulders of Vladimír Mečiar were to be found men of finance and capital, such as well-known Alexander Rezeš with his Košice clan in the mid-1990s and Jozef Majský, who was tried and jailed for asset-stripping during the Dzurinda governments. However, it would be unjust to overlook the presence of the shadowy figures who mediated the sell-off of strategic branches of Slovak industry to foreign partners for low prices, receiving funds destined for the treasury department during both Dzurinda governments. In the most visible cases of corruption, the public figures involved were not tried, but ousted from domestic politics (Pavol Rusko and Jirko Malchárek from the ANO Party) or generously exiled from international financial institutions (Gabriel Palacka from the SDKÚ). While in the 1990s it was politicians who controlled and awarded to their vassals the distribution of state assets, today it is financial magnates—the so-called oligarchs—who seem to completely control Slovak politicians and state institutions. This includes the Slovak National Council, the legislative process, the judicial system and everything else from the political parties' franchises down to the post of general laborer in

---

[48] "Penta uspela na súde: Nicholson nemôže vydať knihu o kauze Gorila" [Penta successful in court: Nicholson not permitted to publish book on Gorilla Affair], *Pravda*, February 3, 2012. As of November 2012, Penta withdrew its objection and permitted the publication of the book: *Gorila* (Havlíčkův Brod: Dixit, 2012).

[49] "Gorila opäť v parlamente" [Gorilla once again in Parliament], www.aktuality.sk, February 7, 2013. "V kauze Gorila sa opäť nikoho nepodarilo obviniť: je to zložitý prípad, tvrdí sa v správe" [No legal action taken in the Gorilla Affair; it is a complicated case, report says], *Čas*, December 3, 2013.

the most underdeveloped regions in East and South Slovakia. This is exactly what makes ordinary people feel helpless and angry. Two questions which have repeatedly been asked on Internet fora and in public can be formulated as: 1) Is this what we wanted in 1989–1990 and 1992? and 2) Is this what we voted for in the 1994, 1998, 2002, 2006, 2010, and 2012 parliamentary elections? These questions do not necessarily insinuate that those who raised them were calling for a return to the "good-old days" of communist Czechoslovakia, when there was no unemployment, no drug problem and no homeless people, and everyone could feed his family.[50] Taking into account this disappointment and the overall disillusion with politics in Slovakia, the most intriguing aspect of current public attitudes is the persistent support for the ruling Smer Party and its leader. In preelection surveys, Fico constantly received the highest percentage of votes as a possible candidate in the 2014 presidential elections (44.6 percent in July 2013) as does the party he leads (42.3 percent, 84 seats in July 2013).[51]

Concerns about this dichotomic situation should not be misread as stemming from sympathy for Fico's opponents. Fico seems to be an exception among the majority of Slovak politicians, who talk a lot and do nothing, regardless of their years of service. Fico, with his socially oriented programs, in which he seems to sincerely believe, still appears to many as the last bastion of stability between acceptance of the rule of political parties and their complete rejection by citizens. The real problems in Slovakia stem from the control of political, legislative, and judicial powers by representatives from financial capital. Today, those

---

[50] "Za komunistov bolo lepšie" [Life was better during communism], published by an author nicknamed Nautilus on his blog affiliated with *Pravda*, January 14, 2014. The article itself is an apt and bitter statement made by an ordinary citizen, which indicates his disappointment with and resignation with regards to the current state of the dysfunctional Slovak state and society. However, it does not call for the return of communism as a system of political rule and government.

[51] Fico announced his bid for the presidency in December 2013. In polls held in January 2014, he received the largest share of the votes—40.1 percent. The candidates in second (Radoslav Procházka) and third (Andrej Kiska) place received 13.6 and 13.2 percent of the votes, respectively. Surprisingly, the latter eventually won the presidential election in March 2014 and became president on June 15 that year.

who control the finances, and stand in Fico's shadow, think that this is what gives them the right to control both politicians and citizens. The continuing fracturing of political parties and the birth of new ones (Rudolf Schuster and the SOP in 1998, Pavol Rusko and the ANO in 2002, Béla Bugár and the Most—Híd, Richard Sulík and the SaS, Marián Kotleba and the ĽSNS in 2010, Daniel Lipšic and Nova in 2013) testify to the overall instability of the political system. Moreover, the quality of new deputies in the National Council remains questionable, as many of them have problems controlling their behavior and put their public image and personal ambitions above the public interest.[52]

If "Gorilla" was chosen as the name of the file linked to unseen corruption scandals associated with the cynicism and arrogance of their major participants, Slovak political parties can be compared to the self-reproducing and self-transforming creature from John Carpenter's classic horror movie *The Thing*.[53] Almost twenty-five years after the fall of communism, the Slovak political system still shows symptoms of political immaturity. These symptoms can be directly linked to the historical evolution of Slovak society. Slovaks respected social hierarchy during the times of feudalism and capitalism. Communism suppressed human individuality and initiative. The post-communist period affected Slovak society and politics in the opposite way. It can be concluded that in current Slovak politics too many want to be heard, but only few want to listen. The lack of party discipline is the pattern showing the inner instability of the existing Slovak political system. This is what leads both the traditional as well as the new political parties to self-destruct. This can be illustrated with the gradual decline of

---

[52] This is the case of the bellicose-by-rhetoric Slovak politicians of younger and middle generations who were elected to the National Council in the 2010 and 2012 parliamentary elections and either initiated or were repeatedly involved in physical conflicts in the parliament, namely Igor Matovič and Alojz Hlina from the OĽaNO—(Hnutie) Obyčajní ľudia a Nezávislé osobnosti [The ordinary men and independent personalities movement]. Meanwhile, Hlina left the party after his quarrels with Matovič, but continues to hold his seat as an MP.

[53] *The Thing*, directed by John Carpenter (1982; Hollywood: Universal Pictures). This metaphor stresses the voter—MP relationship in post-communist Slovakia, while pointing at the transforming ability of an extraterrestrial organism, which pretended to be human, after it had already killed its host.

the HZDS in the late 1990s and early 2000s; today, a similar process seems to plague the SDKÚ and SaS.[54] Until Slovak politicians learn how to build and manage political parties that can survive for at least two elections, while following a common goal, and resolve their leadership problems within party structures, there is a little hope that the political system in Slovakia will improve.

During the writing of this chapter, two classic expressions subconsciously came to mind. Seneca the Younger's classic dictum, "Inhonesta victoria est suos vincere," warns that a victory achieved over fellow citizens is dishonorable. The aim of this presentation has not been to harm Slovakia's international image by underlining the weaknesses of its domestic politics. Such an occurrence, however, was not uncommon in the mid-1990s. The second quotation points to the motivation behind this paper. It says, "Men did not love Rome because she was great. Rome became great because they loved her."[55] Applying Chesterton's observation in a proportionate way, this chapter suggests that ordinary Slovak citizens still have to learn how to become good patriots. A healthy and productive patriotism should not only be manifested during the celebration of the past and future victories of the Slovak national hockey and soccer teams, though such occasions may serve as its valid indicators. A true and effective patriotism should be directly linked to an improved work ethic, the elimination of mutual jealousies based on material disparities, respect for each other and

---

[54] Vladimír Mečiar resigned from the party on December 12, 2013. The party officially dissolved on January 11, 2014. Its successor is expected to become the new Left—Centrist "Strana demokratického Slovenska" (The Party of Democratic Slovakia). See the article, "HZDS po 22 rokoch definitívne skončilo" [After 22 years, the HZDS definitely ceased to exist], *Pravda*, January 11, 2014. For the SDKÚ see "Z SDKÚ odchádzajú poslanci, je medzi nimi aj Žitňanská" [Deputies, including Žitňanská, are abandoning the SDKÚ], www.webnoviny.sk , December 12, 2013. A survey held by the Polis Slovakia polling agency in February 2014 indicated that SaS would not be able to pass the 5 percent threshold having only 4.2 percent support, thus paralleling the fate of its predecessors, the SOP and ANO. "Prieskum: SaS by sa nedostala do parlamentu. Smer by vyhral" [Survey: the SaS would not make it into parliament: Smer would win], *Pravda*, February 4, 2014.

[55] Gilbert Keith Chesterton, *Orthodoxy* (London: The Bodley Head Ltd., 1908). Cited from An Electronic Classics Series Publication, The Pennsylvania State University, 60.

towards others. At the same time, the majority of Slovak politicians and financial gurus should stop pretending they are socially sensitive and philanthropic. They should be fair not only to their sponsors and themselves, but to all citizens. Pompous public events and glamour-fashioned charities cannot solve Slovakia's problems, but effective and well-balanced legislation without the uncontrollable influence of lobbyist groups can. Taking the mood which prevails in Internet discussions as the real *vox populi*, neither the Slovak Left, nor the Slovak Right, have as much time as they think they have.[56] Both of them have too often failed to meet public expectations. None of the Slovak governments or politicians has ever given an account of their work to the public by whom they were elected. The mixture of apathy and disappointment with the current situation among Slovak citizens, regardless of their profession or social status, is ubiquitous. Behind the conditional acceptance of the rule of political parties and their representatives lies social unrest and potentially an economic breakdown, disintegration of state institutions, and the moral collapse of society. Slovak politicians and their close friends in the world of business and finance, with a few exceptions, should become cognizant and more empathetic of the real life of their less prosperous fellow-citizens, and take appropriate measures before it is too late. The image of the tiny, yet daring Stuart Little, who was able to escape imminent danger thanks to his own skills and with the help of his family and friends, suits Slovakia better than that of the mouse that roared for a very short time, or that of a gorilla, which no one cares for, and potentially will be treated as such.

---

[56] See the debates on current political issues on the most visited Slovak Internet fora: www.sme.sk, www.pravda.sk, www.topky.sk, and also on www.necenzurovanenoviny.sk. Some of the contributors expressed their readiness to use physical force and even to attack high-ranking representatives of state institutions and political parties. "V Bratislave sa chystá masový protest: Do ulíc hlavného mesta sa chystajú tisícky demonštrantov" [A massive protest to occur in Bratislava: thousands ready to fill the streets of the Slovak capital], http://debata.pravda.sk/debata/blog-patricia-57-2013-11-01-v-bratislave-hrozi-masovy-protest-do-ulic-hlavneho-mesta-sa-chystaju-tisicky-demonstrantov/, November 1, 2013. Similar initiatives to resist the rule of politicians have appeared on facebook, Facebook, https://www.facebook.com/events/355959211202114/?fref=ts.

CHAPTER 8

Thinking Big about a Small Country: On Juraj Hocman's "People, Mice and Gorillas"

Kevin Deegan-Krause[1]

Juraj Hocman's meditation on Slovakia's political development over the last twenty years makes colorful use of provocative metaphors. His comparisons run the zoological gamut from *mus musculus* to *gorilla gorilla*, and the cinematic range from the "General Audience" rating of *Stuart Little* to the "Restricted" rating of *The Thing*. Woven through his text is a poignant account of the setbacks and successes of a particular country for which Hocman and I share great affection. But seen in the broader European perspective, the story of Slovakia is not a particularly unusual one. Without explicitly making the case, Hocman's account implicitly reinforces the argument that scholars should pay attention to Slovakia not because its experiences have been unique but because they are so typical. Slovakia is fascinating in its own right, but even more so in the way that it provides an important laboratory in which we can look at deeper regional trends and a few worldwide trends as well. As I have argued elsewhere:

> Slovakia is an excellent case to study because its political competition resembles the region in miniature: deep and stable divides between majority and minority ethnic and religious groups, and shallower but wider-reaching conflicts within the majority

---

[1] With particular thanks to Mark Stolarik for hosting the conference, to John Gould, Tim Haughton, and Zsolt Enyedi for their textual suggestions, and to Martin Bútora, Sharon Fisher, Carol Leff, and Sharon Wolchik (along with John Gould) for filling the conference with warm memories and good cheer.

ethnic group over communist legacies, economic policy, mode of democracy and the meaning and relevance of national identity, and emerging conflicts over corruption.[2]

Or, in fewer words, "Slovakia is everywhere."[3] Indeed, Slovakia has become more of an "everywhere" over time as the peculiarities of its political history have either receded or have popped up in other countries. For a more complete analysis, it is useful to reorganize Hocman's chronologically linear account into two pairs of themes, one pair largely retrospective and the other largely prospective.

First among the retrospective issues—the "old fears"—are those related to minorities and the politicization of Hungarian and Roma questions. Hocman alludes only briefly to Slovakia's history of tense domestic relationships between ethnic Slovaks and ethnic Hungarians and the international relationship between Slovakia and Hungary, but the undercurrents of this conflict are present in many of the issues he discusses, and similar questions have emerged in nearly all of the countries of the post-communist world. The presence of a linguistically distinct, geographically compact population with an active kin state just across the border shaped Slovakia's internal politics well into its second decade. The ethnic difference produced two political divides. The most obvious was a firm inter-ethnic division between parties of ethnic Hungarians and those of ethnic Slovaks. Between these two, there was almost no exchange of voters—Hungarians tended to vote only for Hungarian parties and few Slovaks crossed over to vote for Hungarian parties—but there was crossover at the parliamentary level, with Hungarian parties supporting the Slovak parties closest to them and participating in governing coalitions. The second division was *intra*-ethnic and involved a struggle between national exclusivists and national pluralists. The exclusivists identified their own ethnic group as the sole state-forming

---

[2] Kevin Deegan-Krause, "Slovakia," in *The Handbook of Political Change in Eastern Europe*, edited by Sten Berglund, Terje Knutsen, Joakim Ekman, and Kevin Deegan-Krause, 3rd ed. (Cheltenham, UK: Edward Elgar Publishing, 2013), 255.

[3] Kevin Deegan-Krause, *Elected Affinities: Democracy and Party Competition in Slovakia and the Czech Republic* (Stanford, CA: Stanford University Press, 2006), 225.

nation (*štátotvorný národ*) and took the position that non-Slovaks, while not necessarily unwelcome, had no intrinsic claims and had no collective claim to participate in decisions about the country's identity. The pluralists, by contrast, were willing to accord representatives of the Hungarian minority a formal place in the political conversation even when it was not politically expedient. Although few within this group accepted Hungarians as equal co-owners of the state (the position of many Hungarians) and most shied away even from formal group rights for minorities, they did accept arguments about linguistic diversity and were more open to pragmatic solutions and more proportional distribution of resources across groups.[4] This second division had characteristics opposite to the first: the demarcation line among voters was more blurred and there was considerable crossover among voters, but the divisions between the parties of the two sides were quite sharp and coalition patterns showed almost no crossover or even cooperation.

Neither of these patterns disappeared in Slovakia's second decade, though they did fray around the edges. Hungarians did not begin to vote in large numbers for Slovak parties, but some few ethnic Slovaks did cross over to vote for moderate Hungarians, and a new Hungarian party with a name meaning "Bridge" in both Slovak and Hungarian did actively court Slovak politicians and voters (though with limited success). Within the ethnic Slovak camp the division remained, though it lost its rigidity. Ten years of Hungarian parties in national and regional governments led to subtle shifts in the positions of the various sides and changes in the likelihood of their eventual cooperation. The position of many on the exclusivist side shifted from apocalyptic fears of irredentism ("Hungarians seek to destroy the Slovak state") to more prosaic fears of clientelism ("Hungarians seek to siphon off the resources of the Slovak state—and their close ethnic ties give them advantages vis-à-vis Slovaks seeking to do the same thing"). By the twentieth anniversary of Slovak statehood, the parties with hard-line Slovak exclusivist positions had disappeared from parliament and traditionally rousing Hungarian questions had lost their ability to mobilize voters, even though the political landscape in Hungary had taken a genuinely alarming turn

---

[4] Zsuzsa Csergő and Kevin Deegan-Krause. "Liberalism and Cultural Claims in Central and Eastern Europe: Toward a Pluralist Balance." *Nations and Nationalism* 17, no. 1 (January, 2011): 85–107.

toward its own national exclusivism. At the same time, the previous ready cooperation between Hungarians and Slovak pluralists was under stress and the Hungarian minority was itself part fractured between two parties. Slovakia entered its third decade without a major "Hungarian question" but with lots of minor Hungarian questions. The same fate, and many of the same dynamics affected politics in Estonia, Latvia, Romania, and Bulgaria, each of which experienced the emergence of increasingly routine and multi-sided interactions in kin-state ethnic politics.[5] Instead of demarking rigid sides, as time passed, ethnicity created a maze of coalition possibilities and alliances.

Slovakia's "Roma question" did not change nearly as much over time. Although Slovakia's Hungarian and Roma populations are of similar size, the Roma lack a kin state, a coherent political organization, territorial concentration or significant financial or social capital. Therefore Slovakia's Roma faced a more difficult challenge in bringing their own policy issues to the table, and the issues themselves were more difficult. Even though they do not include the complexities of a kin state (as with the Hungarians and neighboring Hungary), Roma issues are complicated further by overlaps between ethnic difference with racial attitudes and extreme differences in social class and education that intensify divisions and make it more difficult to solve (or even to identify) the core problems. With a growing Roma population and relatively few policy initiatives, the problems of concentrated Roma poverty and lack of opportunity seem likely to grow worse over time. Tested policy options exist for dealing with these questions, but these require significant political will and expenditure,[6] and, at the moment, Roma issues are not high on the list of government priorities.[7] Despite these problems, Slovakia has at least, until recently, avoided the worst forms of the region's militant anti-Roma sentiment: the Slovak National Party

---

[5] Ibid.
[6] European Commission. *What Works for Roma Inclusion in the EU: Policies and Model Approaches* (Luxembourg: Publications Office of the European Union, 2012).
[7] Marianne Kneuer, Darina Malová, and Frank Bönker, *2014 Slovakia Report*. Sustainable Governance Indicators (Gütersloh, Germany: Bertlesmann Stiftung, 2014), http://www.sgi-network.org/docs/2014/country/SGI2014_Slovakia.pdf.

(SNS) faced almost universal criticism for ads promising a hard line against Roma (especially since the pictures of Roma in the ads had been visually altered to include tattoos and gold jewelry not in the originals) and the radical People's Party Our Slovakia (ĽSNS) has averaged less than 2 percent of votes in the polls. The major recent exception—the election of ĽSNS leader Marián Kotleba as governor of the Banská Bystrica region—does not seem to have helped his party in the polls or provided a great deal of opportunity for restrictive policies, but it also may have a chilling effect on efforts to assist Roma and an encouraging one on the political organizing of those who feel similarly and seek to emulate Kotleba's path. Whether Kotleba himself becomes a prototype or a footnote, Roma issues will demand the attention of Slovakia's political leaders.

Second among the "old fears" is the authority issue, and the related politicization of democracy. Hocman's chapter devotes considerable attention to the governments led by Vladimír Mečiar between 1992 and 1998, and for good reason. In retrospect, the story seems clear: a leader with a strong desire proceeded to dismantle accountability mechanisms until he had near-complete control over state institutions, justifying his encroachments to voters as necessary to protect a small, new country under siege by ethnic minorities, neighboring countries and the West, with support from a disloyal opposition. Hocman identifies this regime type by the Slovak label "Mečiarism," but he astutely places it within the broader framework of "illiberal democracy" in which leaders take firm control of institutions and public discourse but allow voters to deliver their verdicts at the ballot box (O'Donnell's "delegative democracy" is another, similar model).[8] This conceptual framework acknowledges the similarities to the cases of Franjo Tuđman in Croatia, Slobodan Milošević in Serbia, Leonid Kuchma and Viktor Yanukovych in Ukraine, Alexander Lukashenko in Belarus, Putin in Russia, and other examples throughout the world. Within this elite classification, Mečiar stands out as relatively ineffectual with his failure to seize a constitutional majority or control the presidency and, most

---

[8] Guillermo A. O'Donnell, "Delegative Democracy." *Journal of Democracy* 5, no. 1 (1994): 55–69.

significantly, in his willingness to risk (or inability to avoid) an election the outcomes of which he could not be certain.

Mečiar's loss in the 1998 election helped to reveal previously hidden elements of the pattern of Mečiarism and the delicate balance of delegative and illiberal democracies. The ability of these systems to endure depends on the share of a population that is willing to "vote for thugs," and also depends on the population's ability to see the accountability violations (a question of media), and its willingness to accept the violations as desirable (a question of democratic values) or as a tradeoff necessary for reaching other goals (a question of competing issue dimensions). Outcomes like the Mečiar governments are more likely if voters do not see the violations, do not see them as a problem, or do not see them as too a high a price to pay for achieving other goals.[9]

While they were happening, Mečiar's successes seemed overwhelming—one of the most common metaphors was the "steamroller"—but in retrospect their limits are just as striking. Mečiar controlled the state media, but he could not gain control of the major daily newspapers (despite efforts at influencing them by pressure on the printing and distribution networks), and he could not easily hide or downplay the kidnappings and police misconduct that were part of his political repertoire. He attracted a large share of the population, which preferred non-democratic governments; but those who actually preferred less accountability constituted a relatively small percentage of Slovakia's electorate. Finally, he attracted voters who were willing to exchange some degree of political monopoly for more concrete goals, such as a better standard of living or protection from Hungarian autonomy. But, in the end, his regime did not produce the necessary rewards. As voters drifted away due to discontent with manipulated referenda and fears of international isolation, the rhetoric from Mečiar's party about foreign plots and domestic traitors became increasingly frantic. However, uniting of nationalism and nascent authoritarianism simply did not yield enough voters. Significant credit must also go to Mečiar's diverse opponents, who realized the seriousness of the threat to democracy and managed to put aside their tendency to squabble among themselves, and instead cooperated in

---

[9] Kevin Deegan-Krause, "Voting for Thugs," *Democracy at Large* 2, no. 3 (2006): 24–7.

pursuit of electoral victory. Hocman is right to note that Mečiar's victorious opponents themselves engaged in a significant number of questionable practices, but the corruption and internal dysfunction that appeared during the subsequent governments of Mikuláš Dzurinda should not obscure the marked improvement they represented on questions of accountability and rule of law.

The return of Mečiar's HZDS to government in 2006 was, as Hocman suggests, rather anticlimactic. The party continued to be a source of scandal (three Ministers of Agriculture dismissed under suspicion of corruption in just over three years) and encroachment (particularly in the politicization of the Ministry of Justice), but HZDS and the Slovak National Party (equally tarnished by corruption allegations during this period) played only minor roles in a government dominated by Robert Fico's Smer (Direction) Party. In Fico many saw a "second Mečiar" and others a "new Bolshevism," but Fico's government proved neither as left-wing nor as authoritarian as its opponents anticipated. It employed leftist and national themes but, despite its clear parliamentary majority, did not follow Mečiar's example and rewrite the rules of democracy in its own favor. And it demonstrated its lack of total control by losing its majority four years later in the 2010 parliamentary election.

When Fico returned to the premiership after the early elections of 2012, he did so with the first one-party majority in Slovakia's history, and the same fears resurfaced. But Fico's government began on a relatively moderate note with a number of independent ministers in key posts and perceptible moderation of tone with regard to Hungary and Hungarians. Whether because of Fico's own more moderate inclinations or his awareness of Mečiar's failure, Smer has not taken systematic advantage of its position to make major changes to the rules of the political game. Any tendencies in that direction, furthermore, may have been pushed back by Fico's failure to win Slovakia's presidency, an outcome that simultaneously weakened his own position and installed a political opponent in that office.

If Fico refused to follow Mečiar's path, the same cannot be said of Viktor Orbán in neighboring Hungary. After his election in 2010, Orbán replicated Mečiarism's encroachments on other institutions, but did so more effectively. His government's media message has been more skillfully targeted, and because Hungary's majoritarian electoral system has given him a constitutional majority, he has been able to avoid many of the brute force aspects of Mečiar's rule that caused some Slovaks to withdraw their support. Like Mečiar, Orbán has gained significant support from those who are most willing to dispense with checks and balances in favor of forceful leadership, but he has also been persuasive in using national, religious and economic appeals to attract supporters who might otherwise be troubled by his institutional encroachments. Whether this is a sustainable position is unclear. Should Orbán be unable to provide sustained economic gains (or unable to blame lack of progress on outside forces), he may find it more difficult to win future elections. No matter what, Orbán will certainly be helped by the highly majoritarian outcomes of the country's electoral system, as well as by the presence of an even more extreme party on his rightward flank (allowing him to sustain the support of more moderate nationalists who can claim that "we are not *that* extreme"), and by the collaboration difficulties experienced by Hungary's left, which managed a joint coalition in 2014, but did not achieve close cooperation or find a common, compelling standard-bearer. If Slovakia's experience is any guide, Orbán's eventual fall from power will be a complicated, but not necessarily unproductive, affair. On the one hand, Slovakia's post-Mečiar coalition found it difficult to find a unifying motive beyond Mečiar's defeat; on the other hand, the disagreement was made easier by the 1990–1998 flow of authoritarians, nationalists, and opportunists to the Mečiar camp, leaving its successor relatively free of that burden. Hungary might experience a similar trajectory, but the deeper institutional changes made by Orbán (including changes to the electoral system and district boundaries, nine-year terms for key oversight positions and the constitutionalization of key provisions) will make the transition away from Orbán's style of rule much more difficult.[10]

First among the questions most relevant to Slovakia *today*—the "new fears"—is the issue of volatility and the rise and fall (and rise and fall) of new parties. In his overview of Slovakia's political parties in the post-Mečiar era, Hocman offers a particularly chilling metaphor, "Slovak political parties can be compared to the self-reproducing and the self-transforming creature from John Carpenter's classic horror film,

---

[10] Kim Lane Scheppele, "The Rule of Law and the Frankenstate: Why Governance Checklists Do Not Work," *Governance* 26, no. 4 (2013): 559–62.

The Thing. The analogy is apt because Carpenter's film (like Howard Hawks' 1951 original) is based on John W. Campbell's 1938 story *Who Goes There?* This is a question not only for Slovakia, but for the wider world in which it is increasingly common to find unknown parties that leap rapidly to success (and collapse equally rapidly). Hocman's intentionally exaggerated comparison to alien organisms that consume living creatures and then impersonate them captures some of the fluidity and mutability of these new political formations in Slovakia. And the analogy is specifically applicable in a few cases, most notably that of Robert Fico, who split from the Party of the Democratic Left (SDĽ), pulled away much of its voter base, and then engineered a merger with SDĽ (in which Smer was the dominant partner). In other cases, the metaphors for new are more prosaic and entirely terrestrial. There is no single correct biological metaphor. But many of Slovakia's parties are not unlike an amoeba, to the extent that divisions in the nucleus—over some key programmatic issue or just because of personal dislike—can quickly lead to the formation of a new, independent entity. Slovakia's political history is littered with parties that emerged when mid-level leaders left a party that was in the tight grip of its founder in order to form their own party. Other parties in Slovakia resemble mushrooms or dandelions, which pop up quickly around the germ of a good idea or a compelling leader, but, lacking roots or strong internal structure, disappear just as quickly. The dandelion metaphor is appropriate since Slovakia's system has produced a range of party types: some, like dandelions are "annuals," which do not survive the harsh weather and reproduce by sending out new seeds; other resemble perennials which can survive indefinitely no matter what the temperature. The two coexist side-by-side in Slovakia's party system and together produce a system that changes frequently, but only in part. Of course, the biological examples are only metaphors—unlike plants, parties can both learn and overreach. In the world of parties, perennials can shield themselves against the winter, and annuals may make bad bets that strip them of protection against the cold.[11]

Hocman acknowledges this difference and the apparently limited longevity of newer parties, "Until Slovak politicians learn how

---

[11] Kevin Deegan-Krause and Tim Haughton, "In with the New (Again): 'Annuals,' 'Perennials' and the Patterns of Party Politics in Central and Eastern Europe," *MPSA Conference, Chicago*, 2012, 12–5.

to build and manage political parties which can survive for at least two elections, while following a common goal, and solve their leadership problems within party structures, there is a little hope that the political system in Slovakia will improve." The point is solid, but it is not only Slovakia's politicians who have this difficulty. Across the region, even in countries whose political systems were once thought to be stable as rocks, we see difficulty with new parties. In just the last four years, the Czech Republic has had two successive elections in which new parties received more than 25 percent of the vote, and in Slovenia the share of new party votes in each of the past two elections has approached or exceeded 40 percent.[12] Patterns like those of Slovakia have emerged in countries as widely spaced as Bulgaria and Latvia, and there is strong reason for thinking that such patterns have become the norm. Older parties tend to survive but newer ones, born under the inauspicious signs of institutional fragmentation and mistrust in politicians, often fail to build the kinds of organizations, party-voter relationships, party positioning, and decentralized leadership structures that help parties survive. The problem is not unique to Slovakia or even to the Central and Eastern European region, but true of parties across the world. Naím's *The End of Power* offers insight into global trends that are changing institution-building toward more flexible and ad hoc structures, and if Slovakia and Eastern Europe exhibit these features more than, say, Western Europe or North America, it is because the older parties are more robust and less likely to create room for new parties, and not because the new parties that emerge there are any more robust.[13]

In this regard, Slovakia is slightly exceptional, but in the direction of stability rather than chaos. When dissident social scientists in Slovakia coined the phrase "islands of positive deviation,"[14] they were

---

[12] Lukáš Linek, "Czech Republic," *European Journal of Political Research Political Data Yearbook*, 52, no. 1 (2013): 50–5.

[13] Moisés Naím, *The End of Power: From Boardrooms to Battlefields and Churches to States, Why Being in Charge Isn't What It Used to Be* (New York: Basic Books, 2014).

[14] Martin Bútora, "Vyvzdorúvanie alebo každodennosť pozitívnych deviantov," [Obstinacy or normalcy in positive deviants,] in *Odklínanie* [Lifting the curse], ed. Martin Bútora (Bratislava: Kalligram, 2004), 189–93.

probably not thinking of people like Robert Fico (at the time a rising young star in the state apparatus). But Fico's party Smer has become one of the most successfully institutionalized new parties in the entire region. Early in its existence, Smer had every hallmark of a new party that makes it into parliament, perhaps even into government, and then fails, from the young charismatic leader, to the ambiguous "unparty" name (at a time when this was still fairly unusual), to rather murky initial financing, to the focus on corruption. Smer's initial three priorities were "Order, Justice, and Stability," and its billboards proclaimed it a party of "a new generation" with the "courage to take on theft and selloffs." Similar claims were made by the Movement of Simeon II in Bulgaria, Public Affairs in the Czech Republic, Palikot's Movement in Poland, the Party of National Resurrection in Lithuania, Zatlers' Reform Party in Latvia, Res Publica in Estonia, and many other parties in these and other countries.[15] Yet, Smer was one of the only ones to survive and the only one to grow consistently from one election to the next. How? Research on the more successful new parties in the region gives Smer high marks on at least two of the three strategies that appear to keep new parties alive: building local-level organizational structures, taking a clear position on a key dimension of political competition, and finding ways to change leaders when those in charge become more of a liability than an asset. The not-quite-success of Fico's party in 2002—nearly 14 percent of the vote, but third place, and no invitation to join the government—actually gave it time to address its limitations. The party acquired the organizational assets of the Party of the Democratic Left and began to build a structure of its own. The party also changed its programmatic position and emphasis, adding "Social Democracy" to its name and positioning itself clearly to the left of other major parties (even if it has not developed wholly according to Western models of social democracy).[16] Only in the third area—leadership—has Smer failed to develop a robust structure for handling potential problems.

---

[15] Tim Haughton and Kevin Deegan-Krause, "Hurricane Season: Systems of Instability in Central and Eastern Europe Party Politics," *East European Politics and Societies*, forthcoming.

[16] Tim Haughton, "Exit, Choice and Legacy: Explaining the Patterns of Party Politics in Post-Communist Slovakia" *East European Politics* 30, no. 2 (2014): 210–29.

But as long as Fico remains the most popular politician in Slovakia, the party can do without an ejection seat for the leader. If Fico's second place finish in the 2014 presidential election reflects a long-term decline, then the party may face the same fate in the long run that other similar parties have suffered in the much shorter run. However, its success thus far is worthy of much closer investigation by those who seek more stable party systems.

The second set of "new fears" involves inequality and the rise (and further rise) of powerful money. Hocman's chapter emphasizes the problem corruption and its influence over the political development of the country. Here, too, Slovakia's story is the story of the region as a whole. Like most of the countries in the region, Slovakia has experienced a close interconnection between politics and economics—not surprising since the two were inseparable for forty years—but potentially troubling, since the two realms play by different rules. During the Mečiar period, the connection of the two was assumed, and political leaders were commonly thought to be those calling the shots. By the 2000s, the two were still intertwined, but the assumption became that it is economic actors, both domestic and international, who have the upper hand. The Gorilla scandal that Hocman discusses was not particularly outrageous by the standards of the region and not particularly unusual by Slovak standards. What was perhaps most notable was not that business and politics were intertwined (this had been true in Slovakia since the first days of privatization),[17] or even that the interconnection had not declined much during the 2000s (this was tacitly accepted even by some supporters of the Dzurinda government), but rather that the balance between political and economic interests had clearly shifted in favor of the latter.

A clear sign of the dominance of these assumptions was the seriousness with which even well-connected Slovaks considered rumors that Robert Fico sought the presidency in order to escape potential blackmail by party sponsors. The fear that a prime minister with unrivalled power could be threatened by a nod from financial interests suggests a wholehearted belief in the dominance of the economic sphere

---

[17] John A. Gould, *The Politics of Privatization: Wealth and Power in Postcommunist Europe* (Boulder, CO: Lynne Rienner Publishers, 2011).

over the political one. One of the most striking experiences of daily life throughout the post-communist regions of the European Union is the expectation that politics does not ultimately determine policy.

If economics does shape policy, it has not yet produced a significant net shift in resources toward the upper echelons. Recent studies suggest that neither the openly neoliberal macro-economic policies nor covert political influence have been accompanied by an increase in poverty or inequality.[18] Slovakia has maintained a lower inequality coefficient than most other countries, and levels have stayed relatively low. This does not mean, however, that there is no cause for concern. The same analyses suggest that the recession of 2008–2009 reversed the tendency of decreasing income inequality from the years preceding the recession,[19] and raises the prospect that "[m]ore recent reforms, including the adoption of [a] flat tax rate, funded second pillar of the pension systems, and decreasing social security benefits in Slovakia may lead to increased inequality in the two countries"[20]

It is difficult to find a more heartfelt response than Hocman's own call for probity in government and his faith that it is possible, however difficult, to create a democratic process that listens primarily to the voice of the people and works for the public good:

> Pompous public events and glamour-fashioned charities cannot solve Slovakia's problems, but an effective and well-balanced legislation without the uncontrollable influence of lobbyist groups can….Slovak politicians and their close friends from the world of business and finance…should become cognizant and empathetic of the real life of their less prosperous fellow-citizens and take appropriate measures before it is too late.

---

[18] Martin Kahanec, Martin Guzi, Monika Martišková, Michal Paleník, Filip Pertold, and Zuzana Siebertová. *GINI Country Report: Growing Inequalities and Their Impacts in the Czech Republic and Slovakia*. GINI Country Reports. AIAS, Amsterdam Institute for Advanced Labour Studies, 2012, http://ideas.repec.org/p/aia/ginicr/czech_slovak.html.
[19] Ibid., 134.
[20] Ibid.

Hocman's insistence on greater justice and more concern for citizens is his final and most important charge to the reader, and applies no less to Western Europe or North America. However, in the universality of his call lies his most paradoxical insight into Slovakia's development. The country's biggest dangers now are the ones it shares most closely with others. Had Slovakia started out the transition race in front of others, this "ordinariness" might be seen as a failure. But Slovakia did not start out in front. It faced a potentially disastrous combination of factors—strong ethnic divisions, weak institutions, and an identity crisis that gave opportunities to ambitious leaders—and yet it has not failed.

Amid all of the fears, old and new, there is thus room for great hope. Although there is much work to be done in Slovakia on questions of social justice and political propriety, it is also true that Slovakia has exceeded the expectations of nearly everyone who made predictions about it in the early 1990s (the only predictions it did not exceed were, ironically, those of the parties that nearly kept the predictions from coming true). If Slovakia exceeded expectations simply by becoming an exceptionally normal country, one troubled by political overreach and economic deficiencies but no more so than any of its neighbors, it is a testimony to the low level of expectations of the country's structural strengths, overreach by those who would have made it less than it is, and solid, hard work by those who had the best interests of the country in mind and were able to steer it away at least from the worst dangers. Other dangers loom, particularly regarding questions of social justice and political propriety, but on the country's twentieth birthday, it is perhaps acceptable to risk complacency and accentuate the positive: independent Slovakia is a success.

And should we need a cinematic animal story to encapsulate Slovakia's first two decades, perhaps best is the final line of the George Miller film *Babe*,[21] in which a farmer quietly commends a performance that no one else expected to go so well, "That'll do, pig. That'll do."

---

[21] A film I first saw in Bratislava at the now (sadly) defunct Kino Dukla/YMCA. This cinema, coincidentally, is also where I first saw *Independence Day*, a movie which, given its title and subject matter, is surprisingly absent from Hocman's narrative.

CHAPTER 9

Letting Czechoslovakia Go: Czech Political Developments Since 1993

Adéla Gjuričová

The story of the twenty-year independence of the Czech Republic has a different starting point from the Slovak one. While the latter's narration opens with the founding of a new state, for the Czechs, it begins with first having to let go of the old one. The breakup of Czechoslovakia was traumatic for the Czechs, both for the political elite and for the general population. Czechoslovakia had been a Czech-initiated project. On the one hand, the Czechs accepted, believed in, and identified with it. On the other hand, the Slovaks quite often pointed to imbalances in the distribution of power between the common state institutions and Slovakia. The Czechs played down such complaints and concentrated on dominating and organizing the central, later federal, power. Only after 1989 did Czech politicians invest a lot of energy into finding a form of the federation acceptable to both nations.

By 1992, very little success had been achieved. The Czechs could see themselves slowly departing, if not running away, from both their Slovak counterparts and the federal idea. To hide this fact, they formulated strongly worded interpretations for the general elections of 1992. As Václav Benda, leader of the Christian Democratic Party, a small dissident-based coalition partner of the winning Civic Democratic Party, tried to conclude:

> In the Czech Republic, the democratic forces won a victory over the non-democratic crypto-communist left...But in the Slovak Republic, 85 per cent of the mandates were won by nationalistically or even separatistically-oriented, predominantly left-

wing, and strongly anti-reformist parties. The election results confronted us basically with the decision as to whether we want another relapse of socialism in a common state or a democratic development in an independent Czech Republic.[1]

Benda's conservative followers tried to disseminate a sense of Slovak political immatureness: Slovaks' affinity for nationalist and left-wing thinking was supposed to put the democratic transition at risk. The Czechs, as opposed to that, were described as hardworking, talented, politically realistic and having better prospects by themselves.

But this could hardly have made Czech society feel like winners. As historian Tomáš Zahradníček pointed out,[2] the images recorded in the center of Prague on the night of January 1, 1993 showed only a few dozen people on the street. Rather than welcoming the new Czech Republic on Wenceslas Square, where major political demonstrations took place in the twentieth century, these people came to celebrate the end of the drawn-out misunderstandings with Slovakia. This was in stark contrast with the spectacular celebrations, with fireworks, in the squares of Slovak cities that same night.

The Czech elite kept reassuring people that nothing substantial would change in the new state, and it is striking how many politicians have tried to preserve this interpretation to the present. For example, the outline of Czech parliamentary traditions published by the Czech Parliament in 2011[3] assumes an implicit continuity between the Bohemian Land Diet, the interwar National Assembly, the postwar National and Federal Assemblies and the Parliament of the Czech Republic created in 1993. The Slovaks do not play any part in the

---

[1] Václav Benda in *Lidové noviny*, September 1, 1992, as quoted in Ladislav Holý, *The Little Czech and the Great Czech Nation: National Identity and the Post-Communist Transformation of Society* (Cambridge: Cambridge University Press, 2004), 113.

[2] Tomáš, Zahradníček, "XXIII. Czech Republic (1993–2004)," in *A History of the Czech Lands*, ed. Jaroslav Pánek, Oldřich Tůma, et al. (Prague: Karolinum, 2014), giving the example of *Noc, kdy se rozpadl stát* [The night when the state dissolved] (1993), footage by documentary filmmaker Vladislav Kvasnička.

[3] Petr Kolář & Petr Valenta, *The Parliament of the Czech Republic—The Chamber of Deputies* (Prague: Ivan Král, 2011), 7–26.

story, nor does the text mention the dramatic discontinuity in political elites between 1992 and 1993. In fact, a large number of the Czech elite that worked in federal institutions were replaced by their—until then less influential—colleagues in these years. Until that time, Czech party leaders most often ran for and worked in federal institutions which, in the eyes of the Czechs, ranked higher than the sub-federal republic level (the Slovak approach was exactly the opposite). In 1992, for the first time, even Václav Klaus, Finance Minister in two federal cabinets and winner of the general elections in the Czech lands, decided to become the Czech, rather than Czechoslovak, prime minister. Soon afterwards, the federal parliament was urged to pass a law formally dissolving the Czechoslovak Federation as well as its parliament, whereas members of the sub-federal Czech National Council were going to become the Chamber of Deputies of the new Czech Republic. Along with an electoral disaster experienced by some pro-federal parties, such as the Civic Movement led by Petr Pithart and Jiří Dienstbier, this definitely represented an elite change worth mentioning and analyzing.

Omitting such a substantial shift was part of another rhetorical twist: the Czech Republic announced itself the successor of Czechoslovakia. It kept the Czechoslovak flag and declared October 28, the day Czechoslovakia was established in 1918, a national holiday. The Constitution of the Czech Republic, drafted and adopted in haste by the Czech National Council in December 1992, introduced only two new features into the political system: the Senate as a second chamber of parliament, referring to interwar Czechoslovakia, and regional self-governing districts. In reality, both had to wait several years to come to life. The constitution also reduced the role of the president, who lost the right to propose legislation to the parliament, which was an obvious attempt to isolate President Václav Havel and prevent him from intervening in domestic politics, as he had in previous years.

The following text does not provide a systematic overview of political developments during the period, with lists of election results, government coalitions, or political parties and their ideologies. Instead, it offers several interpretative suggestions, which may reveal the long-term characteristics of Czech politics, as well as specific settings at certain points in time, such as 1993, 2000, and 2013, from a more productive perspective. These interpretative suggestions pertain to the topics of institutional and staffing stability in Czech politics, economic transformation as a political issue, bargaining on the powers of civil society, foreign-policy priorities, and the phenomenon of "politics of the past." In the final part of this chapter, the text will look into new trends in party politics and electoral strategies observable from the results of the most recent parliamentary elections.

Regardless of the subsequent changes in government coalitions or the prevailing topics of public debate, Czech politics after 1993 has been characterized by both institutional and staffing stability. For the entire first decade of the Czech Republic and well into the second, many of the country's political playing fields were formed by three men: Václav Havel, Václav Klaus, and Miloš Zeman. Theirs are three fascinating political biographies. They all share a common start of social and political activity in the 1960s, especially during the Prague Spring of 1968, while following very different trajectories during the 1970s and 1980s, and meeting up again in the first days of the Velvet Revolution. The three men, albeit in different ways and occupying different political positions, even survived the earthquake that hit a part of the Czech political elite working in federal institutions in 1992–1993. Havel's domestic influence in the Czech Republic never reached the dimensions it held during the first months after November 1989 and, although he remained a global symbol and trademark even after his death, his real political style combining artistic and bohemian traits, his anti-political rhetoric, and obvious political goals are still difficult to describe and analyze.[4] Václav Klaus originally came to the revolutionary Civic Forum as an economic expert from the academic community. So did Miloš Zeman. Within months, Klaus was elected chairman of the Civic Forum and transformed its larger membership into the center-right Civic Democratic Party (remaining its chairman until 2002). Zeman was sent by the Civic Forum into the federal parliament, where he chaired the economic committees and earned fame as an excellent speaker. After the breakup of Czechoslovakia, which at the moment meant the end of

---

[4] See the latest analysis of Havel's thought until 1989 in Jiří Suk, *Politika jako absurdní drama: Václav Havel v letech 1975–1989* [Politics as an absurd drama: Václav Havel in the years 1975–1989] (Prague: Paseka, 2013).

Zeman's parliamentary mandate, he became chairman of the Czech Social Democratic Party and slowly transformed it into the strongest center-left party and the most important actor opposing the dominant right-wing coalition discourse represented by Prime Minister Klaus. In 1998, Klaus and Zeman traded positions as prime minister and Speaker of the House of Deputies, then both ran for president in 2003 as the most serious contenders for the office after it had been vacated by Havel. Klaus won and remained in Prague Castle until 2013, when Zeman took his place.[5]

Klaus and Zeman also personified two standpoints regarding the country's economic transformation, which remained a part of the domestic political struggle throughout two decades. The reform agenda in the first years of the transformation was set by one generation of middle-aged economists from Prague's academic community. It involved a specific market discourse, which said that essentially any private owner, no matter where you find him or her, is better than state ownership of previously nationalized property. The new capitalists supposedly used a market logic that helped them make choices which would be beneficial for everybody: the owners, their potential employees, and the state. This combination of near mystical belief and technocratic thinking was highly influential.[6] The discourse dominated center-right politics, stretching from legitimizing the so-called voucher privatization to explaining the structural unemployment resulting from closures in manufacturing as workers' "chance to set up their own business."[7] The belief that Czechs were predestined to succeed, and had the courage to undertake national experiments were other elements

---

[5] Karel von Schwarzenberg, who was Zeman's opponent in the second round of presidential elections, was another long-term phenomenon in Czech politics: Havel's long-time collaborator, senator, Minister of Foreign Affairs from 2007–2013, and leader of the TOP09 party.

[6] Seán Hanley provides a deep analysis of the right-wing dominance and its ideological and societal roots in Seán Hanley, *The New Right in the New Europe: Czech Transformation and Right-Wing Politics, 1989–2006* (Oxon–New York: Routledge, 2008), 40–65 and 91–127.

[7] For striking examples of this discourse prevailing even among obvious losers in the transformation, namely working-class women, see Elaine Weiner, *Market Dreams: Gender, Class, and Capitalism in the Czech Republic* (Ann Arbor: University of Michigan Press, 2007), 95–117.

in the economic reform concept,[8] as well as yet another reaction to the trauma of the Czechoslovak breakup.

Reducing the general political debate, as well as the whole right-left cleavage to economic issues, which Tony Judt referred to as a no-longer-reflected consequence of the neoconservative turn of the 1980s,[9] grew extreme in the Czech Republic. Two of the most powerful political parties in the country were led by economists, mobilizing and radicalizing their followers. Václav Klaus, as finance minister, and later as prime minister, was responsible for the decisive steps taken in the first years of the reforms and retained the task of defending these policies. Miloš Zeman, on the other hand, played the role of a critical expert deputy and eventually the leader of the opposition. However, facing the recent criticism of the post-communist transformation coming from a new generation of the radical left, the two men seem to have reconciled. Other things seemed to matter more than their different rhetoric: after all, they shared the experience of the 1968 reforms, an active part in the country's transformation in the 1990s, as well as their parties' coexistence within the so-called Opposition Agreement starting in 1998.[10] At that point, after a period of long right-wing dominance, the Social Democrats for the first time formed a minority government headed by Miloš Zeman, while Václav Klaus, who became Speaker of the Chamber of Deputies, allowed the minority government to operate. This odd relationship between the two major parties brought about agreements on distribution of political and business positions, strengthening their interconnections, and the interference of business in politics. It was also in the two parties' common interest to limit the influence of other players in the political field, in particular President Havel,

---

[8] Martin Myant argues that this was caused by the provincialism of the local economic elite, as opposed to the situation in Warsaw or Budapest, whose academic institutions had not lost contact with major developments in economic thought. Martin Myant, *The Rise and Fall of Czech Capitalism: Economic Development in the Czech Republic Since 1989* (Cheltenham, UK–Northampton, MA: Edward Elgar Press, 2003), 12–14.

[9] Tony Judt, *Ill Fares the Land* (London–New York: Penguin, 2010), 144–53.

[10] For an analysis of the effects of the Czech Opposition Agreement on the party system, see Hloušek, Vít and Kopeček, Lubomír: *Origin, Ideology and Transformation of Political Parties: East-Central and Western Europe* (Farnham, UK–Burlington, VT: Ashgate Publishing, 2010), 123–9.

the other smaller parties, but also the civil society sector, which drew public attention to cases of corruption occurring at various levels of public administration, as well as to the hidden convergence of business and political spheres.

The position of the civil society sector in a political system is a matter of complex negotiations within each country's political tradition and current setting. In the Czech case, a number of specific characteristics can be discovered. Václav Havel was a conscious and consistent promoter of a relatively radical concept according to which civil society should become a regular political partner of winners of elections. Havel himself was involved in supporting several projects based on this idea, for example, the so-called Czech Television Crisis of 2000–2001, in which public protests joined in the battle for control of the public television broadcasting company, or the "Thank You, Now Leave!" campaign launched on the tenth anniversary of the Velvet Revolution to challenge the "arrogant political power" and calling for "a return to decency, morality, political propriety and human values."[11] To no one's surprise, Václav Klaus was a fierce opponent of such attempts, labeling them "non-political politics, lacking the voters' mandate."

However, neither Havel nor Klaus were consistent in working in the long-lasting Central European tradition of anti-political thinking. So-called "anti-politics" is a multifaceted phenomenon stretching from the Masaryk-style program of socialization of suppressed nationalities within the Habsburg Monarchy at the end of the nineteenth century, via dissident concepts of civic politics as "an objective annihilation of the political sphere as well as a subjective reflection of its emptiness"[12] during the communist era, up to the current concepts of the critical potential of the nongovernmental sector. In Czech politics of the last two decades, the contradictions inherently contained in anti-political thinking had paradoxical consequences. The conflict between the fact that many former dissidents rejected traditional political forms and, at the same time, desperately needed to make use of political power actually underlined the need for political professionalization and building a

---

[11] The manifesto is available at http://www.ce-review.org/99/24/thankyou24.html.
[12] Miloš Havelka, "'Nepolitická politika': kontexty a tradice," [Non-political politics: context and tradition] *Sociologický časopis* 34, no. 4 (1998): 455–66.

party system. In other words, President Havel who sincerely believed and insisted that he was *not* a politician, in spite being the highest ranking state official, in fact contributed to the popularity of Václav Klaus, who proceeded to create a powerful party system and denied civil society any role in public decision-making.

As was argued earlier, in most institutional areas, the Czech Republic tried to appear as the successor to Czechoslovakia. Its foreign policy, however, was an exception. As of 1993, the Czech government distanced itself from the international activism practiced by President Havel and the first Czechoslovak governments after 1989, and began to use the concept of national interest. Instead of regional cooperation within the so-called Visegrád Group (The Czech Republic, Slovakia, Poland, Hungary), Czech policy focused on bilateral relations, predominantly with Germany, and accession into NATO and the European Union. Regional cooperation was supposed to include only a free trade zone. This represented a serious challenge, even to the "special relationship" with Slovakia, fortunately without long-term consequences. What was specific for the "Europeanization" of Czech politics was the coexistence of strong public support for EU entry and EU policies, on the one hand, and the extensive presence of intellectual euroscepticism, on the other. The Czech Republic seems to be the only country in Europe in which eurosceptic stances have been endorsed by both the ruling Civic Democratic Party and President Klaus,[13] not by marginal parties and politicians or parties in opposition.

However, around the year 2000, the EU accession process and relations between Central European countries went through a period of political radicalization and historically legitimized policies. Austria threatened to block EU enlargement because it demanded more consideration for the post-war expulsion of German-speaking communities from Czechoslovakia. Hungary tried to slow down Slovak acces-

---

[13] Adéla Gjuričová, "Poněkud tradiční rozchod s minulostí: Občanská demokratická strana," [A small traditional divorce with the past: the Citizen's Democratic Party] in Adéla Gjuričová *et al.*, *Rozděleni minulostí: Vytváření politických identit v České republice po roce 1989* [Divorce with the past: the evolution of political identities in the Czech Republic after 1989] (Prague: Knihovna Václava Havla, 2011), 107–34. Available online at http://www.usd.cas.cz/wp-content/uploads/2010/01/rozdeleni_minulosti.pdf.

sion because of the alleged discriminatory treatment of the Hungarian minority in Slovakia, while at the same time granting members of the community the legal status of "Hungarians living in neighboring countries." It seemed surprising that the histories of different Central European countries of the twentieth century reached into the European Union in the third millennium.

Although this trend did not remain fierce for long, historical (il)legitimacies, especially those stemming from the communist era, continue to be a key factor in Czech politics. Up to the present, previous membership in the Communist Party is regularly brought up as a way to disqualify candidates for government positions. Accusations regarding public actors' collaboration with the communist Secret Service routinely appear in election campaigns. Andrej Babiš, the entrepreneur of Slovak origin, whose party ANO 2011 finished second in the general elections of 2013, was the latest example: as soon as the country's second richest man entered the political scene, accusations that he had previously collaborated with the Secret Service seemed to matter more to many people than the fact that the politician's company purchased one of the largest publishing houses which runs two influential daily newspapers and a music TV channel. Furthermore, for a part of Czech society, the simplified identification of "left-wing" and "communist," which originated in the early anti-communist statements of the 1980s and 1990s, is still perceived as rational. Consequently, the left as a whole is still considered by many as too suspicious "to deal with the communist past," resulting, for example, in public protests against the Social Democratic Party's involvement in the management of the government-funded (and right-wing dominated) Institute for the Study of Totalitarian Regimes, which administers the files of the communist Secret Service.[14]

Perhaps the most striking example of a contradiction contained in the Czech "politics of the past" is the position of the Communist Party. In spite of the strong presence of anti-communist rhetoric in public debate, the Czech Republic remains the only country in East-Central Europe whose Communist Party did not change its name and

---

[14] For a summary of events in 2013, see for example "Members of Academic Council Resign in Protest of Herman Sacking," *Prague Daily Monitor*, April 12, 2013, http://praguemonitor.com/2013/04/12/members-academic-council-resign-protest-herman-sacking.

consciously built its identity around "not transforming" into a social democratic party.[15] Neither did the party "die out" as was predicted by many in the early 1990s, although its membership and electoral support comes from age groups older than those of other parties.[16] Nonetheless, the Communist Party's position and strength has had a crucial impact on the party system as a whole. On the one hand, the party seems to have no coalition potential and is, to a large extent, isolated within the political system. But, on the other, it regularly wins third place in parliamentary elections, gaining as much as 18.5 percent of the vote in 2002 and 14.9 percent in 2013. Isolating such a large share of parliamentary seats obviously causes tremendous problems for building stable coalitions that can take turns at holding power.

In September 2013, Jacques Rupnik, a French political scientist of Czech origin, told the Czech Press Agency that "the Czech Republic is an exhausted democracy in which the political and party systems have started to disintegrate."[17] The same author previously described the phenomenon of a "tired" democracy, in which people are disgusted by the emptiness of politics and the interconnections between politics and business, parties, and the state.[18] Although this chapter may not share Rupnik's radicalism, part of his argument must be conceded. Many elections over the last fifteen years saw a newly established party making it into parliament on an anti-corruption platform or criticism of "the emptiness of politics." Until 2010, these new parties—as, for example, the Freedom Union or TOP09—were mostly derivatives of the existing

---

[15] Michal Kopeček, "The Stigma of the Past and the Bond of Belonging: Czech Communists in the First Post-1989 Decade," *Czech Journal of Contemporary History* I (2013): 101–30.

[16] Lukáš Linek argues that his quantitative model suggests the Communist Party will "die out" in the future. However, it is impossible to predict the electoral behavior of the youngest, radically left-wing generation that is currently entering Czech universities. See Lukáš Linek, "Kdy vymřou voliči KSČM? K věkové struktuře elektorátu KSČM" [When will the voters of the KSČM die out? The age structure of supporters of the KSČM], *Czech Journal of Political Science/Politologický časopis*, 15, no. 4 (2008): 31836.

[17] "French Analyst Rupnik: Czech Democracy is Exhausted," *Prague Daily Monitor*, September 18, 2013, http://praguemonitor.com/2013/09/18/french-analyst-rupnik-czech-democracy-exhausted.

[18] Jacques Rupnik, "Twenty Years of Postcommunism: In Search of A New Model," *Journal of Democracy* 21, no. 1 (2010): 105–12.

parties. It could be argued that voters were actually shuffling among the established actors, around whom the main topics of campaigns and post-election coalitions were also organized. The 2010 elections, however, produced a significant change in electoral results as well as in the government. Support for two main parties—the Civic Democrats and the Social Democrats—fell to historically low levels, while newly emerged parties not only entered parliament, but went straight into government.[19] Especially the Public Affairs Party, until then an active player in Prague municipal politics, exploited to an unprecedented extent the perceived competence and lack of corruption among their leaders.

Its success did not last. As early as in April 2011, Public Affairs leader Vít Bárta, by that time Minister of Transport, was accused of bribery by his own party colleagues. Internal conflicts not only brought party representatives before the court, but also resulted in a breakup of the political newcomer. A new model was set though: Public Affairs had sought electoral support in a symbiotic relationship with Vít Bárta's security company, in terms of organization, personnel, and financing. The electoral campaign focused on building networks of registered sympathizers coordinated through the Internet and new social media. Its reliance on political marketing made the party closer to the "business firm" model than ever before. And it took only a short time before the following newcomer party, Andrej Babiš's ANO 2011 (YES 2011), sought to apply the same model to public administration as a whole. "Yes, the state must be governed as a business," was one of the slogans that made the party surpass all expectations in the next general elections and finish a close second with 18.6 percent of the vote.[20]

---

[19] Tim Haughton, Tereza Novotná and Kevin Deegan-Krause, "The 2010 Czech and Slovak Parliamentary Elections: Red Cards to the 'Winners'," *West European Politics* 34, no. 2 (2011): 394–402. Compare this to Seán Hanley, "Dynamics of New Party Formation in the Czech Republic 1996–2010: Looking for the Origins of a 'Political Earthquake'," *East European Politics* 28, no. 2 (2012): 119–43.

[20] The party leader went further in his specific anti-political approach for *The Economist*. He said, "I am governing a company in favour of the company and shareholders. Politicians are governing the state in their favour." "Meeting Andrej Babiš," *The Economist*, November 22, 2013, http://www.economist.com/blogs/easternapproaches/2013/11/czech-politics#sthash.ZPR05xxx.dpuf.

The general election of 2013 therefore represented an even stronger reshaping of the political party landscape than the previous election. The Civic Democrats started to disintegrate well before the elections and their 7.7 percent meant getting close to the five-percent electoral threshold. The Social Democratic Party, an expected election winner in a country run by a center-right government introducing harsh austerity measures, was substantially weakened by President Zeman's skilful exploitation of the Czech constitutional system and his own party campaign. The Social Democrats came nowhere near first place, placing not even 2 percent in competition with Andrej Babiš's ANO 2011. The two until-then pivotal actors, the Civic Democrats and the Social Democrats, altogether only attracted slightly more than a quarter of all votes. Using a comparison with other East-Central European states, one can argue that this is only the delayed arrival of a new strong trend, which other countries had experienced much earlier. Voters tend to shift to new parties because of their disillusionment with the existing ones.

So, would it be appropriate to conclude that we are witnessing the dawning of a new era, both in the history of Czech party politics and the political system? Some of the medium-term characteristics that were depicted in this article as holding true for the first two decades of the independent Czech Republic's existence may really be coming to an end: the Czechs do not identify with Czechoslovakia strongly any more, and the party spectrum may be opening up to the segment of ad-hoc, anti-corruption actors known in other countries. This chapter argues, however, that the long-term trends—such as the Czech inclination to anti-political thinking about public administration, the tradition of weak presidential powers bestowed by the constitution—and yet the real-life presidents often enjoy extremely strong positions in the political process, and using references to historical issues and to "past guilt" in politics—will remain integral parts of future Czech politics. As such, they will focus on the issues of the day.

CHAPTER 10

Czech Political Developments Since 1993: Some Comments

Carol Skalnik Leff

Given the excellent framing of post-independence politics in Adéla Gjuričová's discussion, I want to focus on some of the paradoxes and distinctiveness of the Czech political scene suggested by her analysis. I hope to contextualize her examination of Czech politics in comparative perspective, both with regards to the new Slovak state and Central Europe.

I want to begin with perhaps the biggest paradox of all, one that builds additional complexity into Gjuričová's accurate depiction of public responses to the end of Czechoslovakia. On the one hand, both Czechs and Slovaks built successful independent states after 1993; both are among the most democratic of the post-communist region, and both qualified for inclusion in NATO and the European Union. Their citizens are generally quite favorable to the post-communist changes (although not as enthusiastic as their Polish neighbors!).[1] And yet, when the Czech and Slovak opinion research centers (CVVM and IVO) conducted a joint 2012 survey in the two states of five historical watersheds in twentieth-century history, by far the greatest approval was accorded not to independence, or the end of communism in 1989, but rather to the founding of the common state in 1918.

---

[1] Jan Červenka, "Hodnocení zmeny systému v roce 1989 v stredoevropském srovnání—zima 2014" [Important changes in the 1989 revolution—the winter of 2014], *Centrum pro výzkum veřejného mínění*, March 18, 2014, http://cvvm.soc.cas.cz/media/com_form2content/documents/c1/a7198/f3/pd140318.pdf.

Appraisal of Historical events in the Czech Republic and Slovakia[2]
(Percentage regarding favorably)

	Czech Republic	Slovakia
The Establishment of Czechoslovakia 1918	83	71
The Velvet Revolution 1989	63	64
Entry into the European Union 2004	38	59
Establishment of Independent Republics 1993	46	58
The Dissolution of Czechoslovakia	38	45

How should we understand this response? Here are some possible points to consider. The first is that 1918 was meaningful to nearly all Czechs and Slovaks as the release from the Habsburg Empire and, as such, is understandably a rather consensual point of reference. The second is that for Czechs and Slovaks the experience of joint statehood was never marked by the massive bloodshed, deportations, and the levels of repression that deeply tarnished the Yugoslav and Soviet projects. When asked which nationality they feel closest to, both Czechs and Slovaks consistently continue to name the other. Pragmatically, the Czech and Slovak prime ministers even verbally agreed in 2013 to explore reviving "Made in Czechoslovakia" as an export label to remind a geographically challenged world who they are.[3] Finally, most Czechs and Slovaks regarded and continue to regard the state dissolution as a product of a bargaining deadlock among elites and not as a grassroots mobilization.[4] There was a certain all too familiar element of *o nás, bez nás* about a decision that was made without a popular referendum or

---

[2] Source: translated from "Rozdělení Československa: 20 let od vzniku samostatné ČR a SR" [The dissolution of Czechoslovakia: 20 years since the creation of the Czech Republic and the Slovak Republic] Centrum pro výzkum veřejného mínění and Inštitút pre verejné otázky [Center for the Study of Public Opinion and the Institute for Public Opinion] December 4, 2012, http://cvvm.soc.cas.cz/media/com_form2content/documents/c1/a6920/f3/po121204d.pdf.

[3] Radio Praha, July 10, 2014, http://www.radio.cz/en/section/curraffrs/slovak-president-rejects-return-of-made-in-czechoslovakia-label.

[4] The fullest investigation of this point can be found in Abby Innes, *Czechoslovakia—The Short Goodbye* (New Haven: Yale University Press, 2001).

even an election fought over the issue. It is also true, however, that there was a complete lack of consensus on the institutional form of a joint state and no deep investment in the "Czechoslovak" idea as forming any kind of resonant common *ethnic* identity. The "Czechoslovak" project failed in the First Republic, and was subsequently rejected by the communist state, meaning that though many regretted the end of Czechoslovakia, it was not a cause worth fighting for.[5]

A second peculiarity distinctive to Czech politics is the anomalous position of the Communist Party (KSČM) in the political system. Throughout Eastern and Central Europe, Communist Parties rather quickly rebranded themselves as mainstream socialists, exchanged the red star for the red rose of transnational social democracy, and embraced the European integration project. As Gjuričová shows, this was not true in the Czech case, and it is a puzzle worth probing. Instead, there have been two viable parties of the left, both of them more currently functional than some of the reconstructed communist successor parties in neighboring states.[6] The mainstream left-of-center consolidated in the mid-1990s around the Social Democrats (ČSSD), a party that like neighboring left-of-center successor parties, embraced the Europeanization program of democracy, capitalism and EU accession, while the communist electorate continued to return to parliament a sizable KSČM delegation that contends "rightists and social democrats have frittered away what the Communists had built," in part through exposing the country to damaging unequal competition within the European Union.[7]

Why did the Communist Party adhere to its name and its critique of democratic capitalism when all around it other Communist Parties had abandoned this stance? Some historical legacy factors may be at play here. Interwar Czechoslovakia was the most industrially developed of the states to emerge from the dissolution of empires after World War

---

[5] See Carol Skalnik Leff, *National Conflict in Czechoslovakia: The Making and Remaking of a State, 1918–1987* (Princeton: Princeton University Press, 1988).
[6] At present, Poland's major parties are both right of center and can be considered Solidarity successor parties. The Polish Democratic Left Alliance only notched around 8 percent of the vote, finishing fifth in the 2011 elections. Slovakia's successor party disappeared in favor of Robert Fico's *Smer*, and in Hungary Viktor Orbán's *Fidesz* nearly tripled the socialist vote in 2014.
[7] KSČM website, http://www.kscm.cz/political-opinions.

I, with a strong working class in the Czech lands. As a democracy, however flawed in some respects, it was also the only East European state to permit the Communist Party to operate legally and compete (successfully) in elections. The party even placed first in a relatively free post-war multi-party election in 1946, based on its dominant performance in the Czech lands and disillusion with the West after Munich. Opinion polling in the immediate aftermath of the Velvet Revolution showed that, although the Czech public rejected adamantly the course that communism ultimately took, a plurality still approved the egalitarian ideals of the so-called Victorious February of 1948. In short, there was a greater historical rootedness of the party than in most other countries. Probably more directly consequential, however, was the heavily purged and "normalized" party apparatus after the 1968 Warsaw Pact Invasion. In Poland and Hungary, for example, reform elements existed at all levels of the party, and negotiations to exit communism on new terms were possible. Czech communist apparatchiki, heavily purged of "sixty-eighters,"[8] were more rigid and ossified, and more resistant to programmatic change.

The resultant Czech Communist Party is both durably successful and durably reviled, and that has strongly influenced the options and choices in Czech politics over time. In the early years, commentators tended to assume that the KSČM would "vegetate" in isolation "until such time as its voters died off."[9] Although the communist electorate is indeed distinctly older than the norm, the party's electoral share is surprisingly stable after almost a quarter century and won its second highest share of the vote in the 2013 parliamentary elections (in fact, the party's electoral strength is largely the same today as it was in the interwar First Republic!).[10]

---

[8] This is the term applied to those who embraced the Prague Spring reforms of 1968, and subsequently quit or were expelled from the party in the bitter aftermath of the Warsaw Pact Invasion.

[9] Jiří Šindelář, "Izolace KSČM," *Český deník*, June 29, 1993.

[10] Leff, *National Conflict*, 52. See also Tomáš Kostelecký, "Economic, Social and Historical Determinants of Voting Patterns: In the 1990 and 1992 Parliamentary Elections in the Czech Republic," *Czech Sociological Review* 2 (1994): 219. His analysis shows that the best predictor of the *geographical distribution* of the communist vote in the 1990 parliamentary elections was the election result of 1946.

One result is that there is a special vigor to the "regime divide" that has affected Eastern European politics more generally. Everywhere in the region it is still noted when a current politician is found to have coyly omitted Communist Party membership from his or her CV (a frequent practice), and it is still a topic of dismayed comment on the number of communist pedigrees diffused through the party system. In the 2004 Romanian presidential election debates between Traian Băsescu and Adrian Năstase, the populist Băsescu won points with his comment "Romania's problem is that fifteen years after the fall of communism, it could not find people other than two former communists like myself and yourself to run for the highest office."[11] In the Czech case, the regime divide is even more palpable.[12]

After the 2012 regional elections that saw a massive defeat for the ruling coalition, the KSČM did formally participate in government for the first time, forming coalitions with the ČSSD in ten regions, spawning angry localized protests.[13] Proposals to ban the party surface periodically,[14] and the Topolánek government did ban the Communist Youth Organization from 2006 until 2010, when the courts overturned the decision.[15] Interestingly, although a 2009 poll showed a substantial 70 percent of the public inclined to favor banning extremist parties,

---

[11] Monica Ciobanu and Michael Shafir, "The 2004 Romanian Elections: A Test for Democratic Consolidation?" RFE/RL Report 7:3 (April 7, 2005), http://www.rferl.org/content/article/1342447.html.

[12] The public does not think the past divisions have become irrelevant. David Roman, "Twenty Years of Transitional Justice in the Czech Lands," *Europe-Asia Studies* 64 (2012): 761–4.

[13] See "V krajích je hotovo: Koalice ČSSD a KSČM vládne v 9 krajích" [In the provinces it is clear: the coalition of the ČSSD and the KSČM rule in nine provinces], November 23, 2012. http://www.ceskatelevize.cz/ct24/domaci/204725-v-krajich-je-hotovo-koalice-cssd-a-kscm-vladne-v-9-krajich/

[14] See, for example, "Vnitro nenašlo pádné argumenty k zákazu KSČM, na stranu chce dohlížet" [The Ministry of the Interior found no legal arguments to dissolve the KSCM, but it will continue to monitor it], iDNES.cz, November 18, 2011, http://zpravy.idnes.cz/vnitro-nenaslo-padne-argumenty-k-zakazu-kscm-na-stranu-chce-dohlizet-1jg-/domaci.aspx?c=A111118_183732_domaci_brm.

[15] Radio Prague, January 28, 2010, http://www.radio.cz/en/section/curraffrs/court-cancels-ministrys-ban-of-communist-youth-union.

only 10 percent considered the Communist Party to fall into that category, down from 25 percent ten years earlier.[16]

Gjuričová has noted a second effect that warrants further scrutiny, a communist delegation so politically toxic that it has been excluded from coalition negotiations for government formation. Indeed, the Social Democrats were forced to issue public commitments NOT to cooperate with the communists in national government, starting with the Bohumín's declaration of 1996. It is not simply that the ČSSD thereby lost a portion of the left-of-center electorate and a numerically useful coalition partner—this handicap was especially clear when the party came first in the 2010 elections but could not form a majority. The whole governing system was affected. Coalitional bargaining to form a government majority started with around 13 percent of the seats, held by Communist MPs, off the table. This made it hard to construct and retain a government and is one significant reason why Czech cabinets have been so unstable and shaky since 1996. Consider this: twelve Czech governments were formed between 1996 and 2014. Three were caretaker governments; three lacked parliamentary majorities from the start; and only *one* served a full electoral term from start to finish: Miloš Zeman's ČSSD *minority* government of 1998–2002. And the Zeman government, which had to govern with a very controversial "opposition accord" deal with the rival ODS, was a great gift to the Communist Party, allowing it to return with nearly 20 percent of parliamentary seats in 2002. The Communists, who have survived so long perhaps precisely because they have been in opposition, can never be blamed for what goes wrong, and can reap protest votes against the mainstream parties (what was known in the interwar period as *gravamenpolitik*, grievance politics).

A final component of the resonance of communism after 1989 is the highly visible effort to cleanse politics of legacy effects from the communist period. Post-communist Czechoslovakia was the first to enact a so-called lustration (*lustrace*) law that debarred former high-ranking communist officials and security police collaborators from

---

[16] CVVM "Postoj verejnosti k extremistickým stranám" [Public attitudes towards extremist parties], Tisková Zpráva, October 16, 2009, http://cvvm. soc.cas.cz/media/com_form2content/documents/c1/a3683/f3/100959s_pv91016.pdf.

some key public offices.[17] While the law fell into disuse in Slovakia after independence, this was not the case in the Czech Republic: the initial law was slated to phase out after a transition period, but was renewed several times and eventually made permanent in 2000. Although a careful interim study of the law by Kieran Williams raises doubt about the scope of its impact on individual careers,[18] the symbolic impact was immediate and ongoing, engendering major controversies for certain high-profile politicians such as former Foreign Minister Jan Kavan and current Finance Minister Andrej Babiš, whose designation as a security police collaborator was voided by the courts only after he had taken office amid much media scrutiny.[19]

The paradox of an enduring lustration law, coupled with a strong and largely unrepentant Communist Party, is only apparent, of course, since the party's continued presence is a major reason why the law remains on the books.[20] As late as 2014, an attempt to abolish the lustration process foundered on a lack of unity within the government coalition and a broad multi-partisan vote against it that crossed government-opposition lines.

One of the stabilities of Czech politics is historical continuity: Masaryk's Czechoslovakia was an institutional reference point for Czech constitutional revisions after independence; the Czech Republic replicated the First Republic in its key democratic features: a bicameral parliament with proportional representation for elections to the lower house and directly elected senators, and a president elected by

---

[17] Some of the Southeast European countries have yet to undergo serious lustration.
[18] Kieran Williams, "A Scorecard for Czech Lustration," *Central European Review* 19, no. 1 (November 1, 1999), http://www.ce-review.org/99/19/williams19.html.
[19] Because Babiš was originally from Slovakia, the lustration review occurred in the Slovak courts, to the objections of the Slovak press, and the Slovak National Memory Institute, which may appeal the decision. See "Babiša zachránil klamár z ŠtB, podľa súdu nebol agentom," [Babiš saved by liar from State Security, he was not an agent, rules the court], *SME*, June 27, 2014, http://www.sme.sk/c/7254745/babisa-zachranil-klamar-z-stb-podla-sudu-nebol-agentom.html.
[20] See especially Roman David, *Lustration and Transitional Justice: Personnel Systems in the Czech Republic, Hungary and Poland,* Pennsylvania Studies in Human Rights (Philadelphia: University of Pennsylvania Press, 2011).

the legislature. Continuity does not mean satisfaction, however. In all the post-communist countries, public opinion tends to favor popularly elected presidents, and the Czechs were no exception; the complications of legislative bargaining over the presidential office only enhanced that preference, ultimately culminating in the shift to direct elections in 2013. The senate has also been something of a stepchild, instituted only after a four-year delay and chronically subject to low voter turnout, as well as questioning about whether the country is really large and complex enough to require a bicameral legislature. In the following section, I would like to examine some additional continuities and discontinuities in post-independence Czech politics.

Gjuričová notes the high profile of economists in the post-communist leadership. This is not a uniquely Czech phenomenon—the market transition tended to put a premium on economics training for decision-makers (supplanting the engineering degree so typical of the communist period), and almost 20 percent of all East European cabinet ministers between 1990 and 2010 had degrees in economics.[21] What is perhaps more notable compared to other countries in the region is the political durability of the three men she highlights who held the office of president: Václav Havel, Václav Klaus, and Miloš Zeman. Lech Wałęsa and lesser lights of the transition period might come and go, but Klaus and Havel remained politically relevant throughout, Havel arguably even after his death. As president of both Czechoslovakia and the Czech Republic, Havel was wont to be compared with Masaryk as a philosopher-president or even president liberator (Masaryk's title in the first republic).[22] Klaus, of course, as both president and prime minister, spent more than half of the Czech Republic's independence years in the top leadership. Zeman, who remained personally popular with a core constituency, never succeeded in establishing a partisan political

---

[21] Carol Skalnik Leff, *Reconstructing Elites after Authoritarian Rule: The Case of post-Communist Eastern Europe* (Rowman & Littlefield, forthcoming).

[22] Havel's obituaries were rife with references to Masaryk and frequently designated Havel himself as a second "prezident osvoboditel" [president liberator], as, for example "Čeští politici o Havlovi: Navázal na Masaryka, byl známější než Česká republika" [Czech politicians on Havel: he was another Masaryk, and was better known than the Czech Republic], *Ihned.cz* December 18, 2011, http://zpravy.ihned.cz/c1-54233720-cesti-politici-o-havlovi-navazal-na-masaryka-byl-znamejsi-nez-ceska-republika.

platform after he left the ČSSD, but the recent constitutional shift to direct presidential elections allowed him to win the presidency, interestingly with the endorsement of Klaus, despite the divergence in their politics and attitudes toward the European Union.[23]

A second domain of stability, until quite recently, was partisan politics. Czech politics was rather late to a phenomenon that began to surface in Eastern and Central Europe around the turn of the millennium: the emergence (and not uncommonly the subsequent disappearance of) successful new political parties, generally as protest vehicles. The most dramatic early case was the Bulgarian election of 2001, in which the former monarch's recently formed National Movement Simeon II swept to a massive electoral victory two months after its formation. Around that time, it became increasingly common to see the arrival in parliament, or even in government, parties with catchy names, but often-ambiguous platforms centered on antiestablishment and anticorruption themes. Such parties appeared in Slovakia as early as 1998 (ANO, SOP). Indeed, after the most recent elections in 2012, only about a quarter of the seats in the Slovak National Council are held by parties that even existed in 1998.

Scott Mainwaring et al. have shown that both post-communist voters and parties themselves are more volatile in their election-to-election behavior than those in the established advanced industrial democracies.[24] Margit Tavits demonstrates that much of that volatility stems not from a fickle public, but rather from a fickle political elite and their "party tourism" and new party formation.[25] The new party

---

[23] Klaus's antagonism toward the rival candidate, former expatriate and Havel adviser—Foreign Minister Karel von Schwarzenberg—was revealed in attacks on the validity of Schwarzenberg's Czech identity.

[24] Scott Mainwaring, Annabella España, and Carlos Gervasoni, "Extra System Electoral Volatility and the Vote Share of Young Parties" (paper prepared for the Annual Meeting of the Canadian Political Science Association, Toronto, May 28, 2009). See also Eleanor Neff Powell and Joshua Tucker, "Revisiting Electoral Volatility in Post-Communist Countries: New Data, New Results and New Approaches," *British Journal of Political Science* 44 (2013): 1–25.

[25] Margit Tavits, "On the Linkage between Electoral Volatility and Party System Instability in Central and Eastern Europe," *European Journal of Political Research* 47 (2008): 537–55.

phenomenon seems to have aborted any convergence with the West European norm in that regard. The Czechs, however, had the least volatile electoral swings in the region until 2010, when the new party phenomenon finally and firmly took hold. The dominance of established parties was highly stable over the first two decades, with the four main parties capturing over 80 percent of the parliamentary seats; that number plunged to only 57 percent after the 2010 elections[26] and [remained the same?] in 2013. Interestingly, the reason for the continued poor performance of the established parties in 2013 was not that the newcomers of 2010 had gained a solid foothold. Instead, three entirely new parties entered the National Assembly, along with the "seasoned" TOP09.

How can we understand this volatility? In the Czech case and elsewhere, it is clear that many voters, having given both established alternatives a chance, declared a pox on both houses and turned to new, often populist, alternatives that promised a cleanup of corruption and greater responsiveness to the public. Grigore Pop-Eleches describes the new alternatives as "unorthodox parties," defined in opposition to "mainstream" parties with electoral appeals, which are:

> based on a recognizable and moderate ideological platform rather than on the personality of its leader and/or extremist rhetoric. In other words, a mainstream party represents an ideological orientation that can be mapped with reasonable accuracy onto the mainstream ideological spectrum of established Western democracies.[27]

Unorthodox parties, by contrast, may avoid any clear ideology, and are often driven by charismatic leaders who promise a reprieve from politics as usual. This strand of political thinking was foreshadowed in Czech politics as early as the "Thank You, Now Leave!" *("Děkujeme, odejděte!")*

---

[26] See Kevin Deegan-Krause and Tim Haughton, "A Fragile Stability: The Institutional Roots of Low Party System Volatility in the Czech Republic, 1990–2009," *Czech Journal of Political Science/ Politilogický časopis* 7 (2010): 227–41.

[27] Grigore Pop-Eleches. "Throwing Out the Bums: Protest Voting and Anti-Establishment Parties after Communism," *World Politics* 62 (2010): 224.

campaign of 1999 that, not coincidentally, occurred amid the highly unpopular "opposition" accord that combined both major political alternatives in a governance deal. The Czech president, Václav Havel, added his voice to the protest. "Our November [1989] political garniture already seems tired and used up and we have lived through enough of it," he said, calling for "fresh and young blood" to enter the political stage.[28]

The blood has not always been fresh and young. But the message, and even the leadership, in the Czech case are consistent with that of many unorthodox parties elsewhere. One pathway has been the use of media platforms; in Slovakia, we saw the Markíza media magnate Pavol Rusko organize a temporarily successful ANO (Party of the New Citizen—ano means "yes" in Czech and Slovak) and popular television host Volen Siderov launched Ataka in Bulgaria. In the Czech case, the year 2010 saw the success of investigative journalist Radek John and his Public Affairs Party (VV in Czech), and Tomio Okamura launched his political career and ultimately his political party Dawn of Direct Democracy, after gaining visibility as a judge on the widely watched reality TV show called Den D. ANO 2011's[29] Andrej Babiš made his wealth elsewhere, but bolstered his political position by buying two major mainstream newspapers and making efforts to micromanage their campaign coverage, leading to dismal comparisons with Italy's Silvio Berlusconi, as in "Babisconi."

Wealthy entrepreneurs are a second and often overlapping source of fresh political talent; the claim, one often made by the likes of American Ross Perot and even mainstream party candidates, is that businessmen know how to make things work and will focus on efficacy over partisan squabbles. Andrej Babiš and Tomio Okamura represent this curious form of "outsider"—the billionaire populists—who, in the Czech case, are doubly distinctive—Babiš was born in Bratislava and Okamura has a Czech mother and a Japanese father.

As for the populist message of the new parties, it has been "Thank You, Now Leave!" without the thanks. Public Affairs' election posters called for "an end to the political dinosaurs" and ANO's billboards

---

[28] *The Guardian*, December 3, 1999, http://www.theguardian.com/world/1999/dec/04/kateconnolly.
[29] In the Czech case, ANO stands for *Akce nespokojených občanů* [Action of Dissatisfied Citizens].

promised "We Are Not like the Politicians." The most classic populist message currently comes from Dawn of Direct Democracy; as the party name suggests, the programmatic solution to the current corrupt and unresponsive elites includes referendums and direct election to political office at all levels. Such a message is familiar throughout the region, but the irony here, as elsewhere, is the identity of the purveyors of the message, who are often quite prominent and well heeled. Indeed, to the extent that populism is a challenge to the neoliberal economics of the transition and to corruption, it requires some legerdemain—and an American campaign publicity firm—to cast leaders with strong business ties as the rescuers.

A nationalist component, which had arguably not been central to a successful Czech parliamentary party since the republicans of the 1990s, is also part of the populist message in some of the new parties in Eastern and Central Europe. In the Czech case, it is only Dawn of Direct Democracy that brought to light a similar electoral message, with slogans such as "Support Families, not the Incapable," and "Work for Our People, not Immigrants." Most provocative and troubling was the party's appropriation for the 2014 European elections of the notorious Swiss People's Party poster showing white sheep kicking the black sheep off the national flag. Dawn of Direct Democracy's "black sheep" include both immigrants and Roma.

So it is clear that Czech politics has now joined its neighbors in generating new political vehicles. What may be less clear is why Czechs were late to this political game. Kevin Deegan-Krause and Tim Haughton note the programmatic and organizational strengths of the long-dominant parties.[30] The function of the Communist Party as an existing repository for protest votes may also contribute a partial explanation for the delay. At the same time, it is not surprising that many would-be protest voters could not find a home in a party so clearly and defiantly tied to the communist past, and that the ODS electoral hemorrhage, particularly in 2013, would find a more logical home in the new rightist vehicles.[31]

---

[30] Deegan-Krause and Haughton, "A Fragile Stability."
[31] For a discussion of voter behavior in the 2013 election, see Tim Haughton, Teresa Novotna and Kevin Deegan-Krause, "The Czech Paradox: Did the Winner Lose and the Losers Win?" *Washington Post Monkey Cage*,

Czech religious engagement is a final distinctive feature of politics and society worth examining. Although a segment of the population does attend church, and elective religious education and ethics classes funded by the state are part of the public education system, over 70 percent of the adult population in a 2008 survey reported that they do not believe in God.[32] In recent surveys, Czechs have the lowest level of religious affiliation in Europe.[33] In addition to the factors that have driven secularization in post-communist Europe—modernization generally, and the anti-religious propaganda of the communist state—the religious nexus with politics and society in the Czech case is historically distinctive. The Czech nation-building saga that developed in the nineteenth century incorporated the Hussite movement as a national assertion in opposition to the Habsburg Counter-Reformation.[34] More than a million citizens left the Catholic Church after the founding of independent Czechoslovakia in 1918, only half of whom affiliated with new national churches. Hence, even before the communist era, there was a strong thread of anti-imperial anticlericalism in Czech identity politics.[35] Census figures, however, show that religious affiliation did not crash

---

October 30, 2013, http://www.washingtonpost.com/blogs/monkey-cage/wp/2013/10/30/the-czech-paradox-did-the-winner-lose-and-the-losers-win/.

[32] Dana Hamplová, "Česká religiozita—církevní příslušnost a víra ve světle Sčítání lidu a dat ISSP 2008" [Czech religiosity—church affiliation and faith in light of census data and the ISSP 2008], CVVM *Naše společnost* (2010), http://cvvm.soc.cas.cz/2010-1/ceska-religiozita-cirkevni-prislusnost-a-vira-ve-svetle-scitani-lidu-a-dat-issp-2008. A number of earlier studies drawing on other surveys also validate the low levels of Czech religious belief and practice, although differing somewhat in the conclusions they draw. See, for example, Zdeněk R. Nešpor, "Religious Processes in Contemporary Czech Society," *Sociologický Časopis / Czech Sociological Review* 40 (2004): 277–95.

[33] Dana Hamplová and Zdeněk R. Nešpor, "Invisible Religion in a 'Nonbelieving' Country: The Case of the Czech Republic," *Social Compass* 56 (2009): 583.

[34] Nešpor, "Religious Processes in Contemporary Czech Society," 282–5.

[35] In their reformulation of the secularization thesis however, Pippa Norris and Ronald Inglehart argue that post-communist religious trajectories can be explained without reference to the history of church-state relations. They focus rather on the level of societal security, as measured by the UN's Human Development Index and the presence or absence of ethnic conflict. See Norris and Inglehart, *Sacred and Secular: Religion and Politics Worldwide*, 2nd ed. (Cambridge: Cambridge University Press, 2011), 11–32.

until the communist period, when the number of non-affiliated soared from around 6 percent to almost 40 percent.[36] Thus, whereas in neighboring Poland the church was at the core of the Solidarity resistance to communism, and religious pilgrimages were central to late communist-era dissent in Slovakia,[37] Czech dissidence was significantly secular.[38]

The Czech Republic was the last post-communist country in Eastern Europe not to have approved a formal legal framework to regulate church-state relations. The heavily contested act governing the restitution of church property passed only in 2013—almost twenty-five years after the Velvet Revolution—and even that resolution became an election campaign issue for the Social Democratic government that took office in 2014.[39] All of which seems consonant with the limited religious tradition.

And yet the Czech Republic has an effective Christian Democratic Party! The entrenchment of Christian Democracy in the Slovak party system probably does not surprise anyone. But Czech Christian Democracy (KDU–ČSL) seems more counterintuitive. Still, in every post-communist election, except that which occurred in 2010, the KDU–ČSL has won a modestly sized, but politically salient, parliamentary delegation, which has participated in nine out of the country's eleven partisan cab-

---

[36] Český statistický úřad [Czech statistical office], "Náboženské vyznání obyvatelstva podle výsledků sčítání v letech 1921, 1930, 1950, 1991 (v %)" [Religious beliefs of our citizens according to the censuses of 1921, 1930, 1950, and 1991, in percentages], http://notes3.czso.cz/sldb/sldb.nsf/i/F86D A18D33F397A4C1256E6800471FB3/$File/tabulka6.pdf.

[37] See, for example, David Doellinger, *Turning Prayers into Protests: Religious-Based Activism and its Challenge to State Power in Socialist Slovakia and East Germany* (Budapest: Central European University Press, 2013).

[38] However, it is important to note Charter 77's three spokespeople consciously included a former Marxist, an independent cultural figure, and a Christian representative. See Jonathan Luxmoore and Jolanta Babiuch, "In Search of Faith, Part 2: Charter 77 and the Return to Spiritual Values in the Czech Republic," *Religion, State & Society* 23 (1995): 291–304. Charter 77 spokesman Jan Sokol, a Catholic moral philosopher, later lost the presidential election to Václav Klaus.

[39] See for example, "Hra na církevní restituce: Game Over" [The attempt at restitution of church property: Game over], *Týden.cz*, June 5, 2014, http://www.tyden.cz/rubriky/nazory/hra-na-cirkevni-restituce-game-over_309147.html.

inet governments.⁴⁰ This is striking because Christian Democracy has not been particularly successful in most post-communist countries. Anna Grzymala-Busse convincingly demonstrates that the success of Christian Democracy in establishing itself in post-communist electoral politics is not correlated with a country's religiosity.⁴¹ She makes a complex and nuanced argument for the importance of pre-communist partisan legacies as the basis on which a Christian Democratic Party (if viable, effective and nationally conscious in the interwar period) could gain a foothold in post-communist politics and then survive if it can prove itself. One might broaden this argument and note that the strength of Social Democracy and the Communist Party in the interwar period—indeed the similarity of the left-right dimension of interwar Czechoslovak party system to that of Western Europe—may be a clue to the continued resemblance of Czech party families to Western ones thereafter.

The electorate of Czech Christian Democracy is grounded in religious believers (both Catholic and Protestant), especially in Moravia, but also includes those who, regardless of religious belief, embrace traditional family values on issues like gay marriage, abortion, drug use, and education. Nešpor notes, "The party advocates for these stances. While in many other political matters the Christian party behaves just as any political player with no core 'ideological' policy, in matters related to Christian and especially Catholic faith it visualises itself as the defender of 'real-Christian' and traditional norms and values, which are presented as the only medicine for saving society."⁴²

Otherwise the Christian Democratic Party reconfigured itself from the communist-era satellite party to a mainstream moderate advocate of the social market (much like Christian Democracy in northern Europe) in opposition to Klaus's neoliberal conservatism. As Seán Hanley notes:

---

⁴⁰ This ubiquity has been possible because Christian Democrats, with their middle of the road social market economic preferences have been eligible coalition partners for both the right- and left-of-center parties. The party's pronounced anti-communism is not an impediment because ČSSD is not a communist successor party.
⁴¹ Anna Grzymala-Busse, "Why are there are (Almost) No Post-Communist Christian Democratic Parties?" *Party Politics*, 19 (2013): 319–42.
⁴² Nešpor, "Religious Processes in Contemporary Czech Society," 288.

In doing so the Christian Democrats directly challenged the legitimacy of Václav Klaus's conservatism, which they presented as an 'Anglo-Saxon' import inappropriate to the Czech lands and their Central European traditions, de-emphasizing the explicit notion of a distinct Catholic Czech identity in conflict with national identity in favour of a stress on 'self-evident' geo-political and cultural affinities and the more widely acceptable Czech corporatist and 'social' traditions.[43]

Thus, Chytilek and Eibl's study of party policy positions in Czech politics places the KDU–ČSL more or less in the dead center of a two-dimensional policy space defined by the left-right economic dimension and the social liberal dimension, and hence as a compatible coalition partner for both left and right of center parties.[44] Recovering from a loss of both voters and leadership to TOP09, the Christian Democrats are once again in the governing coalition of 2014.

In the 1990s, Czech politics looked perhaps the most West European of the region, with a clear left-right political spectrum anchored by two major parties. More than twenty years after independence, the political arena is far murkier, and public satisfaction with the way democracy is working has dropped. What, then, is the identity of this new state?

During the debate that led to the dissolution of Czechoslovakia, it was not uncommon to see media discussions of the "Czech question," asking whether the Czechs even had a strong national identity, and, if so, whether Czech or Czechoslovak. A sociological study conducted in 1991 found that some 37 percent of Czechs doubted that there was such a thing as a Czech national character.[45] At precisely the same time

---

[43] Seán Hanley "Conservative Sensibilities in Czech Politics Before and After 1989" (Working Paper, Heinrich Boll Stiftung, Prague, 2009), http://www.cz.boell.org/downloads/hanley.pdf.

[44] Roman Chytilek and Otto Eibl. "České politické strany v politickém prostoru" [Czech political parties in the Czech political landscape], *Sociologicky časopis / Czech Sociological Review* 47 (2011): 61–88.

[45] Olga Šmídová, "Svejk after Slovakia: Czech National Identity Now," *East European Reporter* 5 (1992): 23–6. Ladislav Holy's nuanced exploration of Czech identity, *The Little Czech and the Great Czech Nation: National Identity and the post-Communist Social Transformation* (Cambridge: Cambridge University Press, 1996) is an essential starting point for this question.

that those issues were being canvassed, however, it became clear that there were definite triggers to the assertion of identity. Negative attitudes toward the Roma population surfaced both in the citizenship law at the national level[46] and at the local level with episodes of interethnic strife and the building of town walls to define ethnic boundaries.[47] Further evidence of national sentiment surrounds a minority long departed—the Sudeten Germans. Havel's 1989–1990 apologies for the postwar deportation of the German minority provoked a firestorm of criticism that centered on the question of the moral equivalence between the expulsion or deportation (even the terminology was disputed) and the Nazi occupation that preceded and triggered it.[48]

National identity can also be an ephemeral political football. When Zeman squared off against former expatriate Karel von Schwarzenberg, his second-round opponent in the 2013 presidential election, incumbent President Klaus chose sides in an oblique manner, "What's important to me is that the next president is someone who belongs to this country, who ... has spent his life here, has lived through its bad and good times."[49] This was a pointed attack on Schwarzenberg's national identity credentials: he and his noble family had gone into exile when the Communists came to power, returning after the Velvet

---

[46] The so-called "Roma clause" in criminal records was understood to target Roma residents with Slovak citizenship.

[47] This has been a problem with persistent international repercussions, from monitoring during the EU accession process, to the imposition of visa requirements upon Czech travelers to Canada (and the United Kingdom in the case of Slovakia), in response to the high volume of mainly Roma asylum seekers.

[48] The issue was not without material dimensions, of course, since culpability claims opened the door to very practical questions regarding property restitution. See Jan Pauer, "Moral Political Dissent in German-Czech Relations," *Czech Sociological Review* 6 (1996): 173–86.

[49] Radio Prague, "Václav Klaus Insinuates Czechs Should not Vote for 'Foreign' Schwarzenberg," January 17, 2013, http://www.radio.cz/en/section/curraffrs/vaclav-klaus-insinuates-czechs-should-not-vote-for-foreign-schwarzenberg. Klaus had voiced similar reservations about "dual loyalties" before, when Schwarzenberg was appointed Foreign Minister in 2006. See "Senátor Schwarzenberg sedí na dvou židlích" [Senator Schwarzenberg sits on two benches] *euportal*, December 28, 2006, http://euportal.parlamentnilisty.cz/Articles/1152-senator-schwarzenberg-sedi-na-dvou-zidlich.aspx.

Revolution to serve as presidential adviser to Klaus's archrival Havel. For good measure, Klaus insinuated that the aristocratic family had been Nazi collaborators during World War II.[50]

Prominent expatriates have served in high office in a number of post-communist countries; at one time, all three of the Baltic States had North American expatriate presidents. What is distinctive about Schwarzenberg, compared to other returned expatriates, ironically, is not his exile, but the length of his domestic service by the time of the 2013 presidential election: he had been active in Czech politics for more than two decades as presidential adviser, senator, and Foreign Minister.[51] Interestingly, Zeman and Schwarzenberg also clashed during the presidential debates over the Beneš decrees that authorized the postwar deportations of ethnic Germans.[52] The Czechs are not, therefore, devoid of the debates manifest elsewhere in the region over who is a true national loyalist.

Nonetheless, Czechs are hesitant about showing pride in their country—only 40 percent said they were proud of being Czech after the 2013 election, although the normal range of response seems to hover closer to 80 percent.[53] Lest the Czechs appear uniquely self-flagellating, however, cross-national surveys show that people in all the Central European states feel more diffident about national pride than

---

[50] "Historik: Klaus junior neříká pravdu, otec Schwarzenberga byl vlastenec" [A historian: Klaus Junior is not telling the truth, Schwarzenberg Sr. was a patriot], *lidovky.cz*, January 17, 2013, http://www.lidovky.cz/klaus-junior-nerika-pravdu-otec-schwarzenberga-byl-vlastenec-puu-/zpravy-domov.aspx?c=A130117_140304_ln_domov_vsv.

[51] The three were Toomas Ilves of Estonia, Valdas Adamkus of Lithuania and Vaira Vike-Freiberga of Latvia. In the Czech case, Czech-American academic Jan Švejnar was a serious prospect in the 2008 election that was won by incumbent Václav Klaus, and Havel touted former United States Secretary of State Madeleine Albright as a possible presidential successor in 2003.

[52] Rohru, January 21, 2013, http://rohru-web.webnode.cz/news/schwarzenberg-klaus-se-zemanem-tvori-mocenskou-skupinu/.

[53] CVVM, Vztah českých občanů k České republice [The attitudes of Czech citizens towards the Czech Republic], *Naše společnost 13–10*, November 8, 2013, *http://cvvm.soc.cas.cz/media/com_form2content/documents/c1/a7110/f3/ov131108.pdf*. STEM polls tend to show higher levels of pride. See for example, the polling on pride in citizenship from May 28, 2012, http://www.stem.cz/clanek/2458.

those in the established Western countries.[54] In this regard, Czechs are not different from their neighboring Slovaks and Poles. The underlying reason for this cannot be recent independence, since states that have existed longer, like Poland, share this same tentativeness. Rather, it is more likely that Czechs share with other countries in the region the national impact both of communism and of prior imperial rule, and the long history of being the "other Europe"—East Europe—rather than a Europe without adjectives.

---

[54] They *are* different from Hungarians, however, who alone in the region top the national charts on pride, to an extent that, at least under Viktor Orbán, somewhat troubles their neighbors. See Tom W. Smith and Seokho Kim, "National Pride in Cross-National and Temporal Perspective," *International Journal of Public Opinion* 18 (2006): 127–36.

Part III
ECONOMIC DEVELOPMENTS AFTER 1993

CHAPTER 11

Economic Developments in Slovakia Since 1993[1]

Ľudovít Hallon, Miroslav Londák, and Adam Hudek

The societal changes which occurred in post-communist states after 1989 are commonly described as a triple transition—political, economic, and state-national.[2] The transformation of the economy was a complex transformation of the socialist economic system. After the fall of the communist regimes, liberal reformers sought to transform the central-planning (socialist) model quickly into a market-oriented, capitalist economy. Such change involved radical and profound alterations, including the reorientation of exports from East to West, the privatization of state-owned property, the restructuring of industry, and the introduction of foreign investment. This process was crucial to a successful transition and was accompanied by deep changes to the political system and to property relations.

The breakup of the Council for Mutual Economic Assistance (COMECON), the Soviet Bloc's organization for economic coordination (which also cooperated with Yugoslavia) took place in just a few months. Yet, new economic relations with the markets of developed capitalist countries and foreign direct investment from interna-

---

[1] This article is an outcome of the Slovak Research and Development Agency contract no. APVV-0628-11"State Borders and Identities in Modern Slovak History in a Central European Context."
[2] See Claus Offe, "Capitalism by Democratic Design? Democratic Theory Facing the Triple Transition in East Central Europe," *Social Research* 58 (1991): 865–81. Taras Kuzio, "Transition in Post-Communist States: Triple or Quadruple?" *Politics* 21 (2001): 168–77.

tional corporations took much longer to develop. The shift also varied depending on the continuity, rapidity, and depth of the economic policies of individual transforming countries.

The basic conditions for Slovakia's transition from a centrally planned command economy to a free market economy were established in the short period between the fall of the communist regime and the division of Czechoslovakia into two separate states. Measures of revolutionary importance, such as the decentralization of economic regulation, the liberalization of foreign trade and prices, establishing internal currency convertibility, and setting up a framework for privatization opened the Slovak economy to the world. In short, Slovakia undertook a plan for the radical decentralization of the economy ensuring that in the future, the economy would predominantly follow the "laws of the free market." Similar economic reforms were carried out in other post-communist countries.

The main aim of the reformers—to create a consolidated market economy—had to be done through a legal process involving changes to the constitution and enacting new legislation that redefined property laws and the functions of the market.[3] From this point of view, the planned "depolarization of the economy" was, in fact, a highly political process managed and shaped by the new, post-communist elite.[4] Not surprisingly, the ideological orientations of the reformers became an important political factor. In Slovakia, the market oriented liberal ideology of federal formers quickly became the target of a substantial number of Slovak economists who rejected the principles of a "standard economy" in favor of what we can call "national sentiments."[5]

---

[3] See Zdislav Šulc, *Stručné dějiny ekonomických reforem v Československu (v České republice) 1945–1995* [Concise history of economic reforms in Czechoslovakia (in the Czech Republic) 1945–1995] (Brno: Doplněk, 1998).

[4] Pavol Hardoš, "Postkomunistické elity a politika ekonomickej transformácie v Československu" [Post-communist elites and the politics of economic transformation in Czechoslovakia], *Inštitút pre slobodnú spoločnosť*, Working Paper no.12 (2006): 6.

[5] Robert Žitňanský, "Jozef Kučerák: Obavy boli zbytočné, rozhovor" [Jozef Kučerák: doubts were unnecessary], *.týždeň*, issue 4 (2006): 23; see also John A. Gould, *The Politics of Privatization: Wealth and Power in Post-Communist Europe* (Boulder: Lynne Rienner, 2011).

Deep economic reforms in the post-communist states inflicted numerous costs on wider society. This included inflation, the destruction of entire segments of industry, and rising unemployment. In Czechoslovakia, market-oriented economists had a stronghold in the Federal Parliament, which implemented "shock therapy" during the years 1990–1992. The result was the immediate disintegration of economic ties with former Eastern Bloc countries and a reorientation towards West European states. This was actually a common feature of all post-communist countries in which long-term economic connections over a large economic area suddenly ended and businesses were forced to shift their markets from the less competitive markets of Central and Eastern Europe to the more competitive markets of developed Western European countries. Between the years 1988–1992, mutual trade between Hungary, Poland and Czechoslovakia decreased by 42 percent while, between 1989–1991, the GDP in the nine countries of the former Eastern Bloc decreased by approximately 23 percent.[6]

The development of economic policies in Slovakia after the fall of the communist dictatorship covers the electoral mandate of several Slovak governments. However, if we want to understand Slovak economic developments in the past twenty years, we have to understand the historical background of these developments. At the beginning of the twentieth century, the territory of present-day Slovakia was one the most industrialized parts of the Kingdom of Hungary. However, the owners of the factories were almost completely non-Slovak. After 1918, low investment in Slovakia became the central problem of the Slovak economy. The dominant agricultural sector had operated with low productivity and could not provide enough employment possibilities for the Slovak workforce, forcing tens of thousands of Slovaks to look for work abroad (mainly in Western Europe, the USA, and Canada). According to Václav Beneš: "[In the Czech Lands] about 39

---

[6] Ľudovít Hallon and Miroslav Sabol, "Proces globalizácie a vstup Slovenska do medzinárodných hospodárskych štruktúr po r. 1993" [The globalization process and the incorporation of Slovakia into international economic structures after 1993], in *20. rokov samostatnej Slovenskej republiky. Jedinečnosť a diskontinuita historického vývoja* [Twenty years of the independence of the Slovak Republic. The uniqueness and discontinuity of its evolution], eds. Miroslav Londák and Slavomír Michálek (Bratislava: VEDA, 2013), 402.

per cent of their population depended on industrial pursuits, whereas little over 31.3 per cent were employed in agriculture and forestry. In Slovakia the corresponding percentages were 17.1 and 60.4 per cent. Thus, compared to the Czech provinces, Slovakia was an economically undeveloped country."[7] Although, in the interwar years, Slovak industry underwent a process of significant modernization, the number of jobs did not increase. As a result, the emigration of Slovak workers abroad continued during the years 1918–1939.

After the communist coup in February 1948, Slovak political bodies had only minimal competencies over the economy. Strict centralization, typical for all communist states, meant that all relevant decisions were made by the central authorities in Prague who, in turn, followed Moscow's directives. Despite promises that the Czech lands and Slovakia would receive equal status, Slovakia was far behind its Czech counterpart. Experts at the time estimated that the Slovak economy was fifty or even eighty years behind the Czech Lands.[8] Indeed, in 1948, workforce distribution in Slovakia was almost identical to what it was in the 1920s and more than 60 percent of the population still worked in agriculture and only 17 percent in industry. The situation in the Czech Lands was also nearly identical to the interwar period.[9]

According to the dominant postwar Czechoslovak economic discourse (by far not only the communist one), to achieve prosperity, modernization and above all full utilization of the workforce, Slovakia des-

---

[7] Václav Beneš, "Czechoslovak Democracy and its Problems, 1918–1920," in *A History of the Czechoslovak Republic, 1918–1948*, ed. by Victor S. Mamatey and Radomír Luža (Princeton: Princeton University Press, 1973), 49.

[8] For economic developments during the years 1945–1948 see Miroslav Sabol, "Elektrifikácia Československa 1945–1948 s dôrazom na územie Slovenska" [Electrification of Czechoslovakia with emphasis on Slovak territory, 1945–1948], *Věda a technika v Československu v letech 1945–1960* [Science and technology in Czechoslovakia from 1945 to 1960], (Prague: Národní technické múzeum, 2010), 336–48.

[9] Miroslav Londák, *Ekonomické reformy v Československu v 50. a 60. rokoch 20. storočia a slovenská ekonomika* [Economic reforms in Czechoslovakia during the 1950s and 1960s and the Slovak economy] (Bratislava: Historický ústav SAV vo vydavateľstve Typoset, 2012), 43.

perately needed to be industrialized.¹⁰ This process started right after 1948; however, socialist industrialization choices created immense problems for future Slovak economic development. The primary objective of central planners was to build new industrial facilities in Slovakia in order to jump-start its economic and social growth. They made some progress, although the communist government failed to achieve its goal of overcoming the economic differences between the Czech Lands and Slovakia. Despite the rapid industrialization of Slovakia, the majority of industrial investments still went to the Czech part of the republic (e.g., 75–77 percent in the 1950s).¹¹ Nor did socialist industrialization compensate for demographic trends in Slovakia. As a result, Slovakia still lacked the investments needed to provide employment to all its inhabitants and many Slovaks had to look for jobs in the Czech Lands.¹²

These features of the Czechoslovak economy became parts of the discussions during the liberalization process of the 1960s. Slovak economic problems were one of the reasons for the Prague Spring in 1968. Thanks to the Slovak leader of the Communist Party of Czechoslovakia (KSČ), Alexander Dubček, the so-called Action Program of the KSČ (April 1968) stated that, despite twenty years of communist rule, the equalization of the Czech and Slovak economies was mere rhetoric. In reality, according to economic indicators, the differences had grown wider.¹³

This was one of the reasons for strong Slovak support for the federalization of the state. It was generally believed that an economy directed by Slovak political bodies would bring more positive developments to Slovakia. While Slovaks did achieve constitutional changes

---

[10] Miroslav Sabol, "Sociálno-ekonomické koncepcie KSS v rokoch 1921–1948" [Social and economic concepts of the Communist Party of Slovakia in the years 1921–1948], in *Český a slovenský komunismus (1921–2011)* [Czech and Slovak communism (1921–2011)], ed. by Jan Kalous and Jiří Kocian (Prague: Ústav pro soudobé dějiny AV ČR: Ústav pro studium totalitních režimů, 2012), 32–40.

[11] Calculated according to data from *Historická statistická ročenka*, 182, 692.

[12] In 1945, 50,000 people claimed Slovak ethnicity in the Czech Lands. By 1960, this number had risen to 421,000. See ibid., 429.

[13] See Miroslav Londák, *Rok 1968 a ekonomická realita Slovenska* [The year 1968 and the economic reality of Slovakia] (Bratislava: Historický ústav SAV vo vydavateľstve Prodama, 2007), 68.

ensuring a federal state, the decentralization of decision-making remained a formality. Following the Warsaw Pact invasion of Czechoslovakia (August 21, 1968), a centralized Communist Party remained the principal decision-making body.

Slovak reform economists were politically persecuted and lost their jobs during the post-invasion years of "normalization." With advocates for Slovakia sidelined, the Slovak economy still lagged behind that of the Czech Lands, despite the propaganda of the 1980s. Moreover, the economy as a whole increasingly lagged behind its counterparts in the West. State ownership was dominant in all areas of the Czechoslovak economy. Lacking access to the most recent technologies and entrepreneurial incentives, productivity grew very slowly.[14]

Yet, while the structural malfunctions of the economic systems contributed to the fall of the communist regime, the economy was not the decisive factor.[15] Czechoslovakia had the advantage of long-term stable economic development and low inflation.[16] At the end of the Czechoslovak communist dictatorship, the state had only a minimal debt—the gross debt was about 6.9 billion USD, while the net debt was five billion USD. The country was 99 percent self-sufficient in food production—there was a small surplus in animal husbandry and a small deficit in plant production.[17]

Moreover, despite gaps with the Czech lands, forty years of communism did succeed in both industrializing the country and significantly reducing the differences in the structure of the economy in the Czech

---

[14] Miroslav Sabol, "Významný priemysel na Slovensku a jeho výrobné programy v rokoch 1969–1989 [Important industry in Slovakia and its development programmes in the years 1969–1989], in *Věda a technika v Československu od normalizace k transformaci* [Science and technology in Czechoslovakia from normalization to transformation], (Prague: Národní technické muzeum, 2012), 199–215.

[15] Otakar Turek, *Podíl ekonomiky na páde komunismu v Československu* [Contributions of the economy to the downfall of communism in Czechoslovakia] (Prague: Ústav pro soudobé dějiny AV ČR, 1995), 75.

[16] Vladimír Baláž and Allan M. Williams, "Capital Mobility in Transition Countries of Central Europe," *Ekonomický časopis* 49 (2001): 252–253.

[17] However, the average cost of basic agricultural products could be even twice as high as in the most developed countries. See National Archives of the Czech Republic, Praha, fond 02/1, vol. 109, archival unit 113.

Lands and Slovakia. The Slovak share of Czechoslovak industrial production had risen from 8.5 percent in 1937 to 29 percent in 1989.[18] Industry was now the main employer in both lands and only a few more people worked in agriculture in Slovakia than in the Czech lands. Slovak GDP per capita was 87.81 percent of the Czech level in 1989.[19]

The fall of the communist regime in 1989 dramatically changed the long-term plan for Czechoslovak economic development. In the early 1990s, the governments of almost all post-communist countries in Europe introduced plans for the privatization of state-owned enterprises. According to opinion polls conducted in the second half of 1990, 97 percent of the inhabitants of Slovakia preferred the "socialist" or combined form of property. They feared the private ownership of companies, as well as foreign ownership of "national property."[20] Stormy discussions in Czechoslovakia culminated in February 1991, with legislation from the Federal Parliament, to start "voucher privatization." This was a method whereby citizens were given or could inexpensively buy a book of vouchers or "coupons" that represented potential shares in any state-owned company. The main advocate of this method of privatization was the federal Minister of Finance Václav Klaus,[21] one of the ideological leaders of the pro-market right wing in the republic.

In Slovakia 678 enterprises were registered for voucher privatization with a book value of 169 billion Czechoslovak crowns (CSK). Of these, 48 percent were privatized by the coupon method and 7 percent were sold directly to investors. Another 28 percent were placed under the authority of a new institution: the National Property Fund.[22] Simultaneously, small property privatization, referred to as

---

[18] Martin Godfrey, "The Struggle Against Unemployment: Medium-Term Policy Option for Transitional Economies," *International Labour Review* 34 (1995): 6, 8.
[19] According to data from *Historická statistická ročenka*, 655.
[20] Hallon and Sabol, "Proces globalizácie," 404.
[21] His main colleagues were T. Ježek, D. Tříska, R. Češka, J. Mládek, V. Dlouhý, J. Tošovský.
[22] Miroslav Beblavý, "Monetárna politika" [Monetary politics], in *Hospodárska politika na Slovensku 1990–1999* [Economic politics in Slovakia 1990–1999], eds. Anton Marcinčin and Miroslav Beblavý (Bratislava: Centrum pre spoločenskú a mediálnu analýzu, 2000), 97, 109–111.

the so-called "lesser privatization" was carried out by means of public auctions.

While the leading Czech economists preferred rapid privatization and minimal state intervention in the economy, many of their Slovak colleagues advocated for a more gradual form of transformation, producing a socially oriented market economy with relatively strong state participation. There were two main reasons for this. First, very soon after coupon privatization began, it became clear that the transformation of the Slovak economy would be more problematic than the transformation of the Czech economy. While the first round of coupon privatization became quite popular in Slovakia, the economic changes inflicted some significant costs on society. The main cause of the problem was the structure of the Slovak economy.

Second, among Slovak economic elites there were a large number of former reform communists (H. Kočtúch, A. M. Húska) and managers of state-owned firms (P. Baco, J. Ducký, Ľ. Černák) who considered themselves advocates of the "specific needs of Slovak industry."[23] Their idea of transformation was closer to the "market socialism of 1968" than to the market liberalism of the economists surrounding Václav Klaus.[24]

At the end of the 1980s, Czechoslovakia was the seventh largest weapons-exporting country in the world. Slovak factories produced mainly heavy equipment (tanks, artillery, armored vehicles) and primary materials processing, particularly in steel, chemicals, and petroleum. This production peaked in 1988 at the level of 19.3 billion CSK.[25] As late as 1991, 67 percent of Slovak exports consisted of heavy

---

[23] Gil Eyal, *The Origins of Postcommunist Elites* (Minneapolis; London: University of Minnesota Press, 2003), 115–17.

[24] The degree of mutual misunderstanding and even condescension is clearly illustrated in an interview with the Czech right-wing economist and one of the architects of the voucher privatization T. Ježek. See Petr Husák, *Budování kapitalismu v Čechách: Rozhovory s Tomášem Ježkem* [Establishing capitalism in the Czech lands: interviews with Tomáš Ježek] (Prague: Volvox Globator, 1997), 67.

[25] It was two-thirds of Czechoslovak production. For more information of the Czechoslovak weapons industries after 1989], see Jan Štaigl, "Špeciálna výroba na Slovensku a problematika konverzie" [Special production in Slovakia and the problem of industrial conversion], in *20 rokov samostatnej Slovenskej republiky*. 213–38.

industry and metallurgy-produced goods for the Warsaw Pact. Thus, the core of Slovak industry consisted of primary processing of imported raw materials and the heavy armaments industry. Unfortunately, this market largely collapsed at the beginning of the 1990s. Weapons production in Slovakia was nearly completely halted, partly for political reasons, but, more importantly, because demand fell among former Warsaw Pact allies with the breakup of the Eastern Bloc. Slovakia also suffered from growing stagnation in its proportionately larger agricultural sector. These structural differences were quickly reflected in diverging unemployment rates between Slovakia and the Czech Lands.[26] For the first time since 1945, in 1991, the unemployment rate in Slovakia soared to over 10 percent. In the Czech Lands, by contrast unemployment rose only to 2.6 percent.

The post-1989 development of former socialist dictatorships was also shaped by changes in the monetary and financial spheres. A common attribute was steep inflation caused by the liberalization of prices and the devaluation of currencies. The yearly Czechoslovak inflation rate in the 1970s and 1980s was about 2.5 percent. However, by 1991 it had reached 65 percent.[27] Prices and exchange rates soon stabilized in Czechoslovakia at a level that made Slovak labor and goods very cheap for foreigners. However, the low quality of goods produced by previously centrally planned economies hampered their export.[28]

The Visegrád Four (V4) economic bloc formed in 1992[29] with the aim of integrating Central Europe. These goals were to be supported by a Central European agreement concerning the creation of a free-trade zone and an agreement over a customs union between the successor states of Czechoslovakia. After the addition of Slovenia to the group of

---

[26] During the last twenty years, Slovakia has had about double the unemployment rate of the Czech Republic. See Radoslav Peter and Tibor Lalinský, "Slovensko versus Česko: 20 rokov od rozvodu" [Slovakia versus the Czech Republic: 20 years since the divorce], *Biatec*, 21 (November 2013): 5–9.

[27] The inflation rate was stabilized in 1992. See Jan Švejnar, "Czech and Slovak Federal Republic: A Solid Foundation," in *Economic Transformation in Central Europe: A Progress Report*, ed. Richard Portes (London: Centre for Economic Policy Research, 1994), 29–33.

[28] Hallon and Sabol, "Proces globalizácie," 403.

[29] Members of the V4 are Poland, Hungary, the Czech Republic, and Slovakia.

cooperating Central European countries, a bloc called the CEFTA 5 (Central European Free Trade Agreement) came into being. In the years 1992–1998, trade between the CEFTA countries grew by 26 percent.

Slovakia's economic challenges contributed to the growing popularity of new political movements. Some demanded either radical constitutional changes in the Czechoslovak Federation, or even the dissolution of the state. Nationalists used the difficulties suffered by Slovak industry to undermine support for the state. They also demonized the role of international capital, claiming that its aim was to dominate and exploit the Slovak economy. The federal government and the Czech economic sphere were presented as tools of foreign hegemony over Slovakia.

Against this political climate, a group of Slovak economists critical of Václav Klaus's plans for economic reforms became more and more influential. The majority joined the most popular new political party, the Movement for a Democratic Slovakia (Hnutie za demokratické Slovensko—HZDS), led by Vladimír Mečiar, which was also critical of Klaus's concept of privatization. With the support of the HZDS, the economists hoped to implement their own model for transforming the Slovak economy.

From the dissolution of Czechoslovakia in 1993 until late 1995, the economic development of the independent Slovak Republic was rather successful. Monetary stability and fiscal prudence combined with growth in global markets to produce generally good macroeconomic trends. In the sphere of economic policy, devaluation of the new currency and the implementation of a 10 percent import surtax helped secure a positive balance of foreign trade in the years 1994–1995. Following the devaluation, the government stabilized the currency through a fixed exchange rate for the Slovak crown (SKK) set against a basket of seven world currencies. Through these economic tools, complete liberalization of the foreign currency regime was achieved by October 1995.[30]

The main Slovak exports were dominated by commodities, specifically, iron and steel. The share of these commodities as a portion of total exports grew from 14 percent in 1993 to 16 percent in 1994.[31] Slovakia's biggest metallurgical enterprise, (Východoslov-

---

[30] Beblavý, "Monetárna politika," 97, 109–11.
[31] Relatively successful were also the chemical, textile, paper-processing and food-processing industries.

enské železiarne or VSŽ) was also its largest exporter.[32] In 1994–1995, Slovakia achieved a surplus of imports over exports and secured the position as the most open of all post-communist countries in Central Europe. However, the reorientation of exports was not accompanied by a deep structural transformation of the economy and industry.

Part of the problem was delayed privatization and an uncertain investment climate. In 1995, the newly elected governing coalition of Prime Minister Vladimír Mečiar canceled almost all of the privatization decisions of the preceding government and prepared a completely different privatization plan. Citizens, who had been issued privatization coupons in anticipation of investing in state property in the second wave of privatization, had their coupons converted to IOUs, or bonds, guaranteeing a government payout when they came due. This created a new fiscal obligation with a nominal value of 33.3 billion SKK (1.1 billion USD according to exchange rate at that time), plus interest set at the National Bank's discount rate. In place of voucher privatization, the Mečiar government embarked on a series of direct sales, dominated by incumbent managers and political allies. Mečiar's declared purpose was to create a strong group of Slovak businessmen in order to avoid selling "national property" to international investors. This second stage of privatization was largely completed by the middle of 1996. It comprised 610 enterprises with a book value of 136.8 billion SKK (4.5 billion USD).[33]

As noted, the dominant players in this privatization process were the managers of the privatized firms. The greater part of this property, which was 67 percent of the amount of all privatized state property, fell into the hands of supporters of the government. Foreign investors played only a marginal role.[34] From the beginning of the process in 1992 to the elections in the fall of 1998, sales to foreign companies

---

[32] Jacoby, "Zahraničný obchod," 145–6.
[33] Anton Marcinčin, *Zákon o strategických podnikoch: Krok späť?* [The law on strategic companies: a step backwards?], (Bratislava: Slovenská spoločnosť pre zahraničnú politiku, 1997).
[34] In 1993, foreign investments represented 24 percent of the money spent on privatization; in 1994, it was 21 percent and, by 1995, only 11 percent. Anton Marcinčin, "Privatizácia" [Privatization], in *Hospodárska politika na Slovensku*, 291–6.

totaled 7.7 billion SKK (257 million USD), only 9.9 percent the total property purchased. With a few highly politicized exceptions, "strategic companies" (communication, transport, et cetera), with a total asset value of 150 billion SKK (50 billion USD) were completely excluded from privatization, according to a law passed in July 1995.[35]

At the beginning of the second round of privatization, government supporters raided the capital market to secure control of companies that had been privatized in the first stage of the process. They did this by seizing or liquidating investment funds and investment companies which had controlling shares in 73 percent of the companies privatized in the first stage of privatization.[36] A majority of the projects in this "manager's privatization" were marked by rather dubious corporate governance practices, including corruption, nepotism, and the tunneling of the assets of collectively owned privatized firms by the managers of fully owned enterprises. Stripped of value and deeply in debt, these firms were then generally liquidated.[37]

The best-known case of merging politics with economics during this privatization concerned Slovakia's largest company, the VSŽ[38] in Košice. On March 11, 1994, the government decided to sell 10 percent of VSŽ shares to Company Manager Alexander Rezeš. On the same day, the Mečiar government received a vote of no confidence and new elections were called. While the nominal value of the shares was 1.5 billion SKK (48.3 million USD), the government sold them for 314 million SKK (10.1 million USD). The new owner had to pay only the first installment, a mere 15 percent of the purchase price or 47 million SKK (1.5 million USD).[39] After the return of Mečiar's government in late

---

[35] Ibid.
[36] With the argument that it was protecting small investors, the government took control of investment funds which were not guaranteed by banks.
[37] Mikael Olsson, *Ownership Reform and Corporate Governance: The Slovak Privatization Process in 1990–1996* (Uppsala: Uppsala University, 1999), 125–206; Gould, *The Politics of Privatization*, Chapter 6.
[38] Today, it is US Steel Košice.
[39] Even this money was in fact indirectly donated to the manager by the seller, the National Property Fund, which was at that time under Mečiar's direct control. See Vladimír Bačišin, "Ako sa z Rezešovcov stali multimilionári" [How the Rezeš group became multimillionaires], *HNonline.sk*, June 6, 2004, http://hn.hnonline.sk/iformat-188/ako-sa-z-rezesovcov-stali-multimilionari-125183.

1994, and with the government's consent, the owner and former Minister of Transportation Alexander Rezeš, built a web of mutually interconnected companies which bought more VSŽ shares. By March 1997, Rezeš controlled 47 percent of the steel company. The state remained a passive owner of a number of additional shares, giving Rezeš effective control.[40]

The management of the company gradually outsourced its exporting activities to its sister firms, which were in fact underpaying the VSŽ for its products and draining its profits. The company owners utilized a similar strategy—including the Slovak government's supportive votes in shareholder meetings to allow the VSŽ to gain control over its creditor banks. Thus, in June 1996, the Mečiar government decided that the banks would remain state-owned.[41] However, the government defied the National Bank of Slovakia (NBS), and allowed the owners of VSŽ Holding to gain control over the biggest bank in Slovakia, the Investment and Development Bank (Investičná a rozvojová banka—IRB). Not surprisingly, the IRB began to finance the activities of the VSŽ management and their private network of sister firms.

It soon became obvious that the loans given by the bank to its patrons were "problematic" and, in December 1997, the IRB ended under NBS receivership. Without its "own" bank and with external companies taking its profits, VSŽ Holding became dependent on short-term loans. By 1998, the company was on the verge of bankruptcy, with a debt over 13 billion SKK (371.5 million USD at that time).[42] The new creditors used their position to appoint new VSŽ managers, thus ending the "Rezeš era." Finally, in 2000, the VSŽ was sold to a new investor, US Steel.

While the fates of the VSŽ and the IRB were the most visible outcomes of Mečiar's "manager's privatization," the same scenario occurred with many other smaller corporations. Greater damages, espe-

---

[40] At the same time, during the years 1994–1997, he was also Minister of Infrastructure and Communications.
[41] See Juraj Ďurčenka, "História privatizácie a krachu Investičnej a rozvojovej banky" [A history of privatization and the bankruptcy of the Investment and Development Bank], *SME*, December 23, 1997, http://www.sme.sk/c/2046475/historia-privatizacie-a-krachu-investicnej-a-rozvojovej-banky.html.
[42] Bačišin, "Ako sa z Rezešovcov."

cially in the Slovak banking sector, were avoided by the fact that the NBS maintained its independence from the government. This enabled the National Bank to prevent the complete domination of the government and its "oligarchs" over the Slovak banking sector. Had the NBS been under government control, it is quite likely the VSŽ would have secured credits to pay off its debts—generating rapid currency depreciation and high inflation as happened in a number of post-Soviet republics, including Russia.

In the second half of the 1990s, the factors that had helped the Slovak economy rebound vanished. The global recession led to a decrease in the demand for Slovak products. Because of the slowdown in the structural transformation of Slovak industry, Slovakia was particularly vulnerable to a downturn. In 1998, its surplus in the balance of trade had turned into a deficit of 80.9 billion SKK (2.2 billion USD).[43] The government tried to promote economic growth with expansive financial policies. It raised capital to meet its long-term obligations using short-term foreign loans, which increased the country's debt. Yet companies privatized by their old management continued to profit from their tight links with government circles. Where they were guaranteed a profit through politics, they had little interest in structural changes. Nor were they interested in improving governmental transparency and accountability.[44]

Between late 1994 and 1998, representatives of Western European countries, the USA, and numerous international organizations, such as the European Commission, criticized the level of democracy in Slovakia and the authoritarian tendencies of the Mečiar government. Relations with the EU countries and the USA worsened, and Slovakia fell into isolation. This reduced the confidence of foreign investors and further derailed Slovakia's growing economic transformation.

The chief aim of the new government of Mikuláš Dzurinda (1998–2002), led by "anti-Mečiar forces" and consisting of both rightist and leftist parties, was to speed economic reforms in order to get Slovakia back into the first group of countries waiting for admission to the EU.

---

[43] Július Tóth, "Exchange Rate—Is it Really Overvalued?" *Slovak Capital and Money Market Report,* September–October 1999, 35–7.

[44] John Gould, "Vladimír Mečiar and the Politics of Privatization in Slovakia, 1992–1998," *Slovakia* 41 (2013): 102–45.

The planned changes involved restructuring the economy, reforming the banking sector, a new round of privatization, and strong incentives to encourage foreign investment.[45] The government repealed the Law on Strategic Companies, making the privatization of monopolies, larger banks and key industrial concerns possible. Foreign capital was invited by the Law on Establishing Industrial Estates, and especially the Law on Investment Stimulus. The latter provided tax holidays for ten years, state benefits for the requalification of new employees, and incentives for the creation of new jobs. The first wave of investors could even acquire higher levels of tax relief and subsidies, according to the level of unemployment in the region.[46]

Immediately after coming into power, the Dzurinda government replaced the fixed exchange rate for the SKK with a more flexible floating peg (fluctuating within a zone of +/–7 percent). In 1998, the government funded the recovery of key banks and offered them to foreign investors. From June 1999 to June 2000, the state's share in the banks was reduced from 59 percent to 13 percent. Austrian capital dominated this sphere.[47] The Slovak international image was also polished by its acceptance into the OECD in 1999 and by signing an association agreement with the EU in 2000.

The reforms of the Dzurinda government resulted in a 19 percent devaluation of the currency in 1998 and a corresponding rise in inflation as foreign demand grew and the cost of imports rose. However, by 2000, these measures helped boost exports and considerably decreased the deficit. This economic reorientation was supported by the activities of foreign investors and the amount of foreign capital in Slovakia quickly increased. Multinationals stepped in to privatize many of the former strategic companies. As in the early 1990s, however, more rapid economic reforms were accompanied by significant social costs, such as higher inflation, growing social stratification, and Europe's highest unemployment rate, topping 19 percent in 2001.

Parliamentary elections in 2002 resulted in a second Dzurinda government. This time, however, the ruling coalition included only rightist and liberal parties with a strong pro-market orientation. As a result,

---

[45] Hallon and Sabol, "Proces globalizácie," 410.
[46] Ibid., 409.
[47] Baláž and Williams, "Capital Mobility," 250–2.

the new government strengthened and accelerated the reform program started by its predecessor. As before, its principal focus was on admission into Western political, economic and military structures, with a priority on the EU and NATO. The primary economic goals were to complete the privatization of strategic facilities and to increase the amount of foreign investment. In order to lure investors, the government introduced the tax reform of 2003—a flat tax consisting of identical income, corporate, and value-added taxes of 19 percent. Foreign investors also appreciated Slovakia's successful bid to become a member of NATO and the EU in 2004.[48] In 2002, the government introduced the new, liberal Slovak Labor Code. The purpose of deregulating employment laws was to motivate employers to create new jobs. However, the activities of the government resulted in strong protests from the Confederation of Labor Unions (Konfederácia odborových zväzov— KOZ). In 2003 and 2004, its leaders organized a number of protests and strikes against the social costs of the "neoliberal" reforms. This process culminated in the KOZ organizing an unsuccessful referendum to hold new elections, which took place in April 2004.[49] As a result, the government cancelled the Law on Tripartite Consultation.[50] This step worsened the position of the labor unions, which, in turn, started to openly support the leftist party Smer, which was in opposition at that time.

The years of the second Dzurinda government (2003–2006) represented an era of gradual, yet accelerating, economic growth. The steady flow of foreign investments and growing trade made the Slovak economy an integral part of the global economy. In the years 1990–1999, Slovakia attracted 2.3 billion USD in foreign investment. From 2000–2005, by contrast, investment reached 18 billion USD, with the

---

[48] Sharon Fisher, John Gould and Tim Haughton, "Slovakia's Neoliberal Turn," *Europe-Asia Studies* 59, no. 3 (September, 2007): 977–98.

[49] For the summary of KOZ positions and activities during the years 2001–2004, see the document *Správa o činnosti Konfederácie, plnenie programu a uzneseni IV. zjazdu KOZ SR* [Report on the activities of the confederation, fulfilling the program and decisions of the Fourth Congress of KOZ SR], which can be found on the official internet portal of the *KOZ* (kozsr.sk), http://www.kozsr.sk/page_sk/kozsr/dokumenty5zjazd/sprava_o_cinnosti.pdf.

[50] The government had promised that the most important economic and social law proposals were to be vetted by representatives of the labor union and employers prior to adoption.

highest shares coming from Germany and Holland. Next came Austria, Italy, France, the United States, and the Czech Republic.[51]

Automobile production became an essential feature of nearly all the post-communist countries with car production becoming the backbone of much of their exports. Slovakia benefitted from investments by Volkswagen (VW), Peugeot-Citroën, Toyota, Hyundai, Kia, MAN, and Steyer, with dozens of subcontractors. Combined, this sector employs 75,000 workers in Slovakia. The first, and still one of the most important car producing companies in Slovakia, is VW. By 2000, its production had increased to 180,800 automobiles per year, earning 2.2 billion USD and comprising 16 percent of Slovakia's total imports.[52] Today, Slovakia joins the Czech Republic and Belgium as one of the largest per capita automobile manufacturers in the world.[53]

At the same time, the contemporary (post-2008) economic crisis and the growing wages of Slovak workers have helped divert investment to Southeastern and Eastern Europe. A number of investors have canceled their plans to build new processing plants in Slovakia and moved to "cheaper" countries. The chronic problem of the Slovak economy is the slow growth of "sophisticated production," especially high-end information technologies. Foreign investments in the past were motivated primarily by the cheap cost of labor, which was low even in comparison with the other Central and Eastern European countries. While the Slovak gross domestic product during 1989–2005 grew by 33 percent, real wages in 2005 were still below the 1989 level.[54] This is one of the main factors contributing to the competitiveness of the Slovak economy

---

[51] Ivan Okáli, Karol Frank, and Hana Gabrielová, "Hospodársky vývoj Slovenska v roku 2005" [Economic development in Slovakia in the year 2005], *Ekonomický časopis* 53 (2005): 452–7.

[52] "Volkswagen Slovakia a. s. Bratislava," *Trend*, May 2, 2001.

[53] "Automobilky urobili zo Slovenska lídra" [The automobile industry made Slovakia a leader], *Trend*, April 2, 2013, http://ekonomika.etrend. sk/ekonomika-slovensko/slovensko-je-svetovym-lidrom-v-pocte-vyrobenych-aut-na-obyvatela.html.

[54] Okáli, Frank and Gabrielová, "Hospodársky vývoj" [Economic development], 452–7; Sonia Ferenčíková and Marek Vážan, "Nové trendy vo vývoji priamych zahraničných investícií v krajinách strednej a východnej Európy" [New trends in the development of direct foreign investments in countries of Central and Eastern Europe], *Hospodárske rozhľady* 34 (2005): 523–4.

in global markets. On the one hand, since Slovakia has one of the most open economies, its economic performance is increasingly beyond its own control. On the other hand, the fact that productivity is the same as the EU average, but salaries are significantly lower, has created significant pressure on all Slovak governments since 2000, which have had a hard time explaining the necessity of this development to the voters.

The economic and debt crisis in Europe is also uncovering other negative factors associated with economic globalization: Slovakia's most talented workers are now freer to leave, and often do; there is a danger of unexpected transfers of foreign investments and production facilities, and Slovak food producers are losing their share in the supermarkets owned by global corporations. These aspects are perceived in a negative light by a significant number of citizens and leftist politicians.

One of the main effects of the economic crisis in Slovakia was the electoral success of leftists, as well as of resurgent nationalists and populist parties. The leftist government of Prime Minister Robert Fico (2006–2010) strongly criticized the "neoliberal measures" of the past, but it made only small changes to the key reforms made by its predecessors.[55] However, the second Fico government (in office since 2012), emboldened by its majority in parliament, changed the economic conditions in Slovakia more profoundly as a reaction to the continually worsening social situation. The flat tax was abolished, and the overall tax burden was increased, especially for industries and people with high incomes. One of the important plans of the current government is to improve workers' rights and their standard of living through a new labor code. In this respect, the government intends to accept the demands of the Confederation of Labor Unions, to the great dismay of a significant portion of employers' organizations.

In conclusion, while we can say that although there are negative aspects to globalization, Slovakia's integration into world markets has gone better than was predicted in 1993. On the one hand, we have witnessed the one-sided use of cheap labor by investors without making greater investments in technologies. These are also seen in

---

[55] John Gould, "Slovakia's Neoliberal Churn: The Political Economy of the Fico Government, 2006–8." Institute of European Studies and International Relations, Faculty of Social and Economic Sciences, Comenius University, June 2009.

the other transition countries of Central Europe. However, the degree of dependence on internationalization and foreign investments is different in each CEFTA country. Many factories in Slovenia are entering demanding markets using their own technologies. But most of the industries of Slovakia, Hungary, and Poland are penetrating world markets as elements of international corporations. Due to a lack of local capital and technology, most of these countries are dependent upon the further deepening of European integration for future growth; that is why their economic policies encourage integration.

On the other hand, during the twenty years of its existence, the Slovak Republic has demonstrated that it can successfully function as an independent economy. Accession into all crucial European and global structures (including the eurozone) is an undeniable success. In 1990, Slovakia's GDP was only 57 percent of the EU average; in 2013, it was 75 percent. Growth has also helped close the development gap with the Czech Republic. From 1990 to 2013, the Czech Republic's GDP grew by 49 percent, while Slovak GDP grew by 65.6 percent. Slovakia's standard of living, at 73 percent of the EU average, compares well to the Czech's 80 percent.[56] This gap is close to where the two republics started in 1990.

Slovak workers are also more productive, with the average worker producing at 82 percent of the EU average versus the Czechs at 73 percent. Yet, much of this difference is due to lower wages in Slovakia—an important indicator that the convergence is still incomplete. The average monthly wage in Slovakia is still only about 90 percent of the Czech rate. In Slovakia it is 805 euros[57] and in the ČR 900.[58] Moreover, 70 percent of both Slovak and Czech workers still fall below the average European rate. While Slovakia is currently doing better than Poland and Hungary, it is still behind the majority of EU countries.

---

[56] "K životnej úrovni EÚ sme sa od roku 2008 nepriblížili ani o krok" [Since 2008 we have not made any progress in increasing our standard of living as compared to the European Union], *O Peniazoch*, June 25, 2012, http://openiazoch.zoznam.sk/cl/122010/K-zivotnej-urovni-EU-sme-sa-od-roku-nepriblizili-ani-o-krok.

[57] Data from the *Slovak Statistical Office*, http://portal.statistics.sk/showdoc.do?docid=67073.

[58] Data from the *Czech Statistical Office*, http://www.czso.cz/eng/redakce.nsf/i/home.

Unemployment, poverty, and the social exclusion of whole groups of citizens, particularly the Roma, remain chronic problems of the Slovak economy and society.[59]

The current Slovak unemployment rate of 14 percent (about 400,000 people) is one of the highest in the EU. In addition, even before the crisis of the 1990s, about 160,000 Slovak citizens worked abroad. One of the effects of Slovakia's marketization and integration into world markets has been the considerable reduction of traditional branches of production, like food-processing, and the textile and chemistry industries. Communist central planners had created these state enterprises across Slovakia. Yet, foreign investment has focused largely on Bratislava and the western part of the country, which offers the best infrastructure and most qualified work force. As industries failed in other regions, there was little to replace them. Consequently, there are significant and deepening regional differences in Slovakia regarding living standards and the unemployment rate.

In contrast to the non-communist states of Europe, East-Central Europe's integration into the global economy overlapped with radical changes in the economic, political, and state-national spheres. The most visible aspect of the transformation from central planning towards a globally integrated market economy was the privatization of state property. Even today, this process is a source of unending controversy and discussion. In 1990–1992, differing views on privatization were one reason for the dissolution of the federal state. Yet, Slovakia's experience since 1993 has only confirmed the statement of a prominent American journalist, Anne Applebaum, "[P]rivatization was unavoidable and countries which preferred a more 'gradual' transition only got stuck with higher corruption."[60]

---

[59] If Slovakia had had the same unemployment rate as the Czech Republic during the last twenty years, its GDP per capita would be 12 percent higher than that in the ČR.

[60] Anne Applebaum, "Existuje ešte východná Európa?" [Does Eastern Europe still exist?], *SME*, March 29, 2013, http://komentare.sme.sk/c/6751346/existuje-este-vychodna-europa.html#ixzz2bwyQgqAM. The original English version of the lecture "Does Eastern Europe Still Exist?" can be found here: *LSE*, http://www.lse.ac.uk/newsAndMedia/videoAndAudio/channels/publicLecturesAndEvents/player.aspx?id=1821.

CHAPTER 12

To Neoliberalism and Back? Twenty Years of Economic Policy in Slovakia

John A. Gould

The story of Slovakia's economic development since 1918 has been told before, but rarely in a single place and never, as far as I know, in a single article. In that respect, Hallon, Londák, and Hudek's "Economic Developments in Slovakia Since 1993" makes an important contribution to the field of Slovak studies. The title, with its promise to provide a review of Slovakia's economic development since independence, actually understates its scope. Indeed, a good portion of the article concerns the 1918–1989 period. As far as I can tell, they get the communist and pre-communist history right in most of the details, and in spite of the article's remarkable parsimony, they add new insights to our understanding of the period since independence. This is an impressive accomplishment.

As a political scientist, however, I was left wondering what broader lesson we should draw from Slovakia's remarkable economic transformation *since* the country became independent in 1993. What follows here is thus intended to complement rather than critique the authors' story. They cover Slovakia's key economic turning points—or at least mention them. As they correctly point out, the breakup of Czechoslovakia has an economic dimension based on the uneven economic and industrial development of the Czech Lands and Slovakia. From the breakup until the economic crisis of 2008–2009, the major shifts in economic policy roughly mirror electoral turnovers, particularly those of late 1994, 1998, 2002, and 2012. Woven into this story are the processes of European accession and the adoption of the euro—an important surrender of monetary independence just as the 2008–2009 financial crisis began to cripple Slovakia's vital post-communist export markets.

Hallon, Londák, and Hudek rightly begin and end their analysis of the post-communist era with a discussion of privatization. As I have noted elsewhere, so much of the driving impetus behind the politics of the Mečiar years were related to privatization.[1] While it seems remarkable in an era of oligarchs and tycoons, the quaint conceit held by most market economists in the immediate post-communist period was that privatization was not only a vital component of economic reform but could also substitute for political reform in the short term and drive it in the long term.

Privatization, the economists argued, depoliticized the operation of firms. It replaced political operatives with private owners who stood to personally benefit from the firms' profitable operation.[2] By replacing the political motive with the profit motive, they argued, privatization would lead the process of economic restructuring. New owners would have a direct incentive to undertake the difficult measures necessary for firms to compete in global markets.

Yet privatization also had an important political role. Ideally, privatization and enterprise restructuring would be deeply rooted in a broader program of structural adjustment. But, because the reforms would be painful for many in society, many doubted they would have the political will to implement the program in its entirety. In theory, the road to markets began by releasing prices from state controls. The resulting inflation would be difficult, but temporary, thanks to monetary restraint and aggregate demand management. The later would consist of reduced government spending and limits on increases in state wages, pensions and other transfers to rates lower than inflation. Reformers would also break up state monopolies, reduce bureaucratic restrictions on creating new businesses, and invite foreign competitors into the domestic market. Firms would thus be exposed to competitive markets. Many would not be able to withstand the pressure. These firms would be liquidated or transformed under new bankruptcy laws

---

[1] John A. Gould, "Vladimír Mečiar and the Politics of Privatization in Slovakia, 1992–1998" *Slovakia* 41 (2013): 76-7, 102–45.

[2] Maxim Boycko, Andrei Shleifer and Robert Vishny, *Privatizing Russia*, (Cambridge: MIT Press, 1995), 38.

speeding the return of their capital, land, and labor to productive use. A capital friendly financial network would allow many assets—and particularly the country's now cheaper, more flexible labor force—to be employed in foreign joint ventures and green field investments. Ideally, a privatized, commercial banking sector would assist the process by loaning only to those firms that had a prospect of succeeding in the market and disciplining those that floundered. Additional capital could be found as domestic capital markets accumulated and rewarded portfolio capital from both home and abroad.[3]

Such reforms were socially and politically painful, however, and unlikely to be implemented quickly or in their entirety. Experience with the Soviet Union's new republic-level parliaments had taught economists and policy makers alike that there were too many stakeholders in the old ways of doing things to get the full program both passed and implemented. Unless the executive was given some degree of decree power, many argued, economic populism and ongoing self-dealing and theft by politically connected state-owned managers were the likely outcomes.[4]

Against this background of stalled blueprints and state-business connivance in corrupting policy, economists thus emphasized privatization as a potential driver of liberal economic *and political* change. Even if the old corrupt stakeholders gained control of their enterprises in the privatization process, as private owners, it was argued, they would become frustrated with bureaucratic and political roadblocks to higher profits.[5] Indeed, economists frequently argued that without private owners there would be no one to resent the grabbing hand of the politicians and bureaucrats. Privatization thus expanded the group of potential political victims of state theft—a powerful interest group who

---

[3] Michael Mandelbaum, "Introduction," in *Making Markets: Economic Transformation in Eastern Europe and the Post-Soviet States*, eds. Shafiqul Islam and Michael Mandelbaum (New York: CSFR 1993), 1–15; Jeffrey Sachs, *Poland's Jump to a Free Market Economy* (Cambridge: MIT Press, 1994).

[4] John A. Gould, *The Politics of Privatization: Wealth and Power in Postcommunist Europe*, (Boulder: Lynne Rienner, 2011), 31–3.

[5] Andrej Shleifer and Daniel Treisman, *Without a Map: Political Tactics and Economic Reform in Russia*, (Cambridge: MIT Press, 2000); Gould, *The Politics of Privatization*, 41–9.

would fight for political liberalization.⁶ In this respect privatization and associated market reforms were a *democratization* project.

Hallon, Londák, and Hudek provide ample evidence in their history of the 1990s to show that the economists were not so much wrong in these assumptions as incomplete. Many economists discounted the fact that privatization carried large distributive consequences with significant political implications. Yet, by putting ownership of the property of the nation in question, post-communist privatization programs created a short-term, high-stakes battle for the wealth and power of a country. Across the post-communist world, combatants fought extraordinarily hard to win this struggle. They would cheat where necessary, steal where unobserved, and even kill where deeply threatened. Privatization enthusiasts were not exactly unaware of this, but since they assumed that private owners would eventually seek to build the basic institutions of a market democracy, they really didn't care. As chief of Russian privatization, Anatoly Chubais, best put it, "They are stealing absolutely everything and it is impossible to stop them. But let them steal and take their property. They will then become owners and decent administrators of this property."⁷

Yet privatization's distributional aspects carried poorly examined political consequences. Privatization combatants knew that if they could succeed in monopolizing the political process, they would be more likely to succeed in monopolizing the privatization process. The struggle for wealth thus became integral to the struggle for power. This had a negative impact on democratic institutions and the rule of law.⁸

This happened even in the Czech Republic, where privatization was dominated by the initially quite popular voucher privatization program. Guided (or, some would say, blinded) by the economists' pro-privatization ideology, Czech policy makers were not terribly concerned

---

[6] Boycko et al., *Privatizing Russia*, 154; Andrew Schwartz, *The Politics of Greed: How Privatization Structured Politics in Central and Eastern Europe*, (Lanham: Rowman & Littlefield, 2006), 30; Shleifer and Treisman, *Without a Map*, 37.

[7] John Kay, "Don't Mix Politics and Quest for Wealth," *Financial Times*, July 7, 2004.

[8] John A. Gould, "Out of the Blue? Democracy and Privatization in Post-Communist Europe," *Comparative European Politics* 1, no. 3 (November 2003): 277–312.

by cheating. Beginning in late 1992, Czech (and, initially, Slovak) citizens became micro-shareholders in privatizing firms. Small shareholders could not provide effective shareholder oversight, so an important group of new enterprises (called investment privatization companies) established funds that concentrated citizens' micro-share holdings into meaningful ownership stakes in privatized firms. To further speed the process of creating real, vested owners out of tens of thousands of citizen micro-shareholders, Czech Prime Minister Václav Klaus and his capital markets regulators "turned out the light" on the process of share accumulation. To put it less discreetly in words they never used, they refused to regulate or monitor trade in shares for fear it would slow down the process of ownership consolidation and the process of enterprise restructuring that clear ownership would entail. Yet, the process that unfolded in the regulatory dark, was no less than capital markets carnage—a free-for-all in which enterprise and capital market insiders used all possible means (anything that was not explicitly illegal, and many things that were) to convert their fragile control over ownership shares or enterprise management into real assets that they could privately control.[9]

The results were dismal. Rather than restructuring enterprises, managers stripped them of cash; rather than respect minority shareholders of funds, fiduciary managers tunneled assets of value to their fully controlled firms; and rather than repay loans, partial enterprise owners pocketed the money and abandoned their asset-stripped firms to an inefficient bankruptcy process. By 1997, little real enterprise restructuring had occurred and the new banking system was having increasing difficulty with insolvency.[10] The main exceptions to the rule could be found in foreign joint venture and green field investments—

---

[9] Karla Brom and Mitchell Orenstein, "The Privatised Sector in the Czech Republic: Government and Bank Control in a Transitional Economy," *Europe-Asia Studies* 46:6 (1994): 893–928; Raj Desai, Raj, "Financial Market Reform in the Czech Republic, 1991–1994: The Revival of Repression?" Working Paper no. 86, Prague: CERGE-EI, September 1995; Mitchell A. Orenstein, *Out of the Red: Building Capitalism and Democracy in Postcommunist Europe* (Ann Arbor: University of Michigan Press, 2001); Hilary Appel, *A New Capitalist Order: Privatization & Ideology in Russia & Eastern Europe*, (Pittsburgh: University of Pittsburgh Press, 1995).

[10] Gould, *The Politics of Privatization*.

enterprises that thrived by producing real products that Czechs and foreigners wanted to buy.

Slovak Prime Minister Vladimír Mečiar inherited the voucher program from the federal state when he became prime minister for the second time in the summer of 1992. While the full ramifications of the voucher privatization fiasco had yet to be realized, he already had a number of technical reasons to be suspicious of how the program was unfolding. Yet, Mečiar's opposition to voucher privatization was more a response to the program's political implications than to its emerging flaws. Specifically, voucher privatization empowered a new, young class of financial entrepreneurs who in most cases had no loyalty to him or his new party, the Movement for a Democratic Slovakia (HZDS).

Mečiar's primary economic clients, by contrast, lay among industrial managers in Slovakia's heavy industrial and engineering sectors—a group he had been courting since at least February 1990. Hallon, Londák, and Hudek explain in detail how these groups took major hits from a series of federal decisions, including lustration, limitations on exports of heavy weaponry, and deep cuts in domestic procurement, and, finally, a reorientation of markets away from Eastern Europe's Council for Mutual Economic Assistance to the West, where the large German engineering firms had a decisive advantage over Slovakia's outdated enterprises.

The resulting industrial recession was tailor-made for a nationalist backlash to federal reforms. Drawing support from the reeling industrial sector and legitimized by a populist, but economically illiterate, group of "national economists," Vladimír Mečiar argued that federal reforms had been designed with Czech, not Slovak, economic conditions in mind. By devolving federal economic controls to the republic level, he promised, Slovakia could better manage its post-communist transformation.[11]

Mečiar was right, but for the wrong reasons—the country would need more global capital and deeper market integration to grow, not less. Indeed, it would take another ten years to show how the timely

---

[11] Ivan Mikloš, "Economic Transition and the Emergence of Clientalist Structures in Slovakia," in *Slovakia: Problems of Democratic Consolidation*, eds. Soňa Szomolányi and John A. Gould (Bratislava: Friedrich Ebert Stiftung/Slovak Political Science Association, 1997), 57–92.

investor-friendly decisions of an independent Slovak government could drive rapid growth. Still, in the short term, the country failed to collapse economically as many of those opposing independence had warned. It has recently been argued that this validates Mečiar's economic policy, but this badly misreads the history. Slovakia's success was part of a regional trend and came largely in spite of Mečiar's policy innovations, rather than because of them.[12] Slovakia's untested, but independent central bank retained a stable monetary supply throughout the Mečiar era. This ensured that Slovakia did not catch the Russian/Ukrainian disease of hyperinflation: e.g., printing money to recapitalize commercial banks as they repeatedly provided loans to companies that had neither the intention nor the ability to repay. In addition, Mečiar's second government (June 1992–March 1994) and the short-lived successor government of Jozef Moravčík, were, for the most part, fiscally prudent. While Slovakia remained a difficult place for both portfolio and direct foreign investment, Mečiar did nothing to impede trade integration into world markets. These policies were essentially inherited unchanged from the federal state.

It was in privatization where Mečiar undertook his major innovation. Despite the voucher program's great initial popularity, he took measures to delay, scale back and, later, cancel the program (replacing it with a fiscally costly bond guaranteeing a payout to every citizen participating in the voucher privatization program). He then privatized enterprises using an opaque process of direct sales in which his industrial and political allies bought valuable enterprise assets for a fraction of their true value. Corruption also played an important role.[13]

---

[12] David Wemer, "Europe's Little Tiger? Reassessing Economic Transition in Slovakia under the Mečiar Government 1993–1998," *The Gettysburg Historical Journal* 12:1 (2013): 96–112.

[13] Mikael Olsson, *Ownership Reform and Corporate Governance: The Slovak Privatization Process in 1990–1996*, (Uppsala: Uppsala University, 1999); Marcinčin, Anton, Daniela Zemanovičová, and Luboš Vagač, *Privatization Methods and Development of Slovakia* (Bratislava: Center for Economic Development, 1996); Ivan Mikloš, "Privatizácia," [Privatization] in *Slovensko, 1997: Súhrnná správa o stave spoločnosti a trendoch na rok 1998* [Slovakia in 1997. A complete report on the state of society and trends for 1998], eds. Martin Bútora and Michal Ivantyšin (Bratislava: Inštitút pre verejné otázky, 1998).

The scandalous details of privatization were hard to justify in an open, democratic society. Mečiar addressed this with a combination of nationalism (he argued that his privatization winners were Slovak patriots who had the interest of the Slovak nation at heart), and repression of democratic institutions. Privatization was certainly not responsible for the near death of Slovak democracy between 1995 and 1998—the HZDS clearly had hegemonic aspirations to remain in power indefinitely—but it certainly played a contributing role.[14]

But what about the new owners? Remember that initially many economists justified rapid privatization under even corrupt conditions with the understanding the new owners would then form a pro-market, pro-democratic interest group. Slovakia proved that this was only partially true. Indeed, while many owners did seek to turn around their properties and even began to oppose Mečiar, others simply took their discounted properties and sold them to secondary investors at market price. Funds which should have gone to the state (to meet the obligation incurred by the costly privatization bond Mečiar had created) thus went into private accounts—often conveniently located outside of the country. Still, at least in this second case, the firms now had serious investors who needed to turn a profit to survive.[15]

Sadly, a third class of entrepreneurs was not content with simply acquiring state property for next to nothing. Its members now sought to privatize state economic policy as well. To see how this worked, one needs only look at the authors' brief examination of the privatization of Slovakia's largest industrial enterprise, the VSŽ.[16] Hallon, Londák, and Hudek's version is the most complete I have seen and hence a welcome addition to the literature. What they left out is that the manipulations of VSŽ owner Alexander Rezeš were quite typical of how privatization could go badly wrong in post-communist Europe. Rezeš was never 100 percent the owner of his firm. Not content with sharing profits with other owners, including the state, he created his own network of trade companies, which served as gatekeepers for the VSŽ's sourcing and marketing.

---

[14] Gould, *The Politics of Privatization*, 122–5.
[15] For details, see ibid., 125–30.
[16] Gould, "Vladimír Mečiar and the Politics of Privatization," 76–7, 102–45.

I like to call these "tick companies" since Rezeš's private network survived by sucking cash from his only partially owned company, the VSŽ. While the real operations of such scams are quite complex, tick companies generally find some way to overcharge the host company for sales and underpay it for purchases. Rezeš was most likely not the first entrepreneur to have become rich by trading with the VSŽ.[17] Indeed, as early as 1993, Mečiar accused opposition-linked VSŽ officials of using their own tick company to acquire VSŽ cash. But he then replaced them with loyalists who apparently did the same thing. Rezeš's network was simply post-communist business as usual—a timeworn strategy with origins back in the late Gorbachev *perestroika* era.[18]

But Rezeš also took it to a new extreme in Slovakia. By 1997, the VSŽ was running short on cash, forcing Rezeš to find new ways to recapitalize. As Hallon, Londák, and Hudek document, Rezeš used government connivance to gain control over one of Slovakia's leading commercial banks. It provided new cash to the VSŽ that eventually ended up in tick company accounts.

Had this been Ukraine or Russia in the early 1990s, the owners would have then used parliamentary control over the National Bank to print money and recapitalize banks controlled by their enterprise debtors. The result would have been deep inflation of the sort that Russia's "red managers" helped engineer from 1992–1995.[19] But unlike Russia, Slovakia's central bank remained stubbornly independent of the government despite growing pressure from Mečiar's Ministry of Finance. In 1997–1998, the government only narrowly failed in an attempt to gain more direct control over the National Bank of Slovakia (NBS).[20] Had this happened, it is quite likely that Mečiar's privatization "winners" would have ordered the NBS to print money to recapitalize Slovakia's indebted banks in order to feed capital to their con-

---

[17] Gould, *The Politics of Privatization*, 111.
[18] Victor Nee and Peng Lian, "Sleeping with the Enemy: A Dynamic Model of Declining Political Commitment in State Socialism," *Theory and Society* 23, no. 3 (1994): 253–96; Joel S. Hellman, "Winners Take All: Politics of Partial Reform in Post-communist Transition," *World Politics*, 50, no. 2 (1998): 203–34
[19] Shleifer and Treisman, *Without a Map*.
[20] Gould, *The Politics of Privatization*, 130.

trolling enterprises and networks of thirsty tick companies. Slovakia's remarkable decade of recovery, integration and rapid growth (1998–2008) would have been replaced by the destruction of Slovak savings in hyperinflation.

The most important watershed in Slovakia's economic development was, therefore, the mass mobilization and defeat of Mečiar in 1998. The new government of Mikuláš Dzurinda (1998–2002) was a broad coalition that had little ideological coherence beyond an agreement that Mečiar had to go and that Slovakia had to do what it took to get back into the good graces of the European Union and NATO. Beyond that, the presence in the government of the right-wing Slovak Christian and Democratic Union (SKDÚ) and the ex-communist Social Democratic Left (SDL'), ensured that the government bickered over reforms and new steps towards deep economic transformation.

The most pressing task was to clean up the fiscal mess left from the last two years of Mečiar's government. Inheriting a budget deeply in deficit, and with credit markets reeling from the Asian financial crisis, the new government had no choice but to cut expenses—adding to already soaring unemployment. However, the government was also able to use the long strings of VSŽ debt to seize control of the company, stabilize it, and then sell it to US Steel. Similar tactics helped tame a number of Mečiar-era oligarchs. The diverse parties in the government also agreed on the need to make up lost time in accession to the European Union. Slovakia became one of the EU's most willing pupils in negotiations over the *Acquis Communitaire*. Indeed, EU conditions helped resolve a number of issues that the ideologically incoherent first Dzurinda government was otherwise incapable of resolving.[21]

The 2002 parliamentary elections served as the next major turning point in Slovakia's economic development. A collapse of the left (especially the SDL) in the polls allowed Dzurinda to establish a more coherent, center-right coalition government. This provided an opportunity for a well-placed group of neoliberal policy-makers to rewrite aspects of Slovakia's social contract along neoliberal lines. Given the

---

[21] Wade Jacoby, "Tutors and Pupils: International Organizations, Central European Elites and Western Models," *Governance* 14, no. 2 (2001): 169–200; Milada Anna Vachudova, *Europe Undivided: Democracy, Leverage and Integration after Communism* (Oxford: Oxford University Press, 2005).

recovery in global markets and four years of enterprise restructuring in Slovakia, it is quite likely that the country would have fared well over the next five years, even if it had no change in government. However, Slovakia's remarkable performance from 2003–2008 was at the very least abetted by neoliberal reforms passed mostly in 2003–2004.

Neoliberals believe that societies will perform better when individuals are responsible for their own well-being—when there are significant personal rewards for success and clear penalties for failure. As such, they seek to reduce the influence of institutions that socialize the risk of failure in the economy.[22] As a governance philosophy, neoliberalism has a particular appeal in post-communist Europe—especially among a group of communist-era dissidents who, like Friedrich Hayek, associate collectivist governance strategies with communist authoritarianism. Moreover, most of the institutions promoting social solidarity in Slovakia have communist-era roots and share that era's inefficiency, indifference to clients, corruption, and bureaucratic bloat. Neoliberalism promised a decisive blow to institutions that cause entrepreneurs and state clients deeply alienation and frustration.

While neoliberals portrayed their policies as a technocratic improvement over state-orchestrated solutions to social problems, in principle the neoliberal agenda had distributional consequences—clear groups of winners and losers. Neoliberalism's greatest appeal was among young, educated citizens whose work related to Slovakia's growing, globally integrated economic sectors. Naturally, those at most risk of falling on hard times or who relied heavily on state services and transfers were more skeptical. They saw the neoliberal promise to make individuals responsible for their own well-being and less responsible for carrying the burden of others as a clear threat. Given the large population in Slovakia that fell into this latter category, neoliberalism in practice was wide open to a populist counterattack.

Accordingly, Dzurinda's second-term neoliberals never had the power to completely transform society, but they did accomplish a lot. Their main achievements were in fiscal restraint, taxation, and the labor code. Minister of Finance Ivan Mikloš fought hard to meet the

---

[22] Sharon Fisher, John Gould and Tim Haughton, "Slovakia's Neoliberal Turn," *Europe-Asia Studies* 59, no. 6 (2007): 977–8.

EU's Maastricht convergence criteria—especially reducing the annual public finance deficit to below 3 percent. Mikloš also secured a flat corporate and income tax that he argued increased investment while not significantly harming overall revenues. Opponents dissented, arguing that a flat tax was deeply unfair to the poor. Shouldn't the rich pay more? Nevertheless, as Mikloš predicted, tax collection rates increased as the combination of a reasonable 19 percent tax rate and less bureaucracy encouraged people to declare their income and corporations to take their profits in Slovakia. On paper, the new code shifted the burden of taxation from the rich to the middle class. In reality, however, many in both the rich and middle classes were paying into the system for the first time—an important accomplishment.[23]

The new government also passed an important amendment to the labor code that made it easier and cheaper for enterprises to hire and fire workers. Additional reforms were implemented or at least attempted in the areas of health, pensions, and justice education, with mixed success. But the combination of more flexible labor, reasonable bureaucracy, and low taxes proved to be a winner. Foreign and domestic investment boomed and Slovak growth soared. As demand for the Slovak koruna (SKK) grew, the National Bank of Slovakia deftly countered inflation by revaluing the SKK against the euro. In the process, Slovaks became richer international consumers while the currency revaluations kept inflation low. Slovakia's unacceptably high official levels of unemployment began to decline from near 20 percent in 2001 to below 10 percent in 2008 at the start of the financial crisis. The long line of workers seeking new jobs in the official economy kept wage pressures down. Slovak wages grew, but given labor's weakness under the neoliberal Dzurinda government, and heavy foreign investments in technology, worker productivity grew faster. Companies pocketed the difference but often reinvested in the economy.[24]

---

[23] The poor were exempt from paying income tax, but were still taxed on consumption via a 19 percent VAT. Ibid., 981.

[24] John A. Gould, "Slovakia's Neoliberal Churn: The Political Economy of the Fico Government, 2006–8," Institute of European Studies and International Relations, Faculty of Social and Economic Sciences, Comenius University, Working Paper 01/2009, p. 11, http://works.bepress.com/john_a_gould/.

The premature collapse of the Dzurinda coalition in 2006 led to the election of another ideologically incoherent coalition led by Robert Fico, whose party Smer—Social Democracy reconsolidated the electoral power of the left. Fico had campaigned against neoliberalism—emphasizing the popular themes of fairness and social solidarity. Unfortunately, to secure power, he had to rule with Mečiar's HZDS (now a pro-EU centrist party) and the extreme nationalist SNS. Both junior members appeared interested in little more than delivering benefits through corruption or otherwise to their clients. Smer secured the economic ministries, but was occasionally blocked by the HZDS and the SNS from taking major initiatives. More importantly, since Smer had inherited a fiscally sound, growing economy, well on its way to joining the eurozone in 2009, it made sense not to undertake a major policy change—despite Fico's rhetoric. In 2007, Slovak growth peaked at 10.4 percent, with only 2.8 percent inflation, a tight budget and rapidly falling unemployment. Fico took credit for the growth.[25]

Slovakia was now one of Europe's most open, capital friendly countries. The downside of deep global integration is that economic performance is highly dependent on demand in export markets over which the country has no control. Hence, in the fall of 2008–2009, when Europeans stopped buying midsized cars and flat screen TVs and investing in new factories to build them, Slovakia's growth ground to halt. Mečiar-era economists spent a lot of time in 2009 fruitlessly calling for a return to state-led growth strategies. However, with Slovakia's accession to the eurozone in January 2009 and frozen international credit markets, Slovakia could neither print nor borrow the money to do *anything* of consequence. By the time Slovakia's Western markets recovered, Fico's government had fallen, to be replaced with a new center-right coalition led by Iveta Radičová. However, internal bickering led to new elections in the spring of 2012 in which Fico's Smer won an outright majority. It remains to be seen whether this unprecedented one-party hegemony will be enough to balance the strictures of European integration and eurozone membership with Smer's promise to build a social market economy based on the principles of social solidarity.

---

[25] Gould, "Slovakia's Neoliberal Turn."

I began this essay by wondering what broader lessons might be drawn from the first twenty years of Slovak economic independence. My tentative answer is that Slovakia has now fully hitched its wagon to the global economy. The defeat of Mečiar in 1998 permitted deeper European capital and market integration—a project leading to EU membership in 2004. Eurozone accession in 2009 deepened Slovakia's external dependence with the surrender of monetary policy controls to the European Central Bank. For better or for worse, the most important economic development in Slovakia's economy is determined by a group of multinational bankers in Frankfurt and European consumers.

The horse pulling Slovakia's economic wagon is now more likely to follow German than Slovak commands. Yet, economic policy in Slovakia is not meaningless. Poor government choices make the wagon harder to pull and give a more comfortable ride to the few at the expense of the many. Good government choices make the wagon easier to pull and give a more comfortable ride to the many at the expense of the few. Government choices also help determine the number of people that falls off the wagon and how much time, if ever, it takes them to climb back on. These are the challenges of the next twenty years. They will be at the heart of the ongoing contest between left and right, and between individualism and social solidarity. Slovakia may have surrendered economic autonomy over the last twenty years, but its political struggles will continue to have vital importance to its citizens' economic well-being.

CHAPTER 13

Economic Developments in the Czech Republic, 1993–2013

Martin Pospíšil[1]

This paper deals with economic developments in the Czech Republic in the last two decades and attempts to analyze problems related to the historically unprecedented process of transition from a command to a market economy. These twenty years were marked by economic reforms, economic convergence, three crises,[2] and a large inflow of foreign capital, among others. Despite many mistakes, Czech economic development was a success, and the lessons that economists and policy makers have learned from these mistakes can serve as an example for other countries. In this article, we will describe key actors, policies, and outcomes with a focus on the question of what Czech society has gained over the last twenty years. At the same time, the transition was probably not as successful as hoped, especially at the beginning of the 1990s, when the Czechs were expecting a fast economic convergence with Western Europe. The Czech transition became a mix of shocks and gradualist steps and was not as rapid as many had expected.

---

[1] This paper benefited from discussions with Karel Kouba, Lubomír Mlčoch, Jibran Punthakey, Jiří Schwarz, and Iryna Momotenko. Special thanks go to Sharon Fisher, who was kind enough to review the paper in detail, and to Mark Stolarik, who organized the conference entitled "The Czech and Slovak Republics: Twenty Years of Independence, 1993–2013," where this chapter was presented. The author also wishes to thank participants in the conference for their active discussion of its contents. All errors are mine.

[2] The transition crisis, the 1997 currency crisis, and the 2008 global economic crisis.

With a little simplification, we can distinguish three periods of Czech economic development over the recent past: The initial transformation (1991–1997), convergence (1998–2007), and the global crisis (2008–today). We conclude with future prospects for the Czech economy.

Recent Czech economic developments cannot be discussed without analyzing the Czechoslovak economy before 1993 and Slovakia after 1993. During 1918–1939, the Czech Lands belonged to the top fifteen most industrialized countries in the world, and "rivaled their neighbors in Western Europe," while during the communist era its economy almost collapsed. In 1989, at the end of forty years of communist rule, Czechoslovakia was one of the most centrally planned economies in the world. While, for example, neighboring Poland and Hungary had some experience with the introduction of market mechanisms in the 1980s, Czechoslovakia entered the 1990s as an almost fully centrally planned economy. The private sector did not exist; almost all productive assets were owned by the state; and there was neither a concept of corporate governance nor a financial market.[3] The irrational communist administrative price system led to an inefficient allocation of resources and contributed to the failure of the planned Czechoslovak economy. Wages were centrally set; there was no unemployment;[4] and, most of all, price allocation mechanisms were completely missing. The major shortcomings of the command economy were perverse incentives and limited innovation. After fifty years of isolation from Western markets during World War II and the communist regime, Czechoslovakia's industry was in a state of collapse. The 1989 Velvet Revolution, therefore, offered a chance for reforms that could leading to profound and sustained economic growth in Czechoslovakia.

---

[3] Jan Bena and Jan Hanousek, "Rent Extraction by Large Shareholders: Evidence Using Dividend Policy in the Czech Republic," *Czech Journal of Economics and Finance (Finance a Úvěr)* 58, no. 3 (2008): 8.

[4] While in 1990 unemployment was below 1 percent (Jan Švejnar and Milica Uvalic. "The Czech Transition: The Importance of Microeconomic Fundamentals," *UNU-WIDER Research Paper* 17 (2009): 17), it reached more than 10 percent in the 2000s.

As politics has had a strong impact on economics throughout the past twenty years in the Czech Republic, it is worth mentioning the main political players. The political background for economic reform was largely created in the Prognostic Institute of the Czech Academy of Sciences by a generation of economists with free-market views: Václav Klaus—Minister of Finance of the Czech and Slovak Federative Republic (1990–1992), Prime Minister of the Czech Republic (1992–1998), Chairman (Speaker) of the Chamber of Deputies (1998–2002), and President (2003–2013); Karel Dyba—Minister of the Economy (1990–1996); and Vladimír Dlouhý—Deputy Prime Minister of the first government after the Velvet Revolution (1989–1990), Minister of the Economy of the Czech and Slovak Federative Republic (1990–1992) and Minister of Industry and Trade of the Czech Republic (1992–1997). One of the architects of economic reform was another member of the Prognostic Institute, Tomáš Ježek. As the Minister for Privatization in 1990–1992 (and the Chairman of the National Property Fund, 1992–1994), Ježek was publicly associated with the privatization process. Ježek later became a strong critic of Klaus's privatization policies, which effectually ended their long-standing friendship.[5]

The first half of the 1990s however, represented a successful beginning to the Czechoslovak and Czech transition. A fundamental change to the economic environment was needed. The basic elements were privatization, price and international trade liberalization, avoidance of hyperinflation, and the creation of a social welfare system. As there was no ready-made economic (transition) program before 1989, the process was created without real knowledge, under the pressure of time, but with the support of the general public.

At the international level, the theoretical background to the economic transition in Central and Eastern Europe came from neoclassical

---

[5] For an overview of Ježek's criticism of the Czech transition and privatization outcomes, see Tomáš Ježek, *Zrození ze zkumavky. Svědectví o české privatizaci 1990–1997* [Shocked by research: witness to the Czech privatization, 1990–1997] (Prague: Prostor, 2007).

economics and the Washington Consensus legacy.[6] The theory argued that the economy's performance is determined by a rational allocation of scarce resources, market competition, and hard budget constraints. The Washington Consensus[7] was a set of policies for promoting economic growth that were first prepared for Latin American countries in the 1980s. The prescription included trade and investment liberalization, and expansion of markets. As such, it also affected the transition of Czechoslovakia. The adherents of the Washington Consensus basically believed that successful economic transition means privatization, liberalization, and stabilization.[8]

However, the ideas of the Washington Consensus did not fully succeed. For example, policies of liberalization and privatization without a strong institutional framework were not sufficient for long-term growth in Central and Eastern Europe, as they did not take into account different historic and institutional differences,[9] which play a crucial role

---

[6] The Washington Consensus is an informal agreement among the most powerful international institutions based in Washington, D.C., such as the International Monetary Fund and the World Bank.

[7] In the 1950s, Western economies suffered from various problems including macroeconomic instability, high debt, slow economic growth, high inflation, and unemployment. This malfunctioning of the markets was fuelled by the malfunctioning of governments and their expansive fiscal policies, subventions, and high income redistribution. In the 1970s and 1980s, these problems were treated with privatization and liberalization, which in fact forms the Washington Consensus.

[8] Jens Holscher, "Twenty Years of Economic Transition: Successes and Failures," *The Journal of Comparative Economic Studies (JCES)* (The Japanese Society for Comparative Economic Studies (JSCES), 5, (December 2009): 3–17.

[9] The World Bank (2002) defines institutions as the rules of the economic game. These include both formal rules and informal norms. Since institutions "place restrictions on undesired kinds of individual behavior" (Gerard Roland, "Ten Years After...Transition and Economics." *IMF Staff Papers* 48 (special issue, 2001): 29–52), they can reduce uncertainty. Institutions are solutions to asymmetrical information problems, as they secure property rights through legal and judicial systems, competition policy, financial systems, and political institutions (Cristina Matos, "Post-socialist Transformation and Institutions," Paper prepared for the 2005 SASE conference "What Counts? Calculation, Representation, Association," Central European University and Corvinus University of Budapest, Budapest, June 30–July 2, 2005).

in economic development.¹⁰ For example, Karel Kouba et al. argue that the transition programs in Central and Eastern Europe lacked the creation of an institutional framework that would minimize microeconomic weaknesses and support macroeconomic policy.¹¹ Later, even John Williamson, author of the Washington Consensus, admitted that the consensus did not bring the expected results and he argued that "second-generation reforms" were needed. This involved strengthening institutions to allow the first-generation reforms to be fully implemented. At the same time, in the Czech Republic—unlike in other countries of Eastern Europe—Washington Consensus organizations (the International Monetary Fund—IMF and the World Bank) had rather limited influence over the economic policies.¹²

Starting in 1990, the Czechoslovak government decided to create a fixed exchange rate for the CSK vis-à-vis major world currencies, which was complemented with a currency devaluation (the government devalued with respect to convertible currencies and revalued with respect to the Russian ruble). The choice of an exchange rate was made by the central bank and the government. Even left-leaning economists, who did not take part in the decision-making process at the beginning of the 1990s, saw the relatively low exchange rate vis-à-vis Western currencies as quite acceptable. The low exchange rate made people relatively worse off, but it supported exports and economic growth. After several currency adjustments, the CSK remained relatively stable in relation to the USD. The result was a rate of 28 Kčs to the USD with a 20 percent surcharge on imports. The Czechoslovak government also introduced some temporary stabilization and anti-inflationary administrative regulations. The money supply had to be restricted in order to avoid the inflation that occurred in many Central and Eastern European countries. For example, Murrell estimates that Eastern European

---

¹⁰ See for example Dani Rodrik, "Understanding Economic Policy Reform," *Journal of Economic Literature*, (March, 1996). Holscher, "Twenty Years," summarizes the fundamental differences between the Washington Consensus and the evolutionary-institutional approach.

¹¹ Karel Kouba, Ondrej Vychodil, and Jitka Roberts, *Privatizace bez kapitálu. Zvýšené tranzakční náklady české transformace* [Privatization without capital. The increasing costs of the Czech transformation. (Prague, Národohospodářský ústav Josefa Hlávky, 2004).

¹² Švejnar and Uvalic, *The Czech Transition*, 6.

inflation averaged 610% (which excluded Serbia's hyperinflation). In Table 1 we show that in Czechoslovakia, inflation was "only" 52% in 1991 but decreased immediately thereafter. After the price liberalization, the Czech Republic managed to reduce inflation below 10 percent by 1994, much more quickly than occurred in neighboring Poland or Hungary. This avoidance of hyperinflation and the establishment of price stability was a major success.[13] The regulation of wages was also necessary, but took too long and made the economy rigid for longer than necessary.

Despite the stabilization measures, the decrease in the GDP and in industrial production was huge in the early 1990s. With the liberalization of trade at the beginning of 1991 and the collapse of Eastern markets, the downturn was severe. This is often referred to as the "transition recession." Before the collapse of communism in 1989, the Soviet Union accounted for 44 percent of Czechoslovakia's total exports. When the Soviet market collapsed, the shift towards Western countries was difficult for both the Czech and Slovak economies. Local companies were producing goods that did not meet the basic standards required by Western markets. German reunification in 1990 represented another problem because East Germany had been an important trading partner for Czechoslovakia.

Moreover, as a consequence of these shocks, a large part of Slovak industry (mostly heavy industry) collapsed and Slovak unemployment increased from 1.5 percent in 1990 to over 10 percent in 1992, while it remained at around 4 percent in the Czech Republic until the second stage of reforms (see Table 1). This difference contributed to the decision to dissolve Czechoslovakia as of January 1, 1993. The newly formed Czech and Slovak Republics kept close economic ties but their developments over the past twenty years have differed. While Slovakia was much poorer than the Czech lands when Czechoslovakia was cre-

---

[13] In January 1992, the first-ever credit rating (the speculative grade of Ba1) of Czechoslovakia was issued by Moody's through the rating of the State Bank of Czechoslovakia. In March 1993, Moody's upgraded its rating to Baa3 and the Czech Republic thus became the first post-communist country to obtain an investment grade (Czech National Bank, *Inflation Report 2011*). The liberalization of the capital account took place only in 1995 when the Czech Republic entered the OECD.

ated in 1918, by 1989, it had converged strongly to the Czech part. For a few weeks after the split in 1993, the old CSK was still used in both countries, but very soon national currencies were adopted (first with an equal exchange rate but very soon the new SKK became much weaker than its Czech twin). The devaluation of the SKK made the country's goods relatively cheaper and more competitive.

The Václav Klaus governments in the 1990s continued reforming the Czech economy, opening the country towards international trade and in the mid-1990s applied for admission into the European Union and NATO. At the same time, Vladimír Mečiar, who as prime minister of Slovakia had negotiated the Czechoslovak split with Klaus, followed a different path. His government was criticized for its autocratic style, along with nontransparent privatization of national companies to the benefit of his allies, and isolation from the West (with a much slower pace of EU and NATO accession negotiations). In both countries, however, shifting emphasis from the East to the West necessitated restructuring virtually all industries (e.g., manufacturing or telecommunications)[14] for which a well-functioning financial sector was necessary.

Banking reform also needed to become part of the economic transformation. Under communism, the role of banks was to allocate funds to firms according to a central plan. The interest rate did not fulfill any of the functions that it does in a market economy (e.g., reflecting supply of and demand for credit, allocation of risk, price of time preference). During communism, enterprises operated without working capital, paying each other on the basis of permanent credits issued by the state bank. Due to the absence of prices reflecting supply and demand, there was no information on the financial status of individual firms. Therefore, the Czechoslovak banking system entered the transition with virtually nonexistent risk management skills and limited knowledge of the real value of assets. To create a viable financial system, the central bank was separated from commercial banks in 1991, and a year later a stock market was created. However, commercial banks were not

---

[14] The Czech telecommunications industry was partially privatized in 1995 when 27 percent of the shares were sold to international investors for over 1.3 billion USD (EBRD, *Transition Report 1998*, 34).

privatized, which caused a collapse of the economy in 1997, which we will analyze later.

Another important element of the transition was privatization. Klaus's government believed in the free market and preferred to privatize and liberalize quickly in order to prevent the communists from taking control of most enterprises. In the end, Czechoslovakia/the Czech Republic pursued a two-track policy of small-scale privatization (between 1990 and 1993 when tens of thousands of small businesses were auctioned off) and large-scale privatization. Part of the large-scale privatization was the so-called voucher privatization.[15] This privatization was a special mechanism, which allowed the state to hand over (privatize) state enterprises (some 1,500 companies) to the general public (private sector), turning Czechs into a nation of stockholders. The voucher privatization system was chosen mostly to speed up the pace of reform. Also, it was seen as an equitable, transparent and fair way to give purchasing power to the population. According to this plan, every citizen was given the opportunity to buy a book of vouchers that represented potential shares in any state-owned company. The idea was to create a vibrant capitalist economy very quickly. At the same time, voucher privatization was heavily criticized by the opposition. Miloš Zeman, leader of the Social Democratic Party (ČSSD), dismissed voucher privatization as "the fraud of the century" and argued that the Czech Republic would become the first state that "has succeeded in almost completely robbing itself."[16] His views sounded extreme at the beginning of 1990s when Klaus's government still had broad public support and journalists did not question this economic transformation too much. Only later was Zeman able to use this rhetoric to win the elections in 1998.

In general, privatization was expected to bring financial health to companies, generate revenues for the state, and minimize the moral hazard. However, as Tomáš Ježek noted, there was a fundamental difference between the Czechoslovak (or Czech) privatization and priva-

---

[15] See Jan Hanousek and Evžen Kočenda "The Impact of Czech Mass Privatization on Corporate Governance," *Journal of Economic Studies* 30, nos. 3/4 (2003) 278–93 for a brief account of the impact of Czech mass privatization on corporate governance.

[16] Martin Myant, *The Rise and Fall of Czech Capitalism: Economic Development in the Czech Republic Since 1989* (London: Edward Elgar, 2003), 114.

tization in Western countries (e.g., in the UK in 1980s). While in Western Europe, the intention was to increase the efficiency of enterprises, while assuming that private ownership is more efficient than state ownership, in the Czech Republic privatization was a tool to fundamentally change the socioeconomic system.[17] There was no capital in Czech hands at the beginning of the privatization process, no local investors prepared to invest in the enterprises and modernize them to be competitive. This can be defined as "privatization without capital." There is a long-running argument about whether the voucher privatization should have been substituted with privatization using standard methods. On the one hand, privatization using standard methods would have taken much longer (probably more than a decade), and, therefore, state ownership in the economy would have continued; the economy would not have been modernized quickly. On the other hand, if the standard method had been used, several enterprises might have been transformed, saved, and sold later at a higher price. However, Ježek explains that Czech privatization could not have been a revenue-maximizing exercise because it was not possible to wait for the locals to acquire enough capital to invest in enterprises. Moreover, waiting for the highest bidder could have taken too long and speedy privatization was vital to the Czech Republic.

Real estate restitutions also played a role in the Czech transition. The Czech Republic had the strongest restitution program in Central Europe with the period of expropriation defined as the beginning of the communist regime on February 25, 1948. One issue was what kinds of assets should be covered in the restitution program. Because of the difficulties involved in proving the confiscation of movable physical property and financial assets and establishing current values for them, Klaus's government decided to include only real property in the resti-

---

[17] Švejnar and Uvalic, *The Czech Transition*: 67, note that privatization does not necessarily lead to better economic performance if privatized firms can still rely on subsidies without microeconomic restructuring. Stepan Jurajda and Juraj Stancik "Foreign Ownership and Corporate Performance: The Czech Republic at EU Entry," *Czech Journal of Economics and Finance (Finance a Úvěr)* 62, no.4 (August, 2012): 306–24. They find that the impact of foreign investors on domestic acquisitions is small in both services and manufacturing industries competing on international markets and significantly positive only in non-exporting manufacturing industries.

tution. In the end, privatization through real estate restitution to the original owners was quickly completed.

Finally, small businesses that were not returned to their original owners under the restitution were auctioned off. At the same time, since most of the large businesses had been nationalized by the pre-communist regime between 1945 and 1948, only a few large industrial enterprises were restored to their original owners.

In effect, while in 1990, the private sector represented a mere 10 percent of GDP in the Czech Republic, by 1998 it reached 75 percent. This was another Klaus policy success and it was in line with his—at least verbal—focus on the rapidity of the transition as the key success factor.[18]

However, the Czech government had to face several obstacles to successful economic transformation. The financial sector and capital markets were only forming, property rights were not well defined, and market-oriented management was missing. Therefore, market players were unable to evaluate the assets of privatized companies. Centrally planned economies did not leave much room for true financial management and, therefore, the role of accounting was limited. Prices did not accurately represent information and since markets were only forming, it was impossible to estimate the value of privatized enterprises. Lewandowski even noted that privatization in Central and Eastern Europe is when someone who does not know the true owner and the true value of an asset sells something to somebody else who does not have any money. Communist accounting provided only virtual numbers. Thus, it is difficult to estimate how much value was actually shifted from the state to the private sector during privatization in the Czech Republic.

Therefore, a shadow economy grew in the 1990s. In the early 1990s, the informal economy (not taxed, monitored by the govern-

---

[18] The general discussion between academics and policy-makers was whether "shock therapy" or a "gradualist approach" towards reforms was preferred. Sergio Godoy and Joseph E. Stiglitz, "Growth, Initial Conditions, Law and Speed of Privatization in Transition Countries: 11 Years Later," in *Transition and Beyond—Essays in Honour of Mario Nuti*, eds. Saul Estrin, Grzegorz Kolodko and Milica Uvalić, (Basingstoke: Palgrave Macmillan, 2007) even reports that shock therapy could create conditions adverse to the creation of institutions that would themselves in the long run be conducive to growth.

ment, or included in GDP, unlike the formal economy) could not easily be distinguished from the new private sector. Johnson et al. estimate that the share of the informal economy increased from 6 percent to 11.3 percent of the GDP in the Czech Republic in the 1990s.[19] Matos even argues that Central and Eastern European governments, influenced by international agencies, feared that fighting underground activities would worsen the economic crisis.[20] The clash between the informal and the formal economies, between formal rules (legislation) and informal rules (culture, ethics) contributed to higher than expected transition costs in the Czech Republic. Formal rules were changed to a substantial extent at the beginning of the transition; the development of new informal rules was much slower.[21] Laws were passed, but people, mostly newly established businessmen, very often did not obey the rules and this noncompliance went unpunished because of the weak rule of law. Standards of behavior that were formed under communism were different from those formed in a democracy. Therefore, Czech society had to face long-lasting uncertainty and the process of economic development was distracted.[22] While new legislation was important, Alchian,[23] for example, stressed the importance of public moral

---

[19] Johnson Simon, Rafael La Porta, Florencio Lopez-de-Silanes, and Andrei Shleifer, *Tunneling*, NBER Working Paper no. 7523. (February 2000).

[20] Cristina Matos, *Post-Socialist Employment 'Informalisation': Hungary and the Czech Republic*, EAEPE 2002 Conference on Complexity and the Economy (Aix-en-Provence, November 7–11, 2002).

[21] Friedrich Hayek, *Rules and Order. Vol. 1 of Law, Legislation and Liberty* (London: Routledge & Kegan Paul), in which a whole chapter is devoted to the need to develop moral rules, which cannot be easily substituted with formal rules.

[22] In this respect, Chavance explores the relations between change in formal and informal rules and discusses rationality of formal institutions and detrimental inertia of informal institutions (Bernard Chavance, "Formal and Informal Institutional Change: The Experience of Postsocialist Transformation," *The European Journal of Comparative Economics* 5, no. 1 (2008): 57–71). He identifies two not directly compatible theories that influenced the new institutional economics' understanding of transition: Hayek's and North's theories of change, respectively.

[23] Alchian is a pioneer in theories of property rights, which, in 1974, was formally introduced by Svetozar Pejovich, ed., *The Economics of Property Rights* (Cambridge, MA: Ballinger Publishing, 1974).

and social ostracism as well. These elements were underestimated by the reformers.

The Czech (and Slovak) transitions, therefore, showed that institutions are the determining factors in modern economic development. Good institutions (e.g., law enforcement, corporate governance, and also ethics) determine transaction costs, which explain economic performance. Both Czech and Slovak transition programs, however, forgot to stress these institutional factors that would have enabled the economy to cope with fragile microeconomic development. There was a belief that privatization and liberalization would create the demand for market infrastructure on its own. This assumption was criticized by Stiglitz.[24] Roland notes that Czech privatization has led to very nontransparent corporate governance.[25] Moreover, there was a general reluctance to focus on laws governing transparency (e.g., against money-laundering or fraud). Josef Zieleniec, then Minister of Foreign Affairs, noted that if the government had started with anticorruption laws "there would have been no transformation."[26] Czech privatization has simply not been a result of a spontaneous evolutionary processes in the market, as explained by Hayek.[27]

At the same time, privatization without capital was a good example of the need for external investors. Too often a change of ownership from the Czech state to Czech private hands was not sufficient, mostly because new local owners lacked the funds to transform and develop newly acquired companies. These factors led to higher transition costs, since locally privatized enterprises had to be sold abroad after a few years in any case. Foreign capital was needed. However, the approach of the Klaus government to foreign investors was reserved. Foreigners were strangers to most of the general public. It was also not politically feasible to sell all enterprises to foreigners, and foreign investors did

---

[24] Joseph E. Stiglitz, *Globalization and its Discontents* (New York and London: W. W. Norton, 2002).
[25] Roland, "Ten Years After," 29–52.
[26] Myant, *The Rise and Fall*, 117.
[27] See, for example, Friedrich Hayek, *The Constitution of Liberty*, (London: Routledge & Kegan Paul: 1960) or Christian Petsoulas, *Hayek's Liberalism and Its Origins: His Idea of Spontaneous Order and the Scottish Enlightenment* (London, Routledge, 2001).

not have much interest in investing in struggling companies. Despite that, some companies were successfully privatized into foreign hands (such as Škoda Auto) but the state usually had to invest a lot (to lift the companies' debt burden, to modernize, to pay for ecological damages, et cetera) before the investor signed the contract. Western investors brought with them not only capital, but also knowhow, and most importantly, they had access to new markets. This increased the pressure to modernize companies in the Czech Republic.

This first part of Czech economic development was successful when it came to macroeconomic stabilization and fundamental reforms to many parts of the economy. This was also because of a relatively favorable heritage from the late communist era of modest external debt, relatively stable public finances and a limited monetary overhang.

After several years, however, the political reform ethos vanished in the Czech Republic. The reason might have been that the Klaus government feared the social impact of further reforms (linked with necessary increases in unemployment), and suffered from overall political self-confidence or excessive satisfaction with the already achieved results. Unemployment was still relatively low due to the insufficient transformation of many large enterprises. This allowed Klaus's Civic Democratic Party (ODS) to win the largest number of votes again in 1996 (as one of the rare leaders in Central and Eastern Europe who managed to win twice in a row) and to form a minority government tolerated by Zeman's ČSSD.

In the end, the Czech transition became a mix of shocks and gradualist steps. While, for example, the macroeconomic stabilization program consisted of measures typical of shock therapy, the Czech government also implemented a more gradualist approach. For example, the government was reluctant to close large, inefficient, and often economically unviable, state-owned firms and tolerated significant inter-enterprise debt, which prevented a dramatic increase in unemployment.[28] State-owned banks continued to finance inefficient companies and unemployment remained low, leading to overemployment. Labor productivity remained low and microeconomic transformation remained

---

[28] See Dyba and Švejnar, "Stabilization and Transition" or EBRD, *Transition Report 1998*.

largely unfinished. During the 1990s, inefficient firms were not forced into bankruptcy, they faced soft-budget constraints and when they needed state subsidies, they received them. Therefore, a failure to create effective bankruptcy laws that would drive inefficient companies into receivership was also a shortcoming of the reform.

During the transition period, the Czechs gained economic and political liberties, businesses could start accessing Western markets, and citizens could acquire private property (e.g., through voucher privatization). At the same time, weak microeconomic, and especially institutional parts of the Czech economy, contributed to the 1997 currency and banking crisis. Many people lost their jobs during the transition and became poorer in real terms than they had been under communism. It needs to be noted that the Czech Republic reached the average level of its 1989 real GDP only in 2001. This means that for ten years the country effectively stagnated in terms of average income. Moreover, many companies were unable to cope with competition from the West and had to cease operations. Unfortunately, this included many traditional Czech brands (e.g., Eska, Favorit, LIAZ, or Karosa).

By 1997, the level of private ownership in the Czech Republic was close to that of developed market economies. At the same time, the banking sector remained weak and underdeveloped. While the Czech banking system was in better shape than the Polish or Hungarian ones at the beginning of the 1990s, over time it lost this position. Bad loans remained a major obstacle to both microeconomic and macroeconomic development. In the 1990s, Czech banks were owned by privatization funds and these funds entered the system of voucher privatization by buying various enterprises. These enterprises required funding and the banks—which were at the same time partial owners of these enterprises—provided the funding. In economics this is referred to as a "moral hazard." This was caused by a hidden form of stealing assets from a company called tunneling.[29] Many companies received loans without intending to repay them. This process was sometimes referred

---

[29] Edward Glaeser, Simon Johnson and Andrei Shleifer, "Coase Versus the Coasians," *Quarterly Journal of Economics* 116, no. 3 (August, 2001): 2. Note that this form of stealing assets from minority shareholders "was so widespread in the Czech Republic as to acquire a new, Czech-specific name—tunnelling."

to as "state capitalism" or "bank socialism."[30] Therefore, probably the biggest drawbacks of the initial transformation process were the late privatization of banks because state-owned banks were not able to assess risk properly.

Due to this unfinished microeconomic transformation, which increased the current account deficit, and the political crisis of 1997, investors started selling their Czech crowns faster than the government could buy them. The country had to abandon its exchange rate peg, the centerpiece of its macroeconomic strategy since 1991. The formerly pegged currency was forced to float (see Table 1 for the evolution of the exchange rate). This had a negative impact on the economy. The government even had to introduce temporary import barriers to tackle growing macroeconomic instability. In addition, the government had to introduce austerity measures. GDP decreased by 0.85 percent in 1997, and by 0.24 percent in 1998 (see Table 1).

The 1997 banking crisis showed that, despite favorable initial macroeconomic conditions, a country can still fail if it does not reform at the microeconomic level. Due to this additional business cycle in 1997, unexpectedly high transition costs occurred in the Czech Republic. The moral hazard of key players (the state, banks, investors, firms) contributed to the estimated total costs linked with Czech bank socialism of 30 billion EUR. The banking sector remained weak until the early 2000s. For example, in the year 2000, the IPB, one of the largest banks in the country, was forced into receivership.

After being charged with corruption, Klaus's government had to resign in 1997. An interim bureaucratic government, led by the governor of the Czech National Bank, was formed until new elections were held in 1998. Politicians responded to the period of major financial instability in 1997–1998 by setting financial stability as an important goal of the Czech National Bank's policies. In December 1997—after the economic turmoil—the Czech National Bank started targeting inflation, which proved to be a successful monetary policy and led to a gradual decrease in inflation. In 2001, the law changed the main goal of the Czech National Bank from currency exchange rate stability to price

---

[30] See e.g., Lubomír Mlčoch, "Czech Privatization: A Criticism of the Misunderstood Liberalism (A Keynote Address)," *Journal of Business Ethics* 17 (July, 1998): 957.

stability. Thanks to the inflation-targeting regime, Czech inflation has remained around two percent since 2001.

From 1998–2006, the Czech government was led by the ČSSD. The party won the largest number of seats in 1998 and its leader Miloš Zeman formed a minority government. He immediately released a report saying that Czech privatization and the lack of institutions was the "main cause for the structural crisis in the economy."[31] The consequences of the 1997 currency crisis pushed the Zeman government to pursue "long-overdue bank privatizations and reforms in the securities markets, finally tackling the incestuous ties between banks, investment funds and large enterprises that have undermined real progress in corporate governance reform and enterprise restructuring." Banking groups were privatized by Belgian, Italian, Austrian, and French interests. Also, a new bankruptcy law was adopted and business forms were standardized. This was the crucial prerequisite for the strong Czech economic recovery between 1998 and 2007.

It was only during this decade that the Czech Republic's transition from a developing to a developed country was completed. During this period, corporate governance, judiciary administration, bankruptcy laws, banking and capital market regulation and financial oversight were gradually improved, partly in response to pressures from the European Union. (The Czech Republic entered into the EU in 2004.) From about 2000, the Czech Republic returned to continuous growth, which was assisted by strong investment performance. Economic reforms and related integration into the European Union brought income convergence as well. Already in 1998, the country started to negotiate with the European Union and had to fulfill many requirements of the *acquis communautaire* for EU accession. In the post-entry years the country also improved in the area of securities markets and non-banking financial institutions.[32]

In the mid-2000s, the Czech Republic reached record GDP growth rates of over 6 percent, which subsequently led to a decrease in the unemployment rate to around 5 percent (see Table 1). Further decreases were constrained by geographical and skills mismatches and

---

[31] Myant, *The Rise and Fall*, 114.
[32] See, e.g., European Bank of Reconstruction and Development, *Transition Report 2005* (London: 2005).

low labor mobility. The economics of this decade of growth were based on foreign investment, household consumption, gross capital formation, and, to some extent, government consumption. While the Czech Republic's sovereign rating worsened as a consequence of the monetary turbulence of 1997–1998, from around 2002 it steadily improved. This improvement, together with decreasing inflation, fostered a downward trend in yields on Czech government bonds. This cheap borrowing led the ČSSD government to overspend. Little progress was made on fiscal reform during their governments (1998–2006), although the relatively strong economic growth would have provided a good opportunity for reform. The periods of pro-cyclical fiscal policy were dominant, which was against the desirable counter-cyclical fiscal policy.

By comparison, in Slovakia a pro-reformist government did not appear until 1998, when Mikuláš Dzurinda united several center-right wing parties and defeated Vladimír Mečiar in the elections. Soon thereafter Slovakia re-entered the economic and political integration processes with the EU, NATO, and the OECD and most of all, implemented reforms that changed the country. Slovakia joined the EU in 2004, which had seemed unimaginable under Mečiar's government in the 1990s. Slovakia then emerged as the Central European "tiger" and has clearly overtaken the Czech Republic in terms of economic reforms.

Generally speaking, in the Czech Republic (as well as in Slovakia and other countries of the region), the decade of 1998–2007 can be characterized by a large inflow of foreign investment, increasing GDP and wages. When it comes to foreign trade, both countries have benefited from their favorable geographical position. Being located close to Germany and Austria, while having a significantly cheaper labor force, has been very attractive for foreign investors. On top of that, the government even intensified its policies to attract foreign direct investment; the public investment promotion agency CzechInvest played an instrumental role in attracting several the large investors. This inflow of foreign investment also financed the current account deficit. Several instruments were used to attract investors: tax incentives, employment subsidies, financial support for training, and investment incentives in the form of transferring the ownership of land and the related infrastructure at an advantageous price.

After the introduction of these instruments, net FDI inflows increased significantly and the Czech Republic became very successful recipients of foreign investment. One of the most important became the automobile sector, with several large greenfield investments (investments in an area where no previous facilities exist). Strong demand from European important markets led to a significant increase in car exports and profitability in related sectors in both the Czech and Slovak Republics.

Moreover, several remaining large state-owned companies were now privatized (e.g., utilities and telecommunications). Czech exporters managed to learn how to live with the appreciating crown, which also contributed to low inflation. Germany replaced Russia and became the main trading partner of the Czech Republic and Czech trade then became strongly linked to German exports. While external factors (FDI, external borrowing, and international trade) played a relatively minor role at the beginning of the 1990s, their importance increased with higher integration into the European economy. After eight years of leftist governments in the Czech Republic, the ČSSD lost the elections in 2006. The newly formed center-right coalition would have to cope with the upcoming global economic turmoil. At the end of 2007, the Czech Republic graduated from the European Bank of Reconstruction and Development, which unofficially ended the economic transition.

The Czech Republic entered the 2008 crisis with relatively strong fundamentals. Public debt was increasing but still relatively low, and there was virtually no assets price bubble. The first phase of the crisis was avoided in the Czech Republic because Czech banks—having experienced the 1997 banking crisis—were relatively prudent in their lending practices and avoided investments in toxic assets. Moreover, low inflation and macroeconomic stability led to virtually nonexistent foreign currency loans in the Czech Republic. This was important after the fall of Lehman Brothers in New York, when, despite the depreciation of the CZK, the Czech National Bank started cutting interest rates to support economic growth. This was not possible in some other Central and Eastern European countries, where rapid exchange rate depreciation could have threatened firms' and citizens' balance sheets because of foreign exchange borrowing.

From 2006 until 2013, the Czech government was again led by the ODS. This party, founded and led by Václav Klaus in the 1990s, was now chaired by Mirek Topolánek. (Klaus resigned as honorary ODS chairman in 2008 due to his disagreement with the party's politics.)

Topolánek's government tried to catch up on fiscal reform. In 2007, the Czech government announced that public finances were its first priority. The government increased the Value Added Tax (VAT), and implemented savings in social policy. As did many European governments during times of economic crisis, the Topolánek government had to violate the Maastricht criterion (a national budget deficit at or below 3 percent of GDP) and achieved a government deficit of 5.8 percent of GDP in 2009 and 4.8 percent in 2010. At the same time, the impact of fiscal austerity on GDP after the crisis was ambiguous. From today's perspective, the fiscal consolidation might appear as too strong since it most likely contributed to a prolonged economic slowdown in the years after the crisis. The Czech National Bank estimated that the 2009 government's anti-crisis package contributed to the GDP by 1.2 percent; the 2010 austerity package reduced the GDP by -0.9 percent, and the 2011 consolidation decreased the GDP by a further -0.6 percent.[33] Due to high uncertainty related to fiscal constraints, caps on public wages, and cuts to several social benefits, household consumption decreased. While between 2006 and 2008 consumption grew by 14.4 percent, it has stagnated since 2009.[34]

However, it would not be fair to negatively assess Topolánek's fiscal consolidation, which probably did not need to be as dramatic as it was in order to maintain market confidence, especially in 2013. Rather, mistakes were made by the preceding ČSSD-led government, when the fiscal "pillow" was not prepared for an economic slowdown. During the turbulent times of 2009 and 2010, it was, however, necessary to show confidence that the country was not going the "Greek" way of unsustainable public deficits. The "Greek question," i.e., how much the government should be allowed to borrow, was also one of the key topics in the 2010 elections. While the ČSSD won the largest number of seats in 2010, the party was unable to form a government due to limited coalition potential. The ODS-led government, therefore, continued, only with different coalition partners, until 2013.

Due to the export-dependence of the Czech economy, the second phase of the crisis hit the country as soon as the majority of EU coun-

---

[33] Czech National Bank, *Inflation Report 2012* (Prague, 2012), 42.
[34] Novotný, *From Reform to Growth*, 114.

tries started having problems in late 2008. As a reaction to the crisis, the exchange rate fell sharply, but stabilized when investors started to distinguish between the countries of Central and Eastern Europe. Especially in December 2008, the pressure on all Central and Eastern European currencies was very high.[35] The government established the Czech National Economic Council that aimed to prepare anti-crisis measures and to support the Czech EU presidency (the Czech Republic presided over the EU between January and June 2009). To support the local economy, the government also implemented a successful program for the renovation and insulation of buildings.

By November 2012, the Czech National Bank lowered its policy rate to zero. Contrary to many European countries, the Czech financial system (almost entirely foreign-owned) did not require support from the Czech state. (However, it benefitted indirectly from public support given to mother banks in their home countries, e.g., Belgium and France). The main reasons were the traditional orientation of Czech banks on retail banking rather than on investment banking and the virtually nonexistence of foreign currency loans in the Czech Republic. It was observed that the decline in credit after the events of 2008 was due to higher economic uncertainty, more prudent lending because of the pressure of mother banks from abroad, and lower demand for credit in general due to low aggregate demand. It can be argued that the Czech banking crisis of 1997 and subsequent privatization of Czech banks to Western global banking groups helped the Czech banking sector to learn how to better assess risk, which was one of the reasons why the Czech economy weathered the 2008 crisis relatively well.[36]

---

[35] Bakker and Klingen (2012: 295) describe an index that calculates the sum of the deviation of monthly changes in the nominal exchange rate vis-à-vis the euro from its mean and the deviation of the monthly change in international reserves in euros from their mean. The index dramatically increased in December 2008, especially for Ukraine, Poland, Russia, and Bulgaria, but also for the Czech Republic.

[36] Despite the avoidance of major economic shock, the 2008 crisis at first harshly affected firms in the Czech Republic. For example, Czech firms complained in 2009 that they were being hit by a credit crunch from banks reluctant to lend them money (*Czech Radio*, http://www.radio.cz/en/section/curraffrs/czech-companies-complain-credit-crunch-has-begun)

During the 2000s, the Czech economy started to benefit from the strong position of Germany and its deep ties with its economy. During 2006–2011, Germany accounted for around 30 percent of Czech foreign trade, and both exports and imports steadily increased since 2005 (with the exception of the year 2009, due to the global economic crisis, see Table 1). At the same time, Czech trade links with the problematic parts of the eurozone (Spain, Italy, Greece) have remained weak, which has limited the spillovers from the debt turmoil. Moreover, successful disinflations since the 1990s, a trustworthy central bank, and a predictable macroeconomic environment have been crucial prerequisites for the relatively mild immediate impact of the first round of the global financial crisis. The country was, however, hit strongly in consequence to the subsequent eurozone crisis as the Czech Republic is closely tied with the eurozone.

To conclude, due to relatively low internal and external imbalances that characterized other European economies, the direct fiscal impact of the crisis on the Czech economy was relatively limited.[37] However, GDP in 2009 decreased by 4.5 percent (see Table 1) and Czech economic performance after the 2008 crisis was worse than in some countries of the region (e.g., Poland). Czech companies had to face a decline in credit provisions after the fall of Lehman Brothers in 2008. This had an impact on the increased number of bankruptcies in the Czech Republic.[38] One of the reasons why companies went bankrupt was the oft-mentioned difficulties in accessing finances during times of economic distress. Also, the non-banking sector was hit by decreasing asset prices, real estate markets were in trouble, and risk aversion increased. This led to an increase in unemployment to 7.3 percent in 2010 (see Table 1), which was still significantly below the EU27 average.

When we talk about the Czech economy today and its possible future, several factors need to be considered. First, the Czech Republic is a small open economy with a flexible exchange rate. (Both imports and exports of goods and services increased their share from below 40 percent in 1990 to above 70 percent of GDP in 2012. See Table 1).

---

[37] IMF. *Czech Republic IMF Country Report* no. 13 243, (Washington, DC, 2013), 2.

[38] Martin Pospíšil and Jiří Schwarz. *Bankruptcy, Investment, and Financial Constraints: Evidence from a Post-Transition Country* (Mimeo).

As such, the country is vulnerable to external economic shocks (more than less export-oriented Poland, for example), such as the global credit crunch after September 2008. The Czech economy still benefits from a low, stable, and predictable inflation rate because inflation-targeting remains a relatively well-functioning monetary policy. Second, the institutional basis still needs to be improved to further enhance the business environment. While most of the sectors are regionally competitive today, tax codes need to be simplified, and public administration needs to be made more efficient and transparent, so as not to constrain business. Legal and institutional systems have always been a constraint for economic growth in the country and will most likely—despite certain improvements in this area—remain a problem for the foreseeable future. Corruption hampers businesses and consumes precious resources in the Czech Republic, especially in times of economic stagnation. Third, the Czech Republic still belongs to countries possessing underdeveloped financial markets. Stock market capitalization is one of the lowest among OECD countries, and it was further reduced after 2008. As such, the Czech economy remains strongly reliant on bank credit for investment, as other parts of the financial system (e.g., the stock market, private equity) remain underdeveloped.[39] Fourth, over time public debt can become a problem. Public debt as a percentage of GDP increased from 18 percent in 2000 to 46.2 percent (by ESA standards) in 2012.[40] Expecting that the old-age dependency ratio will rise, this will put more pressure on public financing of social and health care systems. Fifth, the cost of labor has been gradually increasing and the country will soon not be able to compete on labor costs. At the same time, its advantageous geographical position, together with a decent industrial base, and relatively skilled labor force will keep the country an attractive destination for foreign investors. It will be necessary, however, for the Czech economy to evolve from labor-intensive to more value-added sectors. Lack of a qualified labor force in these sectors, however, may hamper economic growth, which calls for an improvement in the Czech educa-

---

[39] It is worth noting that even in more developed countries (such as Germany), firms prefer bank loans as a form of funding for the majority of investment projects. At the same time, the German financial market allows firms to be less dependent on banks if their CEOs prefer.

[40] IMF, *Czech Republic IMF Country Report 2013*.

tional system. At the same time, as wages rise to keep up with European levels, it is essential that the economy becomes more efficient and more productive so as to remain competitive.

Finally, what is the Czech approach to the adoption of the common European currency? Upon joining the European Union in 2004, the Czech Republic pledged to eventually join the eurozone and adopt the common currency. However, while before the crisis, support for adopting the euro in the Czech Republic was relatively high among the public, and probably even higher among Czech businessmen (mostly due to higher predictability when it comes to exchange rates and related costs), the crisis significantly reduced Czech willingness to enter the eurozone, which is reflected by those in power. As the economy does not need to import monetary credibility from abroad, there is little support for the euro in the country. It should be noted that Slovakia successfully adopted the euro in 2009, while the Czech Republic is not expected to adopt the European currency in the near future for a lack of political will and public support.

What have Czechs gained since independence? Certainly economic and civic liberties, the ability to work and study abroad, and to live a standard "European" life. After twenty years of independence, the Czech Republic belongs to the group of the most advanced countries in the world. Living standards are gradually rising, and economic change is clearly visible. GDP per capita in purchasing power parity increased from $12,000 in 1990 to almost $27,000 in 2012 (see Table 1). The private sector expanded from a very low level of 10 percent to more than 80 percent of GDP and net inflow of foreign direct investment has been significant.[41] Finally, as Lízal notes, while prosperity is subjective,

---

[41] On top of that, Hanousek and Filer ("Consumers' Opinion of Inflation Bias Due to Quality Improvements," *Economic Development and Cultural Change* 53, no.1, 2004: 235–54) describe the problems with GDP and inflation data due to inadequate accounting for improvements in the quality of goods and services. Due to these accounting problems, Filer and Hanousek indicate a strong downward bias in growth rate estimates for post-communist economies. It is also possible that official data underestimated the growth of increasing informal or shadow sectors of the economy (see also Dyba and Švejnar, "Stabilization and Transition") and, therefore, the actual improvement of standards of living since the fall of communism was even higher than the official statistics suggest.

and it is difficult to objectively assess economic developments over the last twenty years, one measure has symbolized success. Life expectancy at birth, which under communism largely stagnated in Czechoslovakia, increased from age 71 in 1990 to age 78 by 2011 (see Table 1) in the Czech Republic (and slightly less in Slovakia). Since health is undoubtedly associated with happiness, this is a major achievement.[42]

At the same time, several promises have not been fulfilled. The Czech Republic did not become the Switzerland of Central Europe. The Czech currency is not as strong as was promised; and some Czech regions still belong among the much less developed in the European Union. While the Czech economy benefits from its unique geographic position between economically strong Germany and Austria, the inability of the political system to generate strong governments run by well-educated elites and focused on institutional reform still constrains the country from becoming as rich as its Western neighbors.

When comparing the Czech Republic on a relative scale with Slovakia and other post-communist neighbors, we see that the country is not lagging behind but neither is it pulling a great deal ahead of the others. Interestingly, despite using different transition strategies and different privatization methods, the countries of Central and Eastern Europe (at least those that entered the European Union) achieved, on average, similar mixed—but rather positive results: increasing living standards, improving investment climates, and better inclusive institutions (mostly because of pressure from the EU).

We conclude that the Czech Republic has gained a lot since independence, but could have gained much more if its full potential had been used and mistakes avoided. The recent history of Eastern Europe has shown that the underestimation of the institutional environment will most likely lead to high economic costs. Despite mistakes made, Czech economic development over the last two and a half decades has been largely a success.

---

[42] The Czech Republic belongs to the EU, where health is seen as the most important in relation to respondents' notion of happiness (European Commission, *Eurobarometer 69, Values of Europeans*, (2008)).

Table 1

	1990	1991	1992	1993	1994	1995	1996	1997	1998	1999	2000	2001	2002	2003	2004	2005	2006	2007	2008	2009	2010	2011	2012
GDP growth (annual %)		-11.61	-0.51	0.06	2.91	6.22	4.54	-0.85	-0.24	1.68	4.19	3.10	2.15	3.77	4.74	6.75	7.02	5.74	3.10	-4.51	2.49	1.89	-1.32
GDP per capita, PPP (current international $)	12,707	11,632	11,825	12,101	12,714	13,795	14,693	14,911	14,986	15,387	16,298	17,653	18,318	19,584	20,973	22,286	24,428	26,659	27,112	27,119	27,054	28,455	28,397
Private Sector Share of GDP	10	15	30	45	65	70	75	75	75	80	80	80	80	80	80	80	80	80	80	80	80	80	80
Life expectancy at birth, total (years)	71.38	71.90	72.27	72.27	72.97	73.07	73.71	73.82	74.51	74.67	74.97	75.17	75.22	75.17	75.72	75.92	76.52	76.72	76.98	77.08	77.42	77.87	
Imports of goods and services (% of GDP)	36.53	39.24	46.18	46.37	45.68	51.71	51.68	54.31	52.76	53.89	63.07	64.13	58.81	60.29	62.10	61.70	63.96	65.56	62.06	54.92	63.23	68.74	72.68
Export of goods and services (% of GDP)	39.37	45.95	47.66	47.76	44.36	48.08	46.51	49.77	52.25	53.33	60.93	62.62	57.64	59.09	62.98	64.43	66.97	68.22	64.45	58.95	66.58	72.89	78.02
Inflation, consumer prices (annual %)		52	13	18	9.96	9.17	8.80	8.55	10.63	2.14	3.90	4.71	1.79	0.11	2.83	1.85	2.53	2.93	6.35	1.04	1.41	1.94	3.30
Labor participation rate, total (% of total population ages 15+)	60.70	61.40	61.40	61.50	61.60	61.40	61.10	60.90	60.90	60.90	60.40	60.10	59.90	59.60	59.30	59.40	59.30	58.90	58.60	58.70	58.50	58.60	59.20
Unemployment, total (% of total labor force)		2.30		4.30	4.30	4.00	3.90	4.80	6.50	8.70	8.80	8.10	7.30	7.80	8.30	7.90	7.10	5.30	4.40	6.70	7.30	6.70	7.00
Foreign direct investment, net inflow (% of GDP)				1.67	1.91	4.44	2.21	2.16	5.79	10.15	8.48	8.76	10.83	2.12	4.37	8.92	3.72	5.88	2.92	1.45	3.08	1.04	5.41
Official exchange rate (CZK per US$, period average)			29.15	28.79	26.54	27.14	31.70	32.28	34.57	38.60	38.04	32.74	28.21	25.70	23.96	22.60	20.29	17.07	19.06	19.10	17.70	19.58	

Sources: World Bank Open Data. Accessed December 22, 2013 (http://data.worldbank.org/); Estrin, Hanousek, Kočenda and Švejnar, "The Effects of Privatization," 700.

CHAPTER 14

The Czech Economic Transition: From Leader to Laggard

Sharon Fisher

The chapter by Martin Pospíšil titled "Economic Developments in the Czech Republic, 1993–2013" provides a good overview of the country's economic transformation after the fall of communism. In it the author offers a detailed description of three key periods of Czech economic transition, describing key actors, policies and outcomes: the initial transformation (1991–1997); the convergence (1998–2007); and the global crisis (2008–today).

The key question of the chapter relates to what Czech society has gained over the first twenty years of independence. Pospíšil argues that, despite a number of policy mistakes over the past twenty years, the Czech economic transition was a success, adding that the lessons learned can serve as an example for other countries. Nevertheless, it is not clear how exactly Pospíšil defines and measures "success."

I would argue that the transition was far less successful than many had hoped at the time of the Czech-Slovak split. The 1992 parliamentary elections brought governments to power in the Czech Republic and Slovakia that had widely diverging policy approaches, at least in rhetoric. In the former case, Prime Minister Václav Klaus was a self-proclaimed Thatcherite, while Slovakia was led by Prime Minister Vladimír Mečiar, an advocate of gradual reforms that would protect the more vulnerable segments of society. The different approaches to economic reform between the 1992 election victors in the two republics served as a primary motivator for the breakup of Czechoslovakia. This was further compounded by the fact that the Czech Republic benefited from a strong manufacturing tradition that dated back to the Austro-

Hungarian Empire while Slovakia's economic position was relatively disadvantageous, as the country experienced the bulk of its industrialization during the communist era. Many Czechs, including Klaus himself, appeared almost relieved to lose their poorer Slovak cousins in the Velvet Divorce, as the split of Czechoslovakia would ostensibly allow Prague to move forward more quickly toward West European levels of prosperity. Indeed, the Czech Republic was expected to emerge as the Central European tiger.

In reality, however, that is not what happened, and the Czech economic "miracle" never emerged. Eurostat data in purchasing power terms indicate that Czech GDP per capita has improved only modestly as a share of the EU average (reaching 80 percent in 2013, up from 77 percent in 1995).[1] Among ex-communist countries, the Czech Republic was second to Slovenia in 2013 (at 83 percent), but still far behind Austria (at 129 percent) and Germany (at 124 percent). Slovakia, by contrast, has seen a much faster convergence than the Czech Republic, rising to 76 percent of the EU average in 2013, up from just 48 percent in 1995. In fact, Slovakia experienced one of the fastest convergence rates of all new member states. This occurred despite warnings of imminent collapse when Slovakia gained independence in 1993.

While Pospíšil describes the post-communist economic transition in the Czech Republic very well, many of the details have already been discussed in other works (which the author faithfully cites). By focusing primarily on Czech domestic economic developments, the author misses an opportunity to answer some of the big questions of the country's post-communist economic transition. Most importantly, in the context of this conference, how did the Czech-Slovak split impact the Czech economy? Are the Czechs better or worse off following the split with Slovakia than they would have otherwise been? What exactly have the Czechs gained since independence? Why has Slovakia performed better than the Czech Republic in the past decade? What happened to the promised Czech economic miracle?

To answer these questions, we must pay closer attention to Czech politics, which have had a huge impact on economics throughout the

---

[1] These figures are from the *Eurostat Database*, accessed July 2014, http://epp.eurostat.ec.europa.eu. The data are calculated as a share of the EU–28.

past twenty years, making it impossible to separate the two. To start with, it is helpful to look back at Václav Klaus's 1992–1997 governments, examining the differences between words and actions. Adéla Gjuričová nicely lays out the political background for the reforms, which she argues were created by a generation of middle-aged economists who were confident in the Czech Republic's predestined success and had a mystical belief in the free hand. During the mid-1990s, Klaus bragged that the Czech economy was so successful that the European Union would ask to join the Czech Republic rather than the other way around. Moreover, with Slovakia under Mečiar and after the ex-communists won elections in Poland and Hungary, Klaus spoke about the Czechs as a "non-leftist island" in Central Europe,[2] even though the Hungarian left introduced reforms that were much more far-reaching than what Klaus was doing at the time. Klaus claimed as early as October 1993 that the Czech economic transition was complete. Many people in the Czech Republic and abroad believed Klaus's rhetoric about the supremacy of the Czech model of reform, and the country attracted high levels of foreign direct investment (FDI), while Slovakia became an international pariah under Mečiar's leadership.

While Klaus acquired an image as a leading reformist, thanks to policies that were introduced in 1990–1992, in reality there was very little reform after the split of Czechoslovakia. By 1994, Klaus's fairytale story had slowly begun to unravel, as the inconsistencies between his Thatcherite discourse and concrete policies started to become apparent.[3] While Klaus continued to present his approach as right wing, the Czech economy remained largely un-restructured, as Klaus's government delayed key reforms in an effort to maintain social peace. The "free hand" was manifested most notably in weak regulation and institutions. Regulated rents in the Czech Republic remained well below market prices through 2006. On the privatization front, a certain nationalism was evident in the general reluctance to sell companies to foreign investors, particularly in the case of strategic firms such as

---

[2] Czech Radio, May 11, 1994.
[3] See Mitchell Orenstein, "The Political Success of Neo-Liberalism in the Czech Republic," Institute for East West Studies paper, preliminary draft, 1994; and Sharon Fisher, "Czech Economy Presents Mixed Picture," *RFE/RL Research Report* 3, no. 29 (July 22, 1994): 31–8.

banks, telecoms, utilities, and other "family jewels." A voucher scheme, which allowed citizens to buy shares in companies for a nominal fee, was launched in an effort to transfer property to private hands as quickly as possible. The program compensated for the lack of domestic capital by offering shares to the population, a move that was aimed at broadening public support for reforms.

By 1997, the Czech "economic miracle" had disintegrated, as confidence in the economy declined and the currency plummeted.[4] Coupon privatization was eventually seen as a negative phenomenon. A major flaw of the coupon program was that, unlike the Hungarians, the Czechs failed to first create an adequate legal and institutional framework. Insufficient regulation allowed for high levels of abuse, including insider trading and asset stripping. Moreover, because most shares were put in investment funds—many of which were controlled by banks that remained in state hands—corporate governance was absent, unemployment remained unnaturally low (which helped maintain social peace), and the banking system ended up in shambles. Under these circumstances, I would question whether the share of the private sector in GDP actually reached 75 percent by 1997, given the role of state-owned banks as shareholders.

Amid a political and economic crisis, Klaus's cabinet fell in late 1997 due to a corruption scandal. It was not until Klaus and his allies lost power that major economic restructuring was launched, under the temporary leadership of former central bank governor Josef Tošovský. New parliamentary elections in June 1998 were followed by the appointment of a minority cabinet led by Prime Minister Miloš Zeman of the Social Democrats (ČSSD), with tacit support from Klaus's Civic Democratic Party (ODS). The ČSSD led the Czech Republic for two successive terms, although the 2002–2006 cabinet was a majority one, as the ČSSD formed a coalition with center-right Christian Democrats (KDU–ČSL) and Freedom Union (US–DEU). Under ČSSD leadership, the Czech Republic shifted its privatization approach to focus on public tenders, and the country sold key firms in the banking and energy sectors to foreign investors. By the time those privatizations took

---

[4] Jiří Pehe, "Czechs Fall From Their Ivory Tower," *Transitions Online* 4, no. 3 (August, 1997).

place, the Czech banking sector was in such poor shape that there were few protests. The economic recession and second-stage reforms that followed the 1997 crisis contributed to three straight years of weak or negative growth. Even after the Czech economy finally began to recover around the year 2000, growth was not as strong as in several other countries in the region, including Slovakia.

Although the ČSSD-led governments made good progress on privatization and restructuring, the approach to fiscal reform was unambitious, as the successive cabinets failed to take advantage of the period of stable economic growth during 2000–2006 to launch changes. The need for fiscal reforms was heightened by the cost of bailing out the banking sector prior to its privatization. Moreover, delays in approving reforms of such areas as healthcare and pensions put undue strain on the budget, as mandatory expenditures were driven upward by the rapidly aging population. Fiscal responsibility was needed not only to meet the Maastricht criteria for entry into the eurozone (which requires budget deficits of less than 3 percent of GDP), but also to provide a basis for healthy medium and long-term economic growth.

While the Czech Republic was under ČSSD leadership, a center-right coalition government took power in Slovakia from 2002–2006 that launched sweeping fiscal reforms, setting the pace for the region. The Czech Republic lagged behind, and Czech reforms that were approved during that period appear to have been largely stopgap measures, without an overall vision. For example, the government planned to gradually cut the corporate income tax rate to 24 percent by 2006, a step that was widely seen as insufficient since it was being slashed to 18–19 percent in the other three Visegrád countries.[5] It is ironic that just eleven years after the split, in 2004, Slovakia became the regional leader in reforms, while the Czech Republic was the laggard. As the formerly "backward" Slovakia was lauded as the new Central European tiger, a number of Czech commentators looked on with envy.

Unlike many of the ex-communist countries that joined the EU in May 2004, the Czech Republic under the ČSSD did not push for economic reform within the EU and did not protest when France and Germany violated the Stability and Growth Pact by overstepping budget

---

[5] See, for example, ČTK, July 7 and 23, 2003.

limits. Indeed, the ČSSD-led cabinet was a reluctant reformer that saw the "European social model" as one of the key advantages of EU membership. In fact, when German and French leaders accused the new member states of "tax dumping" and called for harmonization of taxation rates within the EU, Prime Minister Vladimír Špidla of the Czech Republic was the only top representative from a new member state to support Germany's Chancellor Gerhard Schröder in that stance.[6]

The need for fiscal reform put the ČSSD in an awkward position vis-à-vis the EU. The party was a strong supporter of the EU as a guarantor of the continuation of social welfare programs. Being forced to cut back on social spending as a way of pleasing the EU thus seemed contradictory, especially as countries like Germany and France were overshooting their deficit targets. The successive ČSSD-led governments that held office after the 2002 elections used their narrow parliamentary majority and falling public support as an excuse to stall on reform. Inevitably, as the 2006 elections approached, the successive governments came up instead with measures that would actually cost the state more money, such as a proposal to implement tax cuts for low- and middle-income citizens.

By 2005, a spate of favorable economic news decreased pressure on the government to make further reforms, as a rising denominator reduced budget deficit/GDP ratios, at least temporarily. Still, the positive fiscal results of 2004–2005 were not expected to last, as mandatory expenditures would continue to rise in the medium- to long-term, putting further strain on deficits. Many experts agreed that it was better for the Czech Republic to implement fiscal reforms before joining the eurozone rather than afterwards, as the authorities would have flexibility in terms of monetary policy and exchange rate adjustments. Nevertheless, the ČSSD lacked the courage to move forward.

The ODS retook control of the Czech Republic in 2006, and successive center-right governments that held power through 2013 tried to catch up with their regional peers on the fiscal reform front. The corporate tax rate was reduced to 19 percent in 2010. Moreover, a flat tax on personal income was introduced, but critics claimed that it did not

---

[6] Jan Macháček, "Špidla vystupuje jako exot" [Špidla behaves as an exotic], *Hospodárske noviny*, May 5, 2004.

actually help simplify the system (and it was effectively canceled at the start of 2013). Pension reform finally took effect at the start of 2013, but it was also controversial, not least because it was introduced just as other countries were backtracking from the three-pillar framework that had been pushed by the World Bank (mandatory public, mandatory private, and voluntary pension plans). Indeed, even the World Bank itself questioned this approach, arguing that post-communist Europe lacks the necessary preconditions for a functioning private pension system.[7]

Czech public finances once again got out of balance amid the economic downturn of 2009, and the governments since then have been eager to demonstrate that they are fiscally responsible. Austerity packages took effect each year in 2010–2013, and the impact has been detrimental to household consumption and investment, contributing to a long-running recession from late 2011 through early 2013. The Czech National Bank complained that fiscal austerity was not well coordinated, meaning that the bank's monetary loosening was ineffective in boosting growth.

The ODS was eventually successful in reducing the government deficit below the Maastricht limit (which finally occurred in 2013), thus meeting a key requirement for eurozone entry. Nevertheless, the party's eurosceptic stance meant that the Czech Republic has yet to set a date for adoption of the common currency, despite the legal obligation to join the eurozone. Indeed, under ODS leadership, the country was reluctant to take on a greater role in the EU and was often openly critical of EU policies. While Slovakia adopted the euro in 2009 (becoming the second country in the region to do so after Slovenia), the Czechs have expressed their desire to maintain nominal independence over monetary and exchange rate policy. Still, the Czech economy is highly intertwined with that of the eurozone, and the country currently has no viable alternatives to further integration.

This raises another key question of the Czech economic transition: How has the country benefited from EU membership? Why has the country seen such a dramatic shift in support for the EU? During his terms as Czech prime minister in 1992–1997, Klaus was largely

---

[7] World Bank, *Pension Reform and the Development of Pension Systems—An Evaluation of World Bank Assistance* (Washington, DC: World Bank, 2006).

pro-European, and it was his government that actually submitted the Czech Republic's application for EU membership in 1996. Even then, however, Klaus took a different approach from other Central and East European candidates, as he emphasized the Czech Republic's "superiority," both toward the country's eastern neighbors and toward the occasionally protectionist West.[8] Klaus's fall from power in 1997, combined with the demonstrated lack of success of his reform model, proved to be instrumental in shifting ODS attitudes toward the EU. The party could no longer talk about Czech "superiority," and it focused instead on spreading fear about the infringements that EU membership would have on Czech national sovereignty.[9] In 2002, the ODS used an openly eurosceptic approach in the parliamentary election campaign for the first time, along the lines of the British Conservative Party. However, despite a relatively low level of support among the Czech population for EU accession, the ODS achieved worse-than-expected results and was forced into opposition as its power-sharing agreement with the ČSSD came to an end.[10]

Recently, the Czech Republic's political leadership has shifted once again. After the last ODS-led government fell in 2013 due to a corruption scandal, the ČSSD has reemerged as the senior partner in the ruling coalition. Under the ČSSD, the cabinet has taken a less ambitious approach to fiscal reform, while also reaffirming the Czech Republic's interest in EU integration. Nevertheless, more steps will be needed to convince Czech citizens, who according to recent public opinion polls appear to be happy with neither EU membership nor the Czech-Slovak split.

---

[8] Milada Anna Vachudova, *Europe Undivided: Democracy, Leverage and Integration After Communism* (Oxford: Oxford University Press, 2005), 196.

[9] Sharon Fisher, "The Czech Republic: Waning Enthusiasm," in *European Union and the Member States*, eds. Eleanor E. Zeff and Ellen B. Pirro (Boulder: Lynne Rienner, 2nd Edition, 2006), 343–60.

[10] See Petr Kopecky, "An Awkward Newcomer? EU Enlargement and Euroscepticism in the Czech Republic" *European Studies* 20 (2004) 238–41; Petr Kopecky and Joop Van Holsteyn, "The grass is always greener…: Mass Attitudes Towards the European Union in the Czech and Slovak Republics," Paper presented at the Public Opinion about the EU in East-Central Europe Conference, University of Indiana, Bloomington, April 2–3, 2004.

Part IV

SOCIAL DEVELOPMENTS AFTER 1993

CHAPTER 15

Reflections on Social Developments in Slovakia, 1993–2013

Martin Bútora and Zora Bútorová

"Social Developments" could mean many different things. This term can be understood as "a transformation of social structures in a manner which improves the capacity of the society to fulfill its aspirations"—says one of the educational websites.[1] It can be perceived as "qualitative changes in the structure and framework of society that help the society to better realize its aims and objectives," claim protagonists of a comprehensive theory of social development.[2] It refers to the alteration of social order within a society, and it is "a process of social change, not merely a set of policies and programs instituted for some specific results," other experts remind us.[3] The historian and archeologist Ian Morris defines social development as "the bundle of technological, subsistence, organizational, and cultural accomplishments through which people feed, clothe, house, and reproduce themselves, explain the world around them, resolve disputes within their communities, extend their power at the expense of other communities, and defend them-

---

[1] *Ask.com*, http://www.ask.com/question/what-does-social-development-mean.
[2] Garry Jacobs and N. Asokan, "Towards a Comprehensive Theory of Social Development," in *Human Choice: The Genetic Code for Social Development*, eds. Harlan Cleveland, Garry Jacobs, Robert Macfarlane, Robert van Harten, and N. Asokan (Minneapolis: The World Academy of Art and Science, 1999), 152.
[3] Uncommon Opportunities: An Agenda for Peace and Equitable Development. *Report of the International Commission on Peace and Food* (London: Zed Books, 1994), 163.

selves against others' attempts to extend power." [4] By social development, he clarifies, "I mean a group's ability to master its physical and intellectual environment to get things done."[5] While there are myriads of definitions, classifications, and characterizations, scholars at least agree that social development can be measured with indicators such as life expectancy, literacy, education, standard of living, Gini coefficient, health status, environment, housing, personal safety, but also with other markers, like freedom of association, gender equality, the level of civic participation, telephone lines, mobile phones, and Internet penetration.

The organizers of the conference did not request an all-inclusive report on Slovakia's achievements, failures, and challenges in this field. Rather, they called for contributions based on relevant research in respective countries in some of the areas related to social developments. That is precisely what we will try to do, using a series of seven snapshots, which monitor and reflect the last twenty years, as well as the current situation.

Coincidence of Anniversaries and Milestones

The conference that brought together the contributors to this book occurred in the year of a major holiday and two milestones for Slovakia. The prevailing tone of the evaluations offered by political scientists, experts on international affairs, and historians was favorable: Slovakia's road from the last two decades to the present has been evaluated as a "success story." To employ a just evaluation to speak for them all, we can refer to historian Roman Holec, who has broadened the time horizon and called the country's development in the twentieth century a successful story "with a fairytale ending." "The Slovaks

---

[4] Ian Morris, *Social Development* (Stanford: Stanford University Press, 2010), 9, http://ianmorris.org/docs/social-development.pdf. Morris recently published *Why the West Rules—For Now: The Patterns of History and What They Reveal about the Future* (New York: Farrar, Straus & Giroux, 2010).

[5] Morris, *Social Development*, 7, http://ianmorris.org/docs/social-development.pdf.

started from nothing," says the narrative, "they obtained an independent state, and then became members of the European Union and NATO."[6]

Second, Slovakia has commemorated another anniversary: fifteen years ago, its citizens were able to cope with the anti-democratic and authoritarian style of governance exercised by then Prime Minister Vladimír Mečiar, marked by a "winner takes all" majoritarianism, an unwillingness to seek consensus, a disrespect for minority rights, and a labeling of critics as "enemies," "anti-Slovak" or "anti-state." In the 1998 parliamentary elections, Mečiar and his entourage were defeated and a broad coalition of pro-democratic forces came into power. The pro-European perspective of Slovakia's future had been reopened.

Third, there is another interesting and important milestone. Indeed, this conference takes place in the middle of two history timelines. Over less than a century—more precisely from the founding of Czecho-Slovakia in the fall of 1918 until now, the fall of 2013—Slovakia has undergone unusually dramatic developments. Six forms of state government, three political systems and, within them, several regimes have alternately taken hold on its territory. And in the year when we celebrate the creation of modern Slovak statehood, the ratio of non-democratic to democratic regimes has evened out. For approximately one half of this period, the inhabitants of Slovakia lived under authoritarian, at times, even totalitarian conditions, and spent the other half, by contrast, in times of greater freedom: about forty-seven years in one type of regime and forty-seven years in another. (The same is true for the Czech lands, where the period from 1939 to 1945 was even more painful than in wartime Slovakia.)

Today, the Slovak Republic enjoys the status of EU, NATO and OECD membership; it is a part of the Schengen Area and the eurozone. The road to this achievement was not even, but rather a cyclical development with ups and downs. A battle was fought over freedom and democracy, over human dignity and over far-reaching societal reforms. However, one feature was always present: the ability of the

---

[6] Michaela Terenzani, "A Common but Contentious History," *The Slovak Spectator* (Bratislava), December 13–19, 2010.

nation to recover, to reinvent itself, to stand up after falling down. Forthcoming decisions and choices made both by the public and the politicians will decide in which direction the pendulum that measures the coming decade of Slovakia will swing.

Framing Successes and Failures

Two decades since the foundation of the Slovak Republic, it is quite natural to ask what independence has brought to its citizens. What has been achieved? Crucial questions can be organized into ten categories:

1. THE QUALITY OF DEMOCRACY: Has independence brought a higher quality of democracy and increased respect for fundamental rights and freedoms?
2. RULE OF LAW: Do we have now, after twenty years, a more stable rule of law, better governance and a functioning public administration? Are public officials held accountable and how efficient is civic control providing a critical feedback to state power?
3. SOCIOECONOMIC STATUS: Are we better off—in terms of economic performance, solving the most pressing social problems, including unemployment, regional differences, the gap between the rich and the poor?
4. CIVIL SOCIETY: Do we see a more robust, more vibrant civil society? Are citizens willing and able to exercise active citizenship and increased civic participation?
5. SOCIAL COHESION: What is the level of social cohesion? Do we see a high incidence of cooperation, deeply anchored bonds that hold society together?
6. SOCIAL CAPITAL, TRUST: What is the level of political and social capital in our society, that is, the level of trust and satisfaction with politics and democracy? Do people believe society is heading in the right direction?
7. INCLUSIVENESS, ACCEPTANCE OF DIVERSITY: How inclusive is our society? How far is tolerance towards others and otherness both an accepted norm and everyday practice? How is our society coping with various new trends—like growing diversity in the lives of people; the declining marriage rate, and the boom in informal part-

nerships; an increase in the divorce rate; the declining birth rate; the aging of the population?
8. HUMAN RIGHTS, MINORITY RIGHTS: What is the status of minorities (ethnic Hungarians, Roma, and other ethnic minorities; religious minorities; and sexual minorities) and various disadvantaged groups? How do we handle various types of discrimination? How do we cope with gender inequalities?
9. THE CAPACITY TO DESIGN, APPROVE AND IMPLEMENT REFORMS: How successful have the adopted social policies and reforms been regarding issues such as unemployment, poverty, social security, housing, the pension system and health care, education, and culture?
10. A SELF-LEARNING SOCIETY, THE CAPACITY OF ELITES FOR SELF-CORRECTION: Is society as a whole and, in particular its elites, able to learn from previous mistakes and failures and to perform better in the next attempts at change?

Slovakia in International Comparative Surveys

Slovakia is doing relatively well in surveys assessing the quality of democracy and quality of life—the *Freedom in the World* survey published by Freedom House,[7] the *Democracy Index* produced by the Economist Intelligence Unit,[8] the *UN Human Development In-*

---

[7] "*Freedom in the World*, Freedom House's flagship publication, is the standard-setting comparative assessment of global political rights and civil liberties. Published annually since 1972, the survey ratings and narrative reports on 195 countries and 14 related and disputed territories are used to monitor trends in democracy and track improvements and setbacks in freedom worldwide," *Freedom House*, http://www.freedomhouse.org/report-types/freedom-world#.UutsafvpjXR; Country ratings and status, FIW 1973–2014.

[8] According to the annual *Democracy Index 2012*, produced by The Economist Intelligence Unit, Slovakia ranked 40th out of 165 independent states and two territories analyzed in the index, which provides a snapshot of the state of democracy worldwide (it covers almost the entire population of the world) (Kavitha A. Davidson, "Democracy Index 2013: Global Democracy at a Standstill, The Economist Intelligence Unit's Annual Report Shows," *The Huffington Post*, 03/21/2013, http://www.huffingtonpost.com/2013/03/21/democracy-index-2013-economist-intelligence-unit_n_2909619.html).

dex,[9] and the *Legatum Institute Prosperity Index*.[10] In all of them, Slovakia (and the Czech Republic, too) is favorably located, usually in the group of the most successful countries in the world. A more critical view—however, concerning one of the most advanced regions of the world, the European Union—was presented in a report prepared by the London-based Demos Think Tank called *Backsliders: Measuring Democracy in the EU*. "A weakening civil society, decline in civic participation, decreasing political and social capital, lower levels of voter turnout, a lack of trust in political elites, and the emergence of grassroots populist movements all point to a deeper malaise underpinning the democratic culture in both new and old democracies of the EU," says the report.[11] This analysis has identified five core areas of democratic backsliding: democratic malaise and public distrust, dissatisfaction with traditional political parties; corruption and organized crime, with corruption "going unpunished"; a justice system that is free from corruption and political influence; media freedom; and human rights and the treatment of minorities (asylum seekers, Roma, and Muslims). In most of the indicators, Slovakia ranks below average, but does not

---

[9] The Human Development Index (HDI) is a comparative measure of life expectancy, literacy, education, standards of living, and quality of life for countries worldwide. It is a standard means of measuring well-being, especially child welfare. It is also used to measure the impact of economic policies on quality of life. In 2013, Slovakia was placed in the highest of four categories ("very high human development"), ranking 35th out of 187 member states of the United Nations, *Wikipedia*, s.v. "List of countries by Human Development," http://en.wikipedia.org/wiki/List_of_countries_by_Human_Development_Index.

[10] The Legatum Prosperity Index is "a unique and robust assessment of global wealth and wellbeing, which benchmarks 142 countries around the world in eight distinct categories: Economy; Education; Entrepreneurship & Opportunity; Governance; Health; Personal Freedom; Safety & Security; and Social Capital." Prepared by the Legatum Institute in London, the index "finds that the most prosperous nations in the world are not necessarily those that have only a high GDP, but are those that also have happy, healthy, and free citizens," *Legatum Institute,* http://www.li.com/programmes/prosperity-index. In 2013, Slovakia ranked 38th out of 142 countries, *Legatum Prosperity Index*, http://www.prosperity.com/#!/ranking.

[11] See *Backsliders: Measuring Democracy in the EU* (London: Demos, 2013).

belong to the most problematic countries. According to this report, the most corrupt EU country is Italy; among the backsliders in most areas are Hungary, Romania, and Bulgaria, and the worst deterioration after the outburst of the crisis was found in Greece.

These views (*Democracy Index 2013* and the Demos study from 2013) correspond to some domestic analyses. For instance, during the last five years, the Institute for Public Affairs (IVO), a think tank based in Bratislava, has regularly evaluated the quality of democracy in the following areas: democratic institutions and the rule of law; legislation; protection and implementation of human rights and minority rights; performance of independent and public service media; and civil society and the third sector. Experts assign an overall rating in each particular area on a scale from 1.00 (the optimum) to 5.00 (the worst). In the period 2008–2012, the overall grade for all areas oscillated between 2.9 in 2008 to 2.8 in 2012, with the worst grade in 2009 (3.3) and the best in 2011 (2.6). While the oscillations are not surprising even in more advanced democracies, the average level is below the required standard in this field.[12]

If we look at another survey, the *Global Competitiveness Report*, prepared regularly by the World Economic Forum,[13] in the overall evaluation, Slovakia ranked 78th out of 148 countries in 2013; however, corruption and inefficient government bureaucracy were considered the

---

[12] See the series *Slovakia: Trends in the Quality of Democracy* (Bratislava: Institute for Public Affairs, 2008, 2009, 2010, 2011, 2012).

[13] Over more than three decades, The Global Competitiveness Report series has evolved into the world's most comprehensive assessment of national competitiveness. The Global Competitiveness Index defines "competitiveness as the set of institutions, policies and factors that determine the level of productivity of a country. GCI scores are calculated by drawing together country-level data covering 12 categories—the pillars of competitiveness: institutions, infrastructure, macroeconomic environment, health and primary education, higher education and training, goods market efficiency, labor market efficiency, financial market development, technological readiness, market size, business sophistication and innovation." See *The Global Competitiveness Index*, http://www3.weforum.org/docs/GCR2013-14/GCI_MethodologyInfographic_2013-2014.jpg.

most problematic factors for doing business.¹⁴ Besides, both Slovakia and the Czech Republic got remarkably bad evaluations regarding "favoritism in decisions of government officials" (out of 148 countries, Slovakia ranked 144th and the Czech Republic 123rd).¹⁵

Also, the area of judicial independence is among those evaluated critically both in international comparative surveys, as well as in domestic public discourse. According to the *Global Competitiveness Report*, Slovakia occupied the 133rd place out of 148 countries. And while the next two indicators did not reveal an ideal situation in the Czech Republic either—"efficiency of legal framework in settling disputes" ranked 115th and "efficiency of legal framework in challenging regulations" ranked 126th—Slovakia's position was worse: the ranking was 143rd and 142nd, respectively.¹⁶

---

[14] The report also summarizes factors seen by business executives as the most problematic for doing business in their economy. The information is drawn from the 2013 edition of the World Economic Forum's Executive Opinion Survey. The survey "captures valuable information on a broad range of factors that are critical for a country's competitiveness and sustainable development, and for which data sources are scarce or, frequently, nonexistent on a global scale…This year's Survey captured the opinions of over 13,000 business leaders in 148 economies between January and May 2013." See *The Global Competitiveness Index*, http://reports.weforum.org/the-global-competitiveness-report-2013-2014/.

[15] From a list of sixteen factors, respondents of the World Economic Forum's Executive Opinion Survey were asked to select the five most problematic and rank them from 1 (most problematic) to 5. The results were then tabulated and weighted according to the ranking assigned by respondents. See *The Global Competitiveness Index*, http://www3.weforum.org/docs/WEF_GlobalCompetitivenessReport_2013-14.pdf.

[16] Also Slovakia's public is very critical of the state of the judiciary. A survey by the Institute for Public Affairs in Bratislava published in July 2012 suggested that mistrust in judicial institutions continues to prevail: the Supreme Court, led by Štefan Harabin, the former Justice Minister and a nominee of Vladimír Mečiar's Movement for a Democratic Slovakia, which was the coalition partner in the first government of Robert Fico in 2006–2010, was trusted by only 37 percent of those polled, while 54 percent said they distrusted it. Only 28 percent of respondents said they trusted the regular courts, with 67 percent saying they did not. See *Slovak Judiciary As Seen by the Public, Experts, and Judges*, http://www.ivo.sk/6856/en/projects/slovak-judiciary-as-seen-by-the-public-experts-and-judges?lang=EN.

The State of Slovakia through the Eyes of Its Citizens

Let us now look at how people in Slovakia view their society and its developments since the fall of communism. What is their perception of crucial social problems in their country? Based on spontaneous answers of respondents in a representative IVO survey, two issues dominated the list of the ten most pressing social problems in 2013: unemployment (71 percent) and the declining standard of living and insufficient social security (55 percent). These were followed by corruption, cronyism, and lack of transparency (32 percent), the unsatisfactory quality of health care (28 percent), inefficient economic policy by the government and the global economic crisis (18 percent), and the social status of the Roma and their problematic relationship with the majority (12 percent). The list of the ten most urgent social problems as seen by the public also included crime and organized crime (11 percent), the state of politics and the quality of democracy (9 percent), the state of education (9 percent) and the state of the judiciary and the rule of law (8 percent).

Chart 1: Top ten most urgent social problems according to Slovak citizens (2006–2013, in %)

	2006	2007	2008	2010	2012	2013
Unemployment	53	37	45	64	64	71
Living standard, social security	79	79	75	53	50	55
Corruption, cronyism, non-transparency	24	25	22	29	29	32
Quality of health care	33	37	23	29	21	28
Economic problems	10	12	21	18	24	18
Ethnic problems*	9	13	19	11	17	12
Crime, organized crime	22	15	16	18	12	11
Politics, quality of democracy	10	9	9	15	13	9
Education	10	12	7	7	11	9
Judiciary, rule of law	6	6	4	4	7	8

* In 2006–2008 mainly Slovak–Hungarians relations, in 2010–2013 mainly coexistence of Roma and the majority.
Source: Institute for Public Affairs, 2006–2013.

In fact, as was confirmed by almost all sociological surveys conducted since the early 1990s, the 2013 findings present a relatively stable pattern of public perception.

Unemployment involves not only losing a job—it is usually accompanied by a worsening of social, psychological and health conditions of the affected individuals and families. The deterioration is deeper in regions with other unfavorable social and economic characteristics, including a low level of education, the outflow of skilled labor into the lucrative parts of the country, and the gradual decline of industries that had provided job opportunities for low-skilled labor. Also, high unemployment, especially long-term unemployment, is more prevalent among the inhabitants of socially excluded localities.

In Slovakia, this is predominantly the case for the Roma. They are a vivid and painful illustration of the very substance of social exclusion—a lack of individual and group participation in the economic, political and social life of society, and a lack of access to resources which can take economic, social, political, territorial and symbolic dimensions.[17] Unemployment permeates all these dimensions.

During the last several years, social scientists and journalists have repeatedly pointed to the continuing deterioration of the quality of life in Roma communities, as well as at increasing tensions between Roma and non-Roma in some areas. As Beata Balogová put it, "The unsolved problems of Slovakia's Roma communities are a ticking time-bomb, the explosion of which will affect the whole of society...Meanwhile, groups of frustrated citizens are calling more frequently for the application of an 'iron fist,' i.e., repressive solutions."[18]

Slovakia ranks among countries with the highest proportion of Roma. According to *Atlas of Roma communities in Slovakia 2013*, they

---

[17] Petr Mareš, "Social Exclusion and Social Inclusion: the Czech Perspective," in *The Challenge of Social Inclusion: Minorities and Marginalised Groups in Czech Society*, ed. Tomáš Sirovátka (Brno: Barrister & Principal, 2006), 11–38.

[18] Beata Balogová, "Anti-Roma Protests Draw Thousands." *The Slovak Spectator*, October 4, 2012, http://spectator.sme.sk/c/20044803/anti-roma-protests-draw-thousands.html.

represent almost 8 percent of Slovakia's population.[19] One of the most comprehensive overviews summarizing reports, findings and analyses from Slovakia, as well as from international sources and organizations, was prepared by the Research Directorate of the Immigration and Refugee Board of Canada in Ottawa.[20] The document clearly shows that Roma suffer disproportionately from poverty, unemployment, illiteracy, crime and disease. They face exclusion and discrimination in numerous areas, including housing, education, health, employment, provision of government services, political participation, loan practices, and access to commercial services.

One of the most critical areas is education. Roma students are often segregated and placed in separate classes or separate schools, even though they have no physical or mental disability, but are only socially disadvantaged. The education received from special needs schools does not provide Roma students with sufficient knowledge or certification to acquire higher education, and this, together with labor market discrimination, contributes to high levels of Roma unemployment.

As for political representation, Roma are underrepresented in all levels of administration and government. This is due to their social marginalization, low levels of education, the lack of cooperation between non-Roma and Roma organizations, the shortage of Roma leaders, and insufficient coordination and cooperation among Roma leaders themselves.

In 2012, the *Strategy of the Slovak Republic for Integration of Roma up to 2020* was adopted by the Slovak government. The goals of the strategy are "to halt the segregation of Roma communities; to facili-

---

[19] *Atlas rómskych komunít na Slovensku 2013* [Atlas of Roma communities in Slovakia, 2013] (Bratislava: UNDP—Regionálne centrum Rozvojového programu OSN pre Európu a Spoločenstvo nezávislých štátov, 2014), http://www.employment.gov.sk/files/slovensky/rodina-socialna-pomoc/socialne-sluzby/atlas_rom-kom.pdf.

[20] *Slovak Republic: Situation of Roma, Including Employment, Housing, Education, Health Care and Political Participation* (Ottawa: Research Directorate, Immigration and Refugee Board of Canada, Responses to Information Requests, 11 July 2012), http://www.irb-cisr.gc.ca/Eng/ResRec/RirRdi/Pages/index.aspx?doc=454087.

tate a significant positive turn in the social inclusion of Roma communities; to foster nondiscrimination; and to change the attitude of the majority population toward the Roma minority."[21] While independent civic experts noticed some improvements, especially in the continuation of already existing programs, they also pointed to the lack of new programs and policies in the new strategy.[22]

In recent years, tensions between Roma and the majority population have increased. In contrast to some other disadvantaged communities or groups (people with disabilities, the elderly or women), whose weaker social position is admitted by the general public, the interpretation of the situation of the Roma is different. Although many non-Roma inhabitants acknowledge the Romas' low levels of education, poverty, unemployment and poor health, they attribute these conditions to their mentality. They do not perceive the Roma as a heterogeneous group, but tend to see them stereotypically as criminals and social parasites, living at the expense of the majority and abusing the social system. Also in the long term, they see relations with the Roma as the most problematic and are very skeptical about the ability of any political representation to improve them. A substantial part of the non-Roma would support stricter legislation and policies concerning only the Roma. They argue that it is the non-Roma who are subject to discrimination.

Keeping in mind all these problems, many of Slovakia's inhabitants are asking themselves: Did we make a good choice in 1989? Is the current system better than the communist regime? As Chart 2 shows, it would be too simplistic to interpret the attitude towards the current system only in terms of material disillusionment. Many people appreciate the positive aspects of the post-1989 transformation. When our respondents compared their situation with that of their counterparts before

---

[21] *Strategy of the Slovak Republic for Integration of Roma up to 2020* (Bratislava: Office of the Plenipotentiary of the Slovak Republic Government for Roma Communities, 2012), http://www.minv.sk/?romske-komunity-uvod. Szilvia Németh, *Strategy of the Slovak Republic for Integration of Roma up to 2020 (critical summary by REF consultant,* (Budapest: Roma Educational Fund 2012), http://www.romaeducationfund.hu/sites/default/files/publications/slovak_strategy_2020_ref.pdf.

[22] Roman Cuprik, "Report Assesses Roma Policies," *The Slovak Spectator*, November 3, 2014, http://spectator.sme.sk/c/20052475/report-assesses-roma-policies.html.

1989, a vast majority of them praised the abolition of the Iron Curtain and the increased freedom to work, study, and travel abroad. They appreciated the freedom of the press and better access to information; they realized that there is much more freedom of expression and they had a much greater chance to freely participate in public life. As expected, they viewed the standard of living more critically—yet almost half of them thought that nowadays people were better off than under communism.

Chart 2: "Compare your life with that of your counterparts before 1989. Is your situation better, the same, or worse?" (opinions of Slovakia's citizens – in %)

	Better	The same	Worse	DK
Chance to study, work and travel abroad	78	11	7	4
Free access to information	70	19	5	6
Chance to express your opinion	63	22	10	5
Chance to freely participate in public life	62	26	6	6
Living standard	48	16	21	4
Chance to influence political decisions	39	36	15	10
Chance to be successfull thanks to honest work	31	26	37	6
Equality before the law	26	37	30	7
Labor opportunities	25	9	61	5

However, other aspects of their lives did not give a reason for enthusiasm. Unemployment is seen as the most troublesome feature of the current era. What is perhaps more surprising is a widespread feeling of civic helplessness. Despite individual political freedoms, only two-fifths of Slovakia's citizens believed that they have a stronger influence on political decision-making now than before 1989. Two decades after the fall of communism, most people felt too weak to defend their rights and to push for their interests. Only about one-third of citizens thought that they had a better chance to be successful through honest work than the generation of their parents before the Velvet Revolution. This is a source of bitter disillusionment, when we take into account that, under communism, this was one of the pivotal dreams of people who were fed up with the political benefits and advantages of Communist Party members on each and every occasion.

Even fewer respondents, one in four, were convinced that the equality of citizens before the law has improved in comparison with the communist era. Once again the ironic Orwellian saying has become popular, "We are all equal, but some of us are more equal than others." Putting it differently, more freedom does not automatically bring less civic alienation and more satisfaction with the state of justice and quality of democracy.

Who are the winners and losers of the transition? Chart 3 addresses these questions. According to the public, on the side of the winners are the entrepreneurs, dissidents, and religious believers persecuted by the communist regime, but also young people and professionals. On the bench of the losers sit old people, blue-collar workers, and farmers. However, among the losers of the new era are also hard-working, honest people—those, who are not cheating, stealing, bribing, or blackmailing; those who try to behave in accordance with good habits and ethics. In other words, according to the prevailing opinion, honest hard work does not bring success and well-being. From this perspective, the country still has a long way to go to build a better society.

Chart 3: "Who has gained and who has lost after 1989?"
(opinions of Slovakia's citizens, in per cent)

	They have gained	No changes	They have lost	I don't know
Entrepreneurs	84	10	2	4
Dissidents	67	17	7	9
Believers	66	25	4	5
Young people	60	21	16	3
Professionals	56	32	6	6
Communist functionaries	24	28	39	9
Hardworking, honest people	16	33	46	5
Farmers	15	29	49	7
Blue-collar workers	13	34	48	5
Older people	11	35	50	4

Source: Institute for Public Affairs/FOCUS, October 2009.

The public perception of winners and losers goes hand-in-hand with the attitudes of various social groups toward the post-1989 system. Its supporters are younger, better educated, and active on the labor market (in contrast to the retired and unemployed). A similar distribution of attitudes is also typical of the other Visegrád Four countries—The Czech Republic, Poland and Hungary.[23]

Chart 4: "In comparison with the pre-1989 period, the current one has more advantages," (opinions of V-4 citizens – by education)

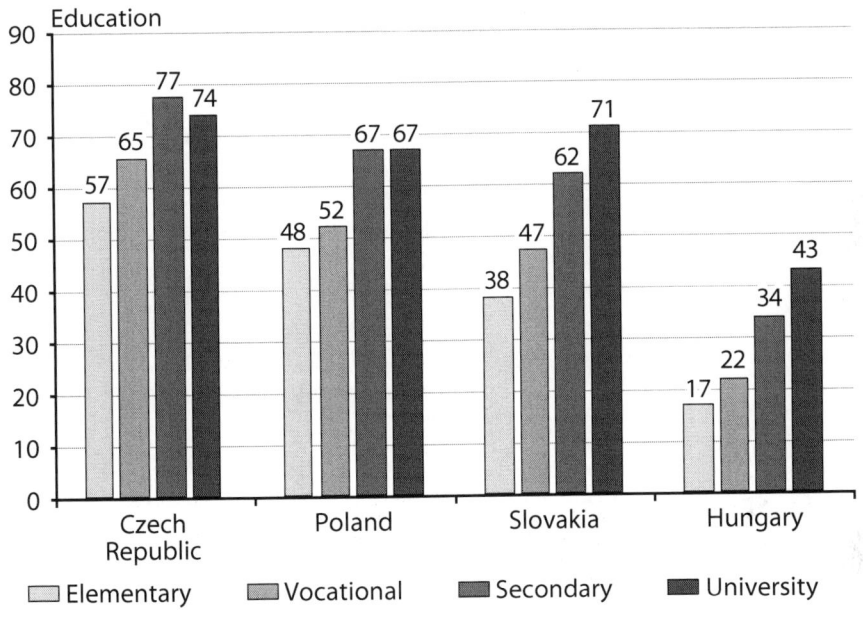

Source: PASOS, October 2009.

---

[23] Zora Bútorová and Oľga Gyárfášová, *Return to Europe: New Freedoms Embraced, But Weak Public Support for Assisting Democracy Further Afield* (PASOS: Policy Brief No. 3, 2009), http://www.ivo.sk/5968/en/news/ivo-and-pasos-published-a-publication-discussing-public-evaluation-of-democratic-transformation-in-the-v4-countries-.

Chart 5: "In comparison with the pre-1989 period the current one has more advantages."
(opinions of V-4 citizens – by age)

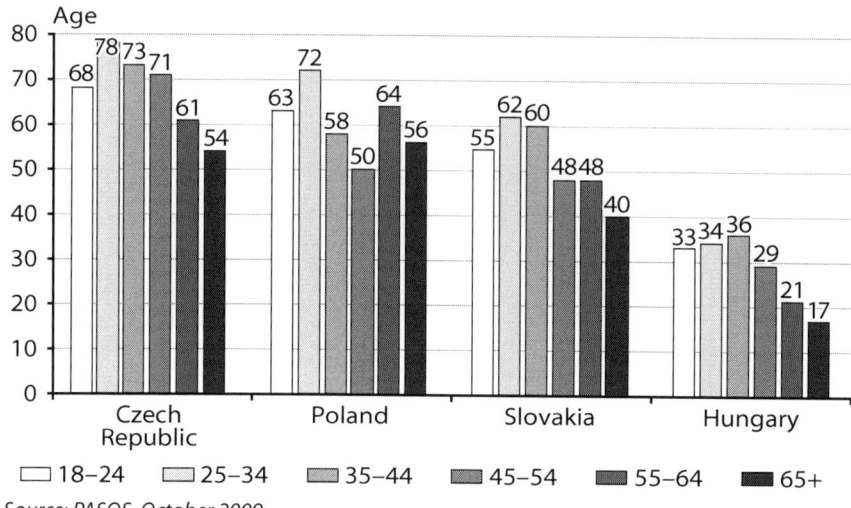

Source: PASOS, October 2009.

Chart 6: "In comparison with the pre-1989 period the current one has more advantages."
(opinions of V-4 citizens – by economic status)

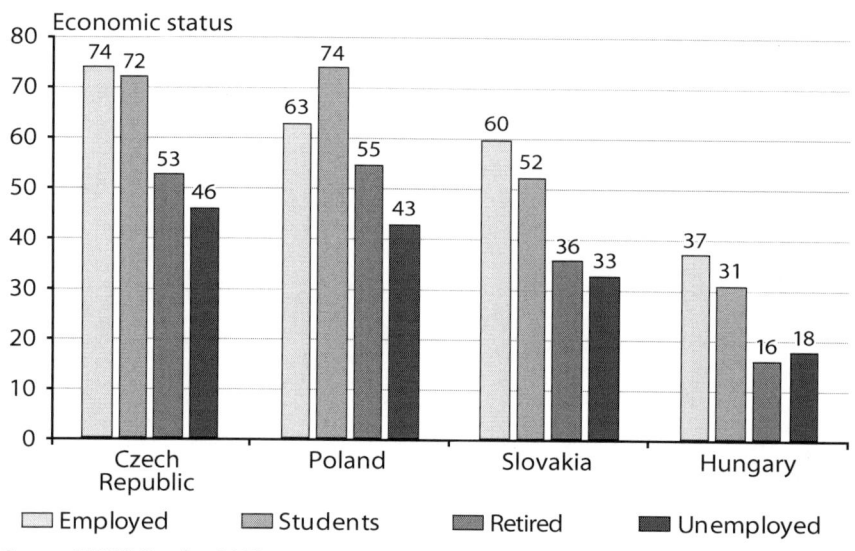

Source: PASOS, October 2009.

In 2013, at the threshold of the third decade of Slovakia's independence, it is worthwhile to ask what are the attitudes of its citizens towards Slovak statehood? As Chart 7 shows, two thirds of citizens (64 percent) were proud of their country's accomplishments. These positive feelings were significantly less frequent than in 2008, shortly before the global economic crisis (77 percent), but much more widespread than in 2011, amid the economic and political crisis in Slovakia, or in 2003, after the first decade of independence (49 percent).

Chart 7: "Looking at Slovakia's accomplishment since its independence, do Slovak citizens have a reason to be proud of their country?" (2003–2013, in %)

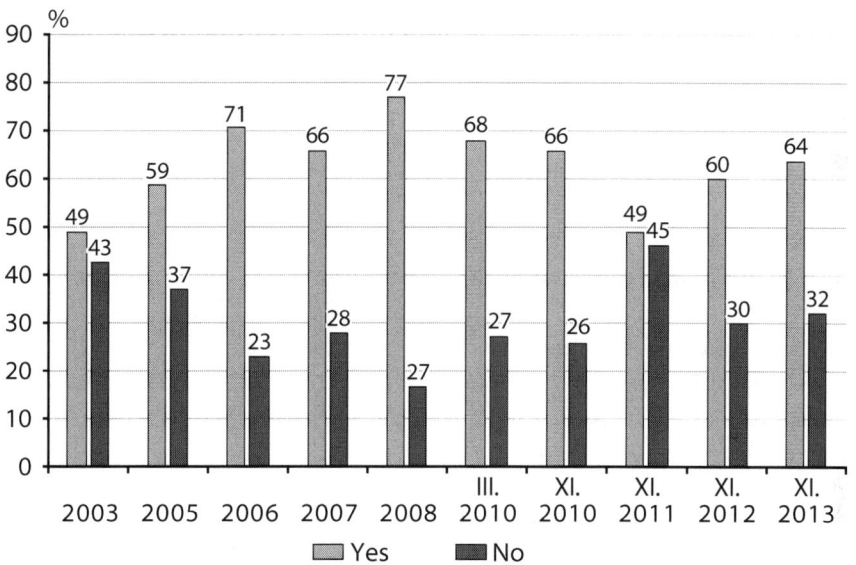

Source: Institute for Public Affairs, 2003–2013

What are the reasons of these feelings? Based on spontaneous statements from respondents (Chart 8), the main source of pride was the international success of Slovakia's sportsmen, especially of the national ice hockey team (a silver medal at the World Championships in 2012), followed by Slovakia's EU membership, the very existence and viability of independent Slovakia, the adoption of the single European currency, as well as the country's economic progress and structural reforms.

Chart 8: Five most frequent reasons why Slovak citizens feel proud and ashamed of their country, respectively (2012)

Sources of pride	%	Sources of shame	%
Success of Slovak sportsmen, particularly hockey players	29	Inability of political parties and their leaders to act in the public interest	23
Membership in the European Union	17	Corruption, cronyism and theft of state assets	19
Existence of an independent state, its viability	10	Unsatisfactory living standards and social security; unemployment	14
Accession to the euro-zone, adoption of single currency	9	Social status of the Roma and their problematic relationship with the majority	8
Economic progress and reforms, arrival of foreign investors, rise of automotive industry	5	Poor condition of the judiciary and law enforcement	6

Source: Institute for Public Affairs, 2012.

Meanwhile, the most frequently cited reason why Slovak citizens felt ashamed of their country was the inability of political parties and their leaders to act in the public interest. This was closely followed by rampant corruption, cronyism, and theft of state assets, poor living standards and insufficient social security, the social status of the Roma and their problematic relationship with the majority and, finally, the poor condition of the judiciary and law enforcement.

In May 2014, Slovakia celebrated the tenth anniversary of its membership in the European Union (EU). An important landmark of Slovakia's EU membership was the adoption of the single European currency (EUR) on January 1, 2009. A number of surveys show that citizens of Slovakia are quite happy about it. The positive attitude that had prevailed long before the country joined the EU further strengthened over the first years of membership. According to the Eurobarometer Survey from the fall 2008, the number of those who considered EU membership "a good thing" reached 62 percent in the autumn of 2008, which was significantly above the EU member states' average of 53 percent. This degree of support was the third highest among the countries that joined the EU between 2004 and 2007. At the same time, 77 percent of respondents believed that EU membership was "beneficial" to Slovakia, which was 21 percent above the EU 27 average.[24]

The above-average positive perception of the EU and its institutions was typical of Slovakia even during the economic crisis. According to the Eurobarometer Survey from the fall of 2010, 71 percent of Slovaks trusted the EU, while the average in the EU was only 43 percent. The general trust of Slovaks in the EU was reflected also in their trust in the EU institutions (76 percent of Slovaks trusted the European Parliament; 67 percent the European Central Bank and 66 percent the European Commission). In a comparative sociological survey carried out in the fall 2012 by the Institute for Public Affairs in Bratislava and the Public Opinion Research Center in Prague,[25] the entry of the country into the European Union was seen as a positive historical event by 59 percent of respondents in Slovakia, compared with only 38 percent in the Czech Republic (see Chart 9).

Chart 9: Evaluation of selected historical events by the citizens of Slovakia and the Czech Republic (% of positive evaluation: "it is good that it happened")

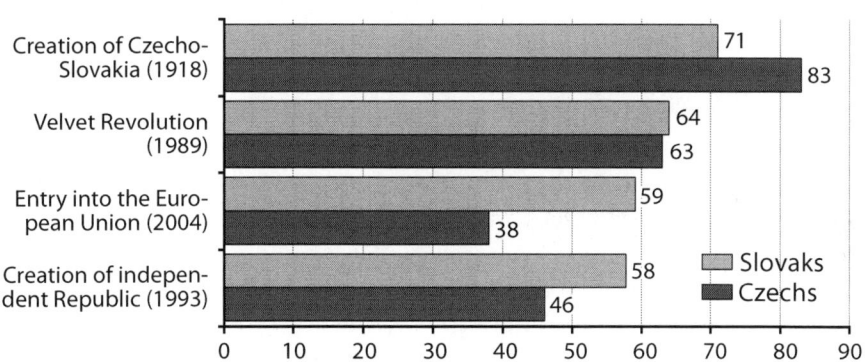

Source: Institute for Public Affairs and Public Opinion Research Center. 2012

---

[24] *Eurobarometer 70. Public Opinion in the European Union*, Fall 2008, http://ec.europa.eu/public_opinion/archives/eb/eb70/eb70_first_en.pdf.

[25] "Dvadsať rokov od rozdelenia—výskumy verejnej mienky v Českej republike a na Slovensku" [Twenty years since the split—a study of public opinion polls in the Czech Republic and Slovakia], http://www.ivo.sk/6914/sk/aktuality/dvadsat-rokov-od-rozdelenia-vyskumy-verejnej-mienky-v-ceskej-republike-a-slovensku.

In the following years, the trust of Slovaks toward the European institutions decreased, following a general trend in the EU countries. However, it remained higher than the EU 28 average. According to the Eurobarometer Survey from the fall 2014, the European Parliament enjoyed the trust of 50 percent of Slovaks (compared to 42 percent of all EU citizens), the European Commission of 47 percent of Slovaks (vs. 38 percent of all EU citizens), the European Central Bank 50 percent (vs. 34 percent of all EU citizens).[26] Despite the decreased trust in EU institutions, most Slovaks endorse the following EU initiatives: economic and monetary union with a single currency (79 percent of Slovaks compared to 56 percent of the EU average); a common foreign policy (74 percent vs. 66 percent) and a common defense and security policy (82 percent vs. 74 percent).

A majority of Slovaks believe in the positive impact of the EU for EU citizens. Sixty-six percent think that the EU contributes to the defense of its citizens; 63 percent believe that the EU has sufficient power and tools to defend the economic interests of Europe in the global economy. Furthermore, most of Slovakia's citizens identify with the EU: 73 percent of them see themselves as EU citizens (compared to a 63 percent average in the EU) and 54 percent feel themselves attached to the EU (vs. an average of 45 percent in the EU). At the same time, 96 percent of Slovaks feel attached to their country (vs. 92 percent in the EU).

On the other hand, Slovak participation in the elections to the European Parliament has been exceptionally low. In 2004, Slovakia recorded the lowest turnout in the history of European elections—only 17 percent. The second European elections in Slovakia brought a slight increase in voter turnout, reaching 19.6 percent. Yet, the country maintained the highest abstention rate among all EU member states. The third European elections in Slovakia attracted even fewer voters—only 13.05 percent and Slovakia remained in last place among all EU countries.

One of the reasons for this discrepancy is that compared to the EU average, Slovak citizens do not feel adequately represented in Brussels. In 2008, for instance, 31 percent of European respondents, but only 17 percent of Slovak respondents subscribed to the assertion, "My voice is heard in the EU." Similarly, the assertion that "Members of the European

---

[26] Public Opinion in the European Union. First Results. Standard Eurobarometer 82, http://ec.europa.eu/public_opinion/archives/eb/eb82/eb82_first_en.pdf.

Parliament listen to my voice regarding European affairs" was endorsed by 25 percent of respondents in the EU, but only 15 percent of respondents in Slovakia.[27] According to a July 2009 post-election survey by the Institute for Public Affairs,[28] respondents gave the following reasons for not taking part in the elections: lack of trust in and dissatisfaction with politics in general (28 percent of non-voters); lack of interest in politics (17 percent); lack of belief in the importance of elections ("my vote does not change anything"—17 percent); inability to vote due to vacation (10 percent), and work obligations (10 percent). Other reasons were directly related to the EU and included lack of information on the EP or EU, lack of interest in the European agenda, and dissatisfaction with the EU or EP as institutions. These findings confirmed a phenomenon well known from years past: abstention from voting is reflective of attitudes toward politics in general, rather than of attitudes toward the EU.

Is the Glass Half Full or Half Empty?

The achievements of the last twenty years can be viewed with reference to the metaphor of the glass being "half full" or "half empty." The more favorable view envisions Slovakia as a successful country that has experienced setbacks and failures, but managed to pick itself up again and to renew democratic rule. The other side sees the situation as a glass "half empty": Slovakia suffers from an ineffective state bureaucracy, widespread bribery, and problematic judicial conduct. A network of public institutions has been put in place, but some of them are not infused with authentically democratic content, and too often they are not occupied by genuine democrats. Parties and leaders of nearly all political stripes have been in power at some point, and practically all

---

[27] *Národná správa. Slovenská republika.* [National report. Slovak Republic] Eurobarometer 69. Verejná mienka v Európskej únii [Public opinion in the European Union], Spring 2008, http://ec.europa.eu/public_opinion/archives/eb/eb69/eb69_sk_nat.pdf.

[28] Zora Bútorová and Oľga Gyárfášová, "Contemporary Slovakia in Public Opinion," in *Slovakia 2009. Trends in Quality of Democracy*, ed. Martin Bútora, Grigorij Mesežnikov and Miroslav Kollár (Bratislava: Institute for Public Affairs 2010).

(including communists and radical nationalists) have made it to parliament at least once. At the same time, many of them have managed to discredit themselves. This is why the public tends to notice only the negative aspects of political life, without taking into account the scale of the problems left over from communist days or associated with the "teething pains" of post-communist democracy. This is also due to the insufficiency of informed public debate on key issues of social, political, and economic transformation.

After the collapse of the communist regime in November 1989, Slovaks lived through a very intense period of history. An enormous number of changes have taken place. For middle-aged and older generations, this has constituted an extraordinary psychological burden, intensified by the competitive and stressful nature of the transition from a command to a free market economy. But even more importantly, given the predominant technocratic-managerial model of reform making, society has not always been able to keep up with the moral dimensions of change. There has been a persistent problem with trust in institutions watching over the moral integrity of public life, as well as an inadequate supply of personalities with undisputed authority to serve as the guardians of moral behavior.

To better understand the underlying background of these phenomena, one has to return to the past, namely to periods of marked discontinuity before 1989. Throughout the twentieth century, hundreds of thousands of people left the country or were forced to change their identity for numerous reasons. Assimilation, migration, political exile, deportations, compulsory transfers, Magyarization, and re-Slovakization have been a part of the Central European and Slovak "political menu." These processes marked the fates not only of ordinary people, but also of domestic elites, who were repeatedly subverted, uprooted, or liquidated. Imprints of times past remain: ruptures, breaks, exoduses and exiles, tectonic shifts, and personal, family, or institutional cataclysms are present in the collective memory. In the language of psychotherapy there is a well-known term: "unresolved issues." Hundreds of thousands of people have such unsettled accounts with previous regimes.

With this perspective in mind, Slovakia today is a country experiencing something unusual. Perhaps for the first time in history, all diverse mentalities openly coexist in one space: conservatives and liberals; étatists and individualists; supporters of state paternalism and admirers of free markets; national populists and global internationalists; greens and technocrats; right-wing extremists and left-wing anarchists; believers in traditional families and supporters of same-sex partnerships. People of various political generations and those with different experiences live here, and in contrast with the past, they live in an independent state, in their own republic that guarantees pluralism and political competition.

The question now is whether society will be able to utilize this pluralism in a productive way. Will it perceive the pluralistic landscape of various convictions, creeds, and lifestyles as an enrichment, rather than as an obstacle to achieving national aspirations of well-being? Will Slovak society welcome the Central European dream of liberty, order, opportunity, equality, and dignity, a dream of success in the form of "normalcy" after long decades of extremes and horrors?

Finally, Slovakia is still struggling with a lack of "democratic modernizers." The challenge is to create an atmosphere in which talents can be nurtured, and to promote institutions that cultivate character through education and social interaction. The country should do more to offer young people opportunities to find a "higher purpose in life," in particular, in public service. Slovakia has a plethora of vibrant first-class individuals and groups capable of competing on a global level. Also, in the economic sphere, top-quality goods are manufactured and new starts-up are emerging. However, what has been missing is strategic thinking and acting at the higher levels of the political establishment by which these "islands of excellence" could combine to become influential agents of change.

Civil Society and Active Citizenship[29]

Shortly after the change of regime in 1989, new laws on the freedom of association and assembly generated a boom in civic mobilization. At the beginning of the 1990s, several thousand associations already operated in Slovakia. In 1994, a steering panel called the Gremium of the Third Sector was established and gained the status of a govern-

---

[29] This analysis is based on the study by Martin Bútora, Zora Bútorová and Boris Strečanský, *Active Citizenship and Nongovernmental Sector in Slovakia. Trends and Perspectives* (Bratislava: Včelí dom association, 2012).

ment partner. The second half of the 1990s was more problematic, as Vladimír Mečiar's semi-authoritarian government attempted to limit the sector's independence. Civil society organizations joined with other actors (political parties, trade unions, the media, and the churches) in a battle over the democratic character of the state. NGOs, organizing a pre-election campaign OK'98, significantly contributed to massive public mobilization, especially of young people, which resulted in an 84 percent voter turnout and in the defeat of Prime Minister Mečiar in the 1998 parliamentary elections.

Since the early 1990s, Slovakia's third sector, as a part of civil society, has created a rich, diverse, and flexible network of forms, organizational schemes, initiatives, and ideas that have moved society forward. It has established an intellectual foundation for societal reforms; provided mechanisms for the control of power; defended the interests of various groups of citizens; opened forums for previously unheard voices; offered useful services; participated in resolving environmental, social, and health issues; and reacted to the needs of villages, towns, communities, and regions. Thousands of small organizations, initiatives, associations, and volunteer groups have proven their usefulness, undertaken work that no one else could do, and attained unique achievements. Civic actors and volunteers engage and motivate a broader public because they offer understandable, acceptable concepts of freedom, solidarity, and activism that are in line with democratic modernization and have challenged the previously prevailing ethos of civic helplessness. They have demonstrated an outstanding ability to weave together meaningful activities, engage in social campaigns, find ways to help socially excluded groups, engage local elites in useful activities in many fields, and find support both at home and abroad.

By the end of the first decade of the twenty-first century there were around forty different platforms, federations, and ad hoc coalitions of civic organizations operating in Slovakia, associated on the basis of common social or regional interests.[30] In 2010, among more than

---

[30] Boris Strečanský et al. "Mimovládne neziskové organizácie a dobrovoľníctvo" [Nongovernmental nonprofit organizations and volunteering], in *Slovensko 2008. Súhrnná správa o stave spoločnosti* [Slovakia 2008. Comprehensive report on the state of society], ed. Miroslav Kollár, Grigorij Mesežnikov and Martin Bútora (Bratislava: Institute for Public Affairs 2009), 609.

37,000 officially registered NGOs there were some 33,000 civic associations.[31] In recent years, we have witnessed an increase of informal, unregistered civic participation as well.

Democracy research institutes, analytical centers, and think tanks, together with human rights NGOs and watchdogs focused on accountability and good governance, have become an indispensable component of a healthy nongovernmental sector. Even if they comprise a relatively small proportion of the whole nonprofit sector, they have a crucial influence on public life. These NGOs have advanced democratization, the observance of human rights, and the realization of economic reforms and good governance, in part by setting the agenda and framing the public debate on important social problems.

Policy institutes, researchers, and ad hoc groups of experts and scholars have also been involved in a number of advocacy initiatives. For instance, the initiative to reform the public administration structures ("For a Real Reform of Public Administration," 2000), the initiative for improving waste management ("For a Good Law on Waste Management," 2001), or those focused on raising public awareness about violence against women ("Every Fifth Woman Campaign," 2002). Civil society organizations have created broader alliances and carried out joint campaigns. Perhaps the most important successful example was the 2000 nationwide campaign *for a good* freedom of information law called "What Is Not Secret Is Public," supported by more than 120 NGOs and bringing together more than 100,000 supporters.

A relatively new phenomenon is the growing role of online social networks and new media in mobilizing citizen activism. Between 2004 and 2012, more than 250 campaigns, calls, petitions, initiatives, declarations, and public reviews of proposed legislation appeared on the website of the Internet-based civic daily *Changenet*.[32] They were supported by tens of thousands of citizens. Signatories usually included well-known personalities in public life, civic activists, and representa-

---

[31] See Register and Records of the Ministry of Interior of the Slovak Republic, http://portal.ives.sk/registre/start.do.
[32] See an overview of campaigns, *Changenet.sk*, http://www.changenet.sk/?section=kampane. By the end of 2014, the number of campaigns had reached almost 400.

tives of NGOs; experts from various fields and professions; members of local governments and other politicians; and many ordinary citizens. These campaigns, initiatives, and controversies have concerned various topics: public policies and issues of democracy, the rule of law and implementation of justice, social and economic problems, public administration and local government, the position of minorities and human rights, nationalist threats, protection of the environment and cultural heritage, conditions for the media, and the employment policies of public institutions. They have encouraged a review of the problems and often included calls to action as well. Mass reviews strive to achieve changes in proposed legislation and usually have a solid level of expertise.

The most visible of these campaigns was an environmentalist initiative by the Slovak branch of Greenpeace and a coalition of allied groups that was able to combine research activities with action. The campaign demanded that the country's local communities have a say in uranium mining projects in their regions. In Slovakia, any petition obtaining 100,000 signatures must be discussed by the national parliament. This petition garnered 113,000 signatures and was delivered to the parliament in September 2009. In March 2010, legislators agreed on legal changes to geological and mining laws that would grant local communities, as well as municipal and regional authorities, more power to limit the development of uranium deposits. This was not only a huge achievement for the Slovak environmental movement and an inspiration for similar groups around the world, but also a strong example of effective action for Slovakia's civil society as a whole.

Third-sector leaders have a clear idea about the workings of the civic sphere, which often clashes with the ideas of state representatives. They consider it important for NGOs to "fill the gaps" and meet the needs of society and individuals through experimentation and the testing of innovations. Third-sector leaders believe that NGOs should serve as a kind of civic control, providing critical feedback to state power. They think it is essential for NGOs to help various disadvantaged groups and to strengthen the voices of those who would otherwise not be heard. NGOs also see it as necessary to achieve mutually beneficial cooperation with the public and business sectors in serving citizens, while respecting the principles of true partnership. In contrast to these beliefs, state representatives tend to reduce the nonprofit sector to a provider of services and to suppress civic participation.³³

However, weakened public rights and barriers to civic participation are at odds with EU norms. For example, after twenty Slovak environmental NGOs submitted a complaint to the European Commission regarding the violation of the right of public participation in decision-making that is essential to environmental protection, in 2008, the commission began an inquiry regarding Slovakia. Facing the potential loss of several billion euros in EU funds, the Slovak Parliament amended the corresponding law so that civic initiatives, associations, and organizations, as well as ordinary citizens, could express their views on the environmental impact of government policies.

The fruits of NGOs have raised the quality of life in Slovakia. They have created, disseminated, and reproduced three specific kinds of wealth in society: cognitive wealth, a wealth of practical experience, and a wealth of pro-social patterns of behavior. They have used several approaches to contribute to cultural change and the democratic modernization of their country.

Other NGOs demonstrated their expert potential by becoming sources of alternative approaches to public policy. The creation of proposals, together with critical reviews of existing state policies, have increased the competition in the "marketplace of ideas" and enabled better-informed public debates and political decisions. A further segment of the third sector has established itself as a service provider. These activities are not just a supplement to state care, but often offer a distinct and a more efficient alternative. NGOs have brought competition to the field of the provision of services and served as a wellspring of innovation and experimentation. They work with a certain "social-risk capital" that allows them to test new approaches on a small scale. Dozens of service innovations have been developed and piloted by Slovak NGOs.

One of the controversial topics in the third sector is civic participation. Civic participation cannot be reduced to electoral participation. It

---

[33] Boris Strečanský, "'We and They'—Slovakia," in *'We and They'. NGOs' Influence on Decision Making Processes in the Visegrad Group Countries*, ed. Tom Nicholson (Bratislava: The Sasakawa Central Europe Fund and Center for Philanthropy 2008), 71–101.

takes various forms, including public debates; demonstrations, strikes, boycotts, or rallies; charitable collections and petitions; engagement in solving local problems; and working for political parties. Comparative data from representative sociological surveys suggest that the ranks of active citizens engaging in public affairs in Slovakia have not expanded since the 1990s.[34] One of the reasons might be a mental shift generated by the onset of a market economy—a growing individualism and weakening interest in the problems of others. Moreover, in a time of crisis, people struggling with poverty and social insecurity concentrate all their energy on making ends meet. Another reason might be an overall decrease in social trust, which is the lubricant of people's willingness to associate and cooperate. And last, but not least, some people put off civic participation because they realize what a major effort is needed to change their conditions and how rarely this kind of effort is crowned with success.

At the same time, several spontaneous civic initiatives have emerged in recent years, especially among young people. In 2011 and 2012, they organized public rallies to criticize the corruption of politicians, the intertwining of business and politics, and the inadequacy of the institutions of representative democracy. They called for more transparency in politics and public life, and for strengthening the elements of direct democracy in the political system.

Also in some other areas, civic activism has shown an upswing. Participation by citizens in community development has increased, and various forms of urban activism are developing as well. Professional organizations are entering the legislative process and fighting for their rights and interests. Formal and informal volunteering is expanding, most intensively in the social and environmental spheres, but also in culture. Internet activism has gained momentum, and thanks to social media, more citizens have become involved in public affairs. Some new initiatives are equipped with entrepreneurial spirit, which has helped them to prove sustainable.

---

[34] Zora Bútorová and Oľga Gyárfášová, "Občianska participácia: trendy, problémy, súvislosti" [Civic participation: trends, problems, and context], *Sociológia* 42, no. 5 (2010): 447–91.

Besides the above-mentioned favorable trends, one cannot ignore persisting problems and challenges in the relationship between the civil sector and the political sphere. These are:

1. Political parties have created a "political class" that operates in closed circles of mutual support and is unwilling to listen to independent voices from civil society.
2. Cooperation between the state and NGOs is marked by formalism. Though government officials invite NGOs to take part in drafting and discussing legislative initiatives and executive policies, in the end their opinions, proposals, and demands are often ignored. The representatives of nonprofit organizations have repeatedly expressed their concerns over the lack of free access to information and insufficient participation by the public in policymaking.
3. The frequent change of state officials, administrators, and staff after general elections results in a loss of "institutional memory," making it difficult to preserve continuity and build on previous achievements.
4. In recent years, most of Slovakia's civic organizations have been struggling with scarce financial resources. The economic crisis has hampered individual and corporate fundraising as well as state support for NGOs. Nonprofits have repeatedly complained of a lack of partnership with the state in planning and implementing the structural EU funds to Slovakia and also of limited access to structural funding, in both the 2002–2006 and 2007–2013 programming periods.
5. Nonprofit organizations providing services in various sectors (health, education, social care) operate at a disadvantage. The legal and regulatory environment prefers state-owned and public service providers at the expense of nonprofits. In general, while the advocacy and activist dimension and the campaigning potential of the Slovak third sector have grown, the service dimension has not had enough space to expand.[35]

---

[35] Boris Strečanský, *The Situation of the Third Sector in Slovakia, The Impacts of Crisis, Trends, Mainstreams and Challenges* (Bratislava: Center for Philanthropy, 2012), 85, http://www.cpf.sk/files/files/Pages%20from%20Civil_Szemle_2012_3.pdf.

6. In addition to civic activism that promotes human rights and a democratic political culture, demonstrations of "uncivil civil society," focusing on installing order with a strong hand and suppressing otherness have become more widespread. Back in 2011, an expert panel that prepared the *Study on Trends in the Development of Civil Society in Slovakia*[36] noted the risk of a more active presence of radical or extremist individuals or groups that use new communication technologies and social networks for communication and mobilization. Those groups have been taking advantage of the deep economic crisis, worsening social situation, and the long-term failure by state organs to solve serious social problems (for example, the social situation of Roma and their relationship with the majority population). In 2012, there were not only more strident expressions of xenophobic rhetoric by extremist groups, but even some city mayors organized petition drives and marches calling for "the defense of the rights of 'decent people' and for stricter legislation and punishment of 'socially unadaptable individuals'."[37] In the 2013 regional elections, Slovakia witnessed another mobilization of the far right: the dissatisfaction with the style of governance, corruption and politics in general resulted in a protest vote of the inhabitants of the region of Banská Bystrica (one of eight Slovak regions), bringing victory to a far-right candidate known for his extremist views on Roma and the Holocaust.

A Need for New Narratives and Visions

Two decades after the birth of Slovak independence, the country—its inhabitants, its elites, its leaders, and society as a whole—needs a new conceptualization of its endeavors in order to move ahead: an active,

---

[36] Martin Bútora et al., *Štúdia trendov vývoja občianskej spoločnosti na Slovensku* [Study of trends in the development of civil society in Slovakia] (Bratislava: Office of the Government of the Slovak Republic, 2011), http://www.ivo.sk/7497/sk/studie/studia-trendov-vyvoja-obcianskej-spolocnosti-na-slovensku.

[37] "Slovakia: Anti-Roma Demos Lead to Warning," *The Slovak Spectator*, 22 October 2012, http://spectator.sme.sk/articles/view/47940/2/anti_roma_demos_lead_to_warning.html. See also the chapter on Slovakia in *Nations in Transit* (New York: Freedom House, 2013), http://www.freedomhouse.org/report/nations-transit/2013/slovakia#.Uu7N2fvpjXQ.

working vision for the future. It should embrace Slovakia's splendor and glamour as well as its setbacks and failures; it should not be based on myths, but should reasonably refer to and evoke the potential for favorable change.

During the last fifty years, several narratives have emerged. In the late 1960s, the Slovak communist writer Vladimír Mináč came up with his own version of a "plebeian hard-working Slovak nation," exposed to constant threat from the outside world. "If history is the history of kings, thieves, bloody battles, and pillaging, then the Slovaks really do not have a history. If, however, the essence of history is everyday hard work, cultivation of the land, and building towns, then our history is one of the most illustrious."[38] His view was a narrative of victims suffering injustice.

In the first decade of the new millennium, after Slovakia's successful reforms and its entry into the EU, NATO and the OECD, a very different, completely opposite conceptualization emerged: that of the "Tatra Tiger"—a dynamic, pro-reform, innovative, successful nation on the rise.[39] It sounded like the victory song of a first-class champion.[40]

Neither of these narratives resonated as truthful, convincing, and mobilizing.

A more promising attempt, even if not designed at length or in detail, has been present in the last quarter of the century mainly among public intellectuals who have challenged the various versions of national populism that abounded in Slovakia after the fall of communism in 1989. It was a narrative close to Jürgen Habermas' concept of constitutional patriotism, as an alternative to ethnic nationalism, emphasizing ideas of civic values, observance of the constitution and the rule of

---

[38] Vladimír Mináč, "Kde sú naše hrady?" [Where are our castles?], *Kultúrny život*, 23, 1968.
[39] Matthew Reynolds, "Slovakia's Awakening: 'Tatra Tiger' is Born," *New York Times*, December 29, 2004.
[40] However, the "Tatra Tiger" nickname was limited mainly to liberal economic reforms that were not positively received by the Slovak public, as they were associated with a need for belt-tightening, *Wikipedia*, http://en.wikipedia.org/wiki/Tatra_Tiger.

law.[41] In the late 1990s, in the era of the struggle with Mečiar's authoritarianism, marked by deep dissatisfaction of the growing majority of citizens with the course the country was heading, Milan Šútovec, a prominent public intellectual, metaphorically expressed the need to endow the state with a new vision and a democratic content in his words "to found the state anew."[42] In other words, these debates have concentrated on a sort of constitutionalism grounded in national sovereignty and constitutional democracy, the idea of fundamental rights and the notion of the rule of law.[43]

However, even if during the years following Mečiar's defeat in 1998 the country progressed significantly in the direction of democratic modernization, the overall climate in society soon began to differ from the euphoria experienced after the 1998 elections. Feelings of fatigue, skepticism, and disenchantment prevailed among the population as a reaction to corruption scandals, political fragmentation, and the half-baked character of some reforms. Citizens' disappointment with the lack of morality in the public sphere became widespread.

And yet, great ideas and visions do help—despite the belief of pragmatists that the nation does not need them. In this regard, it is

---

[41] "After the fall of communism in 1989, the Slovak community was confronted with two basic positions concerning its own story of 'Slovakness,'" writes Kamila Stullerová (citation below). According to Stullerová, the above-mentioned Vladimír Mináč, a well-known author and a prominent figure during communist rule, and Peter Zajac, a literary critic, scientist, and a co-founder of the Public Against Violence Movement in Bratislava that challenged and defeated the communist regime in 1989, represent two opposite approaches to and concepts of contemporary Slovak society, two fundamental alternative positions of the Slovak discourse, "Mináč advocating for perseverance of the national identity based on tradition and common experience and Zajac calling for a non-romantic perception of the nation which should incorporate an idea of civic values and binding rules," (Kamila Stullerová, "National Sentiments, Globalization and Justice. Slovaks Narrating their Democratization Process," *Thinking Fundamentals*, IWM Junior Visiting Fellows Conferences 9 (Vienna, 2000), http://www.iwm.at/publ-jvc/jc-09-08.pdf).

[42] Milan Šútovec, "Kam povedú tie diaľnice?" [Where will those superhighways lead?], *Domino-fórum* 1, 1997.

[43] See Paul Bloker, *Constitutionalism and Constitutional Anomie in the New Europe* (Trento: Universita degli Studi di Trento, Department of Sociology and Social Research, 2010), http://papers.ssrn.com/sol3/papers.cfm?abstract_id=1719095.

useful to recall the words of Pope John Paul II during his visit to Slovakia in 1995, in a time of tension and anxiety over democracy. The man, whose huge impact and appeal had spread well beyond religious boundaries, addressed a crowd of almost one million with the same simple words he used in his native Poland and dozens of other countries throughout five continents. "Don't be afraid," he said, giving people faith that they were not alone, that they had the courage to stand firm, and the strength to press for change.

This message, in combination with the electrifying appeal of Public Against Violence in the first hours of the Velvet Revolution in November 1989—"let us, as citizens, take matters into our own hands"—could provide fertile and inspiring soil for a future narrative. A narrative for a country whose citizens are able to mobilize their potential and have courage to pursue their dream: to anchor Slovakia more firmly in the family of freedom-loving and rule-abiding democratic nations, to build a good society based on equity, fairness, tolerance and compassion.

CHAPTER 16

Social Developments in Slovakia after Twenty Years: The Impact of Politics

Sharon L. Wolchik

As Martin Bútora and Zora Bútorová note in the introduction to their chapter, the social dimension of the transition from communism and a planned economy, as well as of the changes that occurred after Slovakia became independent in 1993, is a huge, multifaceted subject. The authors wisely chose to limit their consideration to several key aspects. Focusing on seven areas related to social changes in the country, their analysis highlights numerous important issues. In this response, I will group my comments into four main areas. These include judgments about the successes and failures of the last two decades; citizens' evaluations of positive and negative changes since 1989 and critical problems; issues related to the development of political and civic life; and the authors' call for a "new narrative." Based, as one would expect in a work by two of Slovakia's preeminent sociologists, on a wealth of empirical data from international as well as domestic sources, the analysis provides an extremely useful and nuanced overview of the areas the authors discuss. As I do not disagree with their interpretations of the data they present or their overall conclusions, my remarks will largely focus on additional questions their snapshots raise.

In dealing with issues of success and failure, the authors use a variety of international and domestic data to document areas in which the country has progressed since 1989, as well as ongoing, and at times, new, problems. On some indicators, Slovakia ranks very well. In the midst of this generally optimistic picture, several problems stand out. One is the issue of corruption. In addition to Slovakia's very low ranking on certain international surveys for corruption and transparency, where the country is near the bottom of all countries surveyed, respondents in Slovakia also identify corruption as one of the most important issues of the day. At the same time, relatively few respondents identify problems with the judiciary and the rule of law, which potentially provide mechanisms to deal with corruption, as significant. How do we explain this pattern, and what if anything have the political elites and NGO leaders done to highlight these connections? This seeming disconnect may be explained somewhat by the information the authors provide on citizens' perceptions and evaluations of the political realm.

In the segments of the chapter that focus more directly on politics and civic life, the authors identify the inability of political parties and their leaders to act in the public interest as one of the main sources of shame citizens feel about their country. They also suggest that Slovakia needs more "democratic modernizers," that is, political leaders who will behave in new, more democratic ways and inspire greater confidence and perhaps activism among citizens. In this area Slovakia is not alone. Levels of trust in political institutions and political leaders are low in many democratic countries, which also share the problem of motivating citizens to engage in what has been described as "unusual activity," that is, politics.[1]

Although they do not address the issue explicitly, the authors' analysis of data concerning citizen evaluations of politics and sources of shame about their country may well reflect the episodic, but ongoing, corruption scandals that have occurred in Slovakia, as well as in other post-communist states in the recent past. The Gorilla scandal that tainted the reputations of some of the leaders thought to be among the most fervent champions of democracy and damaged the electoral fortunes of the center right parties is not dealt with directly in the authors' discussion.[2] It is hard to see how such incidents can fail to influence

---

1 See the results of public opinion studies in the EU, as in Standard European Barometer 809, "Public Opinion in the EU," pp. 48ff., *Eurobarometer*, http://ec.europa.edu/p_o/archives/eb_arch_eu.htm.

[2] The transcripts of secret meetings between Slovak politicians and the financial institution Penta were leaked to the press in late 2012. See "Gorila Pentu nezastavila" [Gorilla did not stop Penta], *Sme*, December 20, 2012. Tom Nicholson, a Canadian journalist resident in Slovakia published a book about the Gorilla Affair. See his *Gorila* (Bratislava: Dixit, 2012).

public views of political leaders and institutions. As the jailing of the former Croatian Prime Minister Ivo Sanader in November 2012, and the forced resignation of Czech Prime Minister Petr Nečas in the summer of 2013 illustrate, problems with elite political values and attitudes, as well as behavior, are not confined to Slovakia.[3] But the disillusionment that the Gorilla scandal caused might be expected to have been especially great, given the association of some of the individuals involved with the ouster of Vladimír Mečiar in 1998 that put Slovakia back on a democratic path after the de-democratization that occurred under Mečiar. This section highlights a problem that many formerly communist countries, as well as those without a communist past, have to deal with, which is the problem of elite political culture. Changes in this area and the development of an elite political culture that emphasizes compromise, collaboration, and service to the nation rather than self-enrichment have been slower to develop than many analysts expected in the early days after the collapse of communism, even though many thought that such changes would take quite some time.

The authors devote special attention to the NGO sector, or civil society. After discussing the vibrancy of this sector and the role of OK'98 (Citizens' Campaign 1998) in removing Vladimír Mečiar in 1998, the authors note both the recent successes and ongoing problems of NGOs. The success of civic initiatives related to environmental issues, as well as the use of new forms of technology, including the Internet, to circulate petitions that elected authorities are required to consider, are encouraging developments. The authors also note, however, the problems that continue to plague this sector after two decades of independence, including a lack of resources, citizen reluctance to participate in organized groups, and the "formalism" that characterizes most of the relationships between the third sector and formal political authorities. They also note the negative, as well as the positive, impact that the ability to communicate easily through the Internet has had, including the growth of xenophobic, anti-democratic discourse and support evident in the recent election of Marián Kot-

---

[3] For information on the conviction of Ivo Sanader, see "Former Premier of Croatia is Sentenced for Graft," *The New York Times,* November 20, 2012; for the Nečas affair, see "Czech PM Petr Necas Resigns Over Major Corruption Scandal," *Deutsche Welle,* June 17, 2013.

leba, the far-right governor of the Banská Bystrica region in Slovakia.[4] In this area, again, Slovakia is not alone, as similar trends exist in other parts of the region.

What is interesting in this area is the fact that, although civic engagement shows some signs of spreading to new forms, the authors also indicate that the overall level of citizens' involvement in civic life has not increased greatly. Here, as in other areas, including the attitudes and behavior of political leaders, it is clear that the negative influence of communism on levels of trust and willingness to be actively engaged in public affairs, including associating with others to deal with communal problems, or pressuring political leaders to do so, has been compounded by the impact of the last twenty-five years after the end of communism. The influence of the more recent past can be expected to be especially great in the case of young people, who although indirectly influenced by pre-1989 trends in these areas through their parents, have direct experience only with post-communist politics.

In this area, as in others, there are issues that one might wish the authors had explored to a greater extent. We are given data about the impact of certain demographic characteristics, such as age, for example, on attitudes and perceptions. But it would have been interesting to know more about the perceptions and values of young people in particular. To what extent has coming of age politically during an era of "transition," with all of its issues, had on young people specifically? How serious is the problem of brain drain in Slovakia? To what extent do young people in Slovakia support any of the extremist views and groups the authors mention? Is there a Slovak equivalent for the support for Hungary's far-right Jobbik Party among educated youth?

Similar questions arise concerning other groups whose views are characterized but not analyzed in depth, such as women, the Roma, and the poor. The authors do pay special attention to the situation of the Roma in Slovakia, but they do not give us information to judge the extent to which Roma citizens share the views of other citizens on the issues discussed. There is yet another aspect of social issues that the authors do not deal with in their discussion, beyond identifying winners

---

[4] "Novým županom je Marián Kotleba" [The new governor is Marián Kotleba], *Sme*, November 23, 2013.

and losers in the transition, which are social problems, including not only poverty and unemployment, but also the various social pathologies that have arisen or been exacerbated by the opening of borders, greater exposure to the rest of Europe, and the decline of rigid political and police control.

The authors conclude their discussion of social and political trends in Slovakia by setting out two competing narratives, which, they argue, have characterized public discussions and perceptions of Slovakia's role in the world. These include the "victim" narrative that emphasizes the role of outside forces in inhibiting positive developments in Slovakia and the "Tatra Tiger" narrative that emphasizes the success of the Slovak economy and its membership in international organizations. They argue that there is a need, instead, for a new narrative that would emphasize democratic, civic values and be inclusive of all the country's citizens. This narrative appears to be very close to that which prevails, at least at the level of the ideal, in most established democratic countries.

The authors' discussion in this section raises several questions. First, they argue that both of the preceding narratives are "problematic," which they undoubtedly are, from the perspective of creating a vibrant civic society and fully democratic political system. But they do not elaborate upon this argument. Nor do they link these views to concrete political parties, leaders, or movements in Slovakia, which would help us to understand the influence and impact of these views. The authors also do not address the issue of how to establish a new narrative, or, perhaps better said, how to make such a narrative, which exists and has been articulated by public intellectuals such as Pavol Demeš, as well as the authors themselves,[5] and individual political leaders in Slovakia over the last twenty years, a more generally accepted view of the nation and its political system.

---

[5] For his profile and some of his ideas, see "Pavol Demeš: Éra dominancie Západu sa končí" [Pavol Demeš: the era of western domination is ending], *Sme*, July 7, 2009. For the ideas and opinions of other public intellectuals, see Martin Bútora et al., eds. *Odkiaľ a kam: Dvadsať rokov samostatnosti* [From where and whither? Twenty years of independence] (Bratislava: Kalligram, 2013).

Their discussion of narratives also raises another issue that the authors do not address directly, but is implicit in the data and analyses they present. There is no direct discussion of an issue of some concern to political scientists and theorists, which is the extent to which Slovakia, as well as other formerly communist European states, should still be considered "post-communist." Václav Havel's argument in the early 1990s that it was not useful to use the term post-communist was judged by many to have been premature.[6] However, twenty years later, it is a question that we need to consider. Given the integration of Slovakia, as well as other formerly communist states, into the EU, NATO, the OECD, et cetera, one might judge the term "post-communist" to be outdated. The evidence the authors provide, however, suggests that, much as Slovakia shares many of the same characteristics and problems of other European states, there are still aspects of political and social life that reflect not only the continued impact of policies, structures, and attitudes dating from the communist period, but also have an impact on the way in which political leaders and citizens have reacted to the problems posed by the process of creating democratic institutions and a market economy in the period since the end of communism and, more specifically, since Slovak independence.

These dual legacies are also related to another question the authors' discussion raises: the extent to which Slovakia should be considered a consolidated democracy. Parts of an answer to this question are included in the authors' initial discussion of success and failures in the last twenty years. As in the question of "post-communist" versus "normal European state," one could simply take the country's membership in the EU and NATO as the equivalent of the Good Housekeeping Seal of Approval, that is, an indication that democracy has indeed been consolidated. If we take a "thin" definition of democracy, which requires free and fair elections and two peaceful alternations of power as our criteria, Slovakia clearly is a democratic state. If, however, we adopt a more ambitious standard that also requires the rule of law, a robust and well-articulated civil society, and the widespread adoption of democratic political values and attitudes on the part of citizens and

---

[6] Václav Havel, "The Post-Communist Nightmare," *The New York Review of Books*, May 27, 1993.

political leaders, the evidence the authors present indicates that Slovakia, as many other countries that have emerged from communism, still has a way to go.

As these comments illustrate, the arguments the chapter presents raise complex issues that are critically important for Slovakia's future. In the short space available, it would have been impossible for the authors to address all the questions their discussion raises. The chapter does an excellent job in providing a taste of the kinds of analyses the authors are known for. One hopes it will be the basis for a more extended, in-depth treatment of the issues it presents.

CHAPTER 17

Social Developments in the Czech Republic Since 1993

Oldřich Tůma

Writing on social developments from a historian's perspective is an extremely demanding task. It is a diverse, multilevel and complex topic, which requires adequate across-the-board research. It is in fact impossible to cover the topic fully without subtopical studies on political, economic or social history, cultural history, and everyday life. Conducting such research and presenting its results is very difficult even for older periods and almost impossible for the last twenty years. Any partial studies, if existing at all, are very preliminary and almost all of them deal exclusively with the 1990s.[1] The following pages are not, and cannot be, the product of focused research, but are based on reflections of public or media discourses or on the perception of and comments regarding changes of the social atmosphere.

First and foremost, it should be noted that Czech society since 1993 is definitely a post-communist society rather than a post-

---

1 On political history see, for example, Adéla Gjuričová et al., *Rozděleni minulostí. Vytváření politických identit v České republice po roce 1989* [Divided by the past. The creation of political identities in the Czech Republic after 1989] (Prague: Václav Havel Library, 2011), or Lubomír Kopeček, *Éra nevinnosti. Česká politika 1989–1997* [The age of innocence. Czech politics, 1989–1997] (Brno: Barrister a Principal, 2010). As to economic history, see, for example, Martin Myant, *The Rise and Fall of Czech Capitalism. Economic Development in the Czech Republic since 1989* (London: Edward Elgar, 2003). On social history see, for example, Jiří Večerník, ed., *Zpráva o vývoji české společnosti 1989–1998* [Report on the development of Czech society in 1989–1998] (Prague: Academia, 1998).

Czechoslovak one. All its metamorphoses, changes, developments, the problems it struggles with take place within a post-communist, rather than a post-Czechoslovak transformation. I dare say that recent developments would have been similar even if Czechoslovakia had not been divided.

It seems to me that the Slovak—or post-Czechoslovak—factor concerns just one aspect of the development of Czech society—that is to say, the spiritual environment of social development, especially in the 1990s. I intend to come back to this aspect at the end of my chapter. Before doing so, however, I have no other option but to present a rather boring explanation of the development of Czech society—it is boring because it essentially does not differ from the stories of Poland, Hungary, Slovakia, or other post-communist European countries. Similarities prevail over differences; all the countries basically represent variants of the same story—a difficult transformation from an unfree, atomized, egalitarian, undifferentiated society toward one that is multilayered, representing many interests and values: a free society, but also a society which is polarized, rapidly changing and developing, and, at the same time, also somehow frozen in one fundamental conflict and unable to look for consensus and pragmatic solutions. The story is—or was—the same, but its accentuations, details, phases, and timings can and did differ.[2]

Czech society at the end of the communist regime was regarded as extraordinarily egalitarian and very homogeneous, at least in the

---

[2] There is an enormous reservoir of publications on the collapse of communist regimes. One covers many of them: Steven Saxonberg, *The Fall. A Comparative Study of the End of Communism in Czechoslovakia, East Germany, Hungary and Poland* (Amsterdam: Harwood Academic Publishers, 2001). The latest publications include Stefan Karner et al., eds. *Der Kreml und die Wende 1989* (Innsbruck: Studien Verlag, 2014). The manner in which the fall of the communist regimes in different Central European countries is perceived in the context of local historiographies is illustrated, for example, by relevant parts of titles available in English: Andrzej Paczkowski, *The Spring Will be Ours: Poland and the Poles from Occupation to Freedom* (University Park: Pennsylvania State University Press, 2003); Ignác Romsics, *Hungary in the Twentieth Century* (Budapest: Osiris 1999); Elena Mannová, ed., *A Concise History of Slovakia* (Bratislava: Historical Institute of the Slovak Academy of Sciences, 2000); and Jaroslav Pánek and Oldřich Tůma, eds. *A History of the Czech Lands* (Prague: Karolinum Press, 2009).

social and economic sense. This was not true, insofar as opinions were concerned. Large segments of society and whole generations or professional groups had alienated themselves from the regime and defied its hardliners long before November 1989, at least in what they thought, but gradually also in what they did. This was confirmed by an increase of critical opinions captured by public opinion polls[3] and the growing number of signatories of anti-regime petitions and, subsequently, also of demonstrations and rallies.[4] The gap was widening not only between the regime and students[5] or intellectuals,[6] but also with respect to social groups upon which the regime was relying the most, in particular, workers.[7] The changing moods within society, but also the diminishing self-confidence and growing doubts within the

---

[3] See Miroslav Vaněk, *Veřejné mínění o socialismu před 17. listopadem 1989. Analýza výsledků výzkumů veřejného mínění prováděných ÚVVM od roku 1972 do roku 1989* [Public opinion on socialism before November 17, 1989. An analysis of public polls conducted by the Institute for Public Opinion Research] (Prague: Ústav pro soudobé dějiny-Maxdorf, 1994).

[4] See Oldřich Tůma, *Zítra zase tady! Protirežimní demonstrace v předlistopadové Praze jako politický a sociální fenomén* [Tomorrow the same place! Anti-regime demonstrations in Prague before November 1989 as a political and social phenomenon] (Prague: Ústav pro soudobé dějiny-Maxdorf, 1994). On the changing relationship and mutual reflections of the opposition and Czechoslovak society, see Tomáš Vilímek, "K otázce vztahu a vzájemné reflexi opozice a společnosti v Československu po roce 1968" [Relations between the opposition and society in Czechoslovakia after 1968 and their opinions of each other], in *Opozice a společnost po roce 1948* [Opposition and society after 1948], ed. Oldřich Tůma and Tomáš Vilímek (Prague: Ústav pro soudobé dějiny, 2009), 176–220.

[5] See Milan Otáhal, Miroslav Vaněk, *Sto studentských revolucí. Studenti v období pádu komunismu—životopisná vyprávění* [A hundred student revolutions. Students during the fall of communism—biographical stories] (Prague: Lidové noviny, 1999).

[6] See Milan Otáhal, *Podíl tvůrčí inteligence na pádu komunismu* [The role of the creative intelligentsia in the downfall of communism] (Brno: Doplněk, 1999).

[7] See the latest publication by Lenka Kalinová, *Dělníci v normalizaci: dělnictvo a sociální stát v Československu* [Workers in the normalization period: the working class and the welfare state in Czechoslovakia], in *Česká společnost v 70. a 80. letech: sociální a ekonomické aspekty* [Czech society in the 1970s and 1980s: social and economic aspects], ed. Tomáš Vilímek and Oldřich Tůma (Prague: Ústav pro soudobé dějiny, 2012), 7–62.

ruling regime, are supported by the results of major oral history projects as well.[8]

Standards of living and property ownership differed as well—although society was egalitarian in terms of official statistical data (particularly wages, salaries, pensions, et cetera). If the average wage was equal to 100 (in the mid-1980s, its typical representatives were workers in processing industries), the best paid employees, at 135, were workers in mining and metallurgical industries, while the lowest wages (83) prevailed in the service sector. The income in the highest category was less than twice of that in the lowest category, which means the difference was not very great.[9] Even in the second half of the 1980s, cautious economic reforms notwithstanding, there were not—save for very rare exceptions—any entrepreneurs or self-employed persons, who were quite common in Poland, and also elsewhere. Still, there were fairly considerable social differences and some people owned quite sizable properties. However, what is most important from the viewpoint of the topic dealt with here is that even at that time, i.e., before 1989, it is possible to identify groups which had the potential for rapid economic and social advancement and who became the source of the new class of entrepreneurs when conditions permitted.

These groups consisted of people closely tied to the communist regime, but who were extremely pragmatic and utilitarian and had no problem in quickly severing their connections with the regime and its ideology. These people had contacts, information, and other forms of social and information capital, which they quickly put to use. They were officials of the Communist Party or other pro-regime organi-

---

[8] Miroslav Vaněk and Pavel Urbášek, eds. *Vítězové? Poraženi? Životopisná interview* [Victors? Vanquished? Biographical interviews] 2 vols. (Prague: Institute of Contemporary History, 2005); Miroslav Vaněk, ed., *Obyčejní lidé...?! Pohled do života tzv. mlčící většiny. Životopisná vyprávění příslušníků dělnických profesí a inteligence* [Ordinary people...?! An insight into the lives of the "silent majority": life stories of manual laborers and the intelligentsia] 3 vols. (Prague: Academia, 2009).

[9] See *Výběrové šetření o mzdách za červen 1984* [Selective analysis of wages in June 1984] (Prague: Federální statistický úřad, 1985). See Lenka Kalinová, *Konec nadějím a nová očekávání. K dějinám české společnosti 1969–1993* [Dashed hopes, new expectations: on the social history of the years 1969–1993] (Prague: Academia, 2012), 274–81.

zations (it is quite remarkable how many names of, for example, of former functionaries of the Social Union of Youth can be found among those who later became very successful businessmen), but also members of the intelligence services or employees of certain exclusive companies, such as foreign trade corporations.

Dozens of names could be used to illustrate the above. Here are a few examples: ex-Minister of Agriculture Miroslav Toman and his sons took control of a number of food companies through his Agrotrade Corporation after privatization; ex-Minister of Foreign Trade Andrej Barčák held high positions (ultimately at the European level) in General Motors; the Slovak Alojz Lorenc, the last chief of state security, worked for Penta, a major Czecho-Slovak investment group; Martin Ulčák, ex-chairman of the Municipal Committee of the Socialist Union of Youth in Prague (and then, for a short time, also the chairman of the Central Committee of the same organization), became a successful wholesaler of tobacco products, a newspaper distributor, and the owner of many companies worth billions of CZK; ex-chairman of the Czech Central Committee of the Socialist Union of Youth Miroslav Šlouf was very successful in consulting and became an immensely powerful lobbyist; Vasil Mohorita, a long-standing chairman of the Central Committee of the Socialist Union of Youth, and for a short time also a member of the supreme bodies of the Communist Party of Czechoslovakia, did business with Russia and Ukraine in the 1990s; Ladislav Adamec Jr., son of the last communist prime minister of the federal government, became a successful businessman in mechanical engineering, sporting goods, and other fields.

A number of today's successful businessmen used to work for former foreign trade corporations: The Slovak Andrej Babiš, now among the top ten richest Czech citizens (owner of the mammoth agrochemical holding Agrofert) and lately also a successful politician, used to work for Petrimex; Jiří Šimáně, owner of Travel Service and Unimex Group, worked at Strojexport; Václav Junek, once managing director of the socialist foreign trade corporation Chemapol, did very well in the chemical industry in the 1990s; Josef Hušek, owner of the huge company Inekon (export of mechanical engineering products), used to work for Pragoinvest before 1989; Tomáš Chrenek, owner of Třinec Ironworks, Moravia Energo Group, and for some time also Barrandov Film Studios, is an ex-employee of Kerametal. Some of them are also registered as former state security secret collaborators—e.g. Václav Junek and Andrej Babiš (the latter, however, brought the matter to court, claiming that his entry in the state security's list of collaborators had been falsified, and his dispute with the Slovak Institute of National Memory has so far gone well for him). Another member of this group is Aleš Hušák, until recently a successful Czech businessman and, inter alia, the CEO of the giant lottery company Sazka.[10]

Another group consisted of those operating within the gray economy/black market environment or selling goods in short supply during the communist era. Perhaps the best—and most profitable—example of black market activities was the trade in the shortest-supply commodity for which, at the same time, one could buy anything—i.e., hard currencies or their local substitute, Tuzex[11] hard currency

---

[10] Detailed information can be found mainly on web pages, in particular (under relevant names) at Česká Wikipedie, http://cs.wikipedia.org/wiki/. On this issue as a whole, see Miroslav Vaněk and Lenka Krátká, eds., *Příběhy (ne)obyčejných profesí. Česká společnost v období tzv. normalizace a transformace v biografických vyprávěních některých profesních skupin* [Narratives of (extra)ordinary occupations. Czech society in the period of "normalization" and transformation: biographical narratives] (Prague: Karolinum, 2014). See also, for example, Petr Matějů, "Determinanty ekonomického úspěchu v první fázi postkomunistické transformace. Česká republika 1989–1992" [Determinants of economic success in the first stage of the post-communist transformation. The Czech Republic, 1989–1992], *Sociologický časopis* 29, no. 3 (1993), 341–66; Petr Matějů and Lim Nelson, "Who Has Gotten Ahead After the Fall of Communism? The Case of the Czech Republic" *Sociologický časopis* 31 no. 2 (1995), 117–36; Eduard Kubů, "České (československé) transformační kontinuity 20. století. Problémy struktury ekonomiky, technicko-technologické vyspělosti a podnikatelsko-manažerských elit" [Czech (Czechoslovak) transformation continuities of the twentieth century. Problems of the structure of the economy, technical and technological development level and entrepreneurial and business elites), *Acta Oeconomica Pragensia* 13, no. 3 (2005): 230–45; Petr Matějů, "Elite Research in the Czech Republic. A Report on Major Research Projects," in *Elites in Transition. Elite Research in Central and Eastern Europe*, ed. Heinrich Best and Ulrich Becker (Opladen: Leske + Budrich, 1997), 61–76.

[11] A government-owned hard currency chain selling Western goods unavailable at regular stores. Similar chains existed in other communist countries as well—Pewex in Poland, Beryozka in the Soviet Union, Intertourist in Hungary, etc.

vouchers. Contacts with foreigners were crucial; it is no coincidence that so many former waiters, cab drivers, car repairmen, and receptionists quickly started their careers as early as 1990. These people had real—not just information or social—capital even before November 1989. Just two names of such businessmen whose success was, however, rather short-lived come to mind: ex-car mechanic Petr Mach, owner of several companies and, in the 1990s, also of the best Czech soccer team Sparta Praha, and Roman Janoušek, later a billionaire, media, and real estate tycoon. At the end of the day, however, both ended up being taken to court.[12]

The last group consisted of pre-1948 property owners, or rather their descendants. Prior to November 1989, hardly any of them had hoped or believed they would get their family property back. However, the early 1990s Czechoslovak and later Czech legal norms to implement relatively extensive restitutions of nationalized property (mainly agricultural land, forests, apartment buildings, hotels, but also small and medium-sized enterprises) provided conditions for a rapid social differentiation, and this is also how a certain segment of the new middle class was born.[13] These were the most extensive property restitutions of all Central and Eastern European post-communist countries. It is estimated that property worth approximately 4 billion USD was transferred to former owners or their descendants under the restitution laws. The restitutions involved more than 100,000 eligible persons.[14] After political changes paved the way for economic and social transformations, Czech society started changing fairly quickly. To quote one of the most respected Czech sociologists, "over a relatively short period of time, the differentiation and structure of wages in the Czech Republic have been moving energetically towards the standard Western pattern."[15]

---

[12] http://cs.wikipedia.org/wiki/Petr_Mach (podnikatel); http://cs.wikipedia.org/wiki/Roman_Janoušek.
[13] See, for example, Jan Kuklík Jr., *Znárodněné Československo* [Nationalized Czechoslovakia] (Prague: Auditorium, 2010), 398–419.
[14] See Jan Urban, *Privatizace a institucionální reformy v České republice* [Privatization and institutional reforms in the Czech Republic] (Prague: Právnická fakulta, 2005), 27.
[15] Jiří Večerník, *Czech Society in the 2000s: A Report on Socio-Economic Policies and Structures* (Prague: Academia, 2009), 87.

Meanwhile, it is good to remember that, when using data pertaining to the Czech Republic as a whole, one should always bear in mind that the "average" figures provide a somewhat distorted picture of reality. As a matter of fact, there is a very significant difference between Prague and the rest of the country. Regional differences are nothing unusual in other countries, and there exist differences between different regions of the Czech Republic as well, but Prague really stands out. It accounts for approximately 12 percent of the Czech Republic's population, but generates approximately 25 percent of the Czech GDP.[16] Prague ranks among the wealthiest regions of the European Union. Prague's average per capita GDP is almost 170 percent of that of the European Union (EU 28).[17] It is thus more than twice the average per capita GDP of the Czech Republic. The average salary is almost 35 percent higher than elsewhere[18] (this is obviously due to the concentration of government, economic, cultural, educational, and other institutions in Prague, which is also reflected in the labor structure); however, the prices of services, housing and some goods are much higher in Prague than in the rest of the country. For a long time, Prague has maintained the lowest unemployment rate of all the Czech regions.[19] All of the above is combined with incomparable offerings of culture and education, tourism, the presence of foreigners and—to some extent—also a different lifestyle and a different standard of living. That is why people living in the capital are not always able to understand or perceive the different economic and social situation in other

---

[16] Prague's population in 2012 was 1,246,780. The whole country had 10,516,025 inhabitants. Prague's GDP in 2012 was 948,844 million CZK. The whole country's was 3,845,900,000. See the web pages of the Regional Office of the Czech Bureau of Statistics in Prague, http://www.czso.cz/x/krajedata.nsf/oblast2/hdp-xa; *Statistická ročenka České republiky 2013* [Statistical yearbook of the Czech Republic, 2013] (Prague: Český statistický úřad 2013), 46–7, 64.

[17] *Eurostat*, http://epp.eurostat.ec.europa.eu/tgm/table.do?tab=table&init=1&plugin=1&language=en&pcode=tec00114

[18] Average monthly gross wage of FTE employees (2011) in Prague: 32,821 CZK; in the whole republic: 24,466 CZK, http://www.czso.cz/x/krajedata.nsf/oblast2/mzdy-xa; *Statistická ročenka 2013*, 50–51.

[19] Prague's unemployment rate in 2012: 3.4 percent, in the whole country: 8.2 percent (*Statistická ročenka 2013*, 332).

parts of the country. And this is also one of the reasons for the aversion of people living in other regions towards the citizens of Prague, which is sometimes downright pathological.

The internal differentiation and regional differences notwithstanding, Czech society as a whole has undergone a significant change during the past two decades. In terms of many measurable and statistically captured data (most of the information presented below is based on data from Eurostat, the European Union's statistical office), it is even becoming increasingly similar to societies of the "old" EU countries (those of the EU 15 before the expansion in 2004), i.e., countries of Western Europe. In fact, it is the most similar to them among all the countries of the former Soviet Bloc (save for a very few exceptions).

The Czech Republic's employment structure is similar to that of Western European countries, although it employs 10 percent to 15 percent fewer people in the tertiary sector (58.9 percent, the EU average is 69.1 percent) and more people in industry (in fact, it has the highest industrial employment of all EU countries, with 38 percent; the EU average is 25.2 percent). However, it has a similarly low agricultural employment rate (3.1 percent; the EU average is 5.1 percent), generally lower than all former communist countries, but also lower than most countries in southern Europe.[20] The structure of household spending is also similar to "Old Europe"; a decreasing, although still higher percentage of expenses for food (15.5 percent compared to 12.4 percent), and increasing shares of expenses for housing: 26.3 percent compared to 24.3 percent, travel, leisure activities, culture (here the Czech Republic almost exactly matches the average figures of the EU: 15—9.1 percent to 8.8 percent), etc.[21]

Since 1989, Czech society has been re-stratified; instead of former categories, there are traditional socioeconomic classes now: the lower, lower middle, middle, upper middle and upper. Sociologists argue that the establishment and growth of the middle class in particular has been

---

[20] For 2010 data, see *Labour Market Statistics* (Luxembourg: Publication Office of the European Union, 2011), 9, *Eurostat*, http://epp.eurostat.ec.europa.eu/cache/ITY_OFFPUB/KS-32-11-798/EN/KS-32-11-798-EN.PDF. For details on the Czech Republic, see *Statistická ročenka 2013*, 326–7.

[21] For 2012 data, see *Eurostat*, http://appsso.eurostat.ec.europa.eu/nui/submitViewTableAction.do.

slower and more problematic than expected and that this class is still smaller than in Western European societies—and, insofar as salaries and property ownership are concerned, they may be right. This may be attributable to the cautious social policy of all Czech governments, both right wing and social democratic, and the slow disappearance of previously existing wage-leveling. As a result, some social and professional groups of employees (but also self-employed tradesmen), who represent a solid segment of the middle class in Western Europe, are not much different from the lower classes in the Czech Republic (this applies, for instance, to teachers, professors, physicians, etc.).[22] Even more remarkably, fewer and fewer people see themselves as belonging to the middle class. While 61 percent of economically active people saw themselves as belonging to the middle class in 1991, their share dropped to less than 37 percent in 2007 (i.e., before the world economic crisis). On the one hand, self-identification with the lower class increased from less than 6 percent to almost 17 percent over the same period—and with the upper middle and upper classes from 3 percent to more than 12 percent.[23] On the other hand, other sociologists argue that the middle class, although not so large and identifiable in terms of income, property ownership, or self-identification in Czech statistical data, is clearly visible in the structure of society in terms of its lifestyle, structure of consumption, the consumption of culture, et cetera.[24]

Moreover, Czech society shows a very low risk-of-poverty rate—a mere 9 percent, the lowest figure of all EU countries! The EU 28 average is about 17 percent. The combined risk of poverty/social exclusion criterion also places the Czech Republic at the lowest level, together with The Netherlands (around 15 percent), while the EU 28

---

[22] For a detailed analysis of the middle class phenomenon in the Czech Republic, see Jiří Večerník, *Czech Society in the 2000s*, 127–43.
[23] Ibid., 139. See also Petr Matějů and Klára Vlachová, *Nerovnost, spravedlnost, politika. Česká republika 1991–1998* [Inequality, justice, politics. The Czech Republic 1991–1998] (Prague: Slon, 2000), 73–97.
[24] E.g., Jiří Černý, Markéta Sedláčková and Milan Tuček, *Zdroje utváření skupinových mentalit v České republice po roce 1989* [Sources for the creation of group mentalities in the Czech Republic after 1989] (Prague: Sociologický ústav AV ČR, 2004); Milan Tuček, ed., *České elity po patnácti letech transformace* [Czech elites after fifteen years of transformation] (Prague: Sociologický ústav AV ČR, 2006).

average is almost 25 percent. Moreover, unlike in most EU countries, there are relatively small differences among densely and thinly populated areas of the Czech Republic.[25] This is surely related to traditional egalitarianism, and even more so to the very cautious and socially sensitive economic transformation of the 1990s, which was a long way from shock therapy, although it was sometimes referred to as such. The Czech Republic also maintained a very low unemployment rate, around 4 percent, practically throughout the 1990s; it only climbed up in the late 1990s due to worldwide economic problems. Since that time, it has been between 6 and 9 percent, depending on economic conditions, which means it is still lower than in most EU countries. However, unemployment is distributed very irregularly among regions, and was a social problem even in the 1990s, particularly in the previously preferred heavy industrial regions of North Bohemia and North Moravia, i.e., today's regions of Ústí nad Labem and Moravia-Silesia.[26]

There is yet another characteristic which produces fairly substantial differences within Czech society and naturally influences the overall picture and overall statistical data, although it is somewhat hidden in them. This is not a territorial characteristic; it concerns the existence of ethnic, or rather ethno-cultural, minorities.[27]

The apparent and also officially reflected existence of minorities is, in fact, also a novelty of the post-communist era. After the expulsion of the Germans after WWII, the Czech Lands were ethnically homogeneous. The Slovak community, the numbers of which had been growing particularly since the late 1960s, was not, due to mutual lan-

---

[25] *Eurostat Regional Yearbook 2013* (Luxembourg: Publications Office of the European Union, 201), 3, 226–35. The data is from 2011. For slightly modified data pertaining to 2012 see *Eurostat*, http://epp.eurostat.ec.europa.eu/statistics_explained/index.php/Social_inclusion_statistics#At-risk-of-poverty.

[26] *Statistická ročenka 2013*, 322.

[27] For the minorities issue see, for example, Yana Leontiyeva, ed., *Menšinová problematika v ČR: komunitní život a reprezentace kolektivních zájmů (Slováci, Ukrajinci, Vietnamci a Romové)* [The issue of minorities in the Czech Republic: community life and the representation of collective interests (Slovaks, Ukrainians, Vietnamese, and Roma)] (Prague: Sociologický ústav, 2006), or Helena Nosková, Petr Bednařík et al., *National Minorities, Identity, Education* (Prague: Institute for Contemporary History 2011).

guage and cultural proximity, perceived as a minority.[28] And the situation did not change even after the birth of the independent Czech and Slovak Republics. During the 2011 census, 147,000 citizens of the Czech Republic[29] proclaimed themselves to be of Slovak ethnic origin; according to 2013 data of the Czech Statistical Office, there were also some 90,000 citizens of the Slovak Republic residing on the territory of the Czech Republic.[30]

Before 1989, even the Roma community had not been perceived as a minority.[31] The assimilation policy of the state, with its forced employment and constant and relatively effective administrative control over every sphere of life, seemed to integrate the community into the "standard" majority society. The end of this policy in 1989, however, brought a disastrous and lasting social slump to most Roma. The skyrocketing unemployment rate, dependence on social welfare and benefits, inferior education, the moving together of numerous Roma families (exacerbated by increasing immigration of their poorer relatives from Slovakia) into special enclaves in the poorest regions of the country, rife with crime and the black economy—all these factors made the Roma problem a frightening social and political issue. Neither the Roma community nor the majority society or the state had a solution to this problem. The Roma, who had been employed mainly as menial (but at that time relatively well-paid) laborers under the old regime, found themselves unable to cope in the labor market, and even less able and willing to do something about it. The effects of the government's attempts at implementing an affirmative action policy were minimal, and the state ultimately proved absolutely helpless, limiting itself to occasional loud rhetoric and continuously increasing social benefits, which created animosity in some segments of society. The Roma problem is the prime mover and fuel for skinhead and radical right-

---

[28] See, e.g., Helena Nosková, *Pražské ozvěny. Minulost a současnost Slováků v českých zemích* [Prague echoes. Past and present of Slovaks in the Czech Lands] (Prague: Ústav pro soudobé dějiny AV ČR, 2014).
[29] *Czech Statistical Office*, https://www.czso.cz/csu/sldb/domov.
[30] *Czech Statistical Office*, https://www.czso.cz/csu/cizinci/4-ciz_pocet_cizincu#cr.
[31] For the Roma see, for example, Dana Bittnerová, Mirjam Moravcová, eds., *Etnické komunity—Romové* [Ethnic communities—the Roma] (Prague: Fakulta humanitních studií, 2013).

wing political movements, which have, however, been very marginal, with their general election results counted in tenths of a percent (except for a short period around the mid-1990s). For the Czech skinheads and radical quasi-nationalists, the Roma community represents the same issue as immigrants for their Western European counterparts, and they use the same methods to win recognition—mainly verbal attacks, but there have also been violent attacks, although their numbers have been dropping in the last decade.

At the same time, it should be noted that the Roma do not constitute an ethnic, language, or even national community with bonds between the successful and the unsuccessful. They are rather a community of numerous, often feuding, family clans with a lifestyle that the majority community sees as unadaptable. Examples of social or cultural mobility do exist,[32] but they have had little effect on the fate and status of others. They rather represent a continuous process in which the successful ones untie themselves from the rest of the Roma community, which thus remains at the same low level and is primarily defined by its social exclusion. It is actually quite symptomatic that most Roma do not perceive their Romaness as an ethnic or nationality attribute, but proclaim themselves to be Czechs or Slovaks on various occasions. During the last census in 2011, only 5,000 citizens identified themselves as Roma (plus 8,000 others in combination with another nationalities),[33]—just a fraction of the Roma community (which the government estimates numbers at some 150,000 to 300,000 people—accurate data is not available). Attempts to create Roma political representation failed miserably—such parties received only fractions of a percent of the votes cast in general elections.

The stories of two other minorities, the Vietnamese and Ukrainians, are quite different (and much more successful). The former had started arriving in then-communist Czechoslovakia under intergovernmental agreements during the 1980s, and were employed mainly as laborers. Many of them have settled permanently in the Czech Republic (in 2013, 57,000 Vietnamese were long-term or per-

---

[32] Laura Fónadová, *Nenechali se vyloučit: sociální vzestupy Romů v české společnosti* [They refused to be excluded: upward social mobility pathways of the Roma in Czech society] (Brno: Masarykova univerzita, 2014).
[33] *Czech Statistical Office*, https://www.czso.cz/csu/sldb/domov.

manent residents of the Czech Republic).[34] They managed to adapt very quickly to, and succeed in, the new economic conditions, and they have taken over a substantial portion of the retail network of food and garment shops—mainly in large cities but also in regions adjacent to the German and Austrian borders. The younger generation, often born in the Czech Republic (according to the 2011 census, there were some 30,000 Czech citizens of Vietnamese descent),[35] is very successful at acquiring education and making its way in the professions.[36] Economic immigration from Ukraine was a phenomenon of the 1990s, and especially of the beginning of the new millennium (in 2013, there were 105,000 Ukrainian citizens living in the Czech Republic).[37] The Ukrainian immigration basically follows the same pattern as immigration to Western Europe—most Ukrainian immigrants found their living as blue-collar workers or in other menial jobs, particularly in the construction industry. Their cultural (and to some extent also language) similarity makes their economic and social integration easier.[38]

Today's Czech society is such that one can basically buy the same goods as in Western Europe—albeit for different prices. This is something that Czechs living in the shortage economy of twenty-five years ago could only dream about. The housing situation has also undergone a significant change. In the first few years after the fall of the communist regime, there were still not enough apartments, particularly in large cities, and especially in Prague (the housing crisis in Prague had lasted practically since 1945 and it used to take years to officially get or

---

[34] *Czech Statistical Office*, https://www.czso.cz/csu/cizinci/4-ciz_pocet_cizincu#cr.
[35] *Czech Statistical Office*, https://www.czso.cz/csu/sldb/domov.
[36] See, for example, Ivona Barešová, ed., *Současná problematika východoevropských menšin v České republice* [Contemporary issues of East-Asian minorities in the Czech Republic] (Olomouc: Univerzita palackého, 2010), especially pp. 7–40.
[37] *Czech Statistical Office*, https://www.czso.cz/csu/cizinci/4-ciz_pocet_cizincu#cr.
[38] On Ukrainians, see Eva Pavlíková and Karel Sládek, eds. *Sociální situace a religiozita ukrajinských migrantů v ČR* [The social situation and religiosity of Ukrainian migrants in the Czech Republic] (Červený Kostelec: Pavel Mervart, 2009).

rustle up a flat in Prague). Now we have a surplus of apartments and the housing supply/demand situation is a textbook example of the efficiency of the market and deregulation. Some fifteen years ago, owners of tenement houses were still willing to pay fairly large sums to their tenants willing to vacate flats with regulated rent; now they face difficulties in renting their apartments, and the actual rent is often lower than the latest regulated limit.

Meanwhile, educational opportunities, especially at the university level, have profoundly changed. In the 1980s, less than 10 percent of the relevant age group studied at universities in the Czech Republic (less than in Slovakia); that number rose to around 50 percent twenty years later.[39] The number of full-fledged universities has more than doubled, and they are now in every regional capital. In addition, dozens of private universities complementing the state-run schools now exist. In 2012, there were 73 universities in the Czech Republic, including 45 private ones (in the 1993–1994 school year, there were 23 universities, none of them private). In 2011–2012, 390,000 students attended universities, with slightly more than one-tenth of that number at private universities (in the 1993–1994 school year, there had been slightly over 125,000 students at universities).[40] The number of students, though it matches Western European standards per capita—is not necessarily congruent with quality.

It is true that, seen purely from the perspective of economic variables characterizing economic growth, the convergence toward the standard of developed Western European countries (the pace of which was, as a matter of fact, quite slow anyway) has ceased. At the same time, the Czech Republic's Eastern neighbors, Poland and Slovakia, have started closing the gap. The Czech Republic's GDP in 2000 was equal to 71 percent of the EU 28 average; it climbed to 79 percent by 2005, but since then it has been stagnating, rising only to 81 percent by 2012. The growth of GDP in Poland, and particularly in Slovakia, was much more dramatic; from 48 percent and 50 percent in 2000 to

---

[39] Kalinová, 243, 361.
[40] *Statistická ročenka 2013*, 638; *Statistická ročenka České republiky 1994* (Prague: Český spisovatel, 1994), 382.

51 percent and 60 percent in 2005, followed by a quantum leap to 68 percent and 75 percent in 2012, respectively.[41]

Nevertheless, the similarity in terms of social stratification, structure of education, et cetera, need not necessarily entail a similar value system, public life, culture, citizens' involvement, et cetera. There are still considerable differences, and, according to rankings evaluating the level of corruption, quality of governance and public services and many other aspects of public life, the Czech Republic is in the company of countries other than those with which it wished to catch up. Czech society has also long been in a state of a permanent conflict of principal political forces, which has assumed the form of an intransigent cultural struggle. This—together with the existing electoral system—results in the repeated formation of weak and unstable government coalitions that are unable to deal with fundamental problems, producing half-baked compromises. While politicians in neighboring Western countries, such as Austria and Germany, can act pragmatically (and society accepts this) and establish, if necessary, broad coalitions, which may not be ideologically homogeneous, but are able to rule effectively, the mere thought of such a pragmatic solution in the Czech Republic is stigmatized as "treason to the voters," even before it can be voiced (this was exactly the tone of the most influential Czech media before the premature parliamentary elections in the autumn of 2013), and political life is spent in endless irreconcilable controversies and disputes.

Although Czech society has made substantial progress toward the fulfillment of its early ambitions, the situation is paradoxical. For instance, while gradually closing the gap with Western Europe in material terms, or from the perspective of statistically comparable data, Czech society seems to be spiritually stagnating in feelings of frustration, failure, and skepticism. These feelings do not reflect economic cycle fluctuations, foreign policy problems, or other serious difficulties. The "bad mood," an apt term coined by Václav Havel in the late

---

[41] *Eurostat*, http://epp.eurostat.ec.europa.eu/tgm/table.do?tab=table&init=1&plugin=1&language=en&pcode=tec00114; *Statistická ročenka 2013*, 749. Data from the Czech Bureau of Statistics is even more pessimistic than the European data: it shows that the Czech GDP actually dropped to the level of 2005 in 2012 (79 percent). Since reaching its record level of 83 percent, it has been declining steadily.

1990s[42] to characterize the general mindset of Czech society, has been continuously poisoning the atmosphere in the Czech Republic for some fifteen years, without any connection to the real situation and, in fact, without any real reason. It is present in the opinions of ordinary people, in the statements of celebrities, and in the way the media describes (and co-creates) the situation.

Insofar as the "bad mood" and its sources are concerned, it might make sense to examine to what extent the term applies to membership in the European Union and the European Union itself. Judging from the tone prevailing in Czech media, it may seem that the Czechs are a nation of dyed-in-the-wool eurosceptics and that they place their trifling objections above the big opportunity that accession to the European Union offers. This opinion is rather difficult to verify. Polls conducted for dozens of years within the framework of the Eurobarometer Surveys have been used to determine opinions of EU citizens, including those concerning the benefits of the European Union. An evaluation of the series of the surveys spanning many years is obviously beyond the scope of the present study; moreover, no historian feels comfortable in a situation in which he or she has to rely on a source which he/she sees as extremely unreliable because of its static and ephemeral nature, i.e., results of public opinion surveys. Nevertheless, some of the results are quite interesting and in fact do not paint the picture of a society full of eurosceptics mentioned above.

It is true that the autumn 2013 Eurobarometer Survey states that only 34 percent and 61 percent of the Czech Republic's citizens tend to trust the EU or not to trust the EU. However, the average figures for the whole European Union are quite similar; 31 percent tend to trust, 58 percent tend not to trust.[43] Another survey carried out in 2011 attempted to discover whether things were going in the right or wrong direction.[44]

---

[42] In his speech to both houses of the Czech Parliament in the Rudolfinum in Prague, December 9, 1997 (Václav Havel, *Spisy, vol. 7, Projevy a jiné texty z let 1992–1999* [Collected works, vol. 7. Speeches and other texts, 1992–1999] (Prague: Torst, 1999), 733–53).

[43] *Eurostat*, http://ec.europa.eu/public_opinion/archives/eb/eb80/eb80_publ_en.pdf, p. 78.

[44] *Eurostat*, http://ec.europa.eu/public_opinion/archives/eb/eb75/eb75_publ_en.pdf, p. 30.

Only 19 percent of Czech respondents believed things were going in the right direction in their country, while 67 percent believed they were not. The average figures for the whole European Union were 28 percent and 51 percent. However, when the question concerned only the European Union, 38 percent of Czechs believed things were going in the right direction, while 38 percent held the opposite opinion. The average figures for the whole European Union were 31 percent and 40 percent, respectively. In 2012, another Eurobarometer Survey focused on opinions regarding the beneficial effects of the European Union on many aspects of life (no/fewer border controls, improved consumer rights, living, working, studying in another EU country, et cetera.).[45] For all eight questions asked in the survey, the opinions of Czech respondents were significantly more positive than the EU averages, and, for most of the questions, more than doubly positive than the opinions of the "old" EU member states (EU 15). Eurobarometer results can (and should be) evaluated in a much more consistent manner and interpreted in different ways; nevertheless, it is obvious that the opinions of Czech citizens regarding the European Union are not overly critical. They are definitely less critical than their opinions of the situation in their own country.

The Czech "bad mood" was preceded by a fairly long period of willingness to make (for the sake of the economic transformation) sacrifices, and be optimistic, with hopes of rapid progress; it was a period of visions and ambitions. This spiritual climate prevailed in the first half of the 1990s, including the years immediately after the division of Czechoslovakia in 1993. This was accompanied by a perhaps naïve, but nonetheless inspiring, concept of "Czech supremacy," i.e., that the Czech Republic would be the first country and society to stand apart from the former Eastern European Bloc, and also the fastest to close the economic, social, and cultural gap with "Old Europe." The reasons why this spiritual atmosphere was lost and why it in fact transformed into its opposite would merit a separate treatise. Here, I am interested in the Slovak angle.

At the beginning of the transformation process, the idea of the future development of Czech society was formed by two fundamental

---

[45] *Eurostat*, http://ec.europa.eu/public_opinion/archives/eb/eb77/eb77_citizen_en.pdf, p. 19.

concepts and—to put it simply—by the two personalities representing them: Václav Havel and Václav Klaus. The former accentuated the role of civic society, the importance of human rights, and European integration; the latter emphasized the free market without any ifs, ands, or buts, the role of traditional political parties, and the nation-state. Havel seemed to be offering an alternative to Western countries. This aspect of Havel's thinking is present in his key texts—from "The Power of the Powerless"[46] of the late 1970s to "Summer Meditations"[47] of the early 1990s, and also in a number of short essays and speeches, particularly from the period immediately after the fall of the communist regime.[48] Klaus simply wanted to transfer, particularly in the technical sense, the basic parameters of the political and economic functioning of Western

---

[46] Václav Havel, *Spisy 4. Eseje a jiné texty z let 1970–1989* [Collected works, vol. 4. Essays and other texts, 1970–1989] (Prague: Torst, 1999), 224–330. In English: *The Power of the Powerless* (London: Hutchinson, 1985).

[47] Václav Havel, *Spisy 6. Projevy z let 1990–1992* [Collected works, vol. 6. Speeches 1990–1992] (Prague: Torst, 1999), 399–549. In English: *Summer Meditations* (New York: A. Knopf, 1993).

[48] For example, Havel's speech to the Congress of the United States in Washington, D.C., February 21, 1990 (ibid., 59–71), in Prague on the occasion of the visit of German President Richard von Weizsäcker, March 15, 1990 (ibid., 94–103) or in Strasbourg before the Parliamentary Assembly of the Council of Europe, May 10, 1990 (ibid., 137–57). In English, see the selection of Havel's speeches: Václav Havel, *The Art of the Impossible. Politics and Morality in Practice. Speeches and Writings, 1990–1996* (New York: A. Knopf, 1997). There also exist a number of publications on Havel in English, including, for example: John Keane, *Václav Havel. A Political Tragedy in Six Acts* (London: Bloomsbury, 1999), in particular, 438–47 and 464–76; Markéta Goetz-Stankiewicz and Phyllis Carey, eds., *Critical Essays on Václav Havel* (New York: G.K. Hall, 1999); the texts of H. Gordon Skilling, Jean Bethke Ebstein, Kenneth S. Zagacki, Dean C. Hammer in the chapter, "Havel's Political Thought," 105–6; Carol R. Strong: *The Role of Charismatic Leadership in Ending the Cold War: The Presidencies of Boris Yeltsin, Vaclav Havel, and Helmut Kohl* (Lewiston : Edwin Mellen Press 2009), 305–88. As to the extensive Czech production, see at least the essential works of Jiří Suk: *Labyrintem revoluce. Aktéři, zápletky a křižovatky jedné politické krize* [Through the labyrinth of revolution. actors, plots and crossroads of a political crisis] (Prague: Prostor, 2003), and *Politika jako absurdní drama. Václav Havel v letech 1975–1989* [Politics as an absurdist drama. Václav Havel between 1975 and 1989] (Prague: Paseka, 2013).

societies to the Czech Republic.[49] In the best-case scenario, these concepts could have been perceived as complementing each other and could have worked as such; unfortunately, the concepts and their representatives became antagonistic; their mutual rejection and disputes have in fact continued till the present day; and sometimes their representatives assume positions so extreme that they seem to be caricatures of the original visions (I am referring to followers and epigones here).

In the years immediately before and after the division of Czechoslovakia, however, each of the above concepts perceived itself as being utterly different from the program represented in Slovakia by Prime Minister Vladimír Mečiar and his accentuation of Slovak conditions. Although an overwhelming majority in Czech society did not want to see the common state divided and felt nostalgic about it even after 1993, most people realized that the end of Czechoslovakia also marked a separation from the problematic situation in Slovakia under Mečiar. Whether from Havel's or Klaus's perspective, it seemed the implementation of their own visions and programs would be easier without Mečiar and his Slovak specifics. As a matter of fact, the growing differences in the internal political situation in the two countries and the way each of them was perceived by the international community fostered the concept of Czech supremacy and imminent victory.

This perception was also nurtured by the media. At that time, the Czech media were covering the situation in Slovakia very extensively and in great detail, but mainly through Slovak journalists (authors writing for the Czech media—whether from Slovakia or from Prague to which they had resettled—included, for example, Milan Žitný, Peter Schutz, Martin Šimečka, Ivan Hoffman, and others) who were, as a

---

[49] Secondary publications on Václav Klaus are not as numerous as those on Havel, and even his own texts are not, as a rule, available in English. The only exception is represented by bilingual editions of his shorter works from the early 1990s—*Cesta k tržní ekonomice* [The road to a market economy] (Prague: Top Agency, 1991), and *Demontáž socialismu. Předběžná zpráva* [Dismantling socialism: a preliminary report] (Prague: Top Agency, 1992). See also Václav Klaus, *Ekonomická teorie a realita transformačních procesů* [Economic theory and the reality of the transformation processes] (Prague: Management Press, 1995), or the miscellany of Marek Loužek, ed., *Patnáct let od obnovení kapitalismu v naší zemi* [Fifteen years since the restoration of capitalism in our country] (Prague: CEP, 2006).

rule, very critical of Mečiar. Logically enough, their articles on the poor situation in Slovakia reflected a certain measure of admiration for the progressing Czech transformation and the impending integration of the Czech Republic into Western structures. At that time, NATO was the important Western structure. It is well known that Mečiar's Slovakia was left out in the first wave of accession talks. Reading articles by some Slovak journalists or the Slovak media from those times could serve as psychotherapy of sorts, boosting Czech self-confidence.

However, this situation did not last long. Czech right-wing politicians, now sitting on opposition benches, started admiring the radical reforms of the Slovak right-wing governments since 1998, which gave them as an example to follow. The use of the Slovak benchmark to assess the Czech situation stopped in the late 1990s. The loss of the Slovak mirror, in which the Czech reality looked a bit better than it actually was, was not the only reason for the onset of skepticism and general self-criticism. But the absence of the relatively low-cost morale-boosting asset might have been one of the secondary factors resulting in the "bad mood" in the Czech Republic. Looking at Czech-Slovak parallels, Czech society will perhaps need a spiritual boost similar to that which Slovak society received by overcoming Mečiar's rule to get rid of its feelings of frustration and general skepticism. This is not to say that I believe that introducing Mečiar's practices, albeit in a somewhat softened form, would benefit Czech political life.

By way of conclusion, when drafting the first version of this chapter, after the fall of the Czech government and during an especially populist campaign before the premature parliamentary elections in the fall of 2013, I was very skeptical. It seemed to me that the Czech Republic was entering a period of soft Mečiarism of sorts. Fortunately, the concerns accompanying the Czech super-election year of 2013 (including the first direct presidential elections and the premature elections referred to above), with the advent of populism and the gradual degeneration of political culture, have not yet materialized. The parliamentary elections in 2013 confirmed a trend toward fragmentation and disintegration of the political scene. The Czech Republic has lost another feature which seemed to set it apart from most post-communist countries of Central and Eastern Europe: permanent political stability for a relatively long time. The period between 1993 and 2003 was characterized by an alternation of left-wing/centrist coalitions led by the Social Democratic Party and the Civic Democratic Party. Although all three center-right governments (Klaus's in 1997, Topolánek's in 2009 and Nečas's in 2013) resigned prematurely and were replaced by caretaker governments, it seemed that the political map of the Czech Republic and the distribution pattern of the sympathies and opinions of Czechs were relatively stable and similar to those in established democracies of Western Europe. However, the last few years have shaken that stability and redrawn the political map; we witnessed a lightning-speed advent of new political entities scoring points by rhetoric focused on criticism of corruption (no matter whether real or imagined) and the incompetence of previous governments, rather than presenting comprehensible political programs along the right-left axis. Their success (we will see whether it will be temporary or more permanent) made the comprehensible right/left division of the political spectrum disappear. Under these circumstances, it would be useful to have a reservoir of civic society élan in the Czech Republic, similar to that which succeeded in Slovakia in 1998, and which returned the situation there to the standard European path. Just in case.

CHAPTER 18

Some Comments on "Social Developments in the Czech Republic"

James W. Peterson

This chapter presents a useful overview of current Czech attitudes regarding key social, political, and economic issues. Oldřich Tůma provides interesting data that demonstrate how economic conditions in Prague have improved to the point that they exceed the average of the European Union. This has had the unfortunate consequence of creating a certain resentment and even animosity towards the capital city in other sections of the country. Further, Tůma offers the central thesis that "post-communist changes are more important than post-Czechoslovak changes." Having an overarching theme lends coherence to his paper and provides a lens for interpreting a variety of conditions and changes during the last two decades in the Czech Republic. Interestingly, Tůma offers the conclusion that Czechs "perhaps need a spiritual boost" to get rid of "feelings of frustration and general skepticism."

There is a wealth of evidence that supports Tůma's proposition that post-communist changes were of overwhelming significance to the Czech Republic. In the political arena, the transitional government that emerged after the fall of the communist system in November 1989 paved the way for the emergence of a plethora of democratic practices that contrasted sharply with the authoritarianism that characterized communist patterns. Former playwright, essayist, and dissident Václav Havel emerged as the near universal choice for the position of president. In previous decades, this office had been very much subordinate to the office of First Secretary of the Communist Party. The record of sacrifice and service of Havel as a dissident, who endured long stretches of time in prison during communist times, was an inspiration that helped to hold the newly freed nation together through the early 1990s. Quickly, a competitive political party system emerged, with the Civic Democrats (ODS), Czechoslovak Social Democrats (ČSSD), and Communist Party (KSČM) taking center stage, a position they would hold for at least the next quarter century.

Change characterized other key sectors of the Czechoslovak policy after 1989. Václav Klaus, prime minster in the early years, embraced shock therapy as the engine of economic conversion from state-centered socialism to free market capitalism. The central planning that was the hallmark of the communist system imposed in 1948 yielded to an economic system that placed the greatest importance on individual incentives and freedom to maneuver and invest in a way that citizens saw fit. The state sale of vouchers led to considerable opportunities for private collections of wealth and subsequent investments in an economy that was now anchored in the entire collective, rather than exclusively in the party elite.

Continuing changes characterized the societal level in the post-communist era as well. Mass demonstrations in November 1989 revealed the capacity of the citizenry to mobilize after four decades of centralized rule and directives.[1] Soon, President Havel began to enunciate the importance of building a "civil society." This significant component of the system had disappeared during the long period of subordination to the communist elite, and its reemergence was likely to take a number of years or even decades. Correspondingly, those who had served the previous communist leadership and regime needed to undergo a vetting process that came under the label of "lustration." Thereby, some who had gained management skills in communist times experienced the opportunity to help guide the new ship of state, as long as their records were not severely compromised.

Post-communist changes also centered on a relocation of the nation's orientation from East to West. By the mid-1990s, the Czech Republic was a Partner for Peace in NATO, a defense organization whose formation in 1949 centered on preventing the expansion of the Communist Bloc further to the west. After the Czech Republic joined that military organization in 1999, the nation's leaders permitted par-

---

1 Leslie Holmes, *Post-Communism: An Introduction* (Durham: Duke University Press, 1997), 76–7.

ticipation in key NATO missions, such as the struggle in Afghanistan against the indigenous Taliban and the foreign fighters known as Al Qaeda. The Western-leaning responsibilities of the newly freed Czech Republic also entailed work with the Bush Administration in the United States to build a missile shield that would offer Europe protection against rogue state onslaughts from nations like Iran. Furthermore, the Czechs sought membership in the European Union, and that ambition came to fruition in 2004, five years after their entry into NATO.

While Tůma's essay centers on the centrality of post-communist transformations in contrast to post-Czechoslovak adjustments, the latter also deserve attention. While many Czechs lamented the loss of the Slovak third of the republic and its territory, the political paralysis that dominated the first four years after the end of communist era controls also disappeared. For example, the complicated mathematical formula that was central to late communist era legislation soon became a distant memory. After 1968, this formula included the requirement that three-fifths of three legislative units agree to any significant legislative outcomes. This inheritance from the communist period tied up meaningful change during the early post-communist years. It had been nearly impossible to garner agreement among the all-Czechoslovak legislature, the Czech representative unit, and the Slovak entity as well. In addition, the West had been more receptive to overtures from the Czech component of the federal state than to those from the Slovak sector, due to the more extreme nationalism of the latter. Being freed from their Slovak partner, the Czechs became one of the first three former Communist Bloc nations to join NATO in 1999. Slovaks waited until 2004, several years after the end of the Mečiar era. Both joined the European Union (EU) in 2004. In these two respects, the changes in the post-Czechoslovak era were important, but not as deeply rooted as those that happened in the post-communist period. In that sense, Tůma's conclusion makes eminent sense.

I would recommend that Tůma further anchor his study in the rich literature on political culture. In their classic work, *The Civic Culture*, Almond and Verba outlined three different types of political culture. They included parochial, subject, and participant political cultures.[2]

---

[2] Gabriel A. Almond and Sidney Verba, *The Civic Culture* (Boston: Little Brown and Company, 1965), 16.

First, parochial political cultures are those in which few citizens have any orientation at all towards the political system. In developing nations with remote villages, many may be totally unaware of the comings and goings of political leaders in the capital city. Such situations are less likely in today's technological world with its extensive use of social media, but people can still be totally wrapped up in struggles to protect their families and livelihood.

Second, subject political cultures are quite different from parochial political cultures, in the sense that persons have a conception of the state and all its political and administrative organizations. However, the political structure is often an authoritarian one or, at times, even totalitarian. For decades or even centuries, citizens may have fallen into the habit of envisioning political leaders as the givers of orders. In addition, there may be few structured organizations, such as interest groups or political parties, and thus the citizenry really does not possess a vehicle for transmitting concerns and demands to the top. Lack of a free press or of the right to demonstrate may compound the problem. One clear illustration of this subject pattern would be Russia under the tsarist system. Many Russians had pictures of the tsar and the Orthodox Patriarch in their homes in remote villages, and this blend of political and religious power kept the system intact. Interestingly, the current regime of Vladimir Putin plays off and depends on the partial continuation of this type of political culture.[3]

Third, a participant political culture is very different because it has a politically aware and actively involved citizenry. Of course, channels for citizen engagement such as robust political parties, energized and well-rooted interest groups, a free press, and the constitutional right to assemble are also necessities. Most Western democracies such as the United States, Canada, the United Kingdom, France, and postwar Germany are vibrant examples. When long periods of authoritarianism end in certain countries, there is often much discussion about developing some form of political democracy through writing a new constitution. This was the case in the former communist nations in the early 1990s and in the Arab Spring successor states in the years since 2011.

---

[3] J. L. Black, *Vladimir Putin and the New World Order: Looking East, Looking West?* (New York: Rowman & Littlefield, 2004), 23–4.

However, in both cases, very disparate results occurred, largely because of the different levels of preparedness of the political culture to take part in the process after a long slumber. In the case of the post-communist countries, Poles under President Lech Wałęsa quickly adopted the values of a participant political culture, while Serbs under President Milošević were slower to do so.[4] Similarly, in recent years, Tunisians were more prepared to establish a secular-based democratic system, while Egyptians experienced a resurgence of Muslim-based political values after the deposal of Hosni Mubarak.[5] In fact, the election of 2012 put the Muslim Brotherhood in power, while the election of 2014 maintained in power the military figure that had carried out a coup against the Muslim Brotherhood one year earlier!

All of this applies very well to the case study of Czechoslovakia after 1989, and the Czech Republic after 1993. During the forty years of communist rule, people retreated into private life, as there would be no positive outcome from efforts to stretch those political muscles that they had used in the interwar period. Leaders such as Klement Gottwald, Antonín Novotný, Gustáv Husák and Miloš Jakeš both expected and reinforced political passivity. During the nearly two decades of rule by Husák, economic progress took place in both the Czech and Slovak Republics. In a sense, the regime bought off the public by increasing the availability and quality of material goods during the 1970s.[6] In other words, as long as citizens accepted their role as subjects, the political leaders would see to it that their basic economic needs were met.

Czechs and Slovaks did experiment with a more participant political culture in 1968, and again in 1977. In 1968, Communist Party leader Alexander Dubček permitted political expressions from the citizenry that were not possible during the previous two decades. He addressed them as "my countrymen," an appellation that was not at all in the spirit of a subject political culture. He tolerated publication

---

[4] Holmes, *Post-Communism*, 71–2, 97–8.
[5] Olivier Roy, "Islamic Revival and Democracy: The Case in Tunisia and Egypt," in *Arab Society in Revolt: The West's Mediterranean Challenge*, ed. Cesare Merlini and Olivier Roy (Washington, D.C.: The Brookings Institution, 2012), 50–2.
[6] Holmes, *Post-Communism*, 71–2, 97–8.

of the "2000 Words Manifesto" that called for considerable expansion of the rights of free speech and political party organizations within the framework of a National Front.[7] Interest groups formed, and the beacon of light from the outreaching Chancellor Willy Brandt of West Germany with his Ostpolitik created a response within Czechoslovakia. The Warsaw Pact invasion of August 1968 halted the growth and emergence of a participant political culture. There was an echo of the protests a decade later, when the Charter 77 movement, headed by dissident Václav Havel, again prodded the citizens to express participant values, but jail sentences placed that movement on hold for ten more years.[8]

Finally, the revolution of 1989 and the move into the post-communist age for Czechoslovakia stimulated growth of a participant political culture for the second time since the early 1930s. President Havel called for the creation of and work on developing a civil society. He realized that the habit of taking an ongoing part in political life did not exist and needed to be nurtured. Furthermore, it would be necessary to supplement a weakening central government with the emergence of a vibrant group of nongovernmental organizations (NGOs). Indeed, participation in political party activity and elections quickly became a regular habit for many Czechs. A significant event in the growth of a competitive party system was the election of 1998, for, at that time, the ruling Civic Democratic Party (ODS) yielded the stage for the first time to the rival Czech Social Democratic Party (ČSSD). Peaceful rotation of parties in power is a key indicator of the important combination of a democratic system and participant political culture.

Tůma's chapter makes perceptive comments on features of the political culture. For example, he notes that there was a sharp decline in the proportion of persons who think of themselves as middle class between 1991 and 2007. Further, trust in the EU was very low, a figure characteristic of the other European countries as well. Significantly, a little less than a fifth of Czechs thought that "things were going in the right direction" within their own country. The plight of the Roma

---

[7] Galia Golan, *Reform Rule in Czechoslovakia: The Dubček Era 1968–1969* (Cambridge: Cambridge University Press, 1973), 156.

[8] J. F. Brown, *Eastern Europe and Communist Rule* (Durham: Duke University Press, 1988), 308.

added another dimension of uncertainty to the wavering political culture. Czechs on the right expressed considerable hostility towards that group, and certain episodes of violence took place. Further, the Roma did not really constitute a recognizable ethnic group according to traditional definitions. Thus, their uncertain self-image undermined efforts to obtain recognizable visibility and corresponding political representation. Specific findings such as these help explain the "bad mood" of so many voices within Czech political culture.

However, it would be good to locate recent political cultural data on such questions as the following: What are elite attitudes about some of the socioeconomic issues that Tůma discusses? What are the perceptions of the general public on the same set of issues? Why is there a constant clash between elite and public perceptions that leads to the "frustration" noted above? The author could develop several hypotheses that could relate economic conditions to the two categories of opinion. Public opinion polls are more likely to center on attitudes of the general public, rather than on those of the elite. Therefore, it may be possible to treat socioeconomic conditions as the independent variable and provide statistics about them for five or ten years. Then, public opinion would become the dependent variable, and perhaps polls about socioeconomic conditions could be found for the same period of time. Perhaps it would also be possible to look at the overall political situation during the same time period. In that case, the alternation of political leaders and the shifting party coalitions would become the independent variable, with public opinion as the dependent one. In the end, conclusions could center on whether there is a relationship between political and economic conditions, on the one hand, and public opinion, on the other. Finally, one would probably discover at least part of the reason for the low level of political involvement by the general public, and this could then be presented as one barrier to the creation of a fully developed "civil society," as President Havel described it in the 1990s.[9]

The political culture does include one variable that deserves exploration on these perplexing topics of Czech political attitudes and

---

[9] Bernard Wheaton and Zdeněk Kavan, *The Velvet Revolution: Czechoslovakia, 1988–1991* (Boulder, CO: Westview Press, 1992), 184.

Czechs' "bad mood" regarding politics. That concept is political efficacy or political competence, and it refers to the growth of a belief among citizens that their participation does matter and could make an impact, if they chose to exercise their citizen rights. Social groups that rank high in that characteristic may not be those in which citizens take part in politics all the time or even frequently. However, their belief that expressed views matter to the elite provides a certain underlying satisfaction with the decision-making process that underpins political stability.[10] People are not generally in a "bad mood" as they currently are in the Czech Republic. Why has a strong sense of political efficacy not accompanied two decades' growth of democracy in the Czech Republic? What steps might nurture it? Does the responsibility lie in the hands of political leaders or the citizenry itself?

In terms of the author's conclusions that post-communist changes are more important than post-Czechoslovak changes, it would be worthwhile to supplement this by conceding that there is evidence that points to the opposite conclusion as well. For example, a number of articles demonstrate the power of the "legacies" of the communist period on Central and Southeast Europe over the last twenty years.[11] An example of such a legacy is the persistent role of the Communist Party. The strength of the party is rooted in areas with high unemployment, high crime rates, and low population density.[12] In mid-October 2013, public opinion polls revealed that the party ranked second in the upcoming elections. In the actual elections, it fell from that position to third, below both the ČSSD and the new ANO Party. The KSČM garnered 14.91 percent of the popular vote and earned 33 out of 200 seats in the lower house of the legislature.[13] The social safety net that existed during communist times still exists in the health care sector, for example, although some benefits are less than they were twenty years ago. Some cultural traditions from the communist era still per-

---

[10] Almond and Verba, *Civic Culture*, 136–9.
[11] Milenko Petrovic, *The Democratic Transition of Post-Communist Europe* (London: Palgrave-Macmillan, 2013), 2–6.
[12] Jiří Lach, James T. LaPlant, Jim Peterson, and David Hill, "The Party Isn't Over: An Analysis of the Communist Party in the Czech Republic," *The Journal of Communist Studies and Transition Politics* 26, no. 3 (2010): 381.
[13] "Czech Legislative Elections," *Wikipedia*, October 5, 2014.

sist. For instance, in Olomouc, the rotating figures on the town clock still represent working class and proletarian values. Thus, there are still important "legacies" from the communist era in political, economic, and cultural life. They also include considerable months and years of time off for either parent after the birth of a child, as well as considerably lower costs and less debt for acquiring a university education than in the United States.

Post-Czechoslovak changes also matter, and this contrasts somewhat with, but also supplements, the author's conclusion downplaying them. The emergence of a formal national border between the Czech Republic and Slovakia is one major change, and it contrasts with the much more fluid separation between the two groups in the old Czechoslovak state. Replacement of internal geographic borders by nation-state borders has resulted in important differences, such as Czech retention of the crown as currency and the Slovak move to the euro. NATO admitted the Czech Republic as a full member in 1999, but Slovakia waited until 2004. Slovak domestic politics in the 1990s were the major reason for that delay. During the history of the Czechoslovak state, majority-minority group relations were characterized by Slovak resentment of Czech dominance and Czech unwillingness to deliver on the promises of the Pittsburgh Agreement.[14] After 1993, the issue of the Roma and their relation to the Czech state became an important minority-majority group problem that caught the attention of outside organizations such as the European Union.[15] Such differences are an important result of the separation of 1993.

In sum, the author has raised some very important issues and presented valuable data on social attitudes and relationships in the Czech Republic. It will be interesting to see how social conditions in the Czech Republic change (or not) over the next twenty years.

---

[14] Rita Klimova, "Current Problems of Transition in Czechoslovakia," in *Transitions from Communism in Russia and Eastern Europe*, ed. Constantine C. Menges (New York: University Press of America, 1994), 115–6.

[15] Holmes, *Post-Communism*, 294.

Contributors

MARTIN BÚTORA, a sociologist by training, is the founder and honorary president of the Institute for Public Affairs (IVO) in Bratislava. In November 1989, he co-founded the Public Against Violence movement in Slovakia, and in 1990–1992, he was the Human Rights Advisor to President Václav Havel. Between 1999 and 2003 he served as Ambassador of the Slovak Republic to the United States. In the last few years, he co-authored and co-edited *Where are We? Mental Maps of Slovakia* (2010); *Active Citizenship and the Nongovernmental Sector in Slovakia. Trends and Perspectives* (2012); *Slovakia 2012: Trends in the Quality of Democracy* (2013); and *From Where to Where? 20 Years of Independence* (2013).

ZORA BÚTOROVÁ is Senior Research Fellow at the Institute for Public Affairs in Bratislava. In 1998, she was one of the founders of the civic campaign of nongovernmental organizations, OK '98, which contributed to free and fair parliamentary elections in Slovakia. She has edited and co-authored a number of books, including *Democracy and Discontent in Slovakia: A Public Opinion Profile of a Country in Transition* (1998); *She and He in Slovakia. Gender and Age in the Period of Transition* (2010); *Where Are We? Mental Maps of Slovakia* (2010); and *Alternative Politics? The Rise of New Political Parties in Central Europe* (2013).

KEVIN DEEGAN-KRAUSE is Associate Professor of Political Science at Wayne State University in Detroit. He has published *Elected Affinities: Democracy and Party Competition in Slovakia and the Czech Republic* (2006) and *The Structure of Political Competition in Western Europe*, co-edited with Zsolt Enyedi (2010). He has won Truman and Fulbright Scholarships, as well as IREX Individual Advanced Research Opportunity grants. He has served as a consultant for the U.S. Department of State on the politics of Central Europe.

SHARON FISHER is Principal Economist with IHS Global Insight in Washington, D.C. In that role, she provides economic and political analysis, risk assessment, and forecasting on a number of countries in Central and Eastern Europe, including the Czech Republic and Slovakia. In the mid-1990s, Fisher spent four years as an analyst at the RFE/RL Research Institute in Munich and the Open Media Research Institute (OMRI) in Prague. Fisher's extensive list of publications includes the book *Political Change in Post-Communist Slovakia and Croatia: From Nationalist to Europeanist* (2006).

JOHN GOULD is Associate Professor of Political Science at Colorado College. He is author of *The Politics of Privatization: Wealth and Power in Postcommunist Europe* (2011) and has published in numerous journals including *Europe-Asia Studies, Slovakia, Comparative European Politics* and *Business & Politics*. His research interests include the political sources of market organization in post-communist Europe, resource politics, and social movements. Gould is associate editor of the *Journal of International Relations and Development.*

ĽUDOVÍT HALLON is a researcher at the Historical Institute of the Slovak Academy of Sciences in Bratislava. He specializes in economic history and the history of technology in Slovakia and in Central Europe. In addition to numerous articles in scholarly journals and book chapters, Dr. Hallon is the author of *Industrializácia Slovenska 1918–1938. Rozvoj alebo úpadok?* (1995) plus either co-author or co-editor of half a dozen books on economics, technology and Slovak history.

JURAJ HOCMAN specializes in the history of East-Central Europe, including Czechoslovakia and Slovakia. He is the Secretary for Research, Science and International Cooperation at the private Hochschule Goethe Uni Bratislava and also teaches history at the private PanEuropean University in Bratislava. Hocman has published *Slovakia from the Downfall of Communism to its Accession into the European Union* (2011) and more than thirty scholarly articles, essays, and newspaper articles on ancient history, diplomacy, international relations, and Slovak politics.

ADAM HUDEK is a researcher at the Institute of History at the Slovak Academy of Sciences in Bratislava. A specialist on historiography, Hudek published *Najpolitickejšia veda. Slovenská historiografia v rokoch 1948–1968* (2010) and is co-author of *Overcoming Old Borders. Beyond the Paradigm of Slovak National History* (2013).

STANISLAV J. KIRSCHBAUM is Professor and Chairman of the Department of International Studies at Glendon College at York University in Toronto. He has published *A History of Slovakia; The Struggle for Survival* (2nd edition, 2005); *Historical Dictionary of Slovakia* (3rd edition, 2013); and over fifty scholarly articles. In 1995, he was made a Chevalier dans l'Ordre des Palmes académiques by the Government of France, and, in 2002, he was elected a Fellow of the Royal Society of Canada. In 2008, he was awarded the Jubilee Medal by Trnavská univerzita for his contribution to the university.

MICHAEL KRAUS is Dirks Professor of Political Science at Middlebury College, Vermont. His publications include *Perestroika and East-West Economic Relations* (1990); *Russia and Eastern Europe after Communism* (1996); and *Irreconcilable Differences? Explaining Czechoslovakia's Dissolution* (2000); as well as book chapters and articles in the *Journal of Democracy*, *Current History*, *Foreign Policy*, and elsewhere. In 2012–2013, he was a Fulbright Visiting Professor at the Institute of Political Studies in the Faculty of Social Sciences at Charles University in Prague.

MIROSLAV LONDÁK is a researcher at the Institute of History of the Slovak Academy of Sciences in Bratislava. He specializes in the economic history of Slovakia. In addition to numerous articles in scholarly journals, Londák is author of *Otázky industrializácie Slovenska* (1999); *Rok 1968 a ekonomická realita Slovenska* (2007); and *Ekonomické reformy v Československu v 50. a 60. rokoch 20. storočia a slovenská ekonomika* (2010).

JOZEF MORAVČÍK taught law and served as Dean of the Faculty of Law at Comenius University in the 1970s and 1980s. In November 1989 he joined Verejnosť proti násiliu (VPN, Public Against Violence), which negotiated the transfer of power from the Communist Party of Slovakia. He was elected a member of both the Slovak and Czechoslovak Parliaments in the period 1991–1992. He briefly served as Minister of Foreign Affairs of both the Slovak Republic and the Czech and Slovak Federative Republic and, in 1994, he was interim Prime Minister of the Slovak Republic. In 1998, he was elected Lord Mayor of Bratislava. Since then, has been in private practice.

JAMES W. PETERSON is Professor and Head of the Department of Political Science at Valdosta State University in Georgia. He is the author of *NATO and Terrorism: Organizational Expansion and Mission Transformation* (2011); *Building a Framework for Security in Southeast Europe and the Black Sea Region: A Challenge Facing NATO* (2013); and *American Foreign Policy: Alliance Politics during a Century of War, 1914–2014* (2014). He has written many articles on Czech politics and foreign policy and serves as editor of *The Czech and Slovak History Newsletter*.

PETR PITHART was educated as a lawyer at Charles University in Prague, expelled from the Communist Party of Czechoslovakia in 1968, and then became a dissident and one of the first signatories of Charter '77 in 1976. During the fall of communism in November 1989, Pithart became one of the founding members of the Občanské forum (OF, Civic Forum) and Prime Minister of the Czech Republic in 1990–1992. He has taught political science at Charles University and also served as President of the Czech Senate for two terms. Pithart has published many books and articles, including *Ptám se, tedy jsem, rozhovor s Martinem T. Zikmundem* (2010) and *Devětaosmdesátý, spisy Petra Pitharta, zvazek druhý* (2009).

MARTIN POSPÍŠIL is an economist at the Organisation for Economic Co-operation and Development in Paris, France. He is also a non-executive board member at the Glopolis Think Tank in Prague. Pospíšil studied economics, econometrics, and management at the Center for Economic Research and Graduate Education—Economics Institute in Prague, the University of Economics in Prague, and at Prague's Charles University. He also studied at the London School of Economics, the University of Bath, and the University of Pennsylvania.

JAN RYCHLÍK is Professor of Modern Czech and Slovak History at the Faculty of Arts of Charles University and a Senior Researcher at the Masaryk Institute and Archives of the Czech Academy of Science in Prague. He specializes in modern Czech and Slovak history and the history of the Balkans and Eastern Europe. He has published many books and articles on these subjects, including *Češi a Slováci ve 20. století* (2 Volumes, 1997–1998) and *Rozpad Československa* (2002).

CAROL SKALNIK LEFF teaches political science at the University of Illinois in Urbana-Champaign. She is the author of *National Conflict in Czechoslovakia: The Making and Remaking of a State, 1918–1987* (1988) and *The Czech and Slovak Republics: Nation vs. State* (1997), as well as book chapters and articles on post-communist Czech and Slovak politics. Her current book project, forthcoming with Rowman and Littlefield, is a study of the transformation of post-communist elites in Eastern Europe.

M. MARK STOLARIK is Professor of History and holds the Chair in Slovak History and Culture at the University of Ottawa. He has published nine books and over sixty articles in the field, including *Growing Up on the South Side: Three Generations of Slovaks in Bethlehem, Pennsylvania* (1985); *Immigration and Urbanization: The Slovak Experience* (1989); and *Where is my Home? Slovak Immigration to North America, 1870–2010* (2012). Founder of the Slovak Studies Association (1977), he edited the *Slovak Studies Newsletter* (1977–1987) and, since 1982, has edited the scholarly annual *Slovakia*.

SHARON L. WOLCHIK is Professor of Political Science and International Affairs at the George Washington University. She is the author, co-author, and co-editor of several books, the most recent of which is *Defeating Authoritarian Leaders in Postcommunist States* (2011), co-authored with Valerie Bunce. She is currently completing the third edition of *Central and East European Politics: From Communism to Democracy* with Jane Curry and editing a volume on comparative mass mobilization and protest that includes the fall of communism in 1989, the "electoral revolutions" in post-communist Europe and Eurasia, the Arab Spring, and recent protests in Russia.

JOZEF ŽATKULIAK is a researcher at the Institute of History at the Slovak Academy of Science in Bratislava. He specializes in contemporary Slovak history. In addition to nearly 100 articles in scholarly journals, Žatkuliak has published numerous monographs, including *Vznik česko-slovenskej federácie v roku 1968* (1996); *November 1989 a Slovensko* (1999); *Novembrová revolúcia a česko-slovenský rozchod* (2002); *November. Medzník vo vývoji slovenskej spoločnosti* (2009); and *Realizácia a normalizačná revízia česko-slovenskej federácie* (2011).

Bibliography

Agnew, Hugh Le Caine. "New States, Old Identities? The Czech Republic, Slovakia and Historical Understandings of Statehood." *Nationalities Papers* 28, no. 4 (December, 2000): 619–50.
Almond, Gabriel A. and Sidney Verba. *The Civic Culture*. Princeton: Princeton University Press, 1966.
Antalová, Ingrid and Mária Mistríková, eds. *Verejnosť proti násiliu 1989–1991: Svedectvá a dokumenty* [Public Against Violence 1989–1991: testimonies and documents]. Bratislava: Nadácia Milana Šimečku, 1998.
Appel, Hilary. *A New Capitalist Order: Privatization & Ideology in Russia & Eastern Europe*. Pittsburgh: University of Pittsburgh Press, 1995.
Atlas rómskych komunít na Slovensku 2013 [Atlas of Roma communities in Slovakia 2013]. Bratislava: UNDP—Regionálne centrum Rozvojového programu OSN pre Európu a Spoločenstvo nezávislých štátov, 2014.
Auer, Stefan. *Liberal Nationalism in Central Europe*. London: Routledge, 2004.
———. "Richard Sulík: A Provincial or a European Slovak Politician?" *Humanities Research* XIX, no.1 (2013): 81–100.
Bakker, Bas B. and Christoph Klingen. *How Emerging Europe Came Through the 2008/09 Crisis: An Account by the Staff of the IMF's European Department*. Washington, DC: International Monetary Fund, 2012.
Baláž, Vladimír and Allan M. Williams. "Capital Mobility in Transition Countries of Central Europe: Macroeconomic Factors and Structural Policies." *Ekonomický časopis* 49, no. 2 (2001): 242–71.
Banáš, Jozef. *Zastavte Dubčeka!* [Stop Dubček!]. Bratislava: Ikarus, 2009.
Barešová, Ivona, ed. *Současná problematika východoevropských menšin v České republice* [Contemporary issues of East-Asian minorities in the Czech Republic]. Olomouc: Univerzita palackého, 2010.
Beblavý, Miroslav. "Monetárna politika" [Monetary politics], in *Hospodárska politika na Slovensku 1990–1999* [Economic politics in Slovakia 1990–1999], ed. by Anton Marcinčin and Miroslav Beblavý. Bratislava: Centrum pre spoločenskú a mediálnu analýzu, 2000: 93–128.

Begg, David. "Pegging Out: Lessons from the Czech Exchange Rate Crisis." *Journal of Comparative Economics* 26, no.4 (December, 1998): 669–90.

Bena, Jan and Jan Hanousek. "Rent Extraction by Large Shareholders: Evidence Using Dividend Policy in the Czech Republic." *Czech Journal of Economics and Finance (Finance a Úvěr)* 58, no. 3 (2008): 106–30.

Beneš, Václav. "Czechoslovak Democracy and its Problems, 1918–1920." *A History of the Czechoslovak Republic, 1918–1948*, ed. by Victor S. Mamatey and Radomír Luža. Princeton: Princeton University Press, 1973: 39–98.

Berglund, Sten, Terje Knutsen, Joakim Ekman and Kevin Deegan-Krause, eds. *The Handbook of Political Change in Eastern Europe*, 3rd ed. Cheltenham, UK: Edward Elgar Publishing, 2013.

Bicha, Karel D. "Settling Accounts with an Old Adversary: The Decatholicization of Czech Immigrants in America." *Histoire sociale—Social History* 8 (November, 1971): 45–60.

Birdwell, Jonathan, Sebastien Feve, Chris Tryhorn and Natalia Vrba. *Backsliders: Measuring Democracy in the EU*. London: Demos, 2013.

Bittnerová, Dana, Mirjam Moravcová, eds. *Etnické komunity—Romové* [Ethnic communities—The Roma]. Prague: Fakulta humanitních studií, 2013.

Black, J. L. *Vladimir Putin and the New World Order: Looking East, Looking West?* New York: Rowman & Littlefield, 2004.

Bloker, Paul. *Constitutionalism and Constitutional Anomie in the New Europe*. Trento: Universita degli Studi di Trento, Department of Sociology and Social Research, 2010.

Bornstein, Morris. "Non-Standard Methods in the Privatization Strategies of the Czech Republic, Hungary and Poland." *Economics of Transition* 5, no. 2 (1997): 323–38.

Boycko, Maxim, Andrei Shleifer and Robert Vishny. *Privatizing Russia*. Cambridge: MIT Press, 1995.

Bradley, John F.N. *Czechoslovakia's Velvet Revolution. A Political Analysis*. Boulder, CO: East European Monographs, 1992.

Brom, Karla and Mitchell Orenstein. "The Privatised Sector in the Czech Republic: Government and Bank Control in a Transitional Economy." *Europe-Asia Studies* 46, no.6 (1994): 893–928.

Brown, J.F.N. *Eastern Europe and Communist Rule*. Durham: Duke University Press, 1988.

Bunce, Valerie. *Subversive Institutions: The Design and the Destruction of Socialism and the State*. Cambridge: Cambridge University Press, 1999.

———. "Peaceful versus Violent State Dismemberment: A Comparison of the Soviet Union, Yugoslavia, and Czechoslovakia." *Politics & Society*, 27, no. 2 (1999): 217–37.

Bunce, Valerie, Michael McFaul, Kathryn Stoner-Weiss, eds. *Democracy and Authoritarianism in the Postcommunist World*, Cambridge University Press, 2010.

Burch, Stuart. "Norway and 1905." *History Today* 55, no. 6 (2005): 2–3.

Busse, Anna Grzymala. "Why are there are (Almost) No Post-Communist Christian Democratic Parties?" *Party Politics*, 19 (2013): 319–42.

Bútora, Martin. "Vyvzdorúvanie alebo každodennosť pozitívnych deviantov" [Obstinacy or normalcy in positive deviants], in *Odklínanie*, ed. by Martin Bútora. Bratislava: Kalligram, 2004: 189–93.
Bútora, Martin, Zora Bútorová, Boris Strečanský, Dušan Ondrušek, Grigorij Mesežnikov, eds. *Štúdia trendov vývoja občianskej spoločnosti na Slovensku* [Study of trends in the development of civil society in Slovakia]. Bratislava: Office of the Government of the Slovak Republic, 2011.
———. *Active Citizenship and Nongovernmental Sector in Slovakia. Trends and Perspectives*. Bratislava: Včelí dom association, 2012.
Bútora, Martin, Zora Bútorová, Grigorij Mesežnikov, Miroslav Kollár, eds. *Odkiaľ a kam? Dvadsať rokov samostatnosti* [From where and whither? Twenty years of independence]. Bratislava: Kalligram, 2013.
Bútorová, Zora and Oľga Gyárfášová. *Return to Europe: New freedoms Embraced, But Weak Public Support for Assisting Democracy Further Afield*. PASOS: Policy Brief No. 3, 2009.
———. "Contemporary Slovakia in Public Opinion," in *Slovakia 2009. Trends in Quality of Democracy*, ed. by Martin Bútora, Grigorij Mesežnikov and Miroslav Kollár (Bratislava: Institute for Public Affairs 2010).
———. "Občianska participácia: trendy, problémy, súvislosti" [Civic participation: trends, problems, and context]. *Sociológia* 42, no. 5 (2010): 447–91.
Buzalka, Juraj. *Slovenská ideológia a kríza* [Slovak ideology and crisis]. Bratislava: Kalligram, 2012.
Černý, Jiří, Markéta Sedláčková, Milan Tuček. *Zdroje utváření skupinových mentalit v České republice po roce 1989* [Sources for the creation of group mentalities in the Czech Republic after 1989]. Prague: Sociologický ústav AV ČR, 2004.
Chavance, Bernard. "Formal and Informal Institutional Change: the Experience of Postsocialist Transformation." *The European Journal of Comparative Economics* 5, no. 1, (2008): 57–71.
Chesterton, Gilbert Keith. *Orthodoxy*. London: The Bodley Head Ltd., 1908.
Chytilek, Roman and Otto Eibl. "České politické strany v politickém prostoru" [Czech political parties in the Czech political landscape]. *Sociologicky časopis / Czech Sociological Review* 47 (2011): 61–88.
Ciobanu, Monica and Michael Shafir. "The 2004 Romanian Elections: A Test for Democratic Consolidation?" *RFE/RL Report* 7, no.3 (April 7, 2005).
Cohen, Shari J. *Politics Without a Past. The Absence of History in Postcommunist Nationalism*. Durham and London: Duke University Press, 1999.
Crane, John O. and Sylvia Crane. *Czechoslovakia: Anvil of the Cold War*. New York: Praeger, 1991.
Csáky, Pál. "Human Rights and Inter-Group Relations in Slovakia," in *The Slovak Republic: A Decade of Independence (1993–2002)*, ed. by M. Mark Stolarik. Wauncondia, IL: Bolchazi-Carducci, 2002: 95–104.
Csergő, Zsuzsa and Kevin Deegan-Krause. "Liberalism and Cultural Claims in Central and Eastern Europe: Toward a Pluralist Balance." *Nations and Nationalism* 17, no. 1 (2011): 85–107.
Czech National Bank. *Inflation Report 2007*. Prague, 2007.

———. *Inflation Report 2011.* Prague, 2011.
———. *Inflation Report 2012.* Prague, 2012.
David, Roman. *Lustration and Transitional Justice: Personnel Systems in the Czech Republic, Hungary and Poland.* Philadelphia: University of Pennsylvania Press, 2011.
Davies, Norman. *Vanished Kingdoms: The Rise and Fall of States and Nations.* New York: Penguin Books, 2012.
Deegan-Krause, Kevin. *Elected Affinities: Democracy and Party Competition in Slovakia and the Czech Republic.* Stanford: Stanford University Press, 2006.
———. "Voting for Thugs," *Democracy at Large* 2, no. 3 (2006): 24–7.
———. "In with the New (Again):'Annuals,' 'Perennials' and the Patterns of Party Politics in Central and Eastern Europe," MPSA Conference, Chicago, 2012, 12–5.
Deegan-Krause, Kevin and Tim Haughton."A Fragile Stability: The Institutional Roots of Low Party System Volatility in the Czech Republic, 1990–2009." *Czech Journal of Political Science/Politilogický časopis* 7 (2010): 227–41.
Democracy Index 2012. London: The Economist Intelligence Unit, 2012.
Democracy Index 2013. London: The Economist Intelligence Unit, 2013.
De Angelis, Paul, ed. *Hope Dies Last: The Autobiography of Alexander Dubcek*, trans. Jiri Hochman. New York: Kodansha International, 1993.
Doellinger, David. *Turning Prayers into Protests: Religious-Based Activism and its Challenge to State Power in Socialist Slovakia and East Germany.* Budapest–New York: Central European University Press, 2013.
Ďurica, Milan S. *Dejiny Slovenska a Slovákov v časovej následnosti faktov dvoch tisícročí* [A chronological history of Slovakia and the Slovaks over two millennia], 5th edition. Bratislava: Lúč, 2013.
Dušek, Libor and Lubomír Lízal. *CERGE-EI Tackles Transition.* Center for Economic Research and Graduate Education—Economics Institute, Prague 2011.
Dyba, Karel and Jan Švejnar. "Stabilization and Transition in Czechoslovakia, NBER Chapters." *The Transition in Eastern Europe* 1. Chicago: National Bureau of Economic Research, Inc, 1994: 93–122.
Estrin, Saul, Jan Hanousek, Evzen Kocenda and Jan Švejnar. "The Effects of Privatization and Ownership in Transition Economies." *Journal of Economic Literature* 47, no. 3 (September, 2009): 699–728.
European Bank of Reconstruction and Development, *Transition Report.* London: European Bank for Reconstruction and Development, 1998.
———. *Transition Report 2001.* London: 2001.
———. *Transition Report 2005.* London: 2005.
European Commission. *Eurobarometer 69, Values of Europeans.* Luxembourg: Publications Office of the European Union, 2008.
———. *Eurobarometer 70. Public Opinion in the European Union*, Fall 2008,
———. *What Works for Roma Inclusion in the EU: Policies and Model Approaches.* Luxembourg: Publications Office of the European Union, 2012.
Eurostat Regional Yearbook 2013. Luxembourg: Publications Office of the European Union, 201.

Eyal, Gil. *The Origins of Postcommunist Elites.* Minneapolis: University of Minnesota Press, 2003.
Ferenčíková, Sonia, Marek Vážan. "Nové trendy vo vývoji priamych zahraničných investícií v krajinách strednej a východnej Európy" [New trends in the development of direct foreign investments in countries of Central and Eastern Europe], *Ekonomické rozhľady* 34 (2005): 522–33.
Fisher, Sharon. "Czech Economy Presents Mixed Picture." *RFE/RL Research Report* 3, no. 29 (July 22, 1994): 31–8.
———. "The Czech Republic: Waning Enthusiasm," in *European Union and the Member States*, ed. by Eleanor E. Zeff and Ellen B. Pirro. Boulder: Lynne Rienner, 2nd Edition, 2006: 343–60.
Fisher, Sharon, John Gould and Tim Haughton. "Slovakia's Neoliberal Turn." *Europe-Asia Studies* 59, no. 3 (September, 2007): 977–98.
Fónadová, Laura. *Nenechali se vyloučit: sociální vzestupy Romů v české společnosti* [They refused to be excluded: upward social mobility pathways of the Roma in Czech society]. Brno: Masarykova univerzita, 2014.
Froese, Paul. "Secular Czechs and Devout Slovaks: Explaining Religious Differences." *Review of Religious Research* 46, no. 3 (March, 2005): 269–83.
Goldman, Minton. *Slovakia since Independence: A Struggle for Democracy.* Westport, CT: Praeger, 1999.
Gál, Fedor. *Aktuálne problémy Česko-Slovenska (Správa zo sociologického výskumu)* [Contemporary problems in Czechoslovakia (Results of sociological research)]. Bratislava: Centrum pre výskum spoločenských problémov, November 1990.
Gjuričová, Adéla. "Poněkud tradiční rozchod s minulostí: Občanská demokratická strana," [A small traditional divorce with the past: the citizen's democratic party] in Adéla Gjuričová et al., *Rozděleni minulostí: Vytváření politických identit v České republice po roce 1989* [Divorce with the past: the evolution of political identities in the Czech Republic after 1989] (Prague, Knihovna Václava Havla: 2011), 107–34.
Gjuričová, Adéla, Michal Kopeček, Petr Roubal, Jiří Suk, Tomáš Zahradníček. *Rozděleni minulostí. Vytváření politických identit v České republice po roce 1993* [Divided by the past. The creation of political identities in the Czech Republic after 1989]. Prague: Václav Havel library, 2011.
Glaeser, Edward, Simon Johnson and Andrei Shleifer. "Coase Versus the Coasians." *Quarterly Journal of Economics* 116, no.3 (August, 2001): 853–99.
Godoy, Sergio and Joseph E. Stiglitz. "Growth, Initial Conditions, Law and Speed of Privatization in Transition Countries: 11 Years Later," in *Transition and Beyond—Essays in Honour of Mario Nuti*, ed. by Saul Estrin, Grzegorz Kolodko and Milica Uvalic. Basingstoke: Palgrave Macmillan, 2007: 89–117.
Godfrey, Martin. "The Struggle Against Unemployment: Medium-Term Policy Option for Transitional Economies." *International Labour Review* 134, no.1 (1995): 3–15.
Goetz-Stankiewicz, Markéta and Phyllis Carey eds. *Critical Essays on Václav Havel.* New York: G.K. Hall, 1999.

Golan, Galia. *Reform Rule in Czechoslovakia: The Dubček Era 1968–1969*. Cambridge: Cambridge University Press, 1973.
Gould, John A. "Out of the Blue? Democracy and Privatization in Post-Communist Europe." *Comparative European Politics* 1, no. 3 (November, 2003): 277–312.
———. "Slovakia's Neoliberal Churn: The Political Economy of the Fico Government, 2006–8." Institute of European Studies and International Relations, Faculty of Social and Economic Sciences, Comenius University, Working Paper 1/2009, 1–33.
———. *The Politics of Privatization: Wealth and Power in Postcommunist Europe*. Boulder, CO: Lynne Rienner Publishers, 2011.
———. "Vladimír Mečiar and the Politics of Privatization in Slovakia, 1992–1998." *Slovakia* 41 (2013): 102–45.
Gyárfášová, Oľga, Grigorij Mesežnikov eds. *Vláda strán na Slovensku: Skúsenosti a perspektívy* [The rule of political parties in Slovakia: experience and perspectives]. Bratislava: IVO, 2004.
Hallon, Ľudovít, Miroslav Sabol. "Proces globalizácie a vstup Slovenska do medzinárodných hospodárskych štruktúr po r. 1993" [The globalization process and the incorporation of Slovakia into international economic structures after 1993], in *20. rokov samostatnej Slovenskej republiky. Jedinečnosť a diskontinuita historického vývoja* [Twenty years of independence of the Slovak Republic. The uniqueness and discontinuity of its evolution], ed. by Miroslav Londák and Slavomír Michálek. Bratislava: VEDA, 2013: 397–439.
Hamplová, Dana. "Česká religiozita—církevní příslušnost a víra ve světle Sčítání lidu a dat ISSP 2008" [Czech religiosity—church affiliation and faith in light of census data and the ISSP 2008], CVVM *Naše společnost* (2010).
Hamplová, Dana and Zdeněk R. Nešpor. "Invisible Religion in a 'Non-believing' Country: The Case of the Czech Republic." *Social Compass* 56 (2009): 581–97.
Hanley, Seán. *The New Right in the New Europe: Czech Transformation and Right-Wing Politics, 1989–2006*. Oxon—New York: Routledge, 2008.
———. "Dynamics of New Party Formation in the Czech Republic 1996–2010: Looking for the Origins of a 'Political Earthquake'," *East European Politics* 28, no. 2 (2012): 119–43.
Hanousek, Jan and Evžen Kočenda. "The Impact of Czech Mass Privatization on Corporate Governance." *Journal of Economic Studies* 30, nos. 3/4 (2003): 278–93.
Hanousek, Jan and Randall Filer. "Consumers' Opinion of Inflation Bias Due to Quality Improvements." *Economic Development and Cultural Change* 53, no.1 (2004): 235–54.
Hardoš, Pavol. "Postkomunistické elity a politika ekonomickej transformácie v Československu" [Post-communist elites and the politics of economic transformation in Czechoslovakia], *Inštitút pre slobodnú spoločnosť*, Working Paper no.12 (2006): 1–76.

Haughton, Tim. *Constraints and Opportunities of Leadership in Post-communist Europe.* Aldershot: Ashgate, 2005.
Haughton, Tim. "Exit, Choice and Legacy: Explaining the Patterns of Party Politics in Post-Communist Slovakia." *East European Politics* 30, no. 2 (2014): 210–29.
Haughton, Tim, Tereza Novotná and Kevin Deegan-Krause. "The 2010 Czech and Slovak Parliamentary Elections: Red Cards to the 'Winners.'" *West European Politics*, 34, no. 2 (2011): 394–402.
Haughton, Tim and Kevin Deegan-Krause, "Hurricane Season: Systems of Instability in Central and Eastern Europe Party Politics," *East European Politics and Societies*, forthcoming
Havel, Václav. *The Art of the Impossible. Politics and Morality in Practice. Speeches and Writings, 1990–1996.* New York: Alfred A. Knopf 1997.
———. *Spisy 4. Eseje a jiné texty z let 1970–1989* [Collected works, vol. 4. Essays and other texts from the years 1970–1989]. Prague: Torst, 1999.
———. *Spisy 6. Projevy z let 1990–1992* [Collected works, vol. 6. Speeches from the years 1990–1992]. Prague: Torst, 1999.
———. *Spisy 7. Projevy a jiné texty z let 1992–1999* [Collected works, vol. 7. Speeches and other texts from the years 1992–1999]. Prague: Torst, 1999.
———. *Prosím stručně: rozhovor s Karlem Hvížďalou, poznámky, dokumenty* [Please be brief: interviews with Karel Hvížď'al, notes and documentation]. Prague: Gallery, 2006.
Havelka, Miloš. "'Nepolitická politika': kontexty a tradice," [Non-political politics: context and tradition]. *Sociologický časopis* 34 , no. 4 (1998): 455–66.
Hayek, Friedrich *Rules and Order. Vol. 1 of Law, Legislation and Liberty.* London: Routledge & Kegan Paul, 1976.
———. *The Constitution of Liberty.* London: Routledge & Kegan Paul, 1960.
Hlavová, Viera, Jozef Žakuliak, eds. *Novembrová revolúcia a česko-slovenský rozchod. Výber dokumentov a prejavov november 1989–december 1992* [The November revolution and the Czechoslovak dissolution. A selection of documents and speeches, November 1989–December 1992]. Bratislava: Národné literárne centrum, 2002.
Heimann, Mary. *Czechoslovakia: The State that Failed.* New Haven: Yale University Press, 2009.
Hellman, Joel S. "Winners Take All: Politics of Partial Reform in Post-communist Transition." *World Politics*, 50, no. 2 (1998): 203–34.
Henderson, Karen. *Slovakia: The Escape from Invisibility.* London: Routledge, 2002.
Hilde, Paal Sigurd. "Slovak Nationalism and the Break-up of Czechoslovakia." *Europe-Asia Studies* 51 (1999): 647–65.
———. "Nationalism in Post-Communist Slovakia and the Slovak Nationalist Diaspora (1989–1992)" (PhD diss., Oxford University, 2003).
Hloušek, Vít and Kopeček, Lubomír. *Origin, Ideology and Transformation of Political Parties: East-Central and Western Europe.* Farnham, UK – Burlington, VT: Ashgate Publishing, 2010.

Hocman, Juraj. *Slovakia from the Downfall of Communism, to its Accession into the European Union, 1989–2004. The Re-Emergence of Political Parties and Democratic Institutions.* Frankfurt am Main: Peter Lang, 2011.

Holmes, Leslie. *Post-Communism: An Introduction.* Durham: Duke University Press, 1997.

Holscher, Jens. "Twenty Years of Economic Transition: Successes and Failures." *The Journal of Comparative Economic Studies (JCES)* 5 (December, 2009): 3–17.

Holub, Tomáš and Jaromír Hurník. "Ten Years of Czech Inflation Targeting: Missed Targets and Anchored Expectations." *Emerging Markets Finance and Trade* 44, no. 6 (November–December, 2008): 67–86.

Holy, Ladislav. "Metaphors of the Natural and the Artificial in Czech Political Discourse." *Man* 29 (1994): 809–29.

———. *The Little Czech and the Great Czech Nation: National Identity in the Post-Communist Social Transformation.* New York: Cambridge University Press, 1996.

Hudek, Adam, ed. *Overcoming the Old Borders: Beyond the Paradigm of Slovak National History.* Bratislava: Historický ústav SAV, 2013.

Innes, Abby. *Czechoslovakia. The Short Goodbye.* New Haven, CT: Yale University Press, 2001.

International Monetary Fund. *Czech Republic IMF Country Report* no. 11/83, (Washington, DC, 2011).

———. *Czech Republic IMF Country Report* No. 13, 243, (Washington, DC, 2013).

Jacobs, Garry and N. Asokan. "Towards a Comprehensive Theory of Social Development," in *Human Choice: The Genetic Code for Social Development*, eds. Harlan Cleveland, Garry Jacobs, Robert Macfarlane, Robert van Harten, and N. Asokan. Minneapolis: The World Academy of Art and Science, 1999.

Ježek, Tomáš and Petr Husák. *Budování kapitalismu v Čechách: Rozhovory s Tomášem Ježkem* [Establishing capitalism in the Czech lands: interviews with Tomáš Ježek]. Prague: Volvox Globator, 1997.

———. *Zrození ze zkumavky. Svědectví o české privatizaci 1990–1997.* [Shocked by research: witness to the Czech privatization, 1990–1997] Prague: Prostor, 2007.

Judt, Tony. *Ill Fares the Land.* London–New York: Penguin, 2010.

Jurajda, Stepan and Juraj Stancik. "Foreign Ownership and Corporate Performance: The Czech Republic at EU Entry." *Czech Journal of Economics and Finance (Finance a Úvěr)* 62, no. 4 (August, 2012): 306–24.

Kahanec, Martin, Martin Guzi, Monika Martišková, Michal Paleník, Filip Pertold, and Zuzana Siebertová. *GINI Country Report: Growing Inequalities and Their Impacts in the Czech Republic and Slovakia.* AIAS, Amsterdam: Institute for Advanced Labour Studies, 2012).

Kalinová, Lenka, "Dělníci v normalizaci: dělnictvo a sociální stát v Ceskoslovensku" [Workers in the normalization period: the working class and the welfare state in Czechoslovakia], in *Česká společnost v 70. a 80. letech: sociální a ekonomické aspekty* [Czech society in the 1970s and 1980s: social and economic aspects], eds. Tomáš Vilímek and Oldřich Tůma. Prague: Ústav pro soudobé dějiny, 2012: 7–62.

———. *Konec nadějím a nová očekávání. K dějinám české společnosti 1969–1993* [Dashed hopes, new expectations: on the social history of the years 1969–1993] (Prague: Academia, 2012).

Kalous, Jan and Jiří Kocian, eds. *Český a slovenský komunismus (1921–2011)* [Czech and Slovak communism (1921–2011)]. Prague: Ústav pro soudobé dějiny AV ČR: Ústav pro studium totalitních režimů, 2012.

Karner, Stefan, Mark Kramer, Peter Ruggenthaler, Manfred Wilke, eds. *Der Kreml und die Wende 1989*. Innsbruck: Studien Verlag, 2014.

Keane, John. *Václav Havel. A Political Tragedy in Six Acts*. London: Bloomsbury, 1999.

Kipke, Rüdeger and Karel Vodička, eds. *Rozloučení s Československem: Příčiny a důsledky česko-slovenského rozchodu* [Goodbye to Czechoslovakia: causes and consequences of the Czechoslovak divorce]. Prague: Český spisovatel, 1993.

Kirkpatrick, Jean. "Dictatorship and Double Standards." *Commentary Magazine* 68 (November, 1979): 34–45.

Kirschbaum, Stanislav J. "The Cleveland and Pittsburgh Documents." *Slovakia* XXXVI (1998): 81–97.

———. "Slovakia: Whose History, What History?" *Canadian Slavonic Papers/ Revue canadienne des slavistes*, XLV, nos. 3–4 (2003): 459–67.

———. *A History of Slovakia. The Struggle for Survival*, 2nd edition. New York: Palgrave Macmillan, 2005.

———. "Whither Slovak Historiography After 1993?" *Canadian Slavonic Papers/ Revue canadienne des slavistes*, LIII, no.1 (2011): 45–63.

———. *Historical Dictionary of Slovakia*, 3rd edition. Lanham, MD: Scarecrow Press, 2014.

Klaus, Václav. *Cesta k tržní ekonomice* [The road to a market economy]. Prague: Top Agency, 1991.

———. *Demontáž socialismu. Předběžná zpráva*. [Dismantling socialism: a preliminary report]. Prague: Top Agency, 1992.

———. *Ekonomická teorie a realita transformačních procesů* [Economic theory and the reality of the transformation processes]. Prague: Management Press, 1995.

Klimova, Rita. "Current Problems of Transition in Czechoslovakia," in *Transitions from Communism in Russia and Eastern Europe*, ed. by Constantine C. Menges. New York: University Press of America, 1994: 112–19.

Kneuer, Marianne, Darina Malová, and Frank Bönker. *2014 Slovakia Report. Sustainable Governance Indicators*. Gütersloh: Bertlesmann Stiftung, 2014.

Kolář, Petr and Olga Gyárfášová. *National Populism in Slovakia*. Bratislava: IVO, 2008.

Kolář, Petr and Petr Valenta. *The Parliament of the Czech Republic—The Chamber of Deputies*. Prague: Ivan Král, 2011.

Kollár, Petr, Milan and Grigorji Mesežnikov, eds. *Slovensko 2000: Súhrnná správa o stave spoločnosti* [Slovakia 2000: global report on the state of society]. Bratislava: IVO, 2000.

Kornai, Janos. *The Road to a Free Economy: Shifting from a Socialist System. The Example of Hungary.* New York and London: W.W. Norton & Company, 1990.
Kopeček, Lubomír. *Éra nevinnosti. Česká politika 1989–1997* [The age of innocence. Czech politics, 1989–1997]. Brno: Barrister a Principal, 2010.
Kopeček, Michal. "The Stigma of the Past and the Bond of Belonging: Czech Communists in the First Post-1989 Decade." *Czech Journal of Contemporary History* I (2013): 101–30.
Kopecky, Petr. *Parliaments in the Czech and Slovak Republics: Party Competition and Parliamentary Institutionalization.* Burlington, VT: Ashgate, 2001.
———. "An Awkward Newcomer? EU Enlargement and Euroscepticism in the Czech Republic." *European Studies* 20 (2004): 238–41.
Kopecky, Petr and Joop Van Holsteyn. "The grass is always greener...: Mass Attitudes towards the European Union in the Czech and Slovak Republics." Paper presented at the Public Opinion about the EU in East-Central Europe Conference, University of Indiana, Bloomington, April 2–3, 2004.
Kořalka, Jiří. "Czechoslovakia." *American Historical Review* 97 (October, 1992): 1026–40.
Kostelecký, Tomáš. "Economic, Social and Historical Determinants of Voting Patterns: In the 1990 and 1992 Parliamentary Elections in the Czech Republic." *Czech Sociological Review*, 2 (1994): 209–28.
Kouba, Karel, Ondřej Vychodil, and Jitka Roberts. *Privatizace bez kapitálu. Zvýšené tranzakční náklady české transformace* [Privatization without capital. The increasing costs of the Czech transformation]. Prague: Národohospodářský ústav Josefa Hlávky, 2004.
Kováč, Dušan. "Nacionalizmus a politická kultúra v Rakúsko—Uhorsku v období dualizmu" [Nationalism and political culture in Austria-Hungary during the period of dualism]. *Historický časopis* 53, no.1 (2005): 45–56.
Kováč, Michal. *Pamäti. Môj príbeh občana a prezidenta* [Memoirs: my role as a citizen and president]. Dunajská Lužná: Milanium, 2010.
Kovács, János Mátyás. *Transition to Capitalism? The Communist Legacy in Eastern Europe.* New York: Transaction Publishers, 1994.
Koźmiński, Maciej, ed. *Európska civilizácia: Eseje a prednášky.* [European civilization: essays and lectures]. Bratislava: Kalligram, 2006.
Kraus, Michael and Allison Stanger, eds. *Irreconcilable Differences? Explaining Czechoslovakia's Dissolution.* Lanham: Rowman and Littlefield, 2000.
Krejčí, Jaroslav. *Czechoslovakia at the Crossroads of European History.* London: Tauris, 1990.
Krivý, Vladimír and Milan Zemko, eds. *Voľby do zákonodarných orgánov na území Slovenska 1920–2006* [Legislative elections in Slovakia from 1920 to 2006]. Bratislava: Štatistický úrad Slovenskej republiky vo vyd. Veda, 2008.
Kubů, Eduard. "České (československé) transformační kontinuity 20. století. Problémy struktury ekonomiky, technicko-technologické vyspělosti a podnikatelsko-manažerských elit" [Czech (Czechoslovak) transformation continuities of the twentieth century. Problems of the structure of the

economy, technical and technological development level and entrepreneurial and business elites], *Acta Oeconomica Pragensia* 13, no. 3 (2005): 230–45.

Kuklík, Jan, Jr. *Znárodněné Československo* [Nationalized Czechoslovakia]. Prague: Auditorium, 2010.

Kusín, Vladimír V. *From Dubček to Charter 77: A Study of Normalisation in Czechoslovakia, 1968–1978.* Edinburgh: Q Press Ltd., 1978.

Kuzio, Taras. "Transition in Post-Communist States: Triple or Quadruple?" *Politics* 21 (2001): 168–77.

Labour Market Statistics. Luxembourg: Publication Office of the European Union, 2011.

Lach, Jiří, James T. LaPlant, Jim Peterson, and David Hill. "The Party Isn't Over: An Analysis of the Communist Party in the Czech Republic." *The Journal of Communist Studies and Transition Politics* 26, no. 3 (2010): 363–88.

Leff, Carol Skalnik. *National Conflict in Czechoslovakia: The Making and Remaking of a State, 1918–1987.* Princeton: Princeton University Press, 1988.

———. *The Czech and Slovak Republics. Nation Versus State.* Boulder, CO: Westview Press, 1997.

———. "Democratization and Disintegration in Multinational States: The Breakup of the Communist Federations." *World Politics* 51, no. 2 (1999): 205–35.

———. *Reconstructing Elites after Authoritarian Rule: The Case of post-Communist Eastern Europe.* Rowman & Littlefield, forthcoming.

Leontiyeva, Yana, ed. *Menšinová problematika v ČR: komunitní život a reprezentace kolektivních zájmů (Slováci, Ukrajinci, Vietnamci a Romové)* [The issue of minorities in the Czech Republic: community life and the representation of collective interests (Slovaks, Ukrainians, Vietnamese, and Roma)]. Prague: Sociologický ústav 2006.

Leška, Vladimír. *Slovensko 1993 –2004: Léta obav a nadějí* [Slovakia in 1993–2004: the years of fears and hopes]. Prague: Ústav mezinárodních vztahů, 2006.

Letz, Robert. *Rozdelenie Česko-Slovenska v roku 1992* [The breakup of Czechoslovakia in 1992]. Bratislava: Polygrafia SAV, 1997.

———. *Slovenské dejiny* [Slovak history]. Bratislava: Literárne informačné centrum, 2008.

Linek, Lukáš. "Kdy vymřou voliči KSČM? K věkové struktuře elektorátu KSČM," [When will the voters of the KSČM die out? The age structure of supporters of the KSČM]. *Czech Journal of Political Science/Politologický časopis*, 15, no. 4 (2008): 318–36.

———. "Czech Republic." *European Journal of Political Research Political Data Yearbook* 52, no. 1 (2013): 50–5.

Londák, Miroslav. *Rok 1968 a ekonomická realita Slovenska* [The year 1968 and the economic reality of Slovakia]. Bratislava: Historický ústav SAV vo vydavateľstve Prodama, 2007.

———. *Ekonomické reformy v Československu v 50. a 60. rokoch 20. storočia a slovenská ekonomika* [Economic reforms in Czechoslovakia in the 1950s and 1960s and the Slovak economy]. Bratislava: Historický ústav SAV, 2012.

Londák, Miroslav and Slavomír Michálek, eds. *20 rokov samostatnej Slovenskej republiky. Jedinečnosť a diskontinuita historického vývoja* [Twenty years of the Slovak Republic. The uniquenes and discontinuity of its historical evolution]. Bratislava: VEDA, 2013.

Loužek, Marek, ed. *Patnáct let od obnovení kapitalismu v naší zemi* [Fifteen years since the restoration of capitalism in our country]. Prague: CEP, 2006.

Luxmoore, Jonathan and Jolanta Babiuch. "In Search of Faith, Part 2: Charter 77 and the Return to Spiritual Values in the Czech Republic." *Religion, State & Society* 23 (1995): 291–304.

Mainwaring, Scott, Annabella España, and Carlos Gervasoni, "Extra System Electoral Volatility and the Vote Share of Young Parties." Paper prepared for the Annual Meeting of the Canadian Political Science Association, Toronto, May 28, 2009.

Malíř, Jiří and Pavel Marek, eds. *Politické strany: Vývoj politických stran a hnutí v českých zemích a Československu 1861 – 2004 II. díl: Období 1938 – 2004* [Political parties: the evolution of political parties and movements in the Czech Lands and in Czechoslovakia, 1861–2004, Volume II, from 1938-2004]. Brno: Doplněk, 2005.

Mandelbaum, Michael. "Introduction," in *Making Markets: Economic Transformation in Eastern Europe and the Post-Soviet States*, ed. by Shafiqul Islam and Michael Mandelbaum. New York: CSFR 1993: 1-15.

Mannová, Elena, ed. *A Concise History of Slovakia*. Bratislava: Historical Institute of the Slovak Academy of Sciences, 2000.

Marcinčin, Anton. *Zákon o strategických podnikoch: Krok späť?* [The law on strategic companies: a step backwards?]. Bratislava: Slovenská spoločnosť pre zahraničnú politiku, 1997.

———. "Privatizácia" [Privatization]. *Hospodárska politika na Slovensku 1990–1999* [Economic policy in Slovakia, 1990–1999], ed. by Anton Marcinčin and Miroslav Beblavý. Bratislava: Centrum pre spoločenskú a mediálnu analýzu, 2000: 291–6.

Marcinčin, Anton, Daniela Zemanovičová and Luboš Vagač. *Privatization Methods and Development of Slovakia*. Bratislava: Center for Economic Development, 1996.

Marés, Antoine. *La Tchécoslovaquie sismographe de l'Europe au XX e siècle*. Paris: Institut d'études slaves, 2009.

Mareš, Petr. "Social Exclusion and Social Inclusion: the Czech Perspective," in *The Challenge of Social Inclusion: Minorities and Marginalised Groups in Czech Society*, ed. by Tomáš Sirovátka (Brno: Barrister & Principal, 2006), 11–38.

Matějů, Petr, "Determinanty ekonomického úspěchu v první fázi postkomunistické transformace. Česká republika 1989–1992" [Determinants of economic success in the first stage of the post-communist transformation. The Czech Republic, 1989–1992]. *Sociologický časopis* 29, no. 3 (1993): 341–66.

Matějů, Petr. "Elite Research in the Czech Republic. A Report on Major Research Projects," in *Elites in Transition. Elite Research in Central and*

Eastern Europe, ed. by Heinrich Best and Ulrich Becker (Opladen: Leske + Budrich, 1997), 61–76.
Matějů, Petr, Lim Nelson. "Who Has Gotten Ahead After the fall of Communism? The Case of the Czech Republic." *Sociologický časopis* 31, no. 2 (1995): 117–36.
Matějů, Petr, Klára Vlachová. *Nerovnost, spravedlnost, politika. Česká republika 1991–1998* [Inequality, justice, politics. The Czech Republic 1991–1998]. Prague: Slon, 2000.
Matos, Cristina. *Post-Socialist Employment 'Informalisation': Hungary and the Czech Republic.* EAEPE, 2002 Conference on Complexity and the Economy. Aix-en-Provence, November 7–11, 2002.
———. "Post-socialist Transformation and Institutions," Paper prepared for the 2005 SASE conference: 'What Counts? Calculation, Representation, Association,' (Central European University and Corvinus University of Budapest, Budapest, June 30–July 2, 2005).
Maxa, Hubert. *Alexander Dubček—člověk v politice (1990–1992)* [Alexander Dubček—the man in politics (1990–1992)]. Bratislava, Brno: Kalligram—Doplněk, 1998.
Mesežnikov, Grigorij, et al. *Slovak Elections 2002: Results, Implications, Context.* Bratislava: IVO, 2003.
Michálek, Slavomír and Miroslav Londák, eds. *Gustáv Husák: Moc politiky—Politik moci* [Gustáv Husák: the power of politics—the politician of power]. Bratislava: Veda, 2013.
Mikloš, Ivan. "Economic Transition and the Emergence of Clientalist Structures in Slovakia," in *Slovakia: Problems of Democratic Consolidation*, ed. by Soňa Szomolányi and John A. Gould. Bratislava: Friedrich Ebert Stiftung/Slovak Political Science Association, 1997: 57–92.
———. "Privatizácia," [Privatization] in *Slovensko, 1997: Súhrnná správa o stave spoločnosti a trendoch na rok 1998* [Slovakia in 1997: A complete report on the state of society and trends for 1998], ed. by Martin Bútora and Michal Ivantyšin]. (Bratislava: Inštitút pre verejné otázky, 1998: 405–32.
Mikloško, František. *Čas stretnutí* [A time of meetings]. Bratislava: Kalligram, 1996.
Mlčoch, Lubomír. "Czech Privatization: A Criticism of the Misunderstood Liberalism (A Keynote Address)." *Journal of Business Ethics* 17 (July, 1998): 951–59.
Morris, Ian. *Why the West Rules—For Now: The Patterns of History, and What They Reveal About the Future.* New York: Farrar, Straus & Giroux, 2010.
———. *Social Development.* Stanford: Stanford University Press, 2010.
Murrell, Peter. "How Far has Transition Progressed?" *Journal of Economic Perspectives* 10, no. 2 (Spring 1996): 25–44.
Musil, Jiří, et al. *The End of Czechoslovakia.* Budapest–New York: Central European University Press, 1995.
Naím, Moisés. *The End of Power: From Boardrooms to Battlefields and Churches to States, Why Being in Charge Isn't What It Used to Be.* New York: Basic Books, 2014.

Myant, Martin. *The Rise and Fall of Czech Capitalism: Economic Development in the Czech Republic Since 1989*. London: Edward Elgar, 2003.
Nations in Transit. New York: Freedom House, 2013.
Nedelsky, Nadya. *Defining the Sovereign Community: The Czech and Slovak Republics*. Philadephia: University of Pennsylvania Press, 2009.
Nee, Victor and Peng Lian. "Sleeping with the Enemy: A Dynamic Model of Declining Political Commitment in State Socialism." *Theory and Society* 23, no. 3 (1994): 253–96.
Németh, Szilvia. *Strategy of the Slovak Republic for Integration of Roma up to 2020 (critical summary by REF consultant)*. Budapest: Roma Educational Fund 2012.
Nešpor, Zdeněk R. "Religious Processes in Contemporary Czech Society." *Sociologický Časopis / Czech Sociological Review* 40 (2004): 277–95.
Nicholson, Tom. *Gorila*. Bratislava: Dixit, 2012.
———. "Je čas dať tomuto štátu zmysel" [It's time to give this state some meaning] in *Odkiaľ a kam? Dvadsať rokov samostatnosti* [From where and whither? Twenty years of independence], ed. by Martin Bútora et al. Bratislava: Kalligram, 2013: 281–91.
———. "Corruption in Slovakia: Time to Reclaim the State." *Slovakia* 42, nos. 78-79 (2015): 112–25.
Norris, Pippa and Ronald Inglehart. *Sacred and Secular: Religion and Politics Worldwide*, 2nd ed. Cambridge: Cambridge University Press 2011.
Nosková, Helena. *Pražské ozvěny. Minulost a současnost Slováků v českých zemích* [Prague echoes. Past and present of Slovaks in the Czech Lands]. Prague: Ústav pro soudobé dějiny AV ČR, 2014.
Nosková, Helena, Petr Bednařík et al. *National Minorities, Identity, Education*. Prague: Institute for Contemporary History, 2011.
Novotný, Vít, ed. *From Reform to Growth*. Delft: Eburon Academic Publishers, 2013.
O'Donnell, Guillermo A. "Delegative Democracy." *Journal of Democracy* 5, no. 1 (1994): 55–69.
Offe, Claus. "Capitalism by Democratic Design? Democratic Theory Facing the Triple Transition in East Central Europe." *Social Research* 58 (1991): 865–81.
Okáli, Ivan, Karol Frank and Hana Gabrielová. "Hospodársky vývoj Slovenska v roku 2005" [Economic development in Slovakia in the year 2005]. *Ekonomický časopis* 53 (2005): 452–57.
Olsson, Mikael. *Ownership Reform and Corporate Governance: The Slovak Privatization Process in 1990–1996*. Uppsala: Uppsala University, 1999.
Ondruš, Vladimír. *Atentát na nežnú revolúciu* [The assassination of the Velvet Revolution]. Bratislava: Ikar, 2009.
Orenstein, Mitchell A. "The Political Success of Neo-Liberalism in the Czech Republic," Institute for East West Studies paper, preliminary draft, 1994.
———. *Out of the Red: Building Capitalism and Democracy in Postcommunist Europe*. Ann Arbor: University of Michigan Press, 2001.
Otáhal, Milan and Miroslav Vaněk. *Sto studentských revolucí. Studenti v období pádu komunismu – životopisná vyprávění* [A hundred student revolutions.

Students during the fall of communism—biographical stories]. Prague: Lidové noviny, 1999.

———. *Podíl tvůrčí inteligence na pádu komunismu* [The role of the creative intelligentsia in the downfall of communism]. Brno: Doplněk, 1999.

Paczkowski, Andrzej. *The Spring Will be Ours: Poland and the Poles from Occupation to Freedom.* University Park: Pennsylvania State University Press, 2003.

Pánek, Jaroslav, Oldřich Tůma, eds. *A History of the Czech Lands.* Prague: Karolinum Press, 2009.

Pauer, Jan. "Moral Political Dissent in German-Czech Relations." *Czech Sociological Review* 6 (1996): 173–186.

Pavlík, Petr. "Economic Transformation in the Czech Republic. What Went Wrong?" in *Post Communist Transition to a Market Economy. Lessons and Challenges,* ed. by D. M. Nuti and Milica Uvalic. Ravenna: Longo Editore, 2003: 231–52.

Pavlíková, Eva, Karel Sládek, eds. *Sociální situace a religiozita ukrajinských migrantů v ČR* [The social situation and religiosity of Ukrainian migrants in the Czech Republic]. Červený Kostelec: Pavel Mervart, 2009.

Pehe, Jiri. "Czechs Fall From Their Ivory Tower." *Transitions Online* 4, no. 3 (August, 1997).

Pejovich, Svetozar. *The Economics of Property Rights.* Cambridge, MA: Ballinger Publishing, 1974.

Peter, Radoslav and Tibor Lalinský. "Slovensko versus Česko: 20 rokov od rozvodu" [Slovakia versus the Czech Republic: 20 years since the divorce]. *Biatec,* 21 (November, 2013): 5–9.

Peterson, James W. "Separate Paths: Czech and Slovak Foreign Policies Since 1993." *Slovakia* 38, Nos. 70-71 (2005): 121–45.

Petrovic, Milenko. *The Democratic Transition of Post-Communist Europe.* London: Palgrave-Macmillan, 2013.

Petsoulas, Christian. *Hayek's Liberalism and Its Origins: His Idea of Spontaneous Order and the Scottish Enlightenment.* London: Routledge, 2001.

Podrimavský, Milan and Dušan Kováč, eds. *Na začiatku storočia, 1901–1914* [The beginning of the century, 1901–1914]. Bratislava: Veda, 2004.

Pop-Eleches, Grigore. "Throwing Out the Bums: Protest Voting and Anti-Establishment Parties after Communism." *World Politics* 62 (2010): 221–60.

Pospíšil, Martin and Jiří Schwarz. *Bankruptcy, Investment, and Financial Constraints: Evidence from a Post-Transition Country* (Mimeo).

Powell, Eleanor Neff and Joshua Tucker. "Revisiting Electoral Volatility in Post-Communist Countries: New Data, New Results and New Approaches." *British Journal of Political Science* 44 (2013): 1–25.

Prameny k dějinám československé krize v letech 1967–1970, Díl 5/1 sv [Sources for the history of the Czechoslovak crisis in the years 1967–1970, part 5, vol. 1]. Prague: ÚSD AV ČR; Brno: Doplněk, 1996.

Pynsent, Robert P. *Questions of Identity: Czech and Slovak Ideas on Nationality and Personality.* Budapest–New York: Central European University Press, 1994.

Raj Desai, Raj. "Financial Market Reform in the Czech Republic, 1991-1994: The Revival of Repression?" Working Paper no. 86, Prague: CERGE-EI, September 1995.
Rodrik, Dani. "Understanding Economic Policy Reform," *Journal of Economic Literature*, 34 (March, 1996): 9–41.
Roland, Gerard. "Ten Years After...Transition and Economics." *IMF Staff Papers* 48 (special issue, 2001): 29-52.
Roman, David. "Twenty Years of Transitional Justice in the Czech Lands." *Europe-Asia Studies* 64 (2012): 761–4.
Romsics, Ignác. *Hungary in the Twentieth Century*. Budapest: Osiris, 1999.
Roy, Olivier. "Islamic Revival and Democracy: The Case in Tunisia and Egypt," in *Arab Society in Revolt: The West's Mediterranean Challenge*, ed. Cesare Merlini and Olivier Roy. Washington, D.C: Brookings Institution Press, 2012.
Rupnik, Jacques. "Twenty Years of Postcommunism: In Search of a New Model," *Journal of Democracy* 21, no. 1 (2010): 105–112.
Rychlík, Jan. *Češi a Slováci ve 20. století. Česko-slovenské vztahy 1945–1992* [The Czechs and Slovaks in the twentieth century: Czechoslovak relations, 1945–1992]. Bratislava: Academic Electronic Press, 1998.
———. "České, slovenské, československé dejiny—vztahy a souvislosti" [Czech, Slovak, Czechoslovak history—relations and consequences]. *Československo 1918–1938. Osudy demokracie ve Střední Evropě I*. [Czechoslovakia, 1918–1938. The fate of democracy in Central Europe, I], ed. by Jaroslav Valenta. Historický ústav ČAV, 1999: 163–9.
———. "Česko-slovenská jednání od roku 1990 do voleb 1992" [Czecho-slovak negotiations from 1990 to the elections of 1992]. *Česko-slovenská historická ročenka 2000*. Brno: Masarykova univerzita, 2002: 167–80.
———. *Rozpad Československa: Česko-slovenské vztahy 1989–1992* [The breakup of Czechoslovakia: Czech-Slovak relations, 1989–1992] Bratislava: AEP, 2002.
———. "Jednání ODS a HZDS o státoprávním uspořádání a rozdělení ČSFR v léte 1992" [The negotiations between the ODS and the HZDS regarding state legal regulations and the dissolution in the summer 1992]. *Česko-slovenská historická ročenka 2003* (Brno: Masarykova univerzita, 2003): 55–72.
———. "Výskum slovenských dějin v České republice," *Historický časopis* 52, No. 2 (2004): 363–74.
———. *Češi a Slováci ve 20. století. Spolupráce a konflikty, 1914-1992* [Czechs and Slovaks in the 20th century: cooperation and conflicts]. Prague: Vyšehrad, 2012.
———. *Rozdělení Československa 1989–1992* [The dissolution of Czechoslovakia, 1989–1992]. Prague: Vyšehrad, 2013.
Sabol, Miroslav. "Elektrifikácia Československa 1945–1948 s dôrazom na územie Slovenska" [Electrification of Czechoslovakia with emphasis on Slovak territory, 1945–1948], *Věda a technika v Československu v letech 1945–1960* [Science and technology in Czechoslovakia from 1945 to 1960]. Prague: Národní technické múzeum, 2010: 336–48.

———. "Významný priemysel na Slovensku a jeho výrobné programy v rokoch 1969–1989" [Important industry in Slovakia and its development programs in the years 1969–1989]. *Věda a technika v Československu od normalizace k transformaci* [Science and technology in Czechoslovakia from normalization to transformation]. Prague: Národní technické muzeum, 2012: 199–215.

Sachs, Jeffrey D. *Poland's Jump to a Free Market Economy*. Cambridge: MIT Press, 1994.

Sachs, Jeffrey D. and Felipe B. Larrain. *Macroeconomics. In the Global Economy*. New York–London–Toronto–Sydney–Tokyo–Singapore: Harvester Wheatsheaf, 1993.

Saxonberg, Steven. *The Fall. A Comparative Study of the End of Communism in Czechoslovakia, East Germany, Hungary and Poland*. Amsterdam: Harwood Academic Publishers, 2001.

Schwarz, Jiří and Jiří Šíma. "The Euro as a Hindrance to Recovery? A Comparative Analysis of the Czech Republic and Slovakia." *Institutions in Crisis: European Perspectives on the Recession*, ed. by David Howden. Cheltenham, UK: Edward Elgar, 2011: 179–99.

———. "Sociálno-ekonomické koncepcie KSS v rokoch 1921–1948" [Social and economic concepts of the Communist Party of Slovakia in the years 1921–1948]. *Český a slovenský komunismus (1921-2011)* [Czech and Slovak communism (1921–2011)], ed. by Jan Kalous and Jiří Kocian. Prague: Ústav pro soudobé dějiny AV ČR : Ústav pro studium totalitních režimů, 2012): 32–40.

Schuster, Rudolf. *Ultimátum* [Ultimatum]. Košice: PressPrint, 1996.

———. *Návrat do veľkej politiky* [Return to serious politics]. Košice: PressPrint, 1999.

Scherpereel, John A. *Governing the Czech Republic and Slovakia: Between State Socialism and the European Union*. Boulder, CO: First Forum Press, 2009.

Shepherd, Robin H. E. *Czechoslovakia. The Velvet Revolution and Beyond*. London: Macmillan, 2000.

Scheppele, Kim Lane. "The Rule of Law and the Frankenstate: Why Governance Checklists Do Not Work." *Governance* 26, no. 4 (2013): 559–62.

Schwartz, Andrew. *The Politics of Greed: How Privatization Structured Politics in Central and Eastern Europe*. Lanham: Rowman & Littlefield, 2006.

Selowsky, Marcelo and Ricardo Martin. "Policy Performance and Output Growth in the Transition Economies." *The American Economic Review* 87, no. 2 (May 1997): 349–53.

Shleifer, Andrej and Daniel Treisman. *Without a Map: Political Tactics and Economic Reform in Russia*. Cambridge: MIT Press, 2000.

Simon, Jeffrey. *NATO and the Czech and Slovak Republics: A Comparative Study in Civil-Military Relations*. Lanham, MD: Rowman & Littlefield, 2004.

Simon, Johnson, Rafael La Porta. Florencio Lopez-de-Silanes, and Andrei Shleifer. *Tunneling*. NBER Working Paper no. 7523 (February 2000).

Skilling, H. Gordon and Paul Wilson, eds. *Civic Freedom in Central Europe. Voices from Czechoslovakia*. New York: St. Martin's Press, 1991.

Slovakia 1998-99: A Global Report on the State of Society. Bratislava: IVO, 1999.
Slovakia: Trends in the Quality of Democracy. Bratislava, Institute for Public Affairs, 2008, 2009, 2010, 2011, 2012.
"Slovenská Gorila: kompletní spis dokumentu" [The Slovak Gorilla: a complete list of the documents]. *Parlamentní listy*, January 9, 2012.
Slovenská národná rada. 6. schôdza, 1. októbra 1990. IV. volebné obdobie. Stenografická správa o schôdzi Slovenskej národnej rady [The Slovak National Council. 6th meeting, October 1, 1990. The 4th electoral period. Stenographic copy of the meeting of the Slovak National Council]. Bratislava: Kancelária SNR, 1990.
Šmidová, Olga. "Švejk after Slovakia: Czech National Identity Now." *East European Reporter* 5 (1992): 23–26.
Smith, Simon, ed. *Local Communities and Post-Communist Transformation: Czechoslovakia, the Czech Republic and Slovakia.* London: Routledge, 2003.
Smith, Tom W. and Seokho. Kim "National Pride in Cross-national and Temporal Perspective," *International Journal of Public Opinion* 18 (2006): 127–36.
Srb, Vladimír and Tomáš Veselý. *Rozdělení Československa: Nejvyšší představitelé HZDS a ODS v procese ČSFR: česko-slovenské spolunažívaní v rokoch 1989–1993* [The dissolution of Czechoslovakia: the leaders of the ODS and the HZDS in the process of the ČSFR: Czechoslovak coexistence in the years 1989–1993]. Bratislava: Karpaty—Infopress, 2004.
Štaigl, Jan. "Špeciálna výroba na Slovensku a problematika konverzie" [Special production in Slovakia and the problem of industrial conversion], *20 rokov samostatnej Slovenskej republiky. Jedinečnosť a diskontinuita historického vývoja* [20 years of the independent Slovak Republic. The uniqueness and discontinuity of its historical development], ed. by Miroslav Londák and Slavomír Michálek. Bratislava: VEDA, 2013: 213–38.
Statistická ročenka České republiky 1994 [Statistical yearbook of the Czech Republic, 1994]. Prague: Český spisovatel, 1994.
Statistická ročenka České republiky 2013 [Statistical yearbook of the Czech Republic, 2013]. Prague: Český statistický úřad, 2013.
Stein, Eric. *Czecho/Slovakia: Ethnic Conflict, Constitutional Fissure, Negotiated Breakup.* Ann Arbor: University of Michigan Press, 1997. (Published also as: *Česko-Slovensko: Konflikt—roztržka—rozpad* [Czecho/Slovakia: ethnic conflict, constitutional fissure, negotiated breakup] Prague: Academia, 2000).
Stiglitz, Joseph E. *Globalization and its Discontents.* New York and London: W. W. Norton, 2002.
Stolarik, M. Mark, ed. *The Slovak Republic: A Decade of Independence (1993–2002).* Wauconda, IL: Bolchazi-Carducci, 2002.
Stolarik, M. Mark and Milan Hauner. "Communications." *American Historical Review* 98 (April 1993): 650–1.
Strategy of the Slovak Republic for Integration of Roma up to 2020. Bratislava: Office of the Plenipotentiary of the Slovak Republic Government for Roma Communities, 2012.

Strečanský, Boris. "'We and They'—Slovakia," in *'We and They'. NGOs' Influence on Decision Making Processes in the Visegrad Group Countries*, ed. by Tom Nicholson (Bratislava: The Sasakawa Central Europe Fund and Center for Philanthropy 2008), 71–101.

———. *The Situation of the Third Sector in Slovakia, the Impacts of Crisis, Trends, Mainstreams and Challenges*. Bratislava: Center for Philanthropy, 2012.

Strečanský, Boris, et al. "Mimovládne neziskové organizácie a dobrovoľníctvo" [Nongovernmental nonprofit organizations and volunteering], in *Slovensko 2008. Súhrnná správa o stave spoločnosti* [Slovakia 2008. Comprehensive report on the state of society], ed. by Miroslav Kollár, Grigorij Mesežnikov and Martin Bútora. Bratislava: Institute for Public Affairs 2009.

Strong, Carol R. *The Role of Charismatic Leadership in Ending the Cold War: the Presidencies of Boris Yeltsin, Vaclav Havel, and Helmut Kohl*. Lewiston: Edwin Mellen Press, 2009.

Stullerová, Kamila. "National Sentiments, Globalization and Justice. Slovaks Narrating their Democratization Process." *Thinking Fundamentals*, IWM Junior Visiting Fellows Conferences 9 (Vienna, 2000).

Suk, Jiří. *Labyrintem revoluce: Aktéři, zápletky a křižovatky jedné politické krize* [Through the labyrinth of revolution: actors, plots and intersections of a political crisis]. Prague: Prostor, 2003.

———. *Politika jako absurdní drama. Václav Havel v letech 1975–1989* [Politics as an absurd drama: Václav Havel in the years 1975–1989]. Prague: Paseka, 2013.

Šulc, Zdislav. *Stručné dějiny ekonomických reforem v Československu (v České republice) 1945–1995* [Concise history of economic reforms in Czechoslovakia (in the Czech Republic) 1945–1995]. Brno: Doplněk, 1998.

Šutaj, Štefan, ed. *Národ a národnosti na Slovensku v transformujúcej sa spoločnosti – vzťahy a konflikty: Stav výskumu po roku 1989 a jeho perspektívy* [Nations and nationalities in the transforming Slovak society—relationships and conflicts: the state of research since 1989 and its prospects]. Prešov: Univerzum, 2004.

Šútovec, Milan. *Semióza jako politikum alebo "pomlčková vojna"* [Semiotics as politics or "the hyphen war"]. Bratislava: Kalligram, 1999.

Švejnar, Jan. "Czech and Slovak Federal Republic: A Solid Foundation," in *Economic Transformation in Central Europe: A Progress Report*, ed. by Richard Portes. London: Centre for Economic Policy Research, 1994: 29–33.

———, ed. *The Czech Republic and Economic Transition in Eastern Europe*. Orlando, FL: Academic Press, 1995.

Švejnar, Jan and Milica Uvalic. "The Czech Transition: The Importance of Microeconomic Fundamentals." *UNU-WIDER Research Paper* 17 (2009).

Tavits, Margit. "On the linkage between electoral volatility and party system instability in Central and Eastern Europe." *European Journal of Political Research* 47 (2008): 537–55.

Teich, Mikuláš, Dušan Kováč, and Martin D. Brown, eds. *Slovakia in History*. Cambridge, UK: Cambridge University Press, 2011.

The Statesman's Year-Book: Statistical and Historical Annual of the States of the World for the Year 1914. London: Macmillan, 1914.
Toma, Peter and Dušan Kováč. *Slovakia. From Samo to Dzurinda*. Stanford: Hoover Institution Press, 2001.
Tóth, Július. "Exchange Rate – Is it Really Overvalued?" *Slovak Capital and Money Market Report* (September–October 1999): 35–7.
Tuček, Milan, ed. *České elity po patnácti letech transformace* [Czech elites after fifteen years of transformation]. Prague: Sociologický ústav AV ČR, 2006.
Tůma, Oldřich. *Zítra zase tady! Protirežimní demonstrace v předlistopadové Praze jako politický a sociální fenomén* [Tomorrow the same place! Anti-regime demonstrations in Prague before November 1989 as a political and social phenomenon]. Prague: Ústav pro soudobé dějiny-Maxdorf, 1994.
Turek, Otakar. *Podíl ekonomiky na páde komunismu v Československu* [Contributions of the economy to the downfall of communism in Czechoslovakia]. Prague: Ústav pro soudobé dějiny AV ČR, 1995.
Uncommon Opportunities: An Agenda for Peace and Equitable Development. Report of the International Commission on Peace and Food (London: Zed Books, 1994).
Urban, Jan. *Privatizace a institucionální reformy v České republice* [Privatization and institutional reforms in the Czech Republic]. Prague: Právnická fakulta, 2005.
Ústava Československé socialistické republiky, Sbírka zákonů Československé socialistické republiky, částka 40, vydána dne 11. července 1960 [Constitution of the Czechoslovak Socialist Republic, Compendium of Documents of the Czechoslovak Socialist Republic, part 40, published on June 11, 1960.]
Vachudova, Milada Anna. *Europe Undivided: Democracy, Leverage and Integration after Communism*. Oxford: Oxford University Press, 2005.
Vaněk, Miroslav. *Veřejné mínění o socialismu před 17. listopadem 1989. Analýza výsledků výzkumů veřejného mínění prováděných ÚVVM od roku 1972 do roku 1989* [Public opinion on socialism before November 17, 1989. An analysis of public polls conducted by the Institute for Public Opinion Research]. Prague: Ústav pro soudobé dějiny-Maxdorf, 1994.
Vaněk, Miroslav, Pavel Urbášek, eds. *Vítězové? Poražení? Životopisná interview* [Victors? Vanquished? Biographical interviews] 2 vols. Prague: Institute of Contemporary History, 2005.
Vaněk, Miroslav, ed. *Obyčejní lidé…?! Pohled do života tzv. mlčící většiny. Životopisná vyprávění příslušníků dělnických profesí a inteligence* [Ordinary people…?! An insight into the lives of the "silent majority": life stories of manual laborers and the intelligentsia] 3 vols. Prague: Academia, 2009.
Vaněk, Miroslav and Lenka Krátká, eds. *Příběhy (ne)obyčejných profesí. Česká společnost v období tzv. normalizace a transformace v biografických vyprávěních některých profesních skupin* [Narratives of (extra)ordinary occupations. Czech society in the period of "normalization" and transformation: biographical narratives]. Prague: Karolinum, 2014.
Večerník, Jiří, ed. *Zpráva o vývoji české společnosti 1989–1998* [Report on the development of Czech society in 1989–1998]. Prague: Academia, 1998.

———. *Czech Society in the 2000s: A Report on Socio-Economic Policies and Structures*. Prague: Academia, 2009.

Vilímek, Tomáš. "K otázce vztahu a vzájemné reflexi opozice a společnosti v Československu po roce 1968" [Relations between the opposition and society in Czechoslovakia after 1968 and their opinions of each other], in *Opozice a společnost po roce 1948* [Opposition and society after 1948], ed. by Oldřich Tůma and Tomáš Vilímek. Prague: Ústav pro soudobé dějiny, 2009: 176–220.

Výběrové šetření o mzdách za červen 1984 [Selective analysis of wages in June 1984]. Prague: Federální statistický úřad, 1985.

Wade, Jacoby. "Tutors and Pupils: International Organizations, Central European Elites and Western Models." *Governance* 14, no. 2 (2001): 169–200.

Weiner, Elaine. *Market Dreams: Gender, Class, and Capitalism in the Czech Republic*. Ann Arbor: University of Michigan Press, 2007.

Wemer, David. "Europe's Little Tiger? Reassessing Economic Transition in Slovakia under the Mečiar Government, 1993-1998." *The Gettysburg Historical Journal* 12, no.1 (2013): 96–112.

Wheaton, Bernard and Zdenek Kavan. *The Velvet Revolution: Czechoslovakia, 1988–1991*. Boulder: Westview Press, 1992.

Williams, Kieran. "A Scorecard for Czech Lustration." *Central European Review* 19, no. 1 (November 1, 1999).

———. *Slovakia after Communism and Mečiarism*. London: School of Slavonic and Eastern European Studies, 2000.

Williams, Kieran and Dennis Deletant. *Security Intelligence Services in New Democracies: The Czech Republic, Slovakia and Romania*. New York: Palgrave, 2001.

Wolchik, Sharon L. *Czechoslovakia in Transition: Politics, Economics and Society*. London: Pinter Publishers, 1991.

Wolf, Karol. *Podruhé a naposled aneb Mírové dělení Československa* [Secondly and finally or the peaceful dissolution of Czechoslovakia]. Prague: G plus G, 1998.

World Bank. *Pension Reform and the Development of Pension Systems—An Evaluation of World Bank Assistance*. Washington, DC: World Bank, 2006.

World Economic Forum. *Executive Opinion Survey*. Geneva: World Economic Forum, 2013.

Young, Robert. *The Breakup of Czechoslovakia*. Kingston: Institute for Intergovernmental Relations, 1994.

———. *The Secession of Quebec and the Future of Canada*. Montreal: McGill-Queen's University Press, 1994.

Za naše Slovensko. Informácie z vlády Slovenskej republiky. [For our Slovakia. Information from the Slovak government], no. 13/90 (Bratislava: ÚV SR), 6; Slovenská národná rada. Stenografická správa o schôdzi Slovenskej národnej rady, 3. schôdza, 27. až 29. augusta 1990 (Bratislava: Kancelária SNR, 1990

Zahradníček, Tomáš. "XXIII. Czech Republic (1993–2004)," in *A History of the Czech Lands*, ed. by Jaroslav Pánek, Oldřich Tůma, et al. Prague: Karolinum, 2014.

Zakaria, Fareed. "The Rise of Illiberal Democracy." *Foreign Affairs*, no. 6 (1997): 22–43.

Žatkuliak, Jozef, et al. *November 1989 a Slovensko: Chronológia a dokumenty (1985–1990)* [November 1989 and Slovakia: chronology and documents (1985–1990)], Bratislava: Nadácia Milana Šimečku—Historický ústav SAV, 1999.

Žatkuliak, Jozef and Ivan Laluha, eds. *Alexander Dubček: Od totality k demokracii: prejavy, články a rozhovory; výber 1963–1992* [From totalitarianism to democracy: a selection of speeches, articles and interviews, 1963–1992]. Bratislava: Historický ústav SAV a Spoločnosť Alexandra Dubčeka vo vyd. Veda, 2002.

Žatkuliak, Jozef et al., eds. *November '89: Medzník vo vývoji slovenskej spoločnosti a jeho medzinárodný kontext* [November '89: a milestone in the development of Slovak society and its international context]. Bratislava: Historický ústav SAV v Prodame, 2009.

———, ed. *Realizácia a normalizačná revízia česko-slovenskej federácie (september–december 1970)* [Realization and revision of the standards of the Czechoslovak Federation (September 1968–December 1970)]. Prague: ÚSD AV ČR, 2011.

Žitňanský, Robert, "Jozef Kučerák: Obavy boli zbytočné, rozhovor" [Jozef Kučerák: doubts were unnecessary], *.týždeň*, issue 4 (2006).

Index

A

Adamec, Ladislav Jr., Czech businessman, 293
Adamkus, Valdas, President of Lithuania, 172n51
Adams, Sean, benefactor, x
Afghanistan, 19n29, 115, 313, Al Qaeda, Taliban, 313
Africa, 19n29
Agnew, Hugh Le Caine, American historian, 2
Albright, Madeleine, American Secretary of State, 107, 172n51
Alchian, Armen Albert, American economist, 221
Alliance of a New Citizen (ANO), Slovakia, 118, 123, 125, 163, 165
Almond, Gabriel A., American political scientist, 313
Applebaum, Anne, American journalist, 196
Arab Spring, 314, 324
Asian financial crisis, 206
Association for the Republic–Republican Party of Czechoslovakia (SPR–RSČ), 40
Auer, Štefan, Slovak political scientist, 58

Austria, 45, 150, 191, 193, 226–227, 234, 238, 302, 304
Austria-Hungary, 7, 44, 82, 87, 108, 237-238, Compromise of 1867, 41

B

Babe, Hollywood movie, 142
Babiš, Andrej, Slovak billionaire and Czech politician, 10–11, 151, 153–154, 161, 165, 293–294, Babisconi, 165
Baco, Peter, Slovak politician, 184
Bakker, Bas B., American economist, 230n35
Balkans, the, 13, 56, 324
Balogová, Beata, Slovak journalist, 256
Baltic States, 172
Banská Bystrica, Slovakia, 133, 276, 284
Barčák, Andrej, Czech politician, 293
Bárta, Vít, Czech politician, 153
Basescu, Traian, Romanian politician, 159
Bata, Sonja, supporter, x
Belarus, 9, 41, 133

Belgium (Belgian), 7, 19, 44, 53, 96, 193, 226, 230
Benda, Václav, Czech politician, 143–144
Beneš, Edvard, Czech politician and President, 95,
  decrees of, 172
Beneš, Václav L., American historian, 179
Beňová, Monika, Slovak politician, 113n21
Berlin, 45
Berlusconi, Silvio, Italian politician, 165
Biľak, Vasil, Secretary of the Central Committee of the Communist Party of Czechoslovakia, 26
Bohemia (ns), 2, 30, 46, 88, 95, 102, 299
Bohumín (Czech Republic) declaration, 160
Bonn, West Germany, 45
Brandt, Willy, Chancellor of West Germany, 316
Bratislava, ix, 26, 35, 40, 42, 62, 76, 80, 105n1, 113, 122, 127, note, 56, 165, 196, 253–254n16, 265, 278n41, 321–323,
  Bratislava Five, 62,
  Hochschule Goethe Uni, 322,
  Hotel Bôrik, 76,
  Movement for Civic Freedom, 62,
  PanEuropean University, 322
Brno, Czech Republic, 38–39, 42
Brubaker, Rogers, American professor of sociology, 51
Brussels, 88, 119, 266
Budmerice, Slovakia, 33
Bugár, Béla, Slovak-Magyar politician, 117, 125
Bulgaria, 132, 138, 165, 230n35, 253, Ataka, 165,
  National Movement Simeon II, 139, 163
Bunce, Valerie, American political scientist, 50–51, 53, 324

Burešová, Dagmar, Czech politician, 30, 32, 35, 67n41, 69
Bush, George H.W., President of the USA, 91
Bush, George W., son of George H.W., President of the USA, 113, 313
Bútora, Martin, Slovak sociologist, 15–16, 50, 247, 281, 321
Bútora (ová), Zora, Slovak sociologist, 15–16, 50, 247, 281, 321
Buzalka, Juraj, Slovak anthropologist, 59

C

Čalfa, Marián, Slovak politician, 29–30, 63n35, 109
Campbell, John W., American writer, 137
Canada (Canadians), ix, 53, 96, 98, 110, 171, 179n47, 257, 314,
  Glendon College at York University in Toronto, 322,
  Global Atomic Fuels Corporation, x,
  Immigration and Refugee Board, 257,
  Slovak Community Circle of Oshawa, ix–x,
  US Steel Canada, x
Captive nations, 18
Čarnogurský, Ján, Slovak politician and Prime Minister of the Slovak Republic, 32, 34, 37, 62, 69–70, 73, 87
Carpenter, John, Hollywood director, 125, 136–137
Čentéš, Jozef, professor at Comenius University, 121
Central Europe, 10–11, 13, 54, 87–88, 95–96, 99, 106, 138, 149–151, 154–155, 157, 163, 166, 170, 172, 179, 185–187, 193, 195-196, 213–215, 219–221, 223, 228, 230, 234, 238–239,

244, 268–269, 295, 309, 318, 321–322
Central European, Switzerland, 95, 234,
tigress, 99, 238, 241
Central European Free Trade Agreement (CEFTA 5), 186, 195
Center for Public Opinion Polling (CVVM), 155
Černák, Ľudovít, Slovak politician, 184
Changenet, website, 271
Charter 77, 61, 168n38, 316, 323
Chavance, Bernard, French economist, 221,
note, 22
Chesterton, Gilbert Keith, British writer, 126
Chrenek, Tomáš, Czech businessman, 293
Christian and Democratic Union—Czechoslovak People's Party (KDU-ČSL), 11, 37, 40, 168, 170, 240
Christian Democratic Movement (KDH), Slovakia, 27, 29–30, 32–37, 40, 42, 67, 70, 88, 111, 113, 117–118, 143, 168
Christian Democratic Party (KDS), Slovakia, 35, 37–38, 40, 168–170
Chubais, Anatoly B., Russian politician and businessman, 200
Chytilek, Roman, Czech political scientist, 170
Čič, Milan, Prime Minister of the Slovak Republic, 29–30, 63n35, 66
Civic Democratic Alliance (ODA), Czech Republic, 34, 37, 40, 99
Civic Democratic Party (ODS), Czech Republic, 7, 10, 32, 35–40, 43, 76–77, 89, 97, 99, 143, 146, 150, 153–154, 160, 166, 223, 228–229, 240, 242–244, 310, 312, 316

Civic Democratic Union (ODÚ), Slovakia, 36
Civic Forum (OF), Czech Republic, 8, 27–32, 63, 67, 70, 76, 88, 109–110, 146, 323
Civic Movement (OH), Czech Republic, 32, 34, 36, 97, 145
Čižnár, Jaroslav, Attorney-General of the Slovak Republic, 122
Cold War, 14n25, 47
Comenius University, 117–118, Faculty of Law, 87–88, 121, 323
Commentary Magazine, 14n25
Communism, 13–14n25, 17–18, 56, 58, 74, 80–81, 108, 125, 155, 158–160, 168, 173, 182–183, 207, 212, 216–217, 219, 224, 237–238, 258–260, 268, 277–278n41, 281, 283–284, 286–287, 302, 307, 311, 313, 315, 319
Communist Party of Bohemia and Moravia (KSČM), 10–11, 17, 40, 151–152, 157–161, 166, 312, 318
Communist Party of Czechoslovakia (KSČ), 6, 8, 25–26, 29, 64, 83, 100, 106, 117, 158–159, 171, 181–182, 259, 292–293, 311, 315, 323,
Action Program of, 181,
Presidium of, 25,
proletarian internationalism, rulers, 86,
Social Union of Youth, 293
Communist Youth Organization, 159
Confederation of Labor Unions (KOZ), Slovakia, 192, 194
Conference on Security and Cooperation in Europe in Helsinki, 91
Conference on 20 years of the independent Slovak Republic, 105n1
Constitutional Law 143/1968 regarding the Czechoslovak Federation, 64–66, 74, 81
Council for Mutual Economic Assistance (COMECON), 177, 202
Croatia, 53, 133

Csáky, Pál, Magyar politician in Slovakia, 9n21
Curry, Jane, American political scientist, 324
Czech and Slovak Federative Republic (ČSFR), 7, 28–29, 31, 44, 55–56, 66, 72–73, 77, 99–100, 323
Czech Academy of Science, 12, 324,
  Prognostic Institute of, 13, 213
Czech National Council (CNC), 28n6, 31–32, 34–37, 42, 66–67n41, 69–74, 77, 97, 100, 144–145, 164, 217–220, 222–223, 225–229, 298, 309, 316,
  Senate, 145, 323
Czech National Economic Council, 230
Czech Socialist Republic (ČSR),
  National Council of, 24
Czech Republic (ČR), Agrofert, Agrotrade Corporation, 293,
  anticlericalism, 167,
  automobile sector, 228,
  bad mood, 16, 304–306, 309, 317–318,
  banking system, 215, 217, 223–225, 228, 230, 232, 240–241,
  Barrandov Film Studios, 293,
  black marketers, 16,
  Chamber of Deputies, 145, 147–148,
  Česko, 101,
  civic nationalism, 51, 57,
  Chemapol, 293,
  Constitution of, 99, 145, 154,
  corruption, 14, 18, 232, 240, 244, 304, 310,
  currency, 10, 38–39, 98, 224, 226, 234, 240,
  CzechInvest, 227,
  decentralized, 3,
  dissidence, 168,
  economic transition, 211–226, 228, 234, 237, 243,
  economy, 12, 181–182, 184, 211, 213, 216–218, 223, 225–227, 229–234, 237–241, 243, 289, 292, 302, 304, 311–312,
  elections, 138,
  Eska, 224,
  Europeanization, 150, 157,
  euroscepticism, 10, 15, 150, 243–244, 305,
  Favorit, 224,
  foreign direct investment (FDI), 227–228, 239,
  foreign policy of, 2,
  GDP, 14, 195, 216, 220–221, 224–226, 229, 231–233, 238, 240, 242, 296, 303,
  homogeneous, 95,
  Inekon, 293,
  inflation, 216, 225–228, 232,
  Institute for the Study of Totalitarian Regimes, 151,
  Investment and Postal Bank (IPB), 225,
  Ironworks, 293,
  Jews in, 96,
  Karosa, 224,
  Kerametal, 293,
  large-scale privatization, 218,
  military policies, 3,
  Moravia Energo Group, 293,
  NGOs, 316,
  Partner for Peace in NATO, 312,
  past guilt, 154,
  Petrimex, Pragoinvest, 293,
  privatization, 3, 13–14, 184, 186, 200–201, 213, 217–220, 222, 225–226, 230, 239–241,
  religious engagement, 167,
  Roma in, 101, 166, 171, 300–301, 316–317, 319,
  Sazka, 294,
  Secret Service, 3, 151,
  Škoda Auto, 223,
  shadow economy, 220, 294,
  small-scale privatization, 218,
  society, 290–292, 295, 297–299, 302, 304–306, 308–309, 312,
  Sparta Praha, 295,

state house, 95–96, 101,
State Security, 16,
Strojexport, 293,
successor of Czechoslovakia, 145, 150,
Television Crisis, 149,
temporal Senate, 99,
tired democracy, 152,
transition recession, 216,
tunneling, 14, 17–18, 224,
Tuzex, 294,
Ukrainians in, 301–302,
unemployment, 14, 16, 147, 185, 216, 223, 226, 231, 240, 299, 318,
Unimex Group, 293,
Vietnamese in, 301–302
Czech(s), centralist, 56,
Catholic identity, 170,
communities in Canada, 4,
economic miracle, 15, 238, 240,
elites, 144–145, 166, 234, 317–318,
federal government of, 186,
identity, 170–171,
individualistic, 2,
media, 304–305, 308,
National Bank, 225, 228–231, 243,
national character, 170,
nationalism, 2, 8, 11, 49, 57, 78,
nation-state, 23, 28, 45, 95, 307,
parliament, 144,
paternalism, 95,
politics, 2, 10, 36, 145–146, 149–151, 154–155, 157–158, 161–164, 166, 170, 172, 238, 304, 309–310,
pragmatic, 60,
Press Agency, 152,
question, 170,
relations with Slovaks, 7, 26–27, 29, 36, 46, 64, 74–75, 86, 299–300,
sovereignty, 24, 64, 70, 227, 244,
Statistical Office, 300,

Sudeten German in, 171, supremacy, 239, 306, 308,
VAT, 229
Czechoslovak, coat of arms, 65–66,
economy, 67, 181, 212,
federation, 7, 24–26, 28, 31, 40, 48, 55, 60, 62–63, 65, 71, 77–78, 145, 186,
Chamber of Nations, 6, 74, identity, 6, 23, 170,
Spring, 61, 108
Czechoslovak People's Party (ČSL), 29–30
Czechoslovak Republic, 6, 28, 65, 83
Czechoslovak Socialist Republic (ČSSR), 6, 24, 28, 62, 124,
Chamber of the Nations, 24–25, 37,
Chamber of the People, 24–25, 37, 44,
federal government of, 29–30, 38, 69,
minority veto, 24, 25, 37, 41,
simple laws of, 24
Czechoslovak (Czech) Social Democratic Party (ČSSD), 10–11, 14–15, 40–41, 43, 147, 148, 151, 153–154, 157, 159–160, 163, 168–169, 218, 223, 226–229, 240–242, 244, 310, 312, 316, 318
Czechoslovakia, Allied recognition of, 86,
asymmetry, 99,
Catholic Church, 167,
centralism, 47, 81,
common state, 49, 77, 83, 85, 87, 90, 308,
communist takeover in 1948, 27,
competency Law, 68,
confederation, 91,
Constitutional Amendment 556/1990, 31,
Constitutional Law Concerning the Dissolution of the Czech and

Slovak Federative Republic, November 25, 1992, 77, 84–85, 99, 102, 156,
Constitutional Law number 143/1968, 24,
Constitutional law 14/1990, 81/1990, 28, 101/1990, 29,
Czech–initiated project, 143,
Czech state, 26, 28,
Czechoslovakism, 83, 95, disintegration, 46,
elites, 83–84, 86, 99, 156,
ethnic identity, 157,
Federal Assembly of, 24, 27–28, 31, 34, 36–37, 40–43, 63, 68–70, 89, 97–100, 179, 183,
federalism, 86,
Germans in, 150,
hyphen war, 7, 29, 65, 88,
industry, 13, 177, 212,
inflation, 216,
lustration (lustrace) law, 160–161, 312,
Made in, 156,
National Front, 316,
national minorities, 86,
nation-state, 23, 47, 86, 90,
new constitution, 42,
normalization, 26, 47, 109n4, 182,
opinion polls, 71,
referendum, 41–42, 71, 98,
self-determination of, 86,
self-sufficient, 182,
sixty-eighters, 158,
split of, ix, 1, 4–6, 8, 15, 18–19, 23–24, 31, 36, 38, 40, 42–44, 52, 56, 58, 65, 70, 73, 85, 88–91, 102, 178, 217, 237–239, 241, 244, 306, 308,
State Bank of, 216n13,
state treaty, 70, 72–73, 77, 100,
unemployment, 124, 179, 212,
velvet divorce, 50, 53, 105, 238,
Velvet Revolution, 63, 85–86, 106, 146, 149, 156, 158, 168, 171, 212, 259, 265, 279,
Victorious February, 158,
voucher privatization, 12–15, 17, 140, 147, 183–184, 187, 196, 200–203, 218–219, 224, 240, 312,
weapon-export, 184–185, 202
Czecho-Slovakia, 6–7, 249, secession from, 83, Second Republic, 7, 28

D

Danube River, water works on, 90
Davies, Norman, British-Polish historian, 50
Dawn of Direct Democracy (Úsvit), Czech Republic, 165–166
Deegan-Krause, Kevin, American political scientist, 2, 9–10, 52, 129, 166, 321
Delegative democracy, 133
Deletant, Dennis, American political scientist, 3
Demeš, Pavol, Slovak politician and public intellectual, 285
Democratic Party (DS), Slovakia, 27, 29, 35–36
Democrats 1992 (D-92), Czech Republic, 36
Demos, Britain's Think-Tank, Backsliders: Measuring Democracy in the EU-report by, 252–253
Den D., Czech TV show, 165
Dienstbier, Jiří, Czech politician, 32, 109, 145,
Dlouhý, Vladimír, Czech politician, 213
Dubček, Alexander, Slovak politician, First Secretary of the Slovak and Czechoslovak Communist Party, 61, 63, 181, 315,
honorary doctorate, "socialism with a human face", 61, 108, 109n11,
Speaker of the Federal Assembly, 63, 69, 74, 2000
Words Manifesto, 316

Index 353

Ducký, Ján, Slovak politician, 184
Dyba, Karel, Czech politician, 99, 213
Dzurinda, Mikuláš, Slovak politician and Prime Minister of the Slovak Republic, 12–13, 93, 107, 111–113, 117–119, 122–123, 135, 140, 190–192, 206–209, 227

E

Eastern Europe, 9–11, 13, 45–46, 55, 106, 108, 138, 151, 154, 157, 159, 162–163, 166, 168, 173, 179, 185, 193, 196, 202, 213–215, 220–221, 223, 228, 230, 234, 244, 295, 309, 318, 322–324
Eastern Slovak Steel Works (VSŽ), 12, 186–190, 204–206
Economist Intelligence Unit, Democracy Index, survey of, 251, 253
Egypt (Egyptians), Muslim-based political values, Muslim Brotherhood, 315
Eibl, Otto, Czech political scientist, 170
Enyedi, Zsolt, Hungarian political scientist, 321
Estonia, 132, 139, 172n51
Eurasia, 324
Eurobarometer Survey, 264–266, 305–306
European, Bank of Reconstruction and Development, 228,
 Central Bank, 210, 265–266,
 Commission, 115, 119, 190, 265–266, 273,
 Court of Justice, 116n30,
 integration, 2, 61, 75, 157, 195–196, 209, 244, 307,
 Parliament, 265–267
European Union (EU), 1, 3, 8, 10, 12–15, 19, 32, 45–46, 53–54, 57, 75, 78, 87–90, 92, 99–101, 105, 107n7, 111–113, 115–116, 119–120, 141, 150–151, 155–157, 163, 167, 169, 171n47, 173, 183, 190–192, 194, 196–197, 206, 208–209, 217, 226–227, 229, 231, 233–234, 238–239, 241–244, 249, 252–253, 263–267, 273, 275, 277, 285–286, 290, 296–299, 303, 305–306, 311, 313, 316, 319,
 Council of Europe, 307n48,
 Eurozone (EUR), 53, 120, 195, 209–210, 231, 233, 242–243, 249, 263–264,
 Schengen Area, 116, 249,
 Stability and Growth Pact, 241
European People's Party, 87
Eurostat Database, 238, 297
Eyal, Gil, American political scientist, 60, 76

F

Fascism, 58
Felak, James Ramon, American historian, ix
Fico, Robert, Slovak politician and Prime Minister of the Slovak Republic, 9, 12–13, 107, 113–122, 124–125, 135, 137, 139–140, 157n6, 194, 209, 254n16
Filer, Randall, American economist, 233n41
First World War, 86, 95, 157–158
Fisher, Sharon, American economist, 14–15, 237, 321–322
France (French), 193, 226, 230, 241–242, 314, 322–323
Frankfurt, 210
Freedom and Solidarity Party (SaS), Slovakia, 117–120, 125–126
Freedom House, Freedom in the World, survey of, 251
Freedom Union—Democratic Union (US–DEU), Czech Republic, 152, 240
Ftáčnik, Milan, Slovak politician, 114

G

Gál, Fedor, Slovak politician, 32, 88
Galko, Ľubomír, Slovak politician, 118
Gašpar, Tibor, President of the Slovak Police Corps, 122
Gašparovič, Ivan, Slovak politician and President of the Slovak Republic, 118, 121
General Motors Europe, 293
Germany, Germans, 14, 45–46, 87, 96, 101, 150, 172, 193, 202, 210, 216, 227–228, 231, 232n39, 234, 238, 241–242, 299, 302, 304, 314,
    Christian Democrats, Confederation of Farmers, 96,
    East of, 216,
    Nazi, 28, 171–172,
    Ostpolitik, 316, Social Democrats, 96
Gini coefficient, 248
Gjuričová, Adéla, Czech historian, 9, 143, 155, 157, 160, 162, 239
Global economic crisis, 13, 106, 117, 193–194, 197, 208, 212, 221, 229, 231, 237, 253, 255, 263, 265, 275
Good Housekeeping Seal of Approval, 286
Gorbachev, Mikhail S., Soviet statesman, 205
Gorilla scandal, 15, 16n27, 105–106, 122, 125, 127, 129, 140, 282–283
Gottwald, Klement, Prime Minister and President of Czechoslovakia, 315
Gould, John A., American political scientist, 3, 13, 197, 322
Greece, 53, 119, 231, 253, Greek question, 229
Green Party (SZ), Slovakia, 29
Greenpeace, Slovak branch of, 272
Gremium of the Third Sector, Slovakia, 269, 272
Grzymala-Busse, Anna, American political scientist, 169

H

Habermas, Jürgen, German sociologist and philosopher, 277
Habsburg Monarchy, 149, 156, Counter-Reformation in, 167
Hallon, Ľudovít, Slovak historian, 11, 177, 197–198, 200, 202, 204–205, 322
Hanley, Seán, British political scientist, 169
Hanousek, Jan, Czech economist, 233n41
Harabin, Štefan, Slovak judge and politician, 254n16
Haughton, Tim, British political scientist, 166
Havel, Václav, Playwright, President of Czechoslovakia and President of the Czech Republic, 6, 10, 27–28, 30–31, 34, 37, 40–42, 49, 52–54, 63, 65, 91, 97, 145–146, 149–150, 162, 165, 171–172, 286, 304, 307–308, 311–312, 316–317, 321
Hawks, Howard, Hollywood director, 137
Hayek, Friedrich, Austrian and British economist and philosopher, 207, 221n22, 222
Hilde, Paal Sigurd, Norwegian historian, 56
Hlina, Alojz, Slovak politician, 125n52
Hlinka, Andrej, Slovak Catholic priest, journalist, and politician, 108
Hocman, Juraj, Slovak historian, 8–9, 105, 129–130, 133, 135–137, 140–142, 322
Hoffman, Ivan, Slovak journalist, 308
Holec, Roman, Slovak historian, 248
Holocaust, 276

Holy, Ladislav, Czech anthropologist, 56
Horák, Jiří, Czech politician, 40
Hrádeček, Czech Republic, 34
Hrušovský, Pavol, Slovak politician, 117
Hudek, Adam, Slovak historian, 7, 11, 55, 79, 84, 177, 197–198, 200, 202, 204–205, 322
Human Development Index (HDI), 251, 252n9
Hungarian coalition (Coexistence and the Hungarian Christian Democratic Movement), Slovakia, 29, 67
Hungarian Civic Party (MOS), Slovakia, 35n14, 36
Hungary, Hungarians, 46, 61, 82, 88, 90, 101, 112, 116, 130, 135–136, 150, 157, 179n6, 158, 173, 179n54, 185n29, 195, 212, 216, 224, 239–240, 253, 261–262, 290,
assimilation, 85, Fidesz, 9, 157n6,
Intertourist, 294n11,
Jobbik Party, 284,
Magyarization, 82, 268,
relations with Slovaks, 88, 90,
television, 61
Hušák Aleš, Czech businessman, 294
Husák, Gustáv, Slovak politician, First Secretary of the Communist Party of Czechoslovakia, President of Czechoslovakia, 26, 63, 100, 108–109n12, 315
Hušek, Josef, Czech businessman, 293
Húska, Augustín Marián, Slovak politician, 184
Hussite movement, 167

I

Icelanders, 95
IHS Global Insight in Washington, 321
Ilves, Toomas, President of Estonia, 172n51
Innes, Abby, British political sociologist, 8, 50, 52, 57, 60, 79
Institute for Public Affairs (IVO), 155, 253–254n16, 255, 260, 264–265, 267, 321
International Court of Justice in The Hague, 90
International Monetary Fund (IMF), 214n6, 215
Iran, 313
Iraq, 113, 115
Ireland, Republic of, 107n7
IREX Individual Advanced Research Opportunity grants, 321
Iron Curtain, 87, 259
Italy (Italian), 61, 165, 193, 226, 231, 253,
University of Bologna, 61

J

Jakeš, Miloš, Czech politician, 315
Janos, Andrew, American political scientist, 51
Janoušek, Roman, Czech businessman and billionaire, 295
Ježek, Tomáš, Czech politician, 213, 218–219
Jihlava, Czech Republic, 43, 77
John Paul II, Pope, 15, 279
John, Radek, Czech journalist, 165
Johnson, Simon, British-American economist, 221
Judt, Tony, British historian, 148
Junek, Václav, Czech businessman, 293–294

K

Kaliňák, Robert, Slovak politician, 122
Kalvoda, Jan, Czech politician, 34
Kavan, Jan, Czech politician and diplomat, 161

Kirkpatrick, Jean, American ambassador to the United Nations, 14n25
Kirschbaum, Stanislav J., Canadian political scientist, 8, 79, 322
Kiska, Andrej, Slovak politician and President of the Slovak Republic, 124n51
Klaus, Václav, Czech politician, Minister of Finance, Prime Minister and President of the Czech Republic, 7–8, 11–15, 32, 35–37, 39–40, 42–43, 45–46, 50, 52, , 71, 76, 85, 89, 96–97, 99–100,145–150, 162–163, 169–172, 183–184, 186, 201, 213, 217–220, 222–223, 225, 228, 237–240, 243–244, 307–308, 310, 312,
  Eurosceptic, 10, 15,
  Thatcherite, 237, 239
Klepáč, Ján, Slovak politician, 33, 35–36, 38
Klingen, Christoph, Deputy Chief of the Emerging Europe Regional Division in the IMF's European Department, 230n35
Kňažko, Milan, Slovak actor and politician, 89, 110
Kočtúch, Hvezdoň, Slovak economist and politician, 184
Kollár, Milan, Slovak ambassador to Canada, ix
Komárno, Slovakia, 116
Kopecky, Petr, Czech political scientist, 2
Košice, Slovakia, 12, 110, 120, 123, 188,
  US Steel, 189, 206
Kotleba, Marián, Slovak politician, 125, 133, 283–284
Kováč, Michal, Slovak politician and President of Slovakia, 39–40, 89, 100, 107n8, 110
Kováč, Michal, Jr., son of the Slovak President, 112

Karel Kouba, Czech economist, 215
Kraus, Michael, American political scientist, 7, 47, 323
Kroměříž, Czech Republic, 30, 33, 71
Kuchma, Leonid, President of Ukraine, 133
Kusý, Miroslav, Slovak political scientist, 57

L

La Maison Slovaque, Montreal, x
Lány, Czech Republic, 33
Latin America, 14n25, 214
Latvia, 132, 138–139, 172n51
Leff, Carol Skalnik, American political scientist, 1–2, 10, 50, 155, 324
Legatum Institute Prosperity Index, 252
Lehman Brothers Holding Inc., 228, 231
Lenin, Vladimir Ilyich, Russian communist revolutionary, 52
Lewandowski, Janusz, Polish politician and economist, 220
Lexa, Ivan, Director of the Slovak Secret Service, 112
LIAZ, Czech and Czechoslovak manufacturer of trucks, 224
Liberal-Social Union (LSU), Czech Republic, 40
Linek, Lukáš, Czech political scientist, 152n16
Lipšic, Daniel, Slovak politician, 125
Lithuania, 172n51, Party of National Resurrection, 139
Lizal, Lubomir, Czech economist, 233
Londák, Miroslav, Slovak historian, 11, 105n1, 177, 197–198, 200, 202, 204–205, 323
London, 252, School of Economics, 324
Lorenc, Alojz, Chief of Czechoslovak State Security, 293

Luhačovice, Czech Republic, 30
Lukashenko, Alexander, President of Belarus, 133

M

Maastricht Treaty, 87, 89, 105, 208, 229, 241, 243
Macek, Miroslav, Czech politician, 38–39, 97
Mach, Petr, Czech businessman, 295
Matos, Cristina, Portuguese economist, 221
Mainwaring, Scott, American political scientist, 163
Majský, Jozef, Slovak businessman, 123
Malchárek, Jirko, Slovak politician, 123
Malinová, Hedviga, Slovak-Magyar student, 115
Marxism-Leninism, 18, 86, 168n38
Masaryk, Tomáš G., Czech politician and founding President of Czechoslovakia, 6, 95–96, 149, 161–162
Matovič, Igor, Slovak politician, 125n52
McKay, James, British political scientist, 60
Mečiar, Vladimír, Slovak politician, Minister of the Interior and Prime Minister of the Slovak Republic, 2, 5–9, 12–13, 30–33, 36–40, 42–43, 45–46, 50, 52, 54, 67–70, 75–76, 85, 88, 90, 92–93, 96–98, 100–101, 110, 112, 114, 117–118, 123, 133–136, 140, 186–190, 198, 202–206, 209, 217, 227, 237, 239, 249, 254n16, 269, 278, 283, 308–309, era, 203, 206, 209, 313,
  illiberal democracy, 133–134,
  Mečiarism, 111–113, 133–135, 309

Mesežnikov, Grigorij, Russian political scientist in Slovakia, 58
Michálek, Slavomír, Slovak historian, ix, 105n1
Middle East, 19n29
Miklas, Dušan, supporter, x
Mikloš, Ivan, Slovak politician, 117–118, 120, 207–208
Mikloško, František, Slovak politician and Speaker of the Slovak National Council, 30, 35, 68–69
Miller, George, Australian film director, 142
Milošević, Slobodan, President of Serbia, 54, 133, 315
Milovy, Czech Republic, 35
Mináč, Vladimír, Slovak writer, 277–278n41
Miškov, Juraj, Slovak politician, 118
Mohorita, Vasil, Czech politician, 293
Moody's, credit rating agency, 216n13
Moravčík, Jozef, Slovak politician and Prime Minister of the Slovak Republic, ix, 5, 85, 89, 110, 203, 323
Moravia (ns), 30, 46, 95, 102, 169, 299
Moric, Víťazoslav, Slovak politician, 27
Morris, Ian, British, historian and archeologist, 247
Moscow, 45, 61, 180
Most—Híd Party, Slovakia, 117–118, 125, 131,
Movement for a Democratic Slovakia (HZDS), 7, 32–33, 36–43, 70, 75–77, 88–90, 92, 97, 102, 110–111, 114, 117, 126, 135, 186, 202, 204, 209, 254n16
Movement for Self-Governing Democracy—the Society for Moravia and Silesia (HSD-SMS), Czech Republic, 29–30, 40

Mubarak, Hosni, President of Egypt, 315
Multinational state(s), 44, 46, 78, 95
Munich, 118, 158,
 Research Institute in, 322,
 University of Ludwig Maximilian, 118
Murrell, Peter, American professor of economics, 215
Musil, Jiří, Czech sociologist, 60, 78

N

Nagyová, Jana, director of Czech Prime Minister Petr Nečas' office, 106
Nastase, Adrian, Romanian politician, 159
NATO, 3, 10, 12, 45–46, 54, 100, 111–113, 115, 150, 155, 192, 206, 217, 227, 249, 277, 286, 309, 312–313, 319
Nečas, Petr, Czech politician and Prime Minister of the Czech Republic, 106–107, 283, 310
Nedelsky, Nadja, American political scientist, 2, 51
Neoliberal(ism), 10, 197, 207–209,
 economics, 166,
 measures, 194,
 reforms, 161, 192, 206–207
Netherlands, 193, 298, University of Leiden, 2
Nešpor, Zdeněk R., Czech sociologist, 169
New York, 228
Nicholson, Tom, Canadian journalist, 15n26, 16n27, 122
Nitra, Slovakia, 115
Nobel Peace Prize, 85
Novotný, Antonín, Czech politician and President of Czechoslovakia, 315
North America, 56, 138, 142, 172
Norway, secession, 19

O

O'Donnell, Guillermo A., Argentine political scientist, 133
Okamura, Tomio, Czech politician and Prime Minister of the Czech Republic, 11, 165
Old Europe, 306, 297, 306
Olomouc, Czech Republic, 319
Open Media Research Institute (OMRI), 322
Orbán, Viktor, Prime Minister of Hungary, 135–136, 157n6, 173n54
Ordinary People and Independent Personalities—New Majority (OĽaNO–NOVA), Slovakia, 125n52
Organization for Economic Cooperation and Development (OECD), 112, 191, 216n13, 227, 232, 249, 277, 286, 323
Orwell, George, English novelist, essayist, journalist, and critic, 260
Ottawa, ix–x, 110, 257,
 University of, 4, 324
Ottoman Empire, 7, 44, 87
Oxford, 120

P

Palacka, Gabriel, Slovak politician, 123
Palikot, Janusz Marian, Polish politician, 139
Paris, 323, Peace Conference, 86
Party of Democratic Slovakia (SDS), 126n54
Party of the Democratic Left (SDĽ), Slovakia, 110–111, 114, 137, 139, 206
Party of the Magyar Coalition (SMK), Slovakia, 111
Party of Civic Understanding (SOP), Slovakia, 111–112, 118, 125, 163

Penta, financial holding company, Slovakia, 123, 282n2, 293
People's Party–Our Slovakia (ĽSNS), 125, 133
Perot, Ross, American politician, 165
Peterson, James W., American political scientist, 2, 17, 311, 323
Petřinová, Irena, Czech journalist, 107n6
Piešťany, Slovakia, 30
Pithart, Petr, Czech politician and Prime Minister of the Czech Republic, ix, 5–6, 17, 29–32, 34, 66–67n41, 70, 95, 145, 323
Pittsburgh Agreement, 319
Poland (Poles), 45, 95, 101, 112, 139, 150, 155, 157n6, 158, 168, 173, 179, 185n29, 195, 212, 216, 224, 230n35, 231–232, 239, 261–262, 279, 290, 292, 303, 315,
  Pewex, 294n11,
  Polish Democratic Left Alliance, Polish political Party, 157n6,
  Solidarity, 157n6, 168
Pop-Eleches, Grigore, American political scientist, 164
Portugal, 119
Pospíšil, Martin, Czech economist, 13–15, 211, 237–238, 323
Post-communist, business, 205,
  changes, 155, 311–312, 318,
  countries, 57, 106, 130, 141, 155, 162, 167–169, 172, 177–179, 183, 187, 190, 193, 198, 200, 204, 207, 216n13, 234, 238, 241, 243, 286, 290, 295, 297, 309, 315, 322, 324,
  Czechoslovakia, 50, 53, 55, 59, 64, 75, 81, 105123, 125, 160, 198, 290, 301, 313, 316,
  economy, 59, 233n41, 238,
  elites, 8, 48, 57, 61, 80–82, 178,
  politics, 47, 52, 78, 111n15, 148, 155, 162–163, 168–169, 202, 268, 284, 311, 323,
  society, 16, 53, 261, 289, 299
Prague, 26, 31, 34, 41, 45, 47, 81, 83, 91–92, 100, 144, 147, 153, 180, 238, 293, 296–297, 302–303, 308, 311, 322,
  Center for Economic Research, 324,
  Charles University in, ix, 324,
  Glopolis Think Tank, 323,
  Graduate Education—Economics Institute, 324,
  housing crisis, 302,
  Masaryk Institute, 324,
  Public Opinion Research Center, 265,
  Spring, 146, 158n8, 181,
  University of Economics in, 323,
  Wenceslas Square, 144
Procházka, Radoslav, Slovak politician, 124n51
Prokeš, Jozef, Slovak politician, 27
Public Affairs Party (VV), Czech Republic, 153, 165
Public Against Violence (VPN), Slovakia, 6, 8, 27–30, 32, 34–36, 63, 67, 70, 75, 88, 109, 278n41, 279, 321, 323
Putin, Vladimir V., President of Russia, 113, 133, 314
Pynsent, Robert P., British literary historian, 2

R

Radičová, Iveta, Slovak politician and Prime Minister of the Slovak Republic, 117–121, 209
Remiáš, Robert, Slovak policeman, 112
Rezeš, Alexander, Slovak billionaire and politician, 12, 123, 188–189, 204–205,
  era, 189
Ridzon, Margaret and Pauline, supporters, x
Roland, Gerard, American economist and political scientist, 222

Romania, 132, 159, 253
Rome, 126
Rupnik, Jacques, French political scientist of Czech origin, 152
Rusko, Pavol, Slovak politician, 123, 125, 165
Russia (n), 9, 45, 87, 100, 133, 190, 200, 205, 228, 230n35, 293, 314, 324,
  hyperinflation, 203,
  Orthodox Patriarch, 313
Ruthenians, 96
Rychlík, Jan, Czech historian and advisor to Petr Pithart, ix, 3, 6, 7, 10, 19, 47–49, 54, 324

S

Samizdat, 61–62
Sanader, Ivo, Prime Minister of Croatia, 283
Schmemann, Serge, American journalist, 107n6
Scherpereel, John A., American political scientist, 3
Schmögnerová, Brigita, Slovak politician, 114
Schröder, Gerhard, Chancellor of Germany, 242
Schuster, Rudolf, Slovak politician, Speaker of the Slovak National Council and President of the Slovak Republic, 63n35, 109–110, 125
Schutz, Peter, Slovak journalist, 308
Schwarzenberg, Karel von, Czech politician and Foreign Minister of the Czech Republic, 11, 147n5, 163n23, 171–172
Scotland, 7n18
Seattle, USA, ix
Seneca the Younger, Roman writer, 126
Second World War (WWII), 46–47, 86, 96, 101, 172, 212, 229
Serbia (Serbs), 51, 53, 133, 315,
  hyperinflation, 216
Siderov, Volen, Bulgarian television host, 165
Silesia (ns), 95, 299,
  Upper and Lower, 45
Šimáně, Jiří, Czech businessman, 293
Šimečka, Martin, Slovak writer and publicist, 308
Simon, Jeffrey, American defense analyst, 3
Slaba, Jaroslav, supporter, x
Slavkov, Czech Republic, 30
Slota, Ján, Slovak politician, 113–114
Šlouf, Miroslav, Czech politician, 293
Slovak Academy of Sciences, 105n1,
  Historical Institute of, ix, 322–324
Slovak Christian and Democratic Union (SDKÚ), 111, 113–114, 117–118, 120, 123, 126, 206
Slovak Christian Democratic Movement (SKDH), 35
Slovak Communist Party (KSS), 27, 29, 38, 42, 67, 100, 323
Slovak-Hungarian conflict, 46
Slovak Intelligence Agency, 122
Slovak National Council (SNC), 28–29, 31–36, 38, 41–42, 62–63, 66, 68–74, 77, 97, 109–110, 118–123, 125, 163, 273, 323
Slovak National Memory Institute (UPN), 161n19, 294
Slovak National Party (SNS), 27, 29, 32–33, 36, 38, 41–42, 67, 97, 111, 113–115, 132–133, 135, 209
Slovak People's Party, 108
Slovak Socialist Republic (SSR), National Council of, 24
Slovak Republic (SR), anti-Roma sentiment, 132, 256–258,
  automobile industry, 193, 264,
  Atlas of Roma communities in, 256,
  banking system, 189–191, 199, 201, 203, 205,

Index

black hole of Europe, Board of Commissioners, 100,
brain drain, 284,
Candle Demonstration, 62, 80,
civic nation, 101, 274–276,
civil society, 15–16, 250, 255, 271–272, 275–276, 286,
confederation, 39–40, 45, 67, 71–72, 75–76,
constitution, 73, 178,
Constitutional Court, 121,
Coordinating Committee of Slovak Students, 63,
corruption, 15–16, 18, 106, 122, 188, 199, 203, 207, 252–253, 255, 264, 274, 276, 278, 281–282,
crony sales, 17,
decentralized, 3, 178, 182,
Declaration of Sovereignty, 42, 70,
de–democratization, 283,
democratization, 52–53, 200,
dissidence, 168,
dysfunctional, 124n50,
Eastern Slovakia, 27, 124,
economy, 12, 178, 181, 184, 186, 190–194, 196–200, 202–203, 206–210, 238, 250, 255, 263, 271–272, 274, 285–286,
Every Fifth Woman Campaign 2002, 271,
federalization, 181–182,
flat tax, 12, 141, 194, 208,
foreign policy of, 2,
free market economy, 178, 185, 198, 268,
For a Good Law on Waste Management 2001, 271,
For a Real Reform of Public Administration 2000, 271,
GDP, 13, 15, 117, 183, 193, 195, 196n59,
Hungarians in, 9, 92, 96, 116, 130–132, 134–135, 151, 251, 255,
hockey team, 263–264,
Hyundai, 193,

independence, 32, 39, 49, 54, 81–82, 92, 98, 102, 197, 203, 210, 238, 250, 263, 269, 276, 281, 286,
industry in, 179, 181, 184–186, 190–191, 256,
inflation, 179, 185, 190–191, 198, 208–209,
Investment and Development Bank (IRB), 189,
judiciary, 16, 255, 264, 282,
Kia, 193,
Law on Establishing Industrial Estates, Law on Investment Stimulus, 191,
Law on Tripartite Consultation, 192,
lower inequality coefficient, 141,
majoritarianism, 249,
MAN, 193,
Markíza TV, 165,
Marshall Plan for, 90,
military policies, 3,
Ministry of Agriculture, 135,
Ministry of Construction and Regional Development, 115,
Ministry of Finance, 205,
Ministry of Justice, 135,
Muslims in, 252,
National Bank of (NBS), 12, 187, 189–190, 205, 208,
national economists, 202,
National Property Fund, 183, 188n39,
national sentiments, 178,
nepotism, 188,
new Bolshevism, 135,
NGOs, 15, 101, 270–273, 275, 282–283,
OK'98, 270, 283, 321,
petition, 272,
Peugeot—Citroen, 193,
policymaking, 275,
Polis Slovakia, 126n54,
politics in, 268–269, 271, 274–276, 278, 281–282, 285–286, 322,

privatization in, 3, 9, 100, 110, 140, 177–178, 187–192, 198–201, 203–204,
Roma in, 9, 15, 130, 132–133, 171, 196n46, 251–252, 255–258, 264, 276, 284, 300,
rule of law, 16, 135, 200, 221, 250, 253, 255, 272, 277–278, 286,
Secret Service, 3,
Social Democrats, 13,
South of, 124,
sovereignty, 33, 278,
notes 10–11, 42, 71–72, 87,
Steyer, 193,
strategic companies, 188,
Tatra Tiger, 107, 227, 241, 277, 285,
Toyota, 193,
traditional society, 59,
Trnavská univerzita, 322,
tunneling, 12, 17–18, 188,
unemployment, 12–13, 15, 117, 179, 185, 191, 196, 206, 208, 216, 250, 255–257, 259, 264, 285,
VAT, 208n23,
Volkswagen (VW), 193,
What Is Not Secret Is Public, 271
Slovak State, 32, 131, 155
Slovak(s), community-oriented, 2,
communities in Canada, 4,
elites, 58, 60, 80–82, 106, 110, 251–252, 268, 276, 283,
environmental movement, 272,
ethnic identity, 2, 300,
ethnic nationalism, 8, 51, 277,
Labor Code, 192, 194, 207–208,
nationalism, 49, 58, 80, 85, 102, 134, 204,
question, 58, 80,
perspective, 80, 84,
plebeian hard-working nation, 277,
populists, 60,
religious, 58,
separatism, 56–57,

Slovak Studies Association, 324
Slovak Studies Newsletter, 324
Slovenia, 138, 195, 238, 243
Smer—Social Democracy, Slovakia, 107, 113–114, 118, 120–123, 135, 137, 139, 157n6, 192, 209
Smith, Simon, American sociologist, 3
Sólyom, László, President of Hungary, 116
Soviet Union (USSR), 7, 41, 44–45, 48, 51, 55, 61, 87,
Beryozka, 294n11, Bloc, 13, 156, 177, 179, 185, 199, 216, 297, 306, 312–313,
Communist Party of, 109,
occupation by, 26n4, 45,
perestroika, 109, 205,
rule, 18,
style of communism, 61
Spain (Spaniards), 7, 19, 44, 53, 96, 119, 231, Catalonia, 53
Špidla, Vladimír, Czech politician and Prime Minister of the Czech Republic, 242
Stanger, Allison K., American political scientist, 48, 52
Stein, Eric, American legal theorist, 78
Stiglitz, Joseph E., American economist, 222
Stolarik, Anne, benefactor, ix
Stolarik, M. Mark, Canadian historian, 1, 7n17, 324
Strasbourg, Germany, 307n48
Stráský, Jan, Czech politician, 40
Stuart Little, Hollywood movie, 108, 127, 129
Stullerova, Kamila, British political scientist, 278n41
Sulík, Richard, Slovak politician, 118–120, 125
Šútovec, Milan, Slovak public intellectual, 278
Švejnar, Jan, USA-based, Czech-born economist, 172n51

Sweden, 19
Switzerland, 44n24,
  Swiss People's Party, 166,
  World Economic Forum, 253–254

T

Tavits, Margit, American political scientist, 163
Taylor, Philip A., benefactor, ix
The Thing, Hollywood movie, 125, 129, 137
Tiso, Jozef, Slovak Catholic priest, and politician, 108
Toman, Miroslav, Czech politician, 293
Topolánek, Mirek, Czech politician and Prime Minister of the Czech Republic, 14, 159, 228–229, 310
Tošovský, Josef, Czech economist and governor of the Czech National Bank, 240
Tradition, Responsibility, Prosperity, 2009 (TOP 09), Czech Republic, 152, 164, 170
Treaty of Trianon, 88
Trenčianské Teplice, Slovakia, 30, 67
Třinec, Czech Republic, 293
Trnka, Dobroslav, Attorney–General of the Slovak Republic, 121
Tuđman, Franjo, President of Croatia, 54, 133
Tůma, Oldřich, Czech historian, 16–17, 289, 311, 313, 316
Tunisia (ns), 315

U

Ukraine, 41, 133, 205, 230n35, 293, 302,
  hyperinflation, 203
Ulčák, Martin, Czech politician, 293
United Kingdom (UK), 7, 19, 44, 53, 171n47, 219, 314,
  Conservative Party of, 244,
  University of Bath, 324

United Nations, 41
USA, 61, 91, 113, 179, 190, 193, 313–314, 319, 321,
  Colorado College, 322,
  Department of State, 321,
  George Washington University, 324,
  First Catholic Slovak Ladies Association, x,
  First Catholic Slovak Union, x,
  Middlebury College in Vermont, 323,
  National Slovak Society, x,
  representatives of, 90,
  Slovak Catholic Sokol, x,
  Truman and Fulbright Scholarships, 321,
  University of Illinois, University of Pennsylvania, 324,
  University of Washington, ix,
  Valdosta State University in Georgia, 323,
  Wayne State University, 321
Ústí nad Labem, Czech Republic, 299

V

Vaculík, Ludvík, Czech intellectual, 96, 100, 107n6,
  Our Slovak Question, 100, 107n6,
Vīķe-Freiberga, Vaira, President of Latvia, 172n51
Visegrád Group (Four–V4), 101, 112, 150, 185n29, 241, 261–262
Verba, Sidney, American political scientist, 313

W

Wałęsa, Lech, dissident and President of Poland, 162, 315
Warsaw Pact, 62, 100, 158n8, 182, 185, 316
Washington, 107n8, 214n6,
  consensus, 13–14, 214–215

Weiss, Peter, Slovak politician, 110, 114
Weizsäcker, Richard von, German politician and President, 307n48
Western Europe, 13, 16, 56, 95, 105, 138, 142, 164, 169–170, 173, 179, 190, 192, 209, 212, 216, 219, 234, 238, 244, 297–298, 301–304, 307, 310,
values, 87
Williams, Kieran, British political scientist, 3, 161
Williamson, John, English economist, 215
Wolchik, Sharon, American political scientist, 15, 58, 281, 324
Workers' Party of Slovakia, 111
World Bank, 214n6, 9, 215, 243
World Ice Hockey Championships, 263

Y

Young, Robert, Canadian political scientist, 49
Yanukovych, Viktor, President of Ukraine, 133

YES 2011 (ANO 2011), Czech Republic, 151, 153–154, 165, 318
Yugoslavia, 7, 44, 48, 51, 53, 55–56, 98, 105, 156, 177

Z

Zahradníček, Tomáš, Czech historian, 144
Zajac, Peter, Slovak literary critic, 278n41
Žatkuliak, Jozef, Slovak historian, 7, 55, 79, 84, 324
Zatlers, Valdis, President of Latvia, 139
Žebrakovský, Karel, Czech ambassador to Canada, ix
Zeman, Miloš, Czech politician, Prime Minister and President of the Czech Republic, 10–11, 43, 89, 146–148, 154, 160, 162, 171–172, 218, 223, 226, 240
Zieleniec, Josef, Czech politician, 222
Žitňanská, Lucia, Slovak politician, 126n54
Žitný, Milan, Slovak journalist, 308